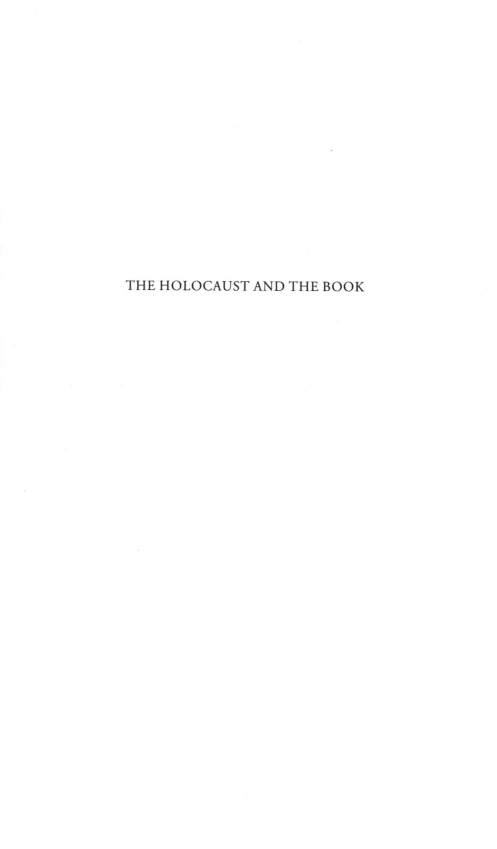

THE HOLOCAUST AND THE BOOK

THE HOLOCAUST
AND THE BOOK

DESTRUCTION AND PRESERVATION

Edited by Jonathan Rose

UNIVERSITY OF
MASSACHUSETTS PRESS
Amherst

Studies in Print Culture and the History of the Book

Copyright © 2001 by University of Massachusetts Press
All rights reserved
Printed in the United States of America
First paperback printing 2008
LC 00-028656
ISBN 978-1-55849-643-9
Set in Adobe Garamond by Graphic Composition, Inc.
Designed by Milenda Nan Ok Lee
Printed and bound by Sheridan Books, Inc.

Library of Congress Cataloging-in-Publication Data
The Holocaust and the book : destruction and preservation / Jonathan Rose, editor.
p. cm. — (Studies in print culture and the history of the book)
Includes bibliographical references (p.)
ISBN 1-55849-253-4 (cloth : alk. paper)
1. Book burning—Germany. 2. Germany—Cultural policy.
3. Censorship—Germany—History—20th century.
4. Jewish literature—Censorship—Germany. 5. Holocaust, Jewish (1939–1945)
I. Rose, Jonathan. II. Series.
Z658.G3 H65 2000
363.3′1′0943—dc21
00-028656

British Library Cataloguing in Publication data are available.

This book is published with the assistance of a generous grant from the Lucius N. Littauer Foundation and with the support and cooperation of the University of Massachusetts Boston.

Frontispiece: Two children sell secondhand books from baby carriages in front of a watchmaker's and a grocery store in the Warsaw ghetto. Photograph by M. Bil. (*YIVO Institute for Jewish Research, courtesy of USHMM Photo Archives*)

CONTENTS

Introduction
Jonathan Rose   I

PART I   DESTRUCTION AND PRESERVATION

   I   The Nazi Attack on "Un-German" Literature, 1933–1945
       Leonidas E. Hill   9

   II Bloodless Torture:
       The Books of the Roman Ghetto under the Nazi Occupation
       Stanislao G. Pugliese   47

   III The Confiscation of Jewish Books in Salonika
       in the Holocaust
       Yitzchak Kerem   59

   IV Embers Plucked from the Fire:
       The Rescue of Jewish Cultural Treasures in Vilna
       David E. Fishman   66

   V   "The Jewish Question" and Censorship in the USSR
       Arlen Viktorovich Blium
       Introduced, translated, and annotated by
       George Durman and Donna M. Farina   79

PART II   CULTURE AND RESISTANCE

   VI The Secret Voice:
       Clandestine Fine Printing in the Netherlands, 1940–1945
       Sigrid Pohl Perry   107

VII   Reading and Writing during the Holocaust as
       Described in *Yisker* Books
       Rosemary Horowitz   128

VIII   Polish Books in Exile:
       Cultural Booty across Two Continents, through Two Wars
       Sem C. Sutter   143

PART III   THE READER IN THE HOLOCAUST: DOCUMENTS

IX   The Library in the Vilna Ghetto
       Dina Abramowicz   165

X   Library and Reading Room in the Vilna Ghetto,
       Strashun Street 6
       Herman Kruk
       Translated by Zachary M. Baker   171

XI   When the Printed Word Celebrates the Human Spirit
       Charlotte Guthmann Opfermann   201

XII   Crying for Freedom:
       The Written Word as I Experienced It during World War II
       Annette Biemond Peck   206

PART IV   PRESENT AND PAST

XIII   Zarathustra as Educator?
       The Nietzsche Archive in German History
       John Rodden   213

XIV   *Convivencia* under Fire:
       Genocide and Book Burning in Bosnia
       András Riedlmayer   266

PART V   BIBLIOGRAPHY

XV   Jewish Print Culture and the Holocaust:
       A Bibliographic Survey
       Joy A. Kingsolver and Andrew B. Wertheimer   295

       Notes on Contributors   311

THE HOLOCAUST AND THE BOOK

INTRODUCTION

Jonathan Rose

THE story of the Six Million is also the story of the One Hundred Million. That is the toll of books destroyed by the Nazis throughout Europe in just twelve years, according to the calculations of one library historian. Of course, this is only the roughest of estimates, which we will probably revise as research progresses. But we can begin with this terrible certainty: the mass slaughter of Jews was accompanied by the most devastating literary holocaust of all time.

Historians of the book all share the working premise that, in literate societies, script and print are the primary means of preserving memory, disseminating information, inculcating ideologies, distributing wealth, and exercising power. The first question they ask about any civilization is how it saved, used, and destroyed documents. From the culture of New England puritanism to the causes of the French Revolution to the implosion of the Soviet Union, this new approach to history has compelled us to rethink how the past worked. It can also, in the case of the Nazi Holocaust, help us to comprehend the incomprehensible.

Film documentaries of the Hitler era commonly open with the book burnings of 1933 and fade out with the death camps. That has become the standard narrative frame, the first and final chapters of the Third Reich. Those who witnessed the bonfires, as well as historians who wrote about them in retrospect, could not help but quote the words of Heinrich Heine: "There where one burns books, one in the end burns men."

But even Heine's premonition, as true as it is terrible, threatens to become a platitude if we pursue it no further. Strikingly, most histories of the Holocaust have nothing more to say about books. We sense that there must be a connection between the book burnings and the gas chambers, but can we explain specifically how one led to the other? Were those bonfires a necessary prelude for what was to follow, and if so, precisely what role did print play in the Holocaust? Though they differ in method and focus, all the essays in this volume confront that question.

For many, the answer is obvious: the book has always been the foundation stone of Jewish theology, Jewish culture, Jewish survival. Joseph Goebbels knew that and proceeded accordingly. The Jews of the Vilna ghetto knew that equally well, when they flocked to their library and tried to find in *War and Peace* some clue to the current horrors. As a survivor, Charlotte Opfermann tells us that even in the camps books were tools for human endurance. Where the rich literary life of Jewish communities was snuffed out, as in Salonika, the communities themselves were effectively destroyed, as Yitzchak Kerem shows. The *yisker* books described by Rosemary Horowitz are not only priceless documents of reading and writing in the Holocaust; they were also a means of preserving what remained of Jewish Europe. The Soviets, as David Fishman illustrates, cultivated their own hostility to expressions of Jewish culture, and after the liberation of Vilna they continued the literary vandalism begun by the Nazis.[1] Before, after, and (incredibly) even during the war with Germany, Soviet authorities suppressed reports of Nazi atrocities against the Jews. Russian scholar Arlen Blium draws on the archives of Soviet censors to show that the crescendo of state-enforced anti-Semitism after the war was spearheaded by the suppression of Jewish authors, publishers, and even literary characters, as well as a complete ban on the publication of Yiddish books. There is good reason to believe that, shortly before his death in 1953, Stalin was planning to deport the Jews of the USSR to the far reaches of Siberia. The destruction of books may have been, once again, a first step toward the destruction of the Jews.

Yet it is equally true that for any nation—and not only for "The People of the Book"—the printed word is essential to survival and identity. That is one of the central insights offered by book history. All of the essays in this collection, and particularly those in Part II, demonstrate that books were indispensable tools of resistance for the Jews as well as for other victims of the Nazis. In occupied Europe, bibliophily was more than a hobby for gentlemen and aesthetes: it became something dangerously political. For the Dutch, writes Sigrid Perry, publishing fine books was an act of resistance to the German invaders. For the Poles, as Sem Sutter relates, the preservation of their incunabula was part of a struggle to preserve their nationhood through the Second World War and the cold war. (By a circuitous route, Poland's early books also became embroiled in the politics of Quebec nationalism.) And András Riedlmayer reminds us that, in the recent Bosnian war, libraries in Sarajevo were shelled as part of a deliberate strategy to strangle a nation at birth—perhaps the largest single book burning in modern times.

Book historians are also discovering that censorship is a more complex phenomenon than we once thought, more than a straightforward matter of destroying all titles listed in an official index. How do tyrannies determine which books will be banned? What are their exact criteria? Even the censors themselves are frequently confused on that point.[2] The essays in Part I address this slippery question. Nazi censorship policies were the ultimate expression of totalitarian conformity, yet they were also inconsistent, muddled, often improvised, and less than airtight, as Leonidas Hill observes. Storm troopers were usually not supplied with rosters of unacceptable books, and many of the volumes they burned were not in fact illegal: they continued to be sold and read during at least the first years of the

Hitler regime. Of course, that uncertainty served Nazi purposes well: anxious readers, booksellers, and publishers often destroyed questionable books rather than risk arrest. That kind of preemptive self-censorship, described by both Hill and Annette Peck, has been observed by book historians in other contexts. Stanislao Pugliese shows that, while the Nazis destroyed many libraries, they confiscated and preserved others, appropriating them for the purposes of anti-Semitic "research." And some Jewish libraries, like Dina Abramowicz's in Vilna, were allowed to function, probably because German authorities thought they would be a useful distraction for ghetto residents.

Library historians once devoted themselves to writing relentlessly happy chronicles of farsighted philanthropists and dedicated keepers of books. More recently, however, they have discovered grimmer issues, such as censorship, racial segregation in the bookstacks, and prison libraries. In the process, a subject that once interested only librarians has become an innovative branch of social history—as well as a remarkably gripping story. The preservation of Poland's oldest and rarest books reads like a Graham Greene thriller. The report filed by the Vilna Ghetto Library is an astonishing document of professional heroism, and more. And when one reads that German firemen poured kerosene on bonfires of "un-German" books, the anticipation of *Fahrenheit 451* (published twenty years later) is stunning.

Recovering the inner experience of ordinary readers may be the most difficult challenge facing book historians. For a long time scholars insisted that the sources for such a history did not exist,[3] yet we are now uncovering documents that can be used to reconstruct reader response. Even in the face of mass extermination, common readers left records, some of which are reproduced in Part III. The Vilna library report, *yisker* books, and the memories of Dina Abramowicz and other survivors are all extraordinary accounts of the uses of literacy in the face of mass extermination. This volume does not attempt to produce a comprehensive history of reading in the Holocaust, but it does show that the materials we need to recover that history have survived.

One type of reading history, the reception history, has long been used to track the responses of critics to particular authors. But reception history can do more than record the booms and busts of literary fashion: applied to the Holocaust, it can address questions of fearsome significance. In *The Politics of Literary Reputation* (1989) John Rodden read the critical response to George Orwell as a barometer of the ideological climate of the cold war era. In this volume Rodden applies the same method to another dark prophet, Friedrich Nietzsche, with disturbing results. The most influential philosopher of the last century, Nietzsche is now enjoying something of a revival in Germany. Throughout the Western world, he has been a font of inspiration for existentialists, psychoanalysts, deconstructionists, anarchists, many Marxists, half of the greatest writers of the twentieth century and, of course, the National Socialists. Now there is no denying that the Nazis hijacked Nietzsche and perverted his message to serve their ideology.

Clearly, he loathed German militarism and anti-Semitism. But in recent years literary critics have shifted their attention away from authorial intention and toward audience response, while book historians have produced a surge of empirical research on the reading experience. Nietzsche himself realized, with utter disgust, that anti-Semites were quoting him in support of their hatreds, and he had an awful premonition that his writings would lead to an unimaginable catastrophe. Today, we are left to confront what may be the most horrifying question of literary influence ever posed: Whatever his intentions, did Nietzsche's works fuel the Holocaust?

The essays in Part IV address the immediate relevance of the Holocaust at the close of the twentieth century, when we are forced to face once again the recurrence of genocide. These essays, along with several others in this collection, necessarily extend the study of the Holocaust beyond the boundaries of purely Jewish history. In so doing, they inevitably raise the question of the uniqueness of the Nazi war against the Jews. With sensitivity and balance, Michael Marrus has argued that it was indeed unique in one critically important sense: the Jews were the victims of the only campaign in modern times that aimed to eradicate an entire people, and to a great extent succeeded. Yet Marrus is careful to add that mass murder as such has been the recurring nightmare of this century. One need only mention Stalin, Mao, and Pol Pot; Armenia, Rwanda, and Kosovo.[4] If we overemphasize the singularity of the Jewish Holocaust, it ceases to have relevance to other great crimes against humanity. Though Hitler's prime motive, his defining passion, was hatred of the Jews, their fate can only be understood in a context that includes nazism's other victims. The German occupation stopped short of the complete extermination of the Polish people, but it did attempt to destroy Poland's nationhood by confiscating her books. The Dutch did not face annihilation, but for them, as for the Jews, books became a means of resistance. The long and larger history of book burning is embodied in the celebrated Sarajevo Haggadah, which has survived no less than four holocausts of books in five centuries, including the Axis invasion of Yugoslavia in 1941 and the Bosnian war of the 1990s. That story provides the essential background to the Nazi war against literature, which was by no means unique in history, though the scale of destruction was unprecedented. András Riedlmayer also suggests how the international community can, as far as possible, repair the devastation caused by such crimes and take action to prevent their recurrence.

Our bibliography, necessarily selective, reveals that not much has been written on this subject, though there is (remarkably) a growing body of scholarship in German. The first book-length study in English is David Shavit's recently published *Hunger for the Printed Word: Books and Libraries in the Jewish Ghettos of Nazi-Occupied Europe*. It is a pioneering work based on impressive research, but it focuses solely on Jewish libraries in Poland, Lithuania, and the Theresienstadt camp in Czechoslovakia. Our volume chronicles the impact of the Holocaust on Gentiles as well as Jews, deals with the often neglected Sephardic Jews of the

Mediterranean as well as the Ashkenazim, and carries the narrative forward to the 1990s. But we cannot pretend to tell the whole story, because we still have so little to draw upon. This book, along with David Shavit's, is a beginning. At this time, we are not ready to write the definitive history of the book in the Holocaust. Our objective is, first, to sketch in as much of this history as we can recover at present. Second, the essays in this volume, and particularly the bibliographic survey, are meant to suggest methods and directions for future researchers.

Versions of the essays by Leonidas E. Hill, Stanislao G. Pugliese, Yitzchak Kerem, Sigrid Pohl Perry, Rosemary Horowitz, Dina Abramowicz, and Annette Biemond Peck were presented at a November 1996 conference on "The Holocaust and the Book," cosponsored by the Center for Holocaust Study and the Center for the History of the Book at Drew University. A considerable debt of gratitude is owed to the program committee that organized that conference: Linda Connors of the Center for the History of the Book; and for the Center for Holocaust Study, Codirectors Jacqueline Berke and Ann Saltzman, and Associates Arlene Kesselhaut and Hildred Nozick. Robin Birnhak, Hedy Brasch, Judy Churgin, Phyllis Diehl, Kerri Durant, Marsha Frank, Valerie Granet, Gerald Gurland, and Elizabeth Pullen—all members of the Center for Holocaust Study—helped with the enormous chores involved in local arrangements. Dean Paolo Cucchi, Prof. J. Perry Leavell, Jr., and Prof. Peter Ochs generously underwrote the costs of the event. The Society for the History of Authorship, Reading and Publishing assisted with publicity.

The essays by David E. Fishman, Sem Sutter, Arlen Blium, Charlotte Guthmann Opfermann, John Rodden, and András Riedlmayer—as well as Herman Kruk's Vilna library report and the bibliography prepared by Joy A. Kingsolver and Andrew B. Wertheimer—were submitted to the editor independently of the Drew University conference. The YIVO Institute for Jewish Research previously published the article by David Fishman, and Maria Kühn-Ludewig supplied explanatory notes to Kruk's library report. We thank them all for permitting us to use their materials. We also thank the editors of *Libraries and Culture* for permission to reprint Stanislao Pugliese's article. Finally, our copy editor, Barbara Palmer, deserves a special commendation for establishing order and consistency in an exceptionally complicated manuscript.

NOTES

1. The destruction actually began when the Red Army first occupied Vilna and eastern Poland in late 1939. Then the Soviets closed most Jewish libraries, purged them of all Hebrew books, and banned the works of ideologically suspect Yiddish authors. David Shavit, *Hunger for the Printed Word: Books and Libraries in the Jewish Ghettos of Nazi-Occupied Europe* (Jefferson, N.C.: McFarland, 1997), 35–39.

2. Some of these complexities are explored in Paul Hyland and Neil Sammells, eds.,

Writing and Censorship in Britain (London: Routledge, 1992), and Robert Darnton, *The Forbidden Best-Sellers of Pre-Revolutionary France* (New York: Norton, 1995).

3. See, for example, Jeffrey Richards, *Happiest Days: The Public Schools in English Fiction* (Manchester: Manchester University Press, 1988), 2.

4. Michael R. Marrus, *The Holocaust in History* (Hanover, N.H.: University Press of New England, 1987), 18–25.

PART ONE

DESTRUCTION AND PRESERVATION

Nazi supporters and SA members unload confiscated materials for the public book burning that is to take place on the Opernplatz in Berlin. The banner on the back of the truck reads: "German students march against the un-German spirit." Photograph by Abraham Pisarek. (*National Archives, courtesy of USHMM Photo Archives*)

I • THE NAZI ATTACK ON "UN-GERMAN" LITERATURE, 1933–1945

Leonidas E. Hill

S CHOLARS continue to debate the actual and symbolic meaning of the public burnings of books on 10 May 1933, the "Action against the Un-German Spirit." Scarcely anyone disputes that the book burnings deserve mention with the Reichstag fire and the boycott of Jewish businesses as among the most striking features of the first months of the Hitler regime. But it was students rather than the new government of the Third Reich who planned and staged these events. Should they still be regarded as symbolic of Nazi cultural policy as they were during the 1930s and World War II? Was this attack on the "un-German" actually a reflection of Nazi racial policies? The Nazis' vicious anti-Semitism and the book burnings made some observers worry that Jews would be burned next. Heinrich Heine was often quoted: "There where one burns books, one in the end burns men."[1] Yet the world reaction was somewhat ambiguous: it combined indignation and condemnation with a propensity to view the burnings as mere student highjinks, in bad taste but a unique occurrence. The stronger international reaction to the boycott made the still vulnerable Nazi regime temporarily cautious. Hence the cultural implications of the 1933 book burnings and book bannings remained unclear for a few years. The various states in Germany designed their own censorship policies and implemented them differently. This chaotic situation ended with the centralization of cultural and racial policy and the introduction of more radical policies. A brief caesura during the 1936 Olympic year was followed by accelerated aggressiveness. After the takeover of Austria in March 1938 and the Kristallnacht pogrom the following November, the Nazis indulged their appetites for plunder and brutality and fulfilled the expectations of their most acute critics by destroying both books and Jews. The destruction was limited compared with the holocaust of books and human beings during the Second World War, but it revealed more fully the crimes implicit in Nazi ideology. The 10 May 1933 book burnings became a powerful symbol of German "barbarism" and helped focus resistance to nazism outside Germany. Only now, however, is the profundity of Heine's perception clear: the burnings of 1933 are an appropriate symbol for and anticipation of the wartime extermination of Jews and Slavs. The "My Life in Germany" collection of autobiographies at the Houghton Library,

Harvard University, vividly illuminates the experiences of German authors, publishers, booksellers, and readers during the continually expanding Nazi war
against everything "un-German."

Two manifestos from April 1933, the "Twelve Theses against the Un-German
Spirit" and the "Feuersprüche" (fire incantations), read and chanted at the burnings, are exemplary distillations of the Nazis' viewpoint. But what were the
sources of their belief in and hatred of the "un-German," and how did they define
that term? Romanticism, nationalism, racism, social Darwinism, and antimodernism were the pillars of National Socialist cultural policy. From romanticism
came the conviction that peoples expressed their special *Geist* (spirit or genius)
in their language, literature, and customs. Early nineteenth-century conservative
romanticism rejected Enlightenment cosmopolitanism and the egalitarian ideas
of 1789. The wars of German unification and the First World War provided an
infusion of militarism and chauvinism. The anti-Western nationalism of the German "ideas of 1914" was hostile to democracy and parliamentarism and was a
baneful force in the Weimar Republic. Nazism combined these elements with
assertions of German superiority based on "race," characterized especially by
"blood," meaning genealogy rather than conventional blood types or genetics.
Although the Nazis considered Jews and Slavs racially inferior, they believed that
only a colossal social Darwinistic struggle could prevent the conspiracy of Jewish
capitalists and financiers from gaining economic control of the globe, and the
conspiracy of Jewish Bolsheviks from fomenting world revolution. In preparation
for this struggle National Socialists would end the political and social disunity of
the hated Weimar Republic and build a politically, socially, racially, economically,
and militarily strong Germany. They intended to liquidate the political parties of
the Jews and their allies in the liberal center as well as on the socialist and communist left; to dissolve classes and unite all Germans in the new discipline of *Gemein-
schaft;* to purify society through eugenic policies, the sterilization of "colored"
and "mentally deficient" people, and the extrusion of Jews and Slavs, who on
racial grounds were non-Germans; to regain control of the economy from the
Jews, whom they accused of dominating banking, the professions, the universities, publishing, and culture; and to build a powerful army capable of aggressive
war for the conquest of *Lebensraum,* virtually the European continent. The population would have to be reeducated for all of these purposes and for war. Nazi
ideology and songs[2] sanctioned or encouraged violence against, even murder of
domestic and foreign enemies. Nazi antimodernism espoused romantic stereo-
types of sturdy, unalienated, racially pure "Nordic" peasants engaged in healthy
agricultural labor and producing "Aryan" children in an idealized countryside. It
condemned the supposed license, decadence, and abstract intellectualism of city
dwellers living unhealthy, alienated, soulless, infertile lives in high-rises and fac-
tories surrounded by asphalt.[3] Nazis preached an idealized vision of the human
soul and fulminated against the elevation of the "base drives" by modern psychology and psychoanalysis, against eroticism and homosexuality in practice as well

as in literature, theater, and the arts. They denounced modern music and architecture, especially the "Bolshevik" Bauhaus, and promoted "traditional," "pure," "German" styles.[4] They despised "un-German," "corrupt," and "materialistic" American culture, sometimes applying the term "nigger culture" to Jews as well as blacks.[5]

Nazi hatred of the Eastern Jews, the *Ostjuden,* was partly cultural (they dressed and looked different and spoke Yiddish) but also racial. Supposedly, Jewish "blood" was so different that it made assimilation impossible, despite the fact that assimilated Jews spoke German, had the same manners, clothing, and habits as other Germans, were usually patriotic, and had fought loyally in World War I with more than proportionate losses. One Jew recalled that during the Weimar period, when he had occasion to disagree with Christian Germans, they would reply, "You will never learn to feel as a German does."[6] This was a milder expression of the Nazi conviction that the German *Geist* and culture could be expressed only in the German language by "true" Germans, that is, non-Jews, and that Jews were imbued with the Jewish "spirit." Hence expression of their thought in the German language was a lie and, in fact, a form of treason. Jews should publish their books in Hebrew or designate them as translations if they appeared in German. Books by Jews or books expressing intellectual currents anathema to the Nazis reflected the Jewish "spirit" and should be purged from bookstores and libraries.[7] Thus would the National Socialist revolution extirpate its enemies and the books expressing their "spirit": the rationalism, materialism, cosmopolitanism, egalitarianism, parliamentarism, pacifism, tolerance, assimilationism, ecumenism, and modernism the Nazis detested.

For a number of years prior to 1933 the National Socialist Society for German Culture, renamed and refounded in 1929 as the Combat League for German Culture, and the Nazi newspapers *Völkischer Beobachter* and *Der Angriff* candidly announced their future cultural policies and denounced "un-German," especially Jewish, ideas and authors. The Nazis disrupted and halted showings of the film version of Erich Maria Remarque's *All Quiet on the Western Front.* In Thuringia Nazi Minister of the Interior and Education Wilhelm Frick forbade the use of Remarque's book in schools; issued an order against "nigger culture" and followed it with bans on some books, plays, and music; approved the whitewashing of a mural by Oskar Schlemmer; ordered the removal of "degenerate art" from the museum in Weimar; and appointed Nazi Prof. Hans F. K. Günther, author of several books on race, to a chair at the University of Jena. Under Nazi pressure the city government of Dessau closed the Bauhaus. Some newspapers already described these actions as the policies of the future "Third Reich."[8]

Nazis disrupted a lecture by Thomas Mann in 1930 and halted a reading by his daughter Erika in 1931. Less noticed were the anonymous threats in telephone calls, letters, graffiti, and constant Nazi patrols that Thomas Mann, Arnold Zweig, Lion Feuchtwanger, Theodor Plievier, Carl von Ossietzky's wife, and others endured. Fritz von Unruh's home was wrecked. In 1930 Nazi ideologist Alfred Rosenberg threatened to bring all "cultural Bolshevists" before a state tribunal. In

April 1932 the *Völkischer Beobachter* published a declaration signed by forty-two professors advocating the protection of culture from "Kulturbolschewismus." In *Der Angriff* Joseph Goebbels listed a number of authors who should be lined up against the wall. Some writers escaped this psychic terror by emigrating before 1933, and others prepared for swift departure if the Nazis came to power.[9]

Between 30 January 1933 and the 10 May book burnings Germany seethed with Nazi activity against writers, their books, publishers, and bookstores. During February the daily articles on culture in the *Völkischer Beobachter* were a chamber of horrors of the kinds of policies that Rosenberg wanted. After the 28 February Reichstag fire and the resulting ban on the Communist Party, the Nazis attacked and arrested Communists, socialists, and pacifists, including authors, and incarcerated some in concentration camps. Months of confiscations of "Marxist" literature briefly intensified after the dissolution of the labor unions on 2 May. Hermann Goering was appointed Prussian commissar for the Nazi campaign against "trash and smut" literature, particularly pornography, especially in lending libraries. The Party and press encouraged action against the "un-German spirit" in books, which resulted in illegal confiscations and destruction of books in Jewish-owned bookstores. In March, the Sturmabteilung (SA) entered the private dwellings of the Jewish owners of the Ullstein and Mosse firms and forced them to fire their Jewish employees and to replace them with Nazis.[10] But when it appeared that Nazis might attempt "wild" actions against research libraries, the Prussian minister of science, art, and education decreed that it was out of the question to remove Jewish, Marxist, and pacifist authors. On the whole, such institutions were protected throughout Germany during the confiscations for the book burnings and later.

The infamous 10 May 1933 public book burnings made the newly composed but unofficial blacklists of condemned ideas, authors, and books more widely known in Germany and the larger world. However, in August 1932 the *Völkischer Beobachter* had already published such a list of authors with a threat to ban their works when the National Socialists came to power. A few days later a committee of professional librarians obsessed with the dangers of lending "Bolshevik, Marxist, and Jewish" literature began compiling a comprehensive list, and by early March the Nazi librarian Wolfgang Herrmann had finished his influential blacklist of authors.[11] Rosenberg's Kampfbund (Combat League) was also making lists, though Goebbels's competing Propaganda Ministry did not officially accept them. These lists were at first sent only to selected Nazis or to student organizations, but one was published in the second half of April. The early lists emphasized 12 notable authors but soon expanded to 71 and then to 131 authors organized in a number of categories. Later in 1933 twenty-one offices had banned more than a thousand books, and by 1934 over forty agencies had lists of 4,100 publications.[12] The Bavarian police had a list of 2,293 authors of 6,843 seized and forbidden books. The first blanket bans of the entire oeuvres of certain authors were instituted by Prussian authorities in November 1934. The Reichsschrifttumskammer (RSK) listed 524 complete bans in 1935, and the number rose to 576 after the invasion of Russia in 1941.[13]

Bookowners knew that possession of the classics of left-wing literature, from Marx through Rosa Luxemburg and Karl Kautsky to Lenin, Leon Trotsky, and Stalin, was dangerous; the Nazis even labeled this "high treason."[14] Before, at, and after the book burnings, Nazis typically classified the "un-German" books in a number of categories: antimilitarist authors Theodor Plievier, Erich Maria Remarque, Arnold Zweig; pacifists Bertha von Suttner, Alfred Hermann Fried, and Friedrich Wilhelm Foerster; left-oriented novelist-critics of bourgeois society Lion Feuchtwanger, Heinrich Mann, Ernst Gläser, and Erich Kästner; "communists" Bertolt Brecht, Gustav Regler, and Anna Seghers; satirists of the bourgeoisie, religion, and the army like George Grosz, photomontagist John Heartfield, essayist Kurt Tucholsky, and dramatists Ernst Toller and Georg Kaiser; the entire "Weltbühne" circle, with Carl von Ossietzky at its center,[15] as well as literary historian Franz Mehring and critic Alfred Kerr; anti-Nazi journalists Theodor Wolff and Georg Bernhard; historians whose views about the origins (Walter Fabian, Hermann Kantorowicz, Emil Ludwig), course (Wilhelm Dittmann, Karl Tschuppik), and end (Martin Hobohm, Gustav Noske, Arthur Rosenberg, Carl Severing) of World War I and the history of the Weimar Republic (Emil Julius Gumbel, Hugo Preuss, Walter Rathenau) were incompatible with Nazi dogma; the founder of psychoanalysis Sigmund Freud; and scientists propounding an incomprehensible worldview, epitomized by the outspokenly anti-Nazi physicist Alfred Einstein, soon under attack for his "Jewish physics."

Although on 10 May 1933 Nazis chanted the "Feuersprüche," nine objectionable characteristics of books followed by the names of some of the authors, while throwing their books on bonfires,[16] few knew the other books that were burned. Whereas anyone aware of the Nazis' views might guess quite accurately which volumes in his or her own library were suspect or condemned, the bookseller Hilde Wenzel knew that not all the books burned on 10 May 1933 were actually banned. In fact, until 1935 the Prussian police had not banned any of the volumes named at the burnings, not even Remarque's *All Quiet on the Western Front*. The regime did not have a master plan when they took office and did not soon design one. For some years Nazi bannings and seizures of books in the fifteen German states were uncoordinated and carried out by many agencies at different levels of government.[17]

The book burnings were a publicity stunt devised by one Nazi student organization, Deutsche Studentenschaft, to upstage another, the Nationalsozialistische Deutsche Studentenbund, and to curry favor with the government. Although the Nazi government had not yet formulated cultural policies, Goebbels's newly founded Ministry of Public Enlightenment and Propaganda welcomed the student initiative without contributing to the preparations. But no government ministry officially approved of the "blacklist" Herrmann first sent to the students on 1 May and frequently extended thereafter.

At the beginning of April the initiating student organization wrote of an

"action against Jewish decomposition of German literature" but on 8 April outlined to its branches at German universities the month-long preparations for
the action "against the Un-German Spirit," beginning with the publication of
"Twelve Theses" on 12 April and ending with the nearly simultaneous book burnings on 10 May. Each university branch was to obtain authorizations and cooperation from the Nazi gauleiter as well as the local university, municipal, and police
authorities; establish local "fighting committees" composed of students, professors, and representatives of the Kampfbund; collect books by the condemned authors; arrange for faculty and student fraternities or corporations to march; find
speakers for the occasion; articulate the specific steps in the ceremony; and release
propaganda about this complex of activities before and after 10 May. During this
month they encouraged erection of *Schandpfähle,* wooden pilings on which they
nailed shaming testimonials against those who did not share their spirit: "Today
the writers, tomorrow the professors." However, the Prussian Ministry of Education, professors in Cologne, and a Hannover Nazi student committee with approval of professor-mentors intervened against installation of these posts.[18]

The planners were very conscious of historical precedents, such as the Inquisition's auto-da-fé, Luther's destruction of the papal bulls, students burning symbols of authority at the Wartburg in 1817, a 1922 burning of *Schundliteratur* at
Berlin's Tempelhof Field, and the burning of the Versailles Treaty with the Dawes
and Young Plans by Nazi students in 1929. During the April preparations they
obliquely referred to these examples and carefully stylized Hitler as a second Luther or as the fearless knight of a famous Dürer drawing.[19] Although the students
copied the methods of propaganda and organization used in the April boycott of
Jewish businesses, they disagreed with its premise. They were steeped in German
idealism and believed that the spiritual crisis symbolized by the book burnings
was the fundamental cause of the economic crisis attacked in the boycott.[20]

Students were asked to purge their own libraries of condemned books and to
press others to do the same. Bookstores and lending libraries were also asked to
contribute such books. Because of the depression far fewer people could afford
books, and with the public library system unable to satisfy popular demand the
gap was filled by more than 15,000 lending libraries with an estimated 30 million
volumes and very low fees. They bought 2 to 3 million books each year, often 10
to 100 copies of best sellers, some by authors the Nazis condemned.[21] On 6 May
"fighting committees" of the two main Nazi student organizations, branches of
the Stahlhelm (a right-wing paramilitary organization) at universities, SA troopers, and police collected and seized books from bookstores and especially lending
libraries, described by Herrmann as "literary bordellos." His characterization reflected the view of professional librarians that the lending libraries spread a dangerous infection with their immoral, sexually explicit, and trashy books. Some of
these books were burned four days later.[22]

Police and the SA rather than students raided private libraries in homes and
seized the "Marxist" contents of workers' libraries.[23] Especially rewarding was an
April SA search of the Berlin apartment house owned by the Schutzverband

Deutscher Schriftsteller, the chief organization of German writers, and occupied by some 500 of its writer-members. Upon finding "communist" books, the SA confiscated others and arrested some occupants. A witness assumed these books were burned in May. The searchers had only a vague idea of the authors and books to be seized: from one apartment they took Thomas Mann's *Buddenbrooks* and Oswald Spengler's *Preussentum und Sozialismus* as well as any other books with titles concerning socialism or revolution. From another virtually destroyed apartment they removed the children's book *Uwe Karsten, Heideschulmeister* by Felicita Rose, despite the owner's protest that it was not banned, because they wanted to examine it.[24]

Many searchers seemed to enjoy rousing half-naked housewives in their bathrobes early in the morning,[25] terrorizing apartment dwellers, and destroying their homes. They often confiscated financial papers, personal correspondence, and large personal libraries, and they stole money, jewelry, and silver. Although a few confiscated books were deposited in restricted collections in libraries, far more landed in the libraries of the Gestapo and Propaganda Ministry. The writer Franz Carl Weiskopf observed that their collectors sold many books abroad for their own profit and that many appeared in secondhand bookstores in towns such as Basel, just beyond the German border.[26]

In Berlin one of the most destructive actions had a particular animus. At 9:30 A.M. on 6 May 100 Nazi students of the Institut für Leibesübungen invaded the Institut für Sexualwissenschaft, founded in 1918 by Magnus Hirschfeld, a physician who specialized in nervous and psychiatric problems. Taken over by the Prussian state government in 1919, his institute studied homosexuality and lesbianism, advocated reform of the criminal code regarding sexuality, prepared briefs for legal cases concerning sexual crimes, and was the first German institution to provide marriage counseling. For three hours the students emptied inkwells onto carpets and broke or vandalized framed paintings and prints, glass, porcelain, or marble vessels, lights, sculptures, and decorations. They confiscated books, periodicals, photographs, anatomical models, a famous wall tapestry, and a bust of Hirschfeld. After music, speeches, and songs outside at noon they departed but were succeeded at 3:00 P.M. by SA men, who removed 10,000 books from the institute's library. A few days later they carried the bust of Hirschfeld on a pole in a torchlight parade before throwing it on the bonfire with the books from the institute.[27]

There was virtually no resistance to any of these actions from the university authorities and faculties, the students, the libraries, bookstores, or publishers. Under the leadership of a dedicated Nazi, the official organization of German booksellers swiftly supported the new regime. At a meeting of scientific librarians in June 1933 a leading speaker accepted the book burnings, applauded the book seizures by police, and advocated the erasure of Jewish and Bolshevik writings. In Prussia, Bavaria, and Saxony various authorities, including teachers, "cleansed" school libraries of unacceptable books. These were eventually replaced in many schools by "model libraries" named Dietrich-Eckart-Bücherei after a

Nazi founding father, which contained thoroughly Nazi books. Teachers played a significant role in promoting this censorship and indoctrination. Thus *Gleichschaltung* (regimentation) was accomplished less through terror than voluntary capitulation by stores, libraries, schools, universities, and public consensus. The announcement on 8 May of the complete reorganization of the Prussian Academy of the Arts and the dissolution of its literary division, resulting in the removal of many authors denounced by the students, was another aspect of *Gleichschaltung* which fit perfectly with the student action.[28]

Books were burned at thirty German universities, mostly on or within a few days of 10 May 1933 but continuing until 21 June. There were two burnings each at Hamburg and Heidelberg; none took place at Danzig, Dillingen, Freiburg im Breisgau, Regensburg, and Tübingen.[29] The students attempted to synchronize the events from eleven until midnight on 10 May in order to exhibit the new technology of radio. The "Deutschland Sender" broadcast the activities in a number of cities, and in Munich all four of the "Bayerischen Rundfunk" carried the story. Led by marching bands, faculty in robes, student corporations in their colored sashes and distinctive caps, uniformed and beflagged Hitler Youth, SA men (many of them students), SS troopers, NSBO members (NS-Betriebszellen-Organisation, or Nazi union cells), and Stahlhelm troops paraded through the streets to the site of the bonfire, where speeches by student, municipal, and university representatives were punctuated with songs. In Frankfurt students collected the books and carried them in rented *Mistwagen* (manure wagons) pulled by beribboned oxen. The volumes in such a wagon symbolically became offal. Trucks usually transported the books, and chains of students passed them hand to hand to be thrown on the fires.[30]

The event was colorful, illuminated bright as day by film company searchlights but soon obscured by smoke and drifting ash, noisy also with the enthusiastic attendance in some cities of more than 15,000 nonuniversity people controlled by police, sometimes on horseback, and the SA. Construction of the pyre, symbolism, and the weather varied greatly. Books usually topped a heap of flammable material resting on wooden scaffolding, but volumes of left-wing daily newspapers were the foundation for one. Decorations included socialist and communist slogans, symbols or acronyms on placards, a photograph of Lenin, the flag of the Weimar Republic. At 11:30 P.M. firemen nourished the flames with kerosene, and as they rose, students chanted the nine Nazi cultural canons of the "Feuersprüche," naming twenty-four authors exemplifying them (including a witness, Erich Kästner), while throwing their books on the fire. At several universities the bonfire sputtered and even died under a downpour, which caused postponements or cancellations.[31]

Some observers dismissed the burnings as a student lark. Leading German critics, writers, and historians such as Hans Mayer, Heinrich Böll, Walter Kempowski, and Golo Mann played down their immediate and long-term symbolic importance. At least one Nazi jested that without occasionally reading a hidden copy of one of the burned books one would lack anything respectable to read.[32]

In Bonn the mayor, the professor for "Germanistik," and the professor of art reportedly said that as the flames devoured the books "the Jewish soul flew into the sky," but such a remark is not in the printed texts of the professors' speeches.[33] Sigmund Freud offered a sardonic reassurance: "Only our books? In earlier times they would have burned us with them."[34] Yet in accordance with their hatred for the "un-German Jewish spirit" and their belief that "the Jews are not human beings,"[35] the Nazis were already sadistically mistreating Jews in jails and concentration camps, then cremating those who died and sending their ashes home in urns. Thus the link between the burning of books and men was forged in Germany as early as 1933. Few Jews made this connection at the time. The pursuit of Communists and Socialists after the Reichstag fire, the boycott and the book burnings, the end of a free parliament and of political parties, the purging of Jews from government, the judicial system, the universities, and the professions, and other anti-Semitic excesses were frequently interpreted as manifestations of an initially radical phase that the Nazis would outgrow.[36]

Nevertheless, well before 10 May, even before Hitler's appointment as chancellor, many Jews and leftists tried to protect themselves from Nazi reprisals by burning their papers and libraries. Some young Communists were warned during the summer of 1932 that it was "five minutes before twelve" and they should destroy all address books or lists in their possession; if they were caught carrying potentially dangerous papers, they must be prepared to swallow them. They also started early with the time-consuming process of sorting their personal effects, the records and traces of their families and their own lives, as well as their libraries.[37] More acted after 30 January 1933, and still more after the Reichstag fire decrees at the end of February resulted in the arrests of many Communists and Social Democrats. The men and women of the Left recognized their peril. The best known of them could not escape identification and arrest by destruction of their papers and books, but they could save others whose names appeared in them. They saved themselves by hiding and fleeing into exile.

Widespread fear of house searches (*Haussuchungen*) by the SA, SS, Gestapo, and police spurred preemptive book burning. On 24 March 1933 an eleven-year-old boy came to Frau Lewinsohn, the wife of a workman who had been a Communist until 1932, and said: "Just think, I met a man who asked me to go at once to tell you to make your house really clean today. He must be crazy, everyone knows your house is clean. He gave me 50 pfennig." The occupants immediately burned their books and papers and the next day endured a search. It was most important to destroy Party membership cards and lists, address books, correspondence and diaries, photographs and memorabilia, then periodicals, pamphlets, and books with a political or aesthetic complexion condemned by the Nazis. However, some who destroyed political materials could not part from their libraries.[38]

And those who did try to burn their books discovered that this cannot be done easily and quickly, as the Nazis themselves found at the end of the war, when they attempted to incinerate enormous collections of documents and simply did not have time. Thick bundles of paper must be separated so that air and flames consume individual sheets, or else the fire has to reach a considerable size and intensity. Otherwise the bundles are only scorched at the edges. A Jewish ophthalmologist in Berlin told of repeatedly combing through his 3,000 books to select those for destruction. Burning large volumes in stoves or fireplaces was tedious and time-consuming. One woman even obtained help from an "Aryan" janitor to burn her compromising documents. Residents of homes and apartments that used gas for heating and cooking disposed of books and pamphlets in the woods, a body of water, or a mailbox on a deserted street, or sent cartons of books to false addresses in another city.[39]

Utilizing a legal loophole, aided by British decisiveness and the grudging cooperation of the Hamburg city government, and escaping by a few weeks the jurisdiction of Goebbels's Ministry of Propaganda, the Warburg family sent most of Aby Warburg's great library to England on two small ships. Late in 1933 carefully chosen anti-Nazi movers packed 80,000 books with thousands of photos and slides, plus the iron shelves and other equipment, into 531 boxes. This became a central scholarly resource of the Warburg-Courtauld Institute in London. Its original home in Hamburg was destroyed by bombing during the war.[40]

Perhaps the largest preemptive removal of documents for destruction took place at the Büro Wilhelmstrasse of the Centralverein deutscher Staatsbürger Jüdischen Glaubens (CV), whose library the Nazis seized later. Devoted mainly to research on the National Socialist Party (NSDAP), the Berlin Büro housed a large archive expanded and organized by a Gentile employee named Walter Gyssling. It contained nearly 800 chronologically organized and cross-referenced dossiers with over 500,000 items. The six divisions of the archive encompassed the NSDAP's national and international policies, relations with other German parties and organizations, anti-Semitic agitation, destructive and criminal acts such as defacing gravestones, the struggle against the Nazis, and records about their leaders and membership. After Hitler's appointment Gyssling helped transport this archive, which contained much compromising material about the Büro and the CV, to Bavaria for eventual destruction.[41] Few organizations were so prescient. The Nazis seized many archives of political parties, special interest groups, and lobbies early in the summer of 1933 when all parties other than the NSDAP were dissolved.

Most of the authors already mentioned had either departed from Germany before Hitler came to power because Nazi harassment made their lives intolerable, or were prepared and escaped soon after. A few died in concentration camps, like Erich Mühsam in 1934, or because of mistreatment there, like Carl von Ossietzky.[42] After their release from concentration camp and escape into exile some of them described their experiences: Willi Bredel in *Die Prüfung*, Gerhard Seger in *Oranienberg*, Karl Billinger in *Schutzhäftling 880*, Walter Hornung in *Dachau*, and Wolfgang Langhoff in *Die Moorsoldaten*.[43] A few publishers and authors chose suicide, others exile. Some committed suicide in exile: Kurt Tucholsky in

Sweden, 1935; Ernst Toller in New York City, 1939; Stefan Zweig, with his second wife, in Petropolis near Rio de Janeiro, 1942.

Yet some who emigrated successfully resumed their literary careers and at the same time contributed from outside to the resistance to Hitler and nazism. Many left-wing publishers and their employees fled early and continued their work abroad. Two from Verlag Gustav Kiepenheuer found places in Amsterdam, Walter Landauer at Verlag Allert de Lange and Fritz Landshoff at Querido Verlag. Wieland Herzfelde reestablished the Malik Verlag in Prague until 1938. Willi Münzenberg was at Editions du Carrefour in Paris. All of these publishers and the Swiss-owned Oprecht Verlag in Zurich, which also used the names Europa Verlag and Aufbruch Verlag in publishing exile authors, were entirely banned at the end of 1938.[44] In June 1934 the Nazis forced the Ullstein family (of Jewish descent) to sell their entire huge complex of newspapers, magazines, and publishing houses, including the Ullstein Verlag and the Propyläen Verlag, though the Ullsteins themselves did not emigrate until 1937 and 1939. Adolf Neumann of Rütten and Loening Verlag fled to Norway in 1934, and the firm was sold in July 1936. The founder of the S. Fischer Verlag died 15 October 1934, but not until April 1936 did his heirs sell to a group financed mainly by a tobacco company, Philipp Reemtsma. They transferred some rights and inventory to Suhrkamp and retained other rights for the refounded firm in Austria, where they shipped 780,000 volumes of their stock.[45] Few exiled authors and publishers prospered. They could not find an audience comparable to the one they had lost.

The impact of Nazi book burning, censorship, anti-Semitism, and repression on German bookstores and readers can be dramatically illuminated through the experiences of a Jewish bookseller, as recounted in the autobiography of Hilde Wenzel, the daughter of a well-known Jewish defense lawyer. After her marriage, her husband, Peter, was listed as the legal owner of their bookstore in Berlin-Charlottenburg from 1933 to 1938, presumably because they hoped he would not be identified as Jewish, as she undeniably was.[46]

Between 1933 and 1937 she and her husband avoided trouble with the authorities about the books they sold, even though booksellers did not have access to the official lists of unacceptable authors and books. The makers of cultural policy in Nazi Germany did not want to provide the outside world with proof that the Nazis systematically censored authors and literature. They also anticipated that if booksellers did not know which books were unacceptable they would censor themselves to avoid possible arrest. However, booksellers knew the names of some authors whose books had been confiscated and burned in 1933, even though those authors were not on a central list until 1935. They realized that books by authors in exile whose citizenship had been revoked were frequently if not always dangerous, and newspapers carried announcements of such revocations. In Berlin the police periodically entered the Wenzels' store and read the names of proscribed authors and books. Hilde Wenzel discerned three grounds for books being banned: their authors were Jewish, or Marxist, or critical of National Socialist rule. In fact, authors were not banned solely for being Jewish until 1940, when all Jewish authors were banned. Although she was right about the other two categories, the Nazis had many more criteria than those she named.[47] She also had a limited understanding of Nazi objections to some authors and their books.

She believed that if Stefan Zweig had not been banned as a Jew he would have sold nicely all along. His *Marie Antoinette* had been the second-best seller at Christmas 1932, but she did not know he was on Nazi lists in 1933. In 1935 their best-selling Christmas book was Zweig's *Baumeister der Welt*, three volumes about Balzac, Dickens, and Dostoyevsky (1920), Hölderlin, Kleist, and Nietzsche (1925), Casanova, Stendhal, and Tolstoy (1928), now republished as one. Unfortunately, Zweig was banned at Easter 1936. Although Wenzel thought he was unpolitical, some of his works in this period had a clear political purpose. Zweig later described his 1934 biography of Erasmus as a "veiled self-portrait" of a "humanist who, though he understood the madness of the time more clearly than the professional world-reformers, for all his sound reason was, tragically enough, unable to oppose unreason."[48] His 1936 study of Castellio versus Calvin also reconstituted humanism as a form of resistance to Hitler and nazism.[49] As humanists, Erasmus and Castellio argued for tolerance in a time of religious wars, but tolerance was ineffectual against nazism, and the new humanism hardly sufficed. Heinrich Mann's huge novel about Henry IV of France, published in German in Amsterdam in 1936 when his books had already been banned in Germany, is another example of this genre.[50] A number of Hilde Wenzel's customers probably read such books in order to reaffirm their own humanistic orientation. But an opponent of nazism inside Germany thought that this kind of humanism and pacifism, which he found in the works of Erich Kästner, lacked a positive "fighting foundation"[51] and was ineffective against national socialism.

Hilde Wenzel assumed that Kästner was banned because he was a Jew (this was incorrect) and was puzzled that the authorities apparently did not even notice until 1938 that the popular travel writer Richard Katz was a Jew. Actually, the Nazis banned Kästner, Arthur Schnitzler, and Gustav Mayrink as "dekadenten Zivilisationsliteratentums," decadent literary people with the values of Western liberal civilization.[52] She apparently did not understand this category. The censors probably considered Richard Katz's travel writings harmless. They may not have known that he was a Jew, but Jewishness was not yet sufficient cause for censorship. The 1935 Nuremberg Laws first provided a legal definition of a Jew. In 1938 the Nazis finally began the "Herculean labor"[53] of compiling a complete list of Jewish authors but never completed it. No wonder the booksellers did not always know why authors were banned or which were Jews.

Her customers also explored a category that Hilde Wenzel described as "wolves in sheep's clothing." First among them was Johann Huizinga's *In the Shadow of Tomorrow: A Diagnosis of the Spiritual Distemper of Our Time,* written by this famous medievalist in Dutch and published in German in Switzerland in 1935, in

English in 1936. She and her husband recognized the author, probably for his classic *The Waning of the Middle Ages* (1924), but could not fathom why at least ten copies of the new book sold until she read it herself. The book analyzes central intellectual traits of national socialism in rather abstract language, without much explicit mention of Hitler or the Nazis. The Nazi authorities eventually grasped its subversiveness and banned it. Also frequently read were Gustav Le Bon's *The Crowd* (1895) and Ortega y Gasset's *Revolt of the Masses* (1929), whose titles suggested explanations of the nature of national socialism. Both were available in cheap German paperback editions. She did not know whether these were banned.

She classified other categories of reading as forms of "flight," such as "Flight into History," though they were more than pure escapism. Her readers might flee the present in reading about Tiberius, Queen Elizabeth, and Napoleon, but they obviously hoped to understand Hitler as well. Nero's persecution of Christians in ancient Rome offered analogies to Nazi persecution of Jews, as did Leopold von Ranke on the sectarian fanaticism and violence of the German Reformation. Books about the French Revolution and Napoleon and Jacob Burckhardt's *Force and Freedom* delineated natural stages in other revolutions, which helped readers understand the Nazi revolution.[54]

Her readers also fled the present into the classics of German literature. In an entire year before the Nazi period she did not sell so many copies of Schiller, Kleist, and Goethe as in one month during the years after Hitler took power. Goethe was much more popular than Schiller, and Kleist was a distant third: thus the less political, the better. The dissolution of numerous households made many used copies available. Heinrich Heine also sold well, at least until 1937. She knew that he was not banned, although many assumed that he was on the Nazi list as a Jew, an exile in Paris, and a critic of repression and censorship in post-Napoleonic Germany.[55]

Another form of flight from Germany was reading about distant parts of the globe. Wenzel's customers read Chinese and Japanese literature, or authors who wrote about China and Japan such as Pearl Buck, Alice Tisdale Hobart, Nora Waln, and the French physician Albert Gervais. They particularly liked Victor George Heiser's *Eines Arztes Weltfahrt,* a best seller in English as *An American Doctor's Odyssey* (1936), which recorded visits to forty-five countries.[56] Also very popular were translations of John Galsworthy, Joseph Conrad, and Romain Rolland, especially *Jean Christophe,* where readers could immerse themselves in the values of better days. Hilde carefully kept Rolland's books out of the display window and sold them only to trusted customers because of his pacifism and his condemnation of nazism. As she remarked, "the more the radio was controlled by the Party and the State, the worse the theater and the movies were, the more the Germans read books." This was not the only reason. Jews were afraid of insults and harassment at the theater and movies even before they were legally excluded from them. Gradually they were being mentally and morally segregated.[57] They might escape in their reading.

There was also considerable demand for the great Russian writers, such as

Tolstoy in the Malik-Verlag edition, which became a rarity. This publisher's books were banned on 31 December 1938 because during the 1920s and in exile after 1933 it published anti-Nazi, left-wing, and modern authors and artists.[58] A good copy of Dostoyevsky did not remain unsold for long either. Although the Nazi regime was bitterly antagonistic toward the Soviet Union, this hostility did not extend to nineteenth-century Russian authors. As Wolfgang Herrmann wrote in 1933, "Not every Russian writer is a cultural Bolshevist. Dostoyevsky and Tolstoy do not belong on the Index (without Dostoyevsky no Moeller van den Bruck!)." At the same time, Hilde Wenzel preferred not to buy Gorky and Lenin, although she knew of no explicit ban on them. A seller might try to trap her, and mere possession of the books might be dangerous. Such self-censorship was one Nazi objective.[59]

On the whole, rather than fearing her customers she grew closer to them as they browsed the shelves and talked. She enjoyed selling new and used books, as well as managing a lending library. The Wenzels kept a card file on their customers' literary interests and searched for the books they wanted. The customers discussed literature and their personal problems and anxieties. The exchange of confidences involved risks, responsibilities, and counsel, especially when Hilde obtained dubious or even forbidden books for her clientele. She was exhilarated by her quietly subversive role as confidante and occasional seller of underground literature.[60] But eventually the authorities realized the Wenzels were Jews.

They had long feared that their failure to fly Nazi flags outside their shop would arouse suspicion. Their neighbors presumably discerned that they either were not Nazis or were Jews. If they had hung the flags to escape attention and had been discovered to be Jews, the Nazis would have punished them severely. But no denunciation was necessary: in a spring 1935 Nazi questionnaire, Peter Wenzel had not concealed his long-dead Jewish grandmother and his Jewish wife. He was classified as a "Mischling II"[61] consonant with the September 1935 Nuremberg Laws, and this was the beginning of the end for them.

The Wenzels were probably not much affected by the centralization and toughening of racial and cultural policies from 1935 to 1937. Between 1933 and 1935 Propaganda Minister Joseph Goebbels waged lengthy bureaucratic wars with his competitors, especially Alfred Rosenberg, for control of German culture. Despite Rosenberg's advantage from his early start with his Kampfbund, plus his imposing title after January 1934 as director of the Office for the Supervision of the Entire Cultural and Ideological Education and Training of the NSDAP, the issue was scarcely in doubt. Goebbels was far more intelligent, flexible, and able, and Rosenberg's power base in offices in the Nazi Party could not match Goebbels's Reich offices. Under the umbrella of his ministry Goebbels created in September 1933 the Reich Chamber of Culture (Reichskulturkammer), which had divisions for Press, Radio, Literature, Theater, Film, Music, and the Plastic Arts. Membership was essential in order to work in these fields. Subdivisions of the Reich Chamber of Literature (Reichsschrifttumskammer) controlled authors, publishers, and booksellers. Goebbels was determined to "Aryanize" the Chamber and make certain that Jews already driven from other professions were not admitted. But in the fall of 1934 Minister of Economics Hjalmar Schacht protested that Goebbels's "Aryanization" would damage the economy. In response Goebbels claimed that he was acting against individuals, not businesses. Starting in 1935 the Chamber excluded approximately 500 authors who were already members and refused the applications of some 1,500 others. The larger number of them were Jews, the previously arrested, and the politically unreliable.[62]

In September 1934 the Nazi Bund Reichsdeutscher Buchhändler (BRB) replaced the old Börsenverein der Deutschen Buchhändler, and it soon had 25,000 members. To establish that none of them were Jews the BRB sent them the questionnaire in May 1935 that Peter Wenzel completed. The BRB gradually terminated the memberships of Jewish publishers and booksellers and removed their names from their address books. Because this ruinously hindered their businesses and Goebbels could not entirely ignore Schacht's protest against economic loss, he agreed to steps minimizing the loss of value and jobs in the forced sales of Jewish businesses to "Aryans."[63] These provisions considerably slowed the process of Aryanization.

On 25 April 1935 Goebbels, as head of the Reich Chamber of Literature, obtained supreme censorship authority at the expense of the censoring agencies in the German states. The Propaganda Ministry compiled the first official "Index" of authors and books applicable throughout Germany but sent it to a restricted number of officials.[64] There followed a second great "cleansing" action until the end of 1936, when the Gestapo and Sicherheitsdienst (the Nazi Party espionage service) periodically purged forbidden volumes on the Index from secondhand bookstores and lending libraries throughout Germany. Heinrich Himmler's appointment on 17 June 1936 as head of the SS and chief of the German police centralized police power, which facilitated censorship operations.[65]

After the promulgation of the Nuremberg Laws against the Jews during the September 1935 Party rally, Goebbels obtained Hitler's approval for tougher measures against publishers and bookstores. The Bund Reichsdeutscher Buchhändler ordered most Jewish bookstore owners to sell their businesses to "Aryans." On economic grounds connected with the heavy demands of rearmament, Schacht apparently persuaded Hitler to reverse himself early in 1936. Goebbels's minions quickly excluded the small Jewish firms from the Chamber and then ordered them to sell all their assets to Aryan owners who would continue the business. They acted much more slowly against the big Jewish publishers and bookstores, in order to minimize the economic damage.[66]

Another motive behind these delays was that the regime wanted to deceive foreign visitors to the 1936 Olympics, both the winter games in Garmisch-Partenkirchen and the summer games in Berlin. The rest of the world disapproved of the Nazis' virulent anti-Semitism. During the Olympics the boxes selling Streicher's offensive *Stürmer* on every street corner were removed, as were signs banning Jews from towns or various facilities.[67] A complement to this was a reverse form of censorship reported in an autobiography by the owner of a lending library. The Nazis forbade the loan or sale of three volumes of Nazi propaganda, apparently to prevent them from coming into the hands of critical visitors. The first was Goebbels's *Das Buch Isador,* an appalling volume of vulgar verses about Dr. Bernhard Weiss, the Social-Democratic (and Jewish) police president of Berlin before 1933. The book was black with gold letters that at first appeared to be Hebrew, but on closer study were the title in German. In the second, *Ernstes und Heiteres aus der Putschzeit* (1928), Manfred von Killinger celebrated the brutality of the Freikorps after the war and the spirit of the Organization Council, in which he plotted the assassinations of Erzberger and Rathenau. Appointed minister president of Saxony by Hitler, during the war he was Nazi minister in Slovakia and Romania. The third, Hanns Heinz Ewers's biography of the supposed Nazi martyr Horst Wessel, described too frankly his life as a procurer and how Hitler had received him in 1931 in the Brown House in Munich.[68] After the Olympics this temporary ban ended; the *Stürmer* boxes on the street corners, and the signs banning Jews reappeared.

During 1936 the authorities hindered Jewish publishers and booksellers in many small ways. They could no longer advertise in important journals, and their books suffered increasingly hostile reviews. As a result approximately 400 fewer Jewish booksellers were listed in the "Booksellers' Address Book" (*Buchhändler-adressbuch*) in January 1937 than a year earlier, and the Propaganda Ministry restricted Jewish publishers to publishing books by and about Jews. Another edict required that Jewish bookstores only sell "Jewish books" by "Jewish authors" to Jews. Otherwise they had to sell their stores to "Aryans." The Wenzels were apparently given a temporary dispensation, perhaps because Peter was a "Mischling II," but they were identified as Jews, and pressures on Jews intensified.[69]

Hilde Wenzel's account reads as though she believed that if her husband had concealed his Jewish grandmother they could have maintained their bookstore. If he or Hilde had concealed their ancestry and had been caught, the consequences would have been severe. However, she may have been right: the Nazis could not easily establish anyone's ancestry without honest answers to the questionnaires. And they did not begin a systematic examination of these documents until 1937, which explains why Peter Wenzel was not caught until two years after he filled out the questionnaire.[70] The authorities punished Peter Wenzel by terminating his membership in the BRD and his listing in the "Booksellers' Address Book."

Although publishers were only allowed to deliver books to members of the BRD, each member had a special number on his or her order slips. The Wenzels continued to use their number and even printed more. However, because they were not in the address book, their deliveries were frequently slowed or denied toward Christmas 1937. To make ends meet, they had to remain open evenings and still complete the bookkeeping after closing. The long hours and worry about the future affected Hilde's health. She slept and ate badly and was near death by the end of 1937. They received a deadline for sale of the bookstore to an "Aryan," a letter most Jewish book dealers had received in October 1935.[71]

In January 1938 the authorities summoned Jews to report with their passports in order to cancel the allowance for travel abroad. Hilde Wenzel already perceived that those who owned little had left Nazi Germany early, whereas those who stayed longer to retain a bigger stake might miss the chance to leave and lose almost everything. Her lawyer urged her to leave. She was the only one in her family who recognized that the March 1938 takeover of Austria was the beginning of a fatal chain of events. At the passport office she promised to go to Italy and was allowed to keep her passport. Instead she went to Zurich with her child, leaving her husband, the bookstore, and her customers. She lamented these losses, but she later realized she had been fortunate to leave with her child before the 10 November 1938 pogrom.

After coming to power the Nazis first attacked literature, but they had always shown a comparable animosity to modernity in art and music. When Hitler sided with Rosenberg's antimodernist views of art, Goebbels ceased defending expressionism. In 1937 he boldly attempted to strengthen his position against competitors for control over the cultural realm, especially Kultusminister Bernhard Rust, who was responsible for museums. Goebbels appointed a commission which during April–October 1937 confiscated 16,000 works of "modern" art and sculpture from German museums. More than 650 of these paintings, sculptures, prints, and books by 112 artists were displayed in the notorious "Degenerate Art Exhibition" in Munich, which later toured other German cities for four years. In 1938 the Nazis mounted a parallel exhibition of "Degenerate Music."[72]

The Nazi belief that Jews subverted modern culture and society was one of many grounds for stealing their wealth and property, which would facilitate the rearmament integral to Germany's more aggressive foreign policy. Hitler's ambitions were clear in his August 1936 memorandum on the Four Year Plan, which harnessed the German economy to accelerated rearmament. This entailed a shift from the protection of Jewish publishers and bookstores demanded by Schacht to confiscations and punitive decrees in 1937–38. During 1937 the Nazis completed the seizure begun in 1933 of the entire property of B'nai B'rith, especially lodges with their handsome libraries and artworks.[73]

In a secret conference on 5 November 1937 Hitler outlined a much more active and grandiose foreign policy, which envisaged the possibility of war over Austria or Czechoslovakia. Schuschnigg's regime in Austria was already protofascist, and under pressure he had conceded the Nazis a greater political role. Many Austrians had long expected Anschluss, and the obvious victims of nazism were apprehensive. In one Jewish household a teenage daughter dreamed that Hitler came into her bedroom, closed the windows and doors, "wrote on the wall that every Jew must be annihilated, [and] fill[ed] the place with poison gas." The maid frantically busied herself burning papers and books, and when a car stopped outside, she ran to the window saying that the Nazis were coming for her. The Nazi invasion of Austria on 9 March 1938 brought in its wake a ferocious pogrom. As Austrian Nazis invaded the apartment of writer Egon Friedell, he leapt through a window to his death. Many famous, primarily Jewish, figures in Austrian intellectual and cultural life committed suicide, frequently with gas.[74]

Like the Germans before them, Austrians now disposed of dangerous papers and books. One of them immediately burned his correspondence, incriminating books by the pacifist Friedrich Wilhelm Foerster, and Konrad Heiden's biography of Hitler. Another destroyed his volumes of Tucholsky. On 12–13 March 1938, a recently married young Viennese couple carried books from their new apartment back to their old one to burn them in a stove. Witnesses thought books were burned in every other home or apartment and that probably more than one Austrian destroyed "harmless written things out of fear that they might contain something incriminating."[75]

The Nazis removed Heinrich Heine from public and private libraries in Vienna. They seized much of the 8,000-volume library of a Viennese Jewish teacher because it contained condemned categories of "Jewish" and "free-thinking" literature. "Jewish" and "Marxist" books were taken out of bookstores, lending libraries, and large private libraries and were frequently burned in the streets and squares of Vienna. Upon finding books in English and French in an apartment, the Nazis characteristically sneered at and punished the owners for their education and cosmopolitanism. A young, blind, Jewish, Social-Democratic teacher, librarian, and editor of a journal in braille, wore his armband for the blind for the first time and experienced only Nazi solicitude when he went to the braille library to save books critical of or banned by the Nazis. He removed the dangerous ones from the shelves and tore labels in normal writing from their spines, then some days later sent them to a friend in Hungary, and in 1939 to London. In Krems, Nazis confiscated a Greek edition of Homer from Paul Brüll's library, apparently in the belief that it might be a secret journal in Hebrew.[76]

With one truck after another the Gestapo removed the records and books from the offices of the chief rabbi of Vienna, Dr. Israel Taglicht, and stole the library of the Jewish community, described by a witness as "one of the most valuable Jewish libraries in the world," which became part of the extraordinary RSHA library in Berlin. Other libraries were added to the collections of the central scientific libraries, which were immediately integrated with the German library system. The head of the Austrian National Library, Josef Bick, was sent to Dachau; twelve of eighty-nine employees, the Jews and politically suspect, were fired and some died in extermination camps. Although part of the Rothschild family managed to flee Austria, Baron Louis de Rothschild was caught at the airport and imprisoned for nine months; he won release only by handing over his property as ransom. Above all the Nazis wanted his large collection of paintings, but he lost substantial libraries, too.[77]

By the end of 1938 the Nazis had confiscated and "Aryanized" or simply liquidated Jewish-owned or politically suspect publishing houses, such as the Freud family's Internationale Psychoanalytische Verlag. The family owners of the German firm of S. Fischer, refounded as Bermann-Fischer in Vienna, left everything at Anschluss and fled to Sweden.[78] The Nazis also "Aryanized" bookstores owned by Jews and usually seized or destroyed their now heavily censored contents. And there was worse to come.

The 10 November 1938 pogrom brought another wave of destruction. Nazis killed ninety-one Jews and burned 267 synagogues with their Torahs and religious books.[79] Outside one burned synagogue they ostentatiously trampled prayer books in the street. Because of the danger of fire spreading from burning synagogues to neighboring houses many survived, but then the Nazis wrecked the interiors and burned the contents in the market square. The district commander in Baden-Baden arrived outside the synagogue and told the assembled Jews that higher authorities had refused his request to burn the building with the Jews inside. Some Nazis in Vienna threw a Torah into the Danube, and SS men seriously considered driving Jews into the Danube to drown.[80]

The attack on a synagogue frequently included destruction or damage to the nearby or attached Jewish community building, containing the administrative offices, a library, the rabbi's dwelling, a Jewish school, and often an orphanage or home for the elderly with an apartment for a teacher or caretaker. The wife of a well-known rabbi in Offenbach recalled how Nazis wrecked their house and confiscated their books while others systematically destroyed the library, classrooms, shop, kitchen, windows, and furniture in the Jewish school. A teacher from a state school led his students through the wreckage, and they took whatever they wanted, although some of these objects were later returned. In a few towns teachers prevented their students from participating in the pogrom.[81]

The Jewish community in Frankfurt am Main suffered especially heavy losses because it was the home of Herschel Grynszpan, whose assassination of the German diplomat Ernst vom Rath was the pretext for Kristallnacht. The police there watched passively while Nazis burned the synagogue and the community house with its library of 16,000 volumes, then wrecked everything in the Jewish school and threw the remains into the streets. They destroyed the teacher's apartment, including his books and records, and arrested and sent to concentration camps a number of Jewish teachers. They completely ruined Jewish orphanages and their books in several towns.[82]

Thirty thousand Jews from Germany and 6,547 from Austria, a high proportion professionals, were sent to concentration camps. Some died from mistreatment or committed suicide on the electric fences or by hanging themselves or were murdered. A number who fell during roll call because of age, illness, exhaustion, or mistreatment died. An SS blockführer kicked a doctor who was lying on a stretcher at roll call and said every day they should brutalize an entire *Judenblock* in that fashion. Another SS man said: "Do you know what a Jew in the Third Reich signifies? Less than a piece of filth lying on the earth." At least one Jew was drowned in a cement mixer and another in excrement in a latrine. The Nazis executed a number of Jews in front of the others and killed by injection many of those taken to the hospital. The camp commander at Buchenwald said loudly

that a dead Jew was merely fuel for the crematorium. The Nazis cremated approximately 1,000 of their victims before returning them by post to their relatives,
who were charged the postage. An SS man shouted that he wished all the emi-
grant ships would sink and the Jews would drown, thus solving the Jewish "question" and saving the Nazis cremation costs. A physician inmate concluded that
the highly organized Germans intentionally incarcerated large numbers in camps
with inadequate water and medical help in order to kill them. These eyewitness
accounts contradict the frequent claim that the Nazis at this time were only pressing Jews to leave Germany in order to confiscate their wealth. Crucial elements
of the Final Solution were already in evidence.[83]

The November 1938 pogrom frightened many German and Austrian Jews into
destroying their books and papers. After a physician was taken by the Gestapo,
his nurse administrator first hid and then burned all of his foreign correspondence. When he returned they packed, married, and immediately departed from
Germany. In order not to compromise anyone, a lawyer and businessman burned
all his papers before his departure.[84] Jews realized that they could take very few
possessions with them and left their libraries and paintings.

By 1937 there were only twenty-seven Jewish publishers in Germany. Founded
in 1909, the Erich Reiss Verlag was a leading publisher of quality literature; from
1933 until 1936 or 1937 it published only Jewish authors and then was sold. A
series of decrees after the November 1938 pogrom excluded Jews from German
economic life, and "Germans" took ownership from the remaining Jewish publishers and booksellers. Salman Schocken Verlag, started by a distinguished department store pioneer, book collector, and cultural Zionist, was liquidated.
Schocken negotiated shipment of 160 tons of books, 80 percent of his stock, to
Haifa in 1939 when he emigrated to Palestine. Owners who had sold their firms
at great loss earlier but had remained in Germany, such as Herman Ullstein, emigrated after the pogrom, as did Ernst Rowohlt, who had published a biography
of Hitler by Konrad Heiden before 1933. Many of the publishers exiled early produced books hostile to the Third Reich and were listed on a 31 December 1938
"Index" of publishers, the first list banning all of their old and new production.[85]
Many of these renowned publishers returned to Germany after 1945 and reestablished themselves; the notes to this essay contain many books published by successor publishing houses with the original names.

The last of the Jewish "ghetto" booksellers were liquidated at the end of 1938
or during 1939. On 31 December 1938 Nazi agencies produced a much fuller list
with eighteen categories of condemned writings, 4,175 single titles of books, and
bans on the entire works of 565 authors. On 15 April 1940 they banned all books
by Jewish authors, although a few scientific works by Jews were sold in Germany
until 1945 because there were no substitutes for them.[86]

The Nazis also sold, exchanged, or auctioned paintings confiscated from Jews
or purged from the museums during 1938–39. But thousands remained, and on
20 March 1939 the Nazis probably burned in secret 1,004 oil paintings and 3,825
water colors, drawings, and prints in a Berlin firehouse courtyard.[87] This was

a mere preliminary to the robbery and destruction of books and art in World War II, in conjunction with the annihilation of peoples.

The Nazi obsession with *Lebensraum*, the "racial inferiority" of Slavs and Jews, and "Jewish bolshevism" resulted in harsher territorial, population, and cultural policies in eastern than in western Europe.[88] The Nazis murdered and starved Polish elites, Polish and Soviet Jews, and more than 3 million Soviet prisoners of war; resettled large annexed areas with Germans after the brutal eviction of Poles; imposed starvation rations and slave labor; limited education to four grades, closed universities, and deported whole faculties to concentration camps; curtailed publishing, destroyed or confiscated libraries, and suppressed Slavic culture.[89] While inflicting colossal losses in the USSR, the Nazis still undertook throughout Europe the extermination of their racial enemy, the Jews, and the eradication of their culture. In northern and western Europe the Nazi occupation regimes at first balanced collaboration and exploitation, although they Germanized and made small population transfers in their annexed territories. A second phase began when the Nazi invasion of the USSR stimulated resistance, initially Communist, in the west. Savage Nazi reprisals, harsher exploitation, defeats in Russia, and Allied landings in the Mediterranean increased resistance. In the final phase the Nazis ended collaboration everywhere and ruled with the gun. But relatively moderate policies toward non-Jewish culture in the west never excluded massive theft of whatever books and art they coveted, which continued even during their evacuations.

During the war two Nazi agencies were central to the theft and destruction of libraries. The first evolved from Alfred Rosenberg's Kampfbund, and the second from the Reich Security Headquarters (Reichssicherheitshauptamt, or RSHA). In July 1940 Hitler commissioned the Einsatzstab Reichsleiter Rosenberg (ERR) to seize books for the library of a postwar Nazi university, the Hohe Schule, at Chiemsee, Bavaria. A 17 September 1940 order covered artworks in France and a Führer order of 1 March 1942 extended this to the eastern front. ERR headquarters was in Berlin, with offices in Brussels, Amsterdam, Paris, Belgrade and Riga; suboffices and mobile units scoured the occupied countries for books. Units of twenty to twenty-five men in special uniforms accompanied the armies in the east, where the ERR investigated 375 archives, 402 museums, 531 institutes, and 957 libraries. In each of the conquered countries the Amt Musik of the ERR took music and theater libraries, music scores, and various instruments, including an estimated 6,000 pianos, harpsichords, and spinets.[90]

On 26 March 1941 Rosenberg opened the Institute for the Investigation of the Jewish Question in Frankfurt. Of ten more planned institutes only three, in Munich, Halle, and Hamburg, achieved any substance.[91] On 1 April 1943 the expropriated Hohe jüdische Schule in Leipzig opened as the Hochschule für Musik. It closed less than a year after bombing in January 1944 forced removal to safety in Silesia of its valuable library and collection of musical instruments, all stolen by the ERR's Amt Musik. Rosenberg's Ostbücherei in Berlin led these mainly stolen libraries with a million volumes. The city library of Frankfurt's excellent Jewish collection was at the disposal of the main institute, without being integrated in its library, which grew from seizures in France, the Netherlands, Poland, Lithuania, and Greece to 550,000 volumes by April 1943.[92]

The RSHA had 2–3 million books concerning the Nazis' enemies: the churches, Freemasons, Marxists, and Jews. The collection on the Jews grew enormously with the seizure of Jewish academic and community libraries from Berlin, Breslau, Gleiwitz, Hamburg, Königsberg, Munich, Warsaw, and Vienna, as well as distinguished private libraries in the new empire.[93]

Both institutions robbed and destroyed the most renowned Jewish, socialist, and Masonic libraries in conquered Europe. In Poland from December 1939 to March 1940 the Nazis plundered more than 100 libraries, plus churches, palaces, manors, museums, and art galleries. Estimates range from 600,000 stolen volumes of Judaica and Hebraica from Lodz alone to a million volumes from the entirety of Poland. Polish librarians shifted the rarest volumes from the National Library and the library of the University of Warsaw to safer storage in the five underground floors of the renowned Krasinski Library, but the Nazis systematically burned the building and the books. In addition to seizing 95 percent of artworks in Poland within six months, the Nazis also plundered or destroyed most libraries in synagogues and Jewish teaching institutions. In Vilna Dr. Johannes Pohl of the ERR, an expert on Hebrew literature who had studied in Jerusalem, ordered a selection of 20,000 of the choicest volumes from 100,000 collected from several towns and 300 synagogues, and the sale of 80,000 as raw material to a paper-shredding mill. Hebrew books published later than 1800 were regularly pulped. But many of the valuable books and manuscripts concealed by forty Jewish workers in the Vilna library before the liquidation of the ghetto in July 1943 survived them.[94]

In September 1940 the ERR in Amsterdam seized the Biblioteca Klossiana of the Freemasons and the libraries in ninety-two Masonic lodges; the Jewish Biblioteca Rosenthaliana (100,000) from the university library; the libraries of the Portuguese-Jewish community, the Sephardic Jewish community, and the Dutch Jewish seminar; and the International Archive of the Women's Movement. They also confiscated collections from a theosophic society (ninety-six crates), from Jewish antiquarian book dealers, and from the famous German exile publishing houses Albert de Lange, Querida, Pegasus, and Bermann-Fischer (seventeen crates). They packed 160,000 volumes from the International Institute for Social History plus its newspaper and periodical collection in 776 crates. From the library of the Societas Spinozana in The Hague they took eighteen crates. In the *Möbel-Aktion* (furniture action) from March 1942 to June 1944 the Nazis seized the contents of 29,000 Jewish deportees' residences, which yielded 700,000 to 800,000 books. In April 1944 they removed a theater library in forty-nine crates.[95]

During the invasion of Belgium German forces destroyed the university library in Louvain for the second time, the first having been in August 1914. The German security police and the ERR confiscated the libraries and archives of Freemasons,

Jews, and socialists in Brussels, Antwerp, Ghent, Liège, Charleroi, Namur, Lille, and Brugge. Especially notable were the Librairie Cosmopolis, the library of the Instituut voor Sociale Geschiedenis, the Jesuit library of 50,000–60,000 volumes and archives in the Enghien Monastery, and the library and archives of the duke of Guise. After deporting the Belgian Jews to their deaths in 1942 the Nazis seized the contents of 4,500 of their homes, including their libraries. They destroyed hundreds of thousands of books and sent large numbers to Germany.[96]

The ERR in France helped seize 723 libraries comprising 1,767,108 volumes, including 12,743 rare books. They took to Rosenberg's institute in Frankfurt the libraries of the Alliance Israélite Universelle (40,000), the Ecole Rabbinique (10,000), and the Fédération de la Société des Juifs de France (4,000), the Polish Library and the Turgenev Library, as well as the contents of the Paris bookstore Lipschütz (20,000), the publisher Calman Levy (15,000), the Collection David Weill (5,000), and the private libraries owned by several Rothschilds. A further 482 boxes of books were taken from Jewish homes. Sonderstab Musik confiscated the books, correspondence, scores, and instruments of musicians and composers, including Wanda Landowska (10,000 volumes, 15 valuable instruments), Darius Milhaud, Gregor Piatigorski, and Arthur Rubenstein. ERR agents opened regional offices in various French cities in December 1940 and again after the occupation of Vichy France in November 1942. By 1942 the ERR had dealt with 1,996 sites. During the *Möbel-Aktion* of 25 March 1942 the Nazis looted 68,441 households owned by deported Jews.[97]

The Nazi agencies in the Soviet Union greedily sought valuable collections, but all of them destroyed more books in the east, because depriving Slavs of education and destroying their culture would make them helots, ripe for ruthless exploitation to extinction. In Ukraine 150 experts working for the ERR stole or destroyed over 51 million books from the central state and university libraries of Kiev, all the regional libraries in other cities, and libraries in palaces, museums, churches, and synagogues. They robbed these sites of their cultural treasures, including archives, then frequently destroyed them. Other German agencies plundered the libraries and archives of Lvov in Galicia. In Belarus more than 200 libraries were plundered; the national library lost 83 percent of its collections, and although 600,000 volumes were later found, 1 million are still missing. Museums, palaces, and churches suffered devastating losses and were often left in ruins.[98]

In Russia comparable plundering and destruction took place. The ERR, the Wehrmacht, and Sonderkommando Künsberg of the Foreign Office loaded trains with state, city, university, museum, and palace libraries and archives from the Leningrad suburbs and from Smolensk, Novgorod, Rostov, Voronezh, Pskov, and Kalinin. They collected from 1,670 Russian Orthodox and 237 Catholic churches, 532 synagogues, and estates in the countryside. As in France they provided special clients, such as other Nazi agencies or leaders, with loot. The Nazis looted 3 to 4 million books from the entire USSR and destroyed many more.[99] Current estimates of German depredations in the USSR must be corrected by research in the recently opened archives there and in Germany. The final estimate will depend on an accurate survey of treasures removed by the Soviet government before the German armies arrived and after they retreated, of destruction by Soviet forces on both occasions, and of the total number of books Soviet forces recovered from occupied Germany.[100] They reportedly found 2 million volumes at Ratibor alone.

When Allied bombing raids on German and Austrian cities threatened or hit libraries, Nazi institutes, and stolen collections in storage centers, the Nazis transferred these holdings to safety in mines or buildings outside the major cities. Such large numbers were difficult to transfer and store safely, but many survived and came under the control of the Allies. During the winter of 1945–46 the contents of all of the depots in the American zone were sent to collecting points in Munich, Wiesbaden, Marburg, and Offenbach for inventory and return to their original owners.[101] The collecting point in Offenbach concentrated on books because the ERR had pillaged so many for Rosenberg's institute in Frankfurt. When twenty bombing raids pounded Frankfurt after October 1943 the books were transferred to nearby towns. After Germany's defeat the Allies returned books to the still intact Rothschild Library in Frankfurt, which was full by the end of 1945. They processed 2.5–3 million books[102] in a five-story I. G. Farben building in Offenbach, on the other side of the Main River, which after 1 May 1946 was the sole western depot for books and archives. But the numbers of books thus far known to have been found are a small fraction of the books that Germany apparently stole, and an even smaller part of one scholar's estimate of 100 million volumes destroyed.[103]

CONCLUSION

Before 1933 various Nazi organizations and publications had frankly expressed their intentions regarding "un-German" literature, theater, art, music, film, and architecture. The Nazis found widespread support for these policies because they tapped powerful historical forces. Nazi cultural policies were implemented in some German states. But the new regime needed time to define its policies, to centralize and assert its control at every level. The widespread confiscations of books and the shocking burnings in the "Action against the Un-German Spirit" on 10 May 1933 combined fierce anti-Semitism with other motives. This action was not national "policy" but perfectly anticipated it. It was appropriate that it became a symbol of Nazi intolerance. Various enemies of the regime as well as owners of bookstores and libraries also destroyed the books and papers believed to be proscribed by the Nazis. Most Jewish (and many non-Jewish) writers and publishers emigrated.

As the dominant figure in cultural affairs, Goebbels pressed for more radical racial and cultural policies beginning in 1935, with temporary delays because of the 1936 Olympics. The Nuremberg Laws, an "Index" of banned "un-German" books, edicts forcing Jews to sell publishing houses and bookstores, and policies against "degenerate" art and music were harshly applied in 1937–38. These measures and the pogroms of March and November 1938 accompanied Hitler's open pursuit of a militarily risky and expansionist foreign policy against Austria and then Czechoslovakia. In both pogroms the Nazis confiscated, stole, and burned books. They also arrested and sent to concentration camps, murdered and cremated many more Jews than in 1933. Many Jews committed suicide with gas; one dreamed that Hitler came to gas her; Nazis talked of gassing Jews and discussed extermination of the Czechs in memoranda. The camps, murderous brutality and deprivation, gassing, extermination: reality and fantasy soon became one in the Final Solution. During the war the Nazis stole and destroyed millions of books and murdered their political and racial opponents. They shot and gassed millions of Jews and burned the bodies. Toward the end of the war they burned considerable numbers alive.[104]

There is not only a symbolic and ideological but also a strong circumstantial connection between the burning of books and the burning of men. The Nazis viewed their ideological and racial enemies and their books as ineluctably one, the living and printed embodiment of the "un-German spirit" and the contemporary civilization they despised. They wanted to destroy and supplant this enemy spirit. They burned and banned its printed and artistic expressions, silenced its creators and exponents within the Reich, denounced and threatened them outside. They classified, identified, and segregated the race and groups that embodied this spirit. After conquering Europe they deported and exterminated the Jews while seizing or destroying their books plus all they owned. In the east they enslaved and killed Slavs, plundered and destroyed their books, indeed, their civilization.

The German writers in exile were quick to recognize the symbolic importance of the 10 May 1933 book burnings, and they reacted by refounding the Organization of German Writers in France. On 10 May 1934 the exiles in Paris commemorated the original event by founding a German Freedom Library under the presidency of Romain Rolland. It soon housed 11,000 volumes: not only those burned, confiscated, and banned in Germany but others on every aspect of fascism in Europe, plus pamphlets, documents, journals, and 200,000 clippings. For six years this was a center of German culture in exile in France. Emigré writers organized, met regularly, publicized mistreatment of writers in concentration camps, and tried to prevent the incorporation of the Saar and Austria into Germany. In June 1935 their writers' congress to defend culture attracted leading writers from the Soviet Union (Boris Pasternak, Ilya Ehrenburg), Austria (Robert Musil), France (Louis Aragon, André Gide, André Malraux), England (Aldous Huxley), as well as German exiles (Bertolt Brecht, Anna Seghers, Ernst Toller, Klaus Mann, Heinrich Mann). Another writers' conference in February 1936 under the chairmanship of Heinrich Mann promoted an anti-fascist coalition. The exiles helped write and publish condemnations of the Reichstag fire trial and *Gleichschaltung,* the book burning and Nazi cultural policies, the murderous purge after the "Röhm Putsch" on 30 June 1934, the boycott and mistreatment of the Jews, and the rearmament of Germany. They condemned Franco's revolt in Spain and supported the Loyalists, whom a number of them joined during the Spanish Civil

War. They deplored the Anschluss, the Munich Accord, the occupation of Prague, and the Nazi-Soviet Pact.

Many who later fled France reached New York City, where the New York Public Library exhibited burned and banned books in December 1942. A 10 May 1943 commemoration there and at 300 other public libraries was accompanied by readings, theatrical and orchestral performances, and radio broadcasts. The speakers frequently quoted Wendell Willkie and Franklin Delano Roosevelt, as did subsequent Allied propaganda emphasizing freedom of speech and publication, the defense of books, and the values of the civilization that the Nazis attacked.[105]

The catastrophic cultural destruction was coupled with unprecedented mass murder of Jews and Slavs, captured in a new word, "genocide." Although the Western governments were very well informed about the extermination of the Jews, they scarcely condemned this as vociferously as they did the destruction of books.[106] The Holocaust should have been trumpeted to the world. Heinrich Heine's perception was true. Through book burnings and the Holocaust the Nazis pursued the same objective, the destruction of the "un-German spirit," which they believed was fundamentally Jewish.[107]

NOTES

I want to thank the Social Sciences Research Council of Canada for its financial support for research on this article; my wife Nancy for endless technical help with the computer; David and Helene Roberts for lodgings in Cambridge while working in the Houghton Library; and Jonathan Rose for his superb editorial help.

1. "Dort, wo man Bücher verbrennt, verbrennt man auch am Ende Menschen." The line is from *Almansor: Eine Tragödie* (1821–23), verse 242; quoted in Leo Löwenthal, "Calibans Erbe," in *"Das war ein Vorspiel nur . . . ," Berliner Colloquium zur Literaturpolitik im "Dritten Reich,"* ed. Horst Denkler and Eberhard Lämmert (Berlin: Akademie der Künste, 1985), 14, hereafter cited as *Das war ein Vorspiel nur* (Berliner), to distinguish it from the 1983 exhibition catalog cited below. Löwenthal's title also quotes Shakespeare, *The Tempest*, act 3, scene 2, where Caliban urges that Prospero's books be burned before his murder.

2. During their marches through cities, Nazi columns sang "fighting songs" attacking Jews and the "Jewish Republic" and threatening that "When the hour of retribution comes some day, we are ready for any wholesale murder." Joseph Wulf, ed., *Musik im Dritten Reich: Eine Dokumentation* (Gütersloh: Mohn, 1963), 244.

3. Gerhard Sauder, *Die Bücherverbrennung: Zum 10. Mai 1933* (Frankfurt: Hanser, 1986). See the section on "Großstadtfeindlichkeit, Agrarromantik und jugendbewegter Antimodernismus" in *"Das war ein Vorspiel nur . . . ," Bücherverbrennung Deutschland 1933: Voraussetzungen und Folgen* (Berlin: Medusa, 1983), Katalog, 118–20; hereafter cited as *Das war ein Vorspiel nur* (Bücherverbrennung). This catalog of an exhibition at the Akademie der Künste, 8 May–3 July 1983, contains introductory essays, followed by lists and reproductions of exhibits; author and title will identify the essays; documents will be identified by "Katalog."

4. The Nazis viewed the Weimar Republic's "Trash and Filth Law" (*Schund-und Schmutzgesetz*) of 1926 as a weak legacy of the period of liberalism. Dietrich Aigner, "Die Indizierung 'schädlichen und unerwünschten Schriftrums' im Dritten Reich," *Archiv für Geschichte des Buchwesens* 11 (1971): 949. For this law, see Detlev Peukert, "Der Schund- und Schmutzkampf als 'Sozialpolitik der Seele': Eine Vorgeschichte der Bücherverbrennung?" in *Das war ein Vorspiel nur* (Bücherverbrennung), 51–63; Klaus Petersen, *Literatur und Justiz in der Weimarer Republik* (Stuttgart: Metzlersche Verlagsbuchhandlung, 1988), 87–97; idem, *Zensur in der Weimarer Republik* (Stuttgart: Metzler, 1995), 56–67, 155–74. For the kinds of titles that the Nazis no doubt wanted to clear from the window of a bookstore in Berlin in July 1932, see Edgar Mowrer, *Germany Puts the Clock Back* (Harmondsworth: Penguin, 1938 [1933]), 149. The Nazis also referred to the Bauhaus as the "Synagogue of Marxism." See Henry Grosshans, *Hitler and the Artists* (New York: Holmes & Meier, 1983), 52.

5. Autobiography 66, Ernest Frank, 33, recollected that Streicher used the term "Neger" for Jews and that a colleague had called Frank, who was a Jew, a "Neger." All the autobiographies cited in these notes are in the "My Life in Germany" collection, Houghton Library, Harvard University.

6. Ibid., 25.

7. As expressed in the "Twelve Theses against the Un-German Spirit," first published in the *Völkischer Beobachter*, 104–5 (April 1933): 14–15, later in *Deutsche Kultur-Wacht* 9 (1933): 15; Dietrich Strothmann, *Nationalsozialistische Literaturpolitik: Ein Beitrag zur Publizistik im Dritten Reich* (Bonn: Bouvier, 1963), 76–77; complete in Joseph Wulf, ed., *Literatur und Dichtung im Dritten Reich: Eine Dokumentation* (Gütersloh: Mohn, 1963), 41–42; with excellent commentary and situated amidst other relevant documents in Sauder, *Die Bücherverbrennung*, 77, 92–93. See also Hans-Wolfgang Strätz, "Die geistige SA rückt ein: Die studentische 'Aktion wider den undeutschen Geist' im Frühjahr 1933," in *10 Mai 1933: Bücherverbrennung in Deutschland und die Folgen*, ed. Ulrich Walberer (Frankfurt: Fischer Taschenbuch, 1983), 90–92 (originally published with notes in *Vierteljahreshefte für Zeitgeschichte* 16 [1968]: 347–72). It is important to realize that this manifesto was published almost a month before the book burnings of 10 May 1933. The students' categories of books were superseded by a much more sophisticated articulation in the regime's later, official lists.

8. Sauder, *Die Bücherverbrennung*, 10; *Das war ein Vorspiel nur* (Bücherverbrennung), Katalog, 148–56; Modris Eksteins, "War, Memory, and Politics: The Fate of the Film *All Quiet on the Western Front*," *Central European History* 13 1 (Mar. 1980): 60–82; Günter Neliba, "Wilhelm Frick und Thüringen als Experimentierfeld für die nationalsozialistische Machtergreifung," in *Nationalsozialismus in Thüringen*, ed. Detlev Heiden and Gunther Mai (Weimar: Böhlau, 1995), 85–91; Barbara Miller Lane, *Architecture and Politics in Germany, 1918–1945* (Cambridge: Harvard University Press, 1968), 171; Mowrer, *Germany Puts the Clock Back*, 158–59; Hildegard Brenner, "Art in the Political Power Struggle of 1933 and 1934," in *Republic to Reich: The Making of the Nazi Revolution*, ed. Hajo Holborn (New York: Random House, 1973), 396. Social Democratic weeklies such as *Reichsbanner* and *Alarm* and dailies such as *Der Volksfreund* (Braunschweig) frequently recognized that such policies presaged the "Third Reich."

9. Volker Dahm, "Die nationalsozialistische Schrifttumspolitik nach dem 10. Mai 1933," in Walberer, *10. Mai 1933*, 37. Anselm Faust, "Die Hochschulen und der 'undeutsche Geist': Die Bücherverbrennung am 10. Mai 1933 und ihre Vorgeschichte," in *Das war ein Vorspiel nur* (Bücherverbrennung), 39–40; Hans-Albert Walter, *Bedrohung und Verfolgung*

bis 1933: Deutsche Exilliteratur 1933–1950 (Darmstadt: Luchterhand, 1972), 1: 53–56; Manfred H. Niessen, "Wie es zu den Bücherverbrennung kam," in Walberer, *10. Mai 1933,* 25–26.

10. Aigner, "Die Indizierung," 939, 943; Volker Dahm, *Das jüdische Buch im Dritten Reich: Erster Teil. Die Ausschaltung der jüdischen Autoren, Verleger und Buchhändler* (Frankfurt: Buchhändler-Vereinigung, 1979), 99; hereafter cited as Dahm, *Das jüdische Buch,* pt. 1. This is a special printing from *Archiv für Geschichte des Buchwesens* 20 (1979), where the pagination is the same.

11. Aigner, "Die Indizierung," 1013; Faust, "Die Hochschulen," 38, 39, 45, 46–47. See Sauder, *Die Bücherverbrennung,* 109–10, 115, 117–19, for Herrmann's life; also in Siegfried Schliebs, "Verboten, verbrannt, verfolgt . . . : Wolfgang Herrmann und seine 'Schwarze Liste, Schöne Literatur' vom Mai 1933," in *Das war ein Vorspiel nur* (Bücherverbrennung), 442–43; Dahm, "Die nationalsozialistische Schrifttumspolitik," 42–43.

12. Aigner, "Die Indizierung," 945, 1008. Dahm, "Die nationalsozialistische Schrifttumspolitik," 57; Sauder, *Die Bücherverbrennung,* 120–44, esp. 126–28, 142–43.

13. Aigner, "Die Indizierung," 951, 955, 986–90.

14. Autobiography 251, Wolfgang Yourgran, 45; Autobiography 92, Edmund P. Heilpern, 117; Sauder, *Die Bücherverbrennung,* 149, in a legal justification for book seizures, 28 Mar. 1933.

15. Istvan Deak, *Weimar Germany's Left-Wing Intellectuals: A Political History of the Weltbühne and Its Circle* (Berkeley and Los Angeles: University of California Press, 1968).

16. For the "Feuersprüche," see Aigner, "Die Indizierung," 1018; Sauder, *Die Bücherverbrennung,* 77. Two German versions are in *Das war ein Vorspiel nur* (Bücherverbrennung), Katalog, 196 (Berlin), 212–13 (Mannheim). A different English version of this document is in J. Noakes and G. Pridham, eds., *Nazism, 1919–1945: A History in Documents and Eyewitness Accounts,* vol. 1, *The Nazi Party, State and Society, 1919–1939* (New York: Schocken, 1990), 402.

17. Autobiography 241, Hilde Wenzel, 14; Aigner, "Die Indizierung," 951, 983; Dahm, "Die nationalsozialistische Schrifttumspolitik," 43; numerous documents in a section entitled "Das organisierte Chaos" in *Das war ein Vorspiel nur* (Bücherverbrennung), Katalog, 255–397.

18. Sauder, *Die Bücherverbrennung,* 71–75, 80, 109–10, 115; Faust, "Die Hochschulen," 40, 42, 44; Strätz, "Die geistige SA rückt ein," 92–96; *Das war ein Vorspiel nur* (Bücherverbrennung), Katalog, 188, #5, 213, #26b, photograph of a *Schandpfahl.*

19. Sauder, *Die Bücherverbrennung,* 9–24, 57, describes precedents dating from ancient times and provides references to the literature on this subject. See *Das war ein Vorspiel nur* (Bücherverbrennung), Katalog, 195; 161, #2c, a photograph of the occasion in 1922.

20. Faust, "Die Hochschulen," 39; Gerhard Sauder, "Akademischer 'Frühlingssturm': Germanisten als Redner bei der Bücherverbrennung," in Walberer, *10. Mai 1933,* 155.

21. Sauder, *Die Bücherverbrennung,* 74–76, 129, 152. For the public library system, see Ladislaus Buzás, *German Library History, 800–1945,* trans. William D. Boyd (Jefferson, N.C.: McFarland, 1986), Popular Libraries, vol. 3, chap. 5; Margaret F. Stieg, *Public Libraries in Nazi Germany* (Tuscaloosa: University of Alabama Press, 1992).

22. Faust, "Die Hochschulen," 45; Strätz, "Die geistige SA rückt ein," 99, 100–106; Aigner, "Die Indizierung," 1011; Sauder, *Die Bücherverbrennung,* 28, 30–31, 56, 105, 152–53, 156–57.

23. Sauder, *Die Bücherverbrennung,* 153; Dahm, *Das jüdische Buch,* pt. 1: 188 n. 698. By 20 May the police had seized 10,000 centners of Marxist books from these libraries. On

"workers' libraries," see Vernon L. Lidtke, *The Alternative Culture: Socialist Labor in Imperial Germany* (New York: Oxford University Press, 1985), 180–91.

24. Autobiography 44, W. M. Citron, 45–46 (I have not been able to verify that the apartment house owned by the Schutzverband was a residence for so many writers or that large numbers of volumes were confiscated there and burned on 10 May); Autobiography 41, Ada Bürger, 36; Autobiography 115, Hilda Koch, 46.

25. Autobiography 41, Ada Bürger, 36, quotes a prurient SA man who admitted this during a first search of her apartment in April 1933. During a second search in July six SA men beat and questioned her for two hours. She was later imprisoned for three years.

26. Autobiography 44, William Citron; Manfred Komorowski, "Die wissenschaftlichen Bibliotheken," in *Bibliotheken Während des Nationalsozialismus*, ed. Peter Vodosek and Manfred Komorowski (Wiesbaden: Harrassowitz, 1992), pt. 1: 13; Dov Schidorsky, "Das Schicksal jüdischer Bibliotheken im Dritten Reich," in ibid., pt. 2: 194; Sauder, *Die Bücherverbrennung*, 108.

27. Hirschfeld's books were banned in the 31 December 1938 list. Aigner, "Die Indizierung," 1027; Sauder, *Die Bücherverbrennung*, 154, 162–66, with sketch of Hirschfeld's life (born 1868 in Kolberg, died 1934 in Nice) and a report published 15 June 1933 in Basel; *Das war ein Vorspiel nur* (Bücherverbrennung), Katalog, 193, 26 f., *Fränkischer Kurier*, 8 May 1933. For the bust on the pole, see Erich Kästner, "Bei Verbrennung meiner Bücher," in Walberer, *10. Mai 1933*, 138. Hermann Weiss, "Besser ein Mühlstein am Halse: Reaktionen in der ausländischen Presse," in ibid., 124–25, prints contemporary reports from several newspapers.

28. Sauder, *Die Bücherverbrennung*, 145; Gabriele Krämer-Prein, "Der Buchhandel war immer deutsch: Das 'Börsenblatt für den deutschen Buchhandel' vor und nach der Machtergreifung," in Walberer, *10. Mai 1933*, 285–302; Komorowski, "Die wissenschaftlichen Bibliotheken," 3; Aigner, "Die Indizierung," 1007; Birgit Dankert, "Die Kinder- und Jugendbibliotheken zur Zeit des Nationalsozialismus," in Vodosek and Komorowski, *Bibliotheken*, pt. 1: 171–72, 177; Geralde Schmidt-Dumont, "Die Jugendschriftenausschüsse in der NS-Zeit," in ibid., 415; Faust, "Die Hochschulen," 47; Hildegard Brenner, "Die Republikaner beugen sich dem Wort der Obrigkeit: Die Umwandlung der Literaturabteilung der Preußischen Akademie der Künste in eine 'Deutsche Akademie der Dichtung,'" in *Das war ein Vorspiel nur* (Bücherverbrennung), 65–71.

29. Sauder, *Die Bücherverbrennung*, 173–218, lists all of them and provides details. On nonparticipation, see Strätz, "Die geistige SA rückt ein," 98–99.

30. Faust, "Die Hochschulen," 45–46. Autobiography 211, Howard Short, 26, describes the entire occasion of the book burning in Marburg. Photographs of the oxen-drawn wagon and the fire in Frankfurt are in Christoph Dorner et al., *Die braune Machtergreifung: Universität Frankfurt 1930–1945* (Frankfurt: Nexus, 1989), 112, 114; *Das war ein Vorspiel nur* (Bücherverbrennung), Katalog, 206, #13b.

31. Sauder, *Die Bücherverbrennung*, 169–71; Weiss, "Besser ein Mühlstein am Halse," 116–37, prints and summarizes a number of vivid contemporary journalistic accounts of the book burnings. On 9 May the students orchestrating the 10 May burnings sent to the various universities a document with a litany of authors and their offenses, but this was too late for use everywhere; see Sauder, *Die Bücherverbrennung*, 77; Strätz, "Die geistige SA rückt ein," 97.

32. Autobiography 250, Eva Wysbar, 14; Sauder, *Die Bücherverbrennung*, 33; Hans Mayer, "Die deutsche Literatur und der Scheiterhaufen," in Walberer, *10. Mai 1933*, 304–15; Pierre Bertraux, "Die Bücherverbrennung in Berlin am 10. Mai 1933," in *Das war*

ein Vorspiel nur (Bücherverbrennung), Katalog, 228–31, #14, a conversation in 1982 with Golo Mann and Gottfried and Brigitte Bermann-Fischer, who attended the 1933 burning in Berlin; Autobiography 108, Harry Kaufmann, 8.

33. Autobiography 101, Maria Kahle, 6; Sauder, *Die Bücherverbrennung*, 182, names Prof. Hans Naumann and Prof. Eugen Lüthgen as speakers, and both speeches are in *Das war ein Vorspiel nur* (Bücherverbrennung), Katalog, 202–6. See also Sauder, "Akademischer 'Frühlingssturm,'" 140–59. Perhaps the mayor mentioned the "Jewish soul," or the remark was ad libbed, or Maria Kahle thought she heard it, or it was reported to her. The remark was certainly in the spirit of the occasion.

34. Sauder, *Die Bücherverbrennung*, 34. See a similar remark in Autobiography 249, Herman Wurzel, 73.

35. Autobiography 68, Martin Freudenheim, 70, who recalled reading this pronouncement in the *Juristischen Wochenschrift* in 1933 or 1934.

36. This was frequently a theme in American newspapers. See Deborah E. Lipstadt, "The American Press and the Persecution of German Jewry: The Early Years, 1933–1935," *Leo Baeck Institute Year Book* 29 (1984): 27–55.

37. Dorner, *Die braune Machtergreifung*, 77; Autobiography 92, Edmund P. Heilpern, 6, started burning personal papers in 1932.

38. Autobiography 137, Marthe Lewinsohn, 1; Autobiography 72, Bruno Gebhard, 37, resigned from the SPD and burned his party membership books; Autobiography 96, Sofoni Herz, 21–22, shortly after 30 January 1933 burned his now illegal books, newspapers, and documents (especially membership lists) relating to the SPD and Reichsbanner (the Socialist Party militia); Autobiography 209, Ernst Schwartzert, pt. 2: 9; Autobiography 251, Wolfgang Yourgran, 45; Autobiography 88, Erich Harpuder [Erich Drucker], 11, 138. Drucker was a Communist and hid his Marxist library before spending years in various prisons after 1933. He then recovered and used it until he fled Germany. He retrieved his manuscript from the "My Life in Germany" collection to revise it for publication and deposited it with later versions in the Leo Baeck Institute, New York. I have cited the 1938 manuscript, written in Paris. Autobiography 182, Max Reiner, 205, a liberal Jewish journalist who worked until 1933 for the Ullstein firm, risked keeping his library in its entirety but presumably had to leave it when he emigrated.

39. Autobiography 157, "Mibberlin" [pseud.], 76; Autobiography 127, Helen Lange, 34; Autobiography 92, Edmund P. Heilpern, 119.

40. Ron Chernow, *The Warburgs: The Twentieth-Century Odyssey of a Remarkable Jewish Family* (New York: Random House, 1993), 405–8.

41. The CV, or Central Association of German Citizens of the Jewish Faith, was the leading non-Zionist Jewish organization in Germany. Its library became part of the Judaica Division of the huge RSHA library. Schidorsky, "Das Schicksal jüdischer Bibliotheken," 195. For Gyssling archive, see Autobiography 86, Walter Gyssling and Leonidas E. Hill, "Walter Gyssling, the Centralverein, and the Büro Wilhelmstraße, 1929–1933," *Leo Baeck Institute Year Book* 388 (1993): 193–208.

42. Dahm, "Die nationalsozialistische Schrifttumspolitik," 37.

43. Karl Billinger was the pseudonym of Paul Massing; see *Das war ein Vorspiel nur* (Bücherverbrennung), Katalog, 402,#14. Walter Hornung, whose *Dachau* was published in 1936 by Emil Oprecht's Europa Verlag, was a pseudonym for Julius Zerfass (1886–1956), editor and trade union functionary; after his release from Dachau he fled to Switzerland; see Peter Stahlberger, *Der Zürcher Verleger Emil Oprecht und die deutsche politische Emigration 1933–1945* (Zurich: Europa, 1970), 151. Wolfgang Langhoff (1901–66) was an actor and

Communist intellectual; after his incarceration at Börgermoor and Lichtenburg he fled to Switzerland in 1934. See the English version of Langhoff, *Rubber Truncheon: Being an Account of Thirteen Months Spent in a Concentration Camp*, trans. Lilo Linke (London: Constable, 1935). The book was banned by the 31 December 1938 list. See Aigner, "Die Indizierung," 1026, and L. E. Hill, "Towards a New History of German Resistance to Hitler," *Central European History* 14/4 (Dec. 1981): 381–82.

44. For an overview, see Hugo Kunoff, "Literaturbetrieb in der Vertreibung: Die Exilverlage," in *Die deutsche Exilliteratur 1933–1945*, ed. M. Durzak (Stuttgart: Reclam, 1973), 183–97. Walter Landauer (1902–44) died of starvation in Bergen-Belsen. Formerly a director in the Kiepenheuer Verlag, Berlin, Fritz H. Landshoff escaped to New York and with Bermann-Fischer established the L.[andshoff] B. Fischer Co. Emanuel Querido (1871–1943) was gassed with his wife at Auschwitz. These details are in Robert E. Cazden's very informative *German Exile Literature in America, 1933–1950: A History of the Free German Press and Book Trade* (Chicago: American Library Association, 1970), 10 11–12, 16 n. 21, 103–16, 129. See also Giuseppe de Siati and Thies Ziemke, eds., *Prag-Moskau: Briefe von und an Wieland Herzfelde 1933–38* (Kiel: Neuer Malik, 1991); Babette Gross, *Willi Münzenberg: Eine politische Biographie*, Schriftenreihe der Vierteljahrshefte für Zeitgeschichte, 14/15 (Stuttgart: Deutsche Verlags-Anstalt, 1967); Stahlberger, *Der Zürcher Verleger Oprecht*; Dahm, *Das jüdische Buch*, pt. 1: 204. For a document from March 1937 showing how closely the SS monitored such publishers abroad, see *Das war ein Vorspiel nur* (Bücherverbrennung), Katalog, 405–7.

45. For Ullstein Verlag, see Dahm, *Das jüdische Buch*, pt. 1: 110–11; Robert M. W. Kempner, "Hitler und die Zerstörung des Hauses Ullstein: Dokumente und Vernehmungen," in *Hundert Jahre Ullstein 1877–1977*, ed. W. Joachim Freyburg and Hans Wallenberg (Berlin: Ullstein, 1977), 3: 267–92; Herman Ullstein, *The Rise and Fall of the House of Ullstein* (New York: Simon & Schuster, 1943). For Rütten and Loening, see Dahm, *Das jüdische Buch*, pt. 1: 111; idem, "Die nationalsozialistische Schrifttumspolitik," 55. For S. Fischer Verlag, see Peter de Mendelssohn, *S. Fischer und sein Verlag* (Frankfurt: S. Fischer, 1970), 1259–1331; Dahm, *Das jüdische Buch*, pt. 1: 109. Suhrkamp was a "gallant and honorable" manager of S. Fischer's affairs from 1936 to 1950; see Cazden, *German Exile Literature*, 172 n. 23. For the shipment of the books to Vienna, see Volker Dahm, "Das jüdische Buch im Dritten Reich:2. Salman Schocken und sein Verlag," *Archiv für Geschichte des Buchwesens* 22 (1981): 810; hereafter cited as Dahm, *Das jüdische Buch*, pt. 2.

46. The store is listed under Peter Wenzel, Mischling II, in Dahm, *Das jüdische Buch*, pt. 1: 246.

47. Dahm, "Die nationalsozialistische Schrifttumspolitik," 61–62, 64–65, covers these points and summarizes eighteen categories of authors and books, which have been examined at length by Aigner, "Die Indizierung," 990–1002; and more briefly in Noakes and Pridham, *Nazism*, 1: 405.

48. Krämer-Prein, "Der Buchhandel war immer deutsch," 299; Stefan Zweig, *The World of Yesterday: An Autobiography* (New York: Viking, 1943), 444, 381–82.

49. On this theme, see Thomas Koebner, "'Militant Humanism': A Concept of the Third Way in Exile, 1933–45," in *German Writers and Politics, 1918–39*, ed. Richard Dove and Stephen Lamb (London: Macmillan, 1992), 121–48 (on Zweig, 130–36).

50. Ibid., 136–37. See the long analysis of Wolf Jöckel, *Heinrich Manns "Henri Quatre" als Gegenbild zum nationalsozialistischen Deutschland*, Deutsches Exil: Eine Schriftenreihe, 9 (Worms, 1977); Hill, "Towards a New History," 384.

51. Autobiography 227, Rudolf Steiner, 68.

52. Kästner was banned because of the content of his writings. From 1933 to shortly before the war he was in exile in Zurich, in Dresden during the war, and in Munich after it; he died in 1974. For 1936 Nazi documents on the ban of Kästner's "Emil und die Detektive," see *Das war ein Vorspiel nur* (Bücherverbrennung), Katalog, 297–301. Richard Katz (1888–1968) was a journalist and writer, who from 1922 to 1924 was a correspondent in Prague (his birthplace) for the *Vossische Zeitung*, an Ullstein newspaper, and from 1926 to 1930 he worked for Ullstein in Berlin. In 1933 he emigrated through Switzerland to Brazil, returning to Switzerland in 1945. See Freyburg and Wallenberg, *Hundert Jahre Ullstein*, 3:571. Hilde Wenzel might have sold Katz's *Ein Bummel um die Welt: 2 Jahre Weltreise auf Kammel und Schiene, Schiff und Auto* (Erlenbach: Rentsch, 1927; new ed. 1935); *Heitere Tage mit braunen Menschen: Ein Südseebuch* (Berlin: Ullstein, 1930); *Schnaps, Kokaine und Lamas: Kreuz und quer durch wirres Südamerika* (Erlenbach: Rentsch, 1931); *Japan von heute: Erlebnisse eines Weltenbummlers* (Reutlingen: Ensslin und Laiblin, 1933); *Funkelnder Fernen Osten! Erlebtes in China, Korea, Japan* (Erlenbach: Rentsch, 1935). See also Dahm, "Die nationalsozialistische Schrifttumspolitik," 63.

53. Aigner, "Die Indizierung," 1003; Dahm, *Das jüdische Buch*, pt. 1: 197.

54. L. E. Hill, ed., *Die Weizsäcker Papiere 1933–1950* (Frankfurt: Propyläen, 1974), 61, 11 March 1933; 70, 30 March 1933; 71, 22 April 1933, letters of Ernst von Weizsäcker to his mother.

55. Autobiography 75, Emil Glas, says that he took refuge in the classics, probably meaning the Greek and Roman classics. That Heine was not banned is confirmed by Dahm, "Die nationalsozialistische Schrifttumspolitik," 67; at length in *Das jüdische Buch*, pt. 1: 179–85. Although police seized 258 copies of Heine's works in Munich bookstores in May 1938, on 13 January 1939 they confirmed that there was no complete ban on Heine; see Aigner, "Die Indizierung," 1005.

56. Buck: *The Good Earth [Die gute Erde]*. Hobart: *Oil for the Lamps of China [Petroleum für die Lampen Chinas]*, and *River Supreme [Strom, Du Schicksal: Roman um die Tangtsekian]*. Waln: *Süsse Frucht, bittre Frucht China and Sommer in der Mongolei*, translated from the original English. Gervais: *Ein Arzt erlebt China, Malven auf weisser Seide, and Im Schatten des MA-KUE: Als Arzt im Banne chin. Geisterwelt*. Heiser: *An American Doctor's Odyssey: Adventures in Forty-five Countries*.

57. Autobiography 212, Hilde Sichel, 67.

58. Dahm, *Das jüdische Buch*, pt. 1:204; idem, "Die nationalsozialistische Schrifttumspolitik," 65.

59. Herrmann quoted by Krämer-Prein, "Der Buchhandel war immer deutsch," 297. Most of Lenin was on the "blacklist" of 10 May 1933; Sauder, *Die Bücherverbrennung*, 135. Gorky was on the 31 December 1938 list; Aigner, "Die Indizierung," 1026. And see Dahm, "Die nationalsozialistiche Schrifttumspolitik," 61–62.

60. Erich Drucker, who became an antiquarian book dealer in New York City, has described how, like a psychoanalyst, he learned about the inner life of his customers and viewed them as patients; he recommended and obtained books for them as therapy. See, among his papers, "Erinnerungen eines deutschen Buchhändlers," 8, Leo Baeck Institute, New York.

61. Dahm, *Das jüdische Buch*, pt. 1: 107–8.

62. Aigner, "Die Indizierung," 952–53, 963–64; Dahm, "Die nationalsozialistische Schrifttumspolitik," 44, 72, 54–55; Brenner, "Art in the Political Power Struggle," 408, 417–18. Dahm, *Das jüdische Buch*, pt. 1: 60–72.

63. Dahm, *Das jüdische Buch,* pt. 1: 100–104 (founding of BRB), 112 (questionnaire), 107 (Schacht's protest).

64. Aigner, "Die Indizierung," 970; Noakes and Pridham, *Nazism,* 1: 403–4. For the format of the Index, see *Das war ein Vorspiel nur* (Bücherverbrennung), Katalog, 279 (1934), 280 (1935), 289 (1938); for the officials, see Dahm, "Die nationalsozialistische Schrifttumspolitik," 61.

65. Aigner, "Die Indizierung," 982, 957; "Die nationalsozialistische Schrifttumspolitik", 59, and see 62–63, about 898 firms ransacked for 37,040 volumes.

66. Dahm, *Das jüdische Buch,* pt. 1: 108, 115–16; idem, "Jüdische Verleger, 1933–1938," in *Die Juden im Nationalsozialistischen Deutschland/The Jews in Nazi Germany 1933–1945,* ed. Arnold Paucker, Schriftenreihe wissenschaftlicher Abhandlungen des Leo Baeck Instituts, 45 (Tübingen: Mohr, 1986), 273.

67. Dahm, *Das jüdische Buch,* pt. 1: 130; Autobiography 208, Oscar Schwartz, 49; *Das Tagebuch der Hertha Nathorff: Berlin-New York Aufzeichnungen 1933 bis 1945,* ed. Wolfgang Benz (Frankfurt: Fischer Taschenbuch, 1989), 86, 8 Aug. 1936; and see Ralf Georg Reuth, *Goebbels* (Munich: Piper, 1990), 344.

68. Goebbels's coauthor was Hans Schweitzer (pseud. Mjölnir, the old Germanic name for Thor's hammer). A year later Goebbels edited *Knorke: Ein neues Buch Isidor für Zeitgenossen* (Munich, 1929). Weiss sued Goebbels seventeen times for defamation of character. Goebbels evaded short prison sentences because of his parliamentary immunity, but periods of suspension for *Angriff,* fines, and legal fees forced him to discontinue his attacks in 1930. See Russel Lemmons, *Goebbels and Der Angriff* (Lexington: University Press of Kentucky, 1994), 26, 112, 118, 120–21, 126; Reuth, *Goebbels.* See also Autobiography 237, Käthe Vordtriede, 79 (a journalist). H. H. Ewers, *Horst Wessel: Ein deutsche Schicksal* (1933); a photograph of Ewers (1871–1943) is in *Das war ein Vorspiel nur* (Bücherverbrennung), Katalog, 145.

69. Dahm, *Das jüdische Buch,* pt. 1:113–34, 139–52; Dahm, "Die nationalsozialistische Schrifttumspolitik," 55–57. The pressure on Jews is reflected in Nathorff, *Das Tagebuch,* 88, 10 Oct. 1936.

70. Dahm, *Das jüdische Buch,* pt. 1: 138.

71. Ibid., 236.

72. Stephanie Barron, "1937: Modern Art and Politics in Prewar Germany," in *"Degenerate Art": The Fate of the Avant-Garde in Nazi Germany,* ed. Barron (Los Angeles: Los Angeles County Museum of Art; New York: Abrams, 1991), 9–23; Christoph Zuschlag, "An 'Educational Exhibition': The Precursors of *Entartete Kunst* and Its Individual Venues," in ibid., 83–97; Andreas Hüncke, "On the Trail of Missing Masterpieces: Modern Art from German Galleries," in ibid., 121–33. (An excellent synopsis of this story is in Jonathan Petropoulos, *Art as Politics in the Third Reich* [Chapel Hill: University of North Carolina Press, 1996], chap. 2); Wulf, *Musik im Dritten Reich,* 414 ff.; Michael Meyer, "A Musical Facade for the Third Reich," in Barron, *"Degenerate Art,"* 171–83, and *The Politics of Music in the Third Reich* (New York: Lang, 1990); Fred K. Prieberg, *Musik im NS-Staat* (Frankfurt: Fischer Taschenbuch, 1982).

73. Autobiography 135, Joseph B. Levy, 48–59, detailed account for Frankfurt, 52; Autobiography 28, Rudolf Bing, 36–37.

74. Autobiography 9, Miriam Arrington, 6. Friedell's works were banned in the 31 December 1938 list; Aigner, "Die Indizierung," 1027. See Eckart Früh, "'Erstarrt und erstorben': Terror und Selbstmord in Wien nach der Annexion Österreichs," *Wiener*

Tagebuch 3 (Mar. 1988): 15–19; Gerhard Botz, *Wien vom "Anschluß" zum Krieg: Nationalsozialistische Machtübernahme und politisch-soziale Umgestaltung am Beispiel der Stadt Wien 1938/39* (Vienna: Jugend & Volk, 1978), 98–105; Herbert Rosenkranz, *Verfolgung und Selbstbehauptung: Die Juden in Österreich 1938–1945* (Vienna: Herold, 1976); Konrad Kwiet, "The Ultimate Refuge: Suicide in the Jewish Community under the Nazis," *Leo Baeck Institute Year Book* 29 (1984); Elisabeth Klamper, "Der schlechte Ort zu Wien: Zur Situation der Wiener Juden vom 'Anschluß' bis zum Novemberpogrom 1938," in *Der Novemberpogrom 1938: Die "Reichskristallnacht" in Wien* (Vienna: Historisches Museum, 1988); idem, "Der 'Anschlußpogrom'" in *Der Pogrom 1938: Judenverfolgung in Österreich und Deutschland,* ed. Kurt Schmid and Robert Streibel (Vienna: Picus, 1990), 25–33.

75. Autobiography 130, Gertrud Wickerhauser-Lederer, 60–61; Autobiography 175, Rose Marie Papanek-Akselried, 58; Autobiography 224, Herbert Stein, 208, 274; Autobiography 170, "Old Glory" [pseud.], VII A.

76. Autobiography 249, Herman Wurzel, 73. Autobiography 218, Helena Spera, 20; Autobiography 226, Margarete Steiner, 6, 22; Autobiography 73, Max Geffner, 53–54; Autobiography 40, Paul Brüll, 76. See also Robert Streibel, "'Und plötzlich waren sie alle weg': Die Juden in Krems 1938," in Schmid and Streibel, *Der Pogrom 1938,* 54–55, "Der Terror gegen Dr. Paul Brüll."

77. Autobiography 175, Rose Marie Papanek-Akselried, 85–86; Schidorsky, "Das Schicksal jüdischer Bibliotheken," 194, 196; Komorowski, "Die wissenschaftlichen Bibliotheken," 19; Peter Malina, "Zur Geschichte der wissenschaftlichen Bibliotheken Österreichs in der NS-Zeit," in Vodosek and Komorowski, *Bibliotheken,* pt. 1: 447–49. Petropoulos, *Art as Politics,* 84. Acting on a law passed in 1998, Austria agreed in February 1999 to return to the Rothschild family some 250 paintings, drawings, furniture, weapons, and coins that had been looted by the Nazis and incorporated into state museums after the war. Carol Vogel, "Austrian Rothschilds Decide to Sell," *New York Times,* 10 Apr. 1999, A17, A22.

78. On the treatment of Jewish firms in Austria, see Dahm, *Das jüdische Buch,* pt. 1:156–62. Expelled from Sweden in 1940 because of anti-Nazi activity, the Fischer family traveled by way of Moscow to New York City. They began again and published Thomas Mann, Franz Werfel, Stefan Zweig, and Annette Kolb, among others. Mendelssohn, *S. Fischer und sein Verlag,* 1259–1331; Brigitte B. Fischer, *My European Heritage: Life among Great Men of Letters,* trans. Harry Zohn (Boston: Branden, 1986), 111–26.

79. Jonny Moser, "Depriving Jews of Their Legal Rights in the Third Reich," in *November 1938: From "Reichskristallnacht" to Genocide,* ed. Walter H. Pehle (New York: Berg, 1991), 126, provides these figures. See also Hermann Graml, *Reichskristallnacht: Antisemitismus und Judenverfolgung im Dritten Reich* (Munich: Deutscher Taschenbuchverlag, 1988); Leonidas E. Hill, "The Pogrom of November 9–10, 1938, in Germany," in *Riots and Pogroms,* ed. Paul R. Brass (New York: New York University Press, 1996), 89–113. For the synagogues, see Saskia Rohde, "Die Zerstörung der Synagogen unter dem Nationalsozialismus," in *Verdrängung und Vernichtung der Juden unter dem Nationalsozialismus,* ed. Arno Herzig and Ina Lorenz (Hamburg: Christians, 1992), 153–71.

80. Autobiography 171, Mara Oppenheimer, 9; Wolf-Arno Kropat, *Kristallnacht in Hessen: Der Judenpogrom vom November 1938, eine Dokumentation,* Schriften der Kommission für die Geschichte der Juden in Hessen, 10 (Wiesbaden: Kommission für die Geschichte der Juden in Hessen, 1988), 148–52; Autobiography 239, Frederick Weil, 124; Autobiography 156, Siegfried Merecki, 95; Autobiography 226, Margarete Steiner, 24.

81. Autobiography 50, Mally Dienemann, 12. Autobiography 138, Heinrich Friedrich

Lichtenstein, 91–93, described the wrecking of the Jewish school in detail; some parents gave the books and tools that their children had taken from the school to the police, who returned them to the school. See also Joseph Walk, *Jüdische Schule und Erziehung im Dritten Reich* (Frankfurt: Hain, 1991), 206.

82. Schulamith Schmidt, "Jüdische Bibliotheken in der Zeit des Nationalsozialismus," in Vodosek and Komorowski, *Bibliotheken*, pt. 1: 510–12; Autobiography 135, Joseph B. Levy, 79; Kropat, *Kristallnacht in Hessen*, 96, 98–99, 120, 127; Walk, *Jüdische Schule*, 206; Autobiography 96, Sofoni Herz, 32.

83. Klamper, "Der Anschlußpogrom," 31; Gerhard Botz, "The Jews of Vienna from the Anschluß to the Holocaust," in *Jews, Antisemitism, and Culture in Vienna*, ed. Ivar Oxaal, Michael Pollak, and Gerhard Botz (London: Routledge & Kegan Paul, 1987), 195; Autobiography 207, Karl Schwabe, 77; Autobiography 239, Frederick Weil, 94, 90; Autobiography 247, Annamaria Wolfram [pseud.], 47, part of 10 pages written by Mr. Wolfram on his experience in a concentration camp; Autobiography 199, David Schapira. It is worth noting that in 1934 guards said to prisoners in a concentration camp that they were "subhuman beings," that they should "be put against the wall and shot," that "It's all the same to me if you rot here or die like dogs; not one of you will get out" (Langhoff, *Rubber Truncheon*, 132, 254). Such remarks were obviously intended to intimidate the prisoners but were also honest. The guards frequently beat prisoners savagely, even killed them, or subjected them to other conditions which killed them.

84. Autobiography 142, Margot Littauer, 31; Autobiography 159, Hugo Moses, 18.

85. For the Erich Reiss Verlag and other Jewish publishers, see Dahm, "Jüdische Verleger, 1933–1938," 273–82. For Schocken, see Dahm, *Das jüdische Buch*, pt. 2: 301–916, esp. 798, 806. For Rowohlt, see Walther Kiaulehn, *Mein Freund der Verleger: Ernst Rowohlt und seine Zeit* (Reinbek bei Hamburg: Rowohlt, 1967). For publishers on Index, see Dahm, *Das jüdische Buch*, pt. 1: 204, and "Die nationalsozialistische Schrifttumspolitik," 65.

86. For the "Aryanization" of the last Jewish booksellers, see Dahm, *Das jüdische Buch*, pt. 1: 163–68, 174–79, 197, 215–23; idem, "Die nationalsozialistische Schrifttumspolitik," 57; Aigner, "Die Indizierung," 1003.

87. Stephanie Barron, "The Galerie Fischer Auction," in Barron, *"Degenerate Art,"* 135–46; Petropoulos, *Art as Politics*, 82, 338 n. 50; Strothmann, *Nationalsozialistische Literaturpolitik*, 74 n. 40; Sauder, *Die Bücherverbrennung*, 172. Concerning the question of whether or not this burning took place, see Barron, *"Degenerate Art,"* 23 n. 2, 117 n. 43, 132 n. 136.

88. Still a good comparison of Nazi occupation policies in the east and the west is Norman Rich, *Hitler's War Aims: The Establishment of the New Order* (New York: Norton, 1974), vol. 2.

89. Martin Broszat, *Nationalsozialistische Polenpolitik 1939–1945* (Stuttgart: Deutsche Verlagsanstalt, 1961); Richard C. Lukas, *The Forgotten Holocaust: The Poles under German Occupation, 1939–1944* (Lexington: University Press of Kentucky, 1986); Czeslaw Madajczyk, "Deutsche Besatzungspolitik in Polen, in der UdSSR und in den Ländern Südosteuropas," in *Deutschland 1933–1945: Neue Studien zur nationalsozialistischen Herrschaft*, ed. Karl Dietrich Bracher, Manfred Funke, and Hans-Adolf Jacobsen, Bonner Schriften zur Politik und Zeitgeschichte, 23 (Düsseldorf: Droste, 1992), 426–39; Christian Streit, *Keine Kameraden: Die Wehrmacht und die sowjetischen Kriegsgefangenen 1941–1945*, Studien zur Zeitgeschichte, 13 (Stuttgart, 1980); idem, "Sowjetische Kriegsgefangene—Massendeportationen—Zwangsarbeiter," in *Der Zweite Weltkrieg: Analysen—Grundzüge—Forschungs-*

bilanz, ed. Wolfgang Michalka (Munich: Piper, 1990), 747–60; Peter Longerich, "Vom Massenmord zur 'Endlösung': Die Erschießungen von jüdischen Zivilisten in den ersten Monaten des Ostfeldzuges im Kontext des nationalsozialistischen Judenmords," in *Zwei Wege nach Moskau: Vom Hitler-Stalin Pakt zum "Unternehmen Barbarossa,"* ed. Bernd Wegner (Munich: Piper, 1991), 251–74; Rolf-Dieter Müller, *Hitlers Ostkrieg und die deutsche Siedlungspolitik: Die Zusammenarbeit von Wehrmacht, Wirtschaft und SS* (Frankfurt: Fischer Taschenbuch, 1991).

90. Donald E. Collins and Herbert P. Rothfelder, "The Einsatzstab Reichsleiter Rosenberg and the Looting of Jewish and Masonic Libraries during World War II," *Journal of Library History* 18:1 (1983): 21–36; Schidorsky, "Das Schickal jüdischer Bibliotheken," 197–98; Willem de Vries, *Sonderstab Musik: Music Confiscations by the Einsatzstab Reichsleiter Rosenberg under the Nazi Occupation of Western Europe* (Amsterdam: Amsterdam University Press, 1996), 91–92, 49, 52, 151; Petropoulos, *Art as Politics*, 130, 145–46.

91. A document from 6 November 1940 locating seven of these future institutes and describing their work, and others on the opening of the institute in Frankfurt, can be found in Leon Poliakov and Josef Wulf, eds., *Das Dritte Reich und seine Denker* (Berlin-Grünewald: Arani, 1959), 132–39, 140–44. The eleven institutes are named in Reinhard Bollmus, "Zum Projekt einer nationalsozialistischen Alternativ-Universität: Alfred Rosenbergs 'Hohe Schule,'" in *Erziehung und Schulung im Dritten Reich,* ed. Manfred Heinemann, Veröffentlichungen der Historischen Kommission der Deutschen Gesellschaft für Erziehungswissenschaft, 4, pt. 2 (Stuttgart: Klett, 1980), 138, 141–42 n. 24. Schidorsky, "Das Schicksal jüdischer Bibliotheken," 192, mentions institutes for the study of Jews or "race" in Paris, Innsbruck, and Budapest, without making clear which Nazi agency controlled them.

92. Vries, *Sonderstab Musik,* 78–79, 108; Schidorsky, "Das schicksal jüdischer Bibliotheken," 192, 199–206; Bollmus, "Zum Projekt," 138; Collins and Rothfeder, "Einsatzstab," 31.

93. Schidorsky, "Das Schicksal jüdischer Bibliotheken," 194–96. At least 250,000 volumes, including the collections from Warsaw and Vienna, were almost completely destroyed in a bombing on 22–23 November 1943. Some 350,000 volumes, mainly periodicals, survived.

94. Jan P. Pruszynski, "Poland: The War Losses, Cultural Heritage, and Cultural Legitimacy," in *The Spoils of War: World War II and Its Aftermath: The Loss, Reappearance, and Recovery of Cultural Property,* ed. Elizabeth Simpson (New York: Abrams, 1997), 51, 253–54 n. 19. Petropoulos, *Art as Politics,* 106; Collins and Rothfeder, "Einsatzstab," 29, 30; Schidorsky, "Das Schicksal jüdischer Bibliotheken," 203–4 n. 27 (on Johannes Pohl), 204–5.

95. Seventy-seven Masonic lodges were raided. See Vries, *Sonderstab Musik,* 157, 161–65. See also the ERR report on its work in the Netherlands, in Poliakov and Wulf, *Das Dritte Reich und seine Denker,* 156–58; Collins and Rothfeder, "Einsatzstab," 27–28; Josefine Leistra, "A Short History of Art Loss and Art Recovery in the Netherlands," in Simpson, *Spoils of War,* 55–56. See Schidorsky, "Das Schicksal jüdischer Bibliotheken," 203, for a longer description of these famous collections, which survived the war nearly intact and were returned to the Netherlands; Lynn H. Nicholas, *The Rape of Europa: The Fate of Europe's Treasures in the Third Reich and the Second World War* (New York: Vintage, 1995), 98. Petropoulos, *Art as Politics,* 140, emphasizes the "minor role" of the ERR in collecting art in the Netherlands.

96. See Nicholas, *Rape of Europa,* 85–86, with a photograph of the ruined Louvain

library in 1940. After World War I the Treaty of Versailles obligated Germany to provide the library with material equal in value to the irreplaceable manuscripts, incunabula, and books that had been destroyed. Great Britain and the United States contributed many books, and a host of institutions and governments, especially the United States, rebuilt the library, which reopened in 1928. Vries, *Sonderstab Musik*, 171, 179, 172; Jacques Lust, "The Spoils of War Removed from Belgium during World War II," in Simpson, *Spoils of War*, 58–60, 62.

97. Collins and Rothfeder, "Einsatzstab," 27; Schidorsky, "Das Schicksal jüdischer Bibliotheken," 202; Marie Hamon, "Spoliation and Recovery of Cultural Property in France, 1940–94," in Simpson, *Spoils of War*, 65; Vries, *Sonderstab Musik*, 94, 97, 130, 210–27, 101.

98. Petropoulos, *Art as Politics*, 145–150; Alexander Fedoruk, "Ukraine: The Lost Cultural Treasures and the Problem of Their Return," in Simpson, *Spoils of War*, 73–74; Nicholas, *Rape of Europa*, 187–201; Patricia K. Grimsted, "The Fate of Ukrainian Cultural Treasures during World War II: Archives, Libraries, and Museums under the Third Reich," *Jahrbücher für Geschichte Osteuropas* 39:1 (1991): 71; Adam Maldis, "The Tragic Fate of Belarusan Museum and Library Collections during the Second World War," in Simpson, *Spoils of War*, 79.

99. A Führer order of 1 March 1942 extended the mandate of the ERR from archives and libraries to artworks, although after the war ERR operatives lied in order to make it appear that they had remained restricted to books and papers. See Nicholas, *Rape of Europa*, 186, 191, 197–98; Petropoulos, *Art as Politics*, 145–46, 148–49; Mikhail Shvidkoi, "Russian Cultural Losses during World War II," in Simpson, *Spoils of War*, 68–71, which contains vivid photographs of wrecked interiors and buildings; Marlene P. Hiller, "The Documentation of War Losses in the Former Soviet Republics," in ibid., 83. It is not clear how the 3–4 million books shipped from the USSR relate to the 51 million that "disappeared" in the Ukraine. Grimsted, "Fate of Ukrainian Cultural Treasures," 67, states that the ERR took a half-million books from the occupied parts of the USSR to the Ostbücherei Rosenberg in Berlin.

100. This is a major argument of Grimsted, "Fate of Ukrainian Cultural Treasures."

101. Schidorsky, "Das Schicksal jüdischer Bibliotheken," 207; Craig Hugh Smyth, "The Establishment of the Munich Collecting Point," in Simpson, *Spoils of War*, 126–30; Walter I. Farmer, "Custody and Controversy at the Wiesbaden Collecting Point," in ibid., 131–34.

102. Schidorsky, "Das Schicksal jüdischer Bibliotheken," 207–10, provides the first figure, Collins and Rothfeder, "Einsatzstab," 34, the second.

103. Pamela Spence Richards, "Deutschlands wissenschaftliche Verbindungen mit dem Ausland 1933–1945," in Vodosek and Komorowski, *Bibliotheken*, pt. 2: 129.

104. See Hill, "Pogrom of November 9–10, 1938," 99. See also Robert H. Abzug, *Inside the Vicious Heart: Americans and the Liberation of Nazi Concentration Camps* (New York: Oxford University Press, 1985), 72–74, 75–79, on Gardelegen and Thekla, with photographs of prisoners burned by the SS.

105. For a glimpse of the work of the exiles, see the essays by Ursula Büttner, "Alfred Kantorowicz: Sein Beitrag zum geistigen Widerstand," and Wolfgang Benz, "Emil J. Gumbel: Die Karriere eines deutschen Pazifisten," in Walberer, *10. Mai 1933*, 160–220; and *Das war ein Vorspiel nur* (Bücherverbrennung), Katalog, 429, #20, for quotation from Willkie, #21 for Alfred Kantorowicz speech on 10 May 1943, with quotation from Roosevelt (429 German, 431 English).

106. Richard Breitman, *Official Secrets: What the Nazis Planned, What the British and Americans Knew* (London: Penguin, 1998).

107. Contemporary Nazi witnesses of the book burnings ascribed quite different symbolic meanings to them, such as obliteration of the "un-German" elements of the past, erasure of the names of the authors and their books, purification from diseases of modernity and "racial pollution," and rebirth of the true "German spirit" from the ashes of its destroyed opponents. Because they missed the fundamentally anti-Semitic nature of Nazi campaigns against the "un-German spirit," recent interpretations have not emphasized the close connections of the book burnings with the Holocaust. See Löwenthal, "Calibans Erbe," in *Das war ein Vorspiel nur* (Berliner), 17–23; Klaus Vondung, "Autodafé und Phönix: Vom Glauben an den deutschen Geist," in ibid., 94–98.

II • BLOODLESS TORTURE: THE BOOKS OF THE ROMAN GHETTO UNDER THE NAZI OCCUPATION

Stanislao G. Pugliese

> From days immemorial books played an important, even vital role in our nation's life. Rightly we were considered in the Diaspora the people of the book when the book served as a loyal companion of our nation.
>
> Librarian, Sholem Aleichem Library, Radomsko, Poland

WHEN I began research into the fate of the books of the Roman ghetto under the Nazi occupation, I had in mind the line from John Milton's *Areopagitica* of 1644: "As good almost kill a man as kill a good book; who kills a man kills a reasonable creature, God's image; but he who destroys a good book kills reason itself." Or perhaps—as another epigraph for the essay—Heinrich Heine's thought in 1823 that "wherever they burn books they will also, in the end, burn human beings." For the more contemporary-minded, Ray Bradbury's *Fahrenheit 451* might seem appropriate. Burned into our collective consciousness are the searing images of Nazi bonfires consuming—with the twin scourges of fire and hatred—the intellectual patrimony of an entire civilization: from the "decadent" liberals to the "diseased" Jews to the "traitorous" Thomas Mann. For historical precedents, I thought of the burning of the ancient library at Alexandria, the sack of Rome by the Vandals, Savonarola's "bonfire of the vanities" in Renaissance Florence, and even Umberto Eco's fictional account of the destruction of a magnificent medieval library in his novel *The Name of the Rose*.

In the winter of 1939, Jewish scholars were already aware of what the Nazi war would mean, at least as far as Jewish material culture was concerned. An article had appeared in the *Deutsche Allgemeine Zeitung* titled "Books, Books, Books," which prompted Chaim Aron Kaplan to note in his diary the ironic similarity between the Germans and the Jews:

> We are dealing with a nation of high culture, with a "people of the Book." . . . The Germans have simply gone crazy for one thing—books. . . . Germany has become a madhouse for books. Say what you will, I fear such people! Where plunder is based on an ideology, on a world outlook which in essence is spiritual, it cannot be equaled

in strength and durability. . . . The Nazi has robbed us not only of our material possessions, but also of our good name as "the people of the Book."[1]

In Turin, a city with a Jewish population of little more than 4,000 in 1938, Jewish books *were* burned—by Italian Fascists. Before the Nazis ever set foot in occupied Italy, the Fascists of Turin forced their way into the Jewish Community Library, seized much of the collection, and used it to feed a great bonfire in the Piazza Carlina.[2] Yet the story of the books of the Roman ghetto reveals that the two libraries—that of the Synagogue and that of the Rabbinical College—were *not* burned; another fate awaited them. Their story is part of the crime against Rome's Jewish community that began with the Nazi occupation of Rome in July of 1943, only hours after King Victor Emmanuel III had removed Mussolini from office. The Fascist regime had come to power more than two decades earlier, in October 1922, without any trace of official anti-Semitism. Indeed, Italian Jews— as middle-class citizens, not as Jews—supported the regime and were present in the highest echelons of the Fascist hierarchy: Guido Jung as finance minister; Aldo Finzi as undersecretary of the interior. It was not until the Rome–Berlin Axis of 1936 that the anti-Semites within fascism were released from their leashes. In 1938 the Fascist regime passed extensive anti-Semitic legislation; most Gentile Italians, to their credit, did their best to circumvent the new laws. In fact, until the Nazi occupation of Italy, not one Italian Jew was transported to the death camps, even though the Nazi leadership was insistent on this point.

In September of 1943, the SS (Schutzstaffel) commander in charge of Rome, Herbert Kappler, summoned the leaders of the Jewish community to his office. He demanded a ransom of fifty kilos of gold, to be paid within thirty-six hours, in exchange for the safety of the Jewish community. On the international gold market in 1943, fifty kilos of gold were worth approximately $56,000; with 12,000 Jews in Rome, a ransom of $4.50 seemed a small price to pay for the life of a person.[3] At his trial after the war, Kappler defended his action as preferable to deportation. What he did not reveal was that the order for the deportation of Roman Jews had already been sent and that his "humanitarian gesture" was merely extortion.

Within hours, word of the extortion demand had spread beyond the ghetto. Jew and Gentile alike presented themselves at the Roman Synagogue to contribute whatever they could. The receipts that were issued reveal that most contributions were pathetically small: a ring, bracelet, earring, or some other precious family heirloom. Yet the fifty kilos were collected well before the deadline and deposited at the SS office in Via Tasso. The community breathed a collective sigh of relief, confident that the atrocities that were rumored to be taking place on the eastern front and the reports of death camps must be exaggerations. In addition, it was inconceivable that here in the Eternal City the pope would allow "his Jews" to be subject to deportation. A few quietly suggested that the Germans would not be content only with gold; they were ignored.

On the morning after the payment of the gold ransom—the eve of Rosh Hashana—officers from Kappler's office knocked on the door of Ugo Foà, president of the Jewish community. The Germans quickly assured Foà that they were not there to arrest him; instead, they had orders to search the premises of the Synagogue; rumor had it that the Synagogue was harboring anti-Fascists and collaborating with the enemy. The Germans were thorough in their search: they broke open the alms boxes, entered the oratorio for the Spanish rite, and destroyed the ark, throwing the two Torahs inside to the ground. More importantly, they carried away thousands of records and documents, including the name and address of virtually every Jew in Rome.[4]

The next day, 30 September 1943, the first day of the Jewish New Year 5704, two representatives from the Einsatzstab Reichsleiter Rosenberg (ERR) appeared at the Synagogue. The ERR was a special commando unit established in 1940 by the official theoretician of national socialism, Alfred Rosenberg, and was an integral part of his plan to refashion German and European culture after the war.[5] The ERR was composed of two formal divisions: regional organizations called Work Groups, and Sonderstäbe (Special Staffs) whose responsibility included the fields of art and historical artifacts.[6] A German historian has called it a "commando organization of cultural robbery."[7] Its chief function was to confiscate, plunder, and loot objects of art during the war and may have been the philosopher's most successful endeavor.[8] Rosenberg already had years of experience in the field of cultural policy. In August of 1927, at the first of the great Nuremberg rallies, a National Socialist Society for Culture and Learning was established; two months later, Rosenberg was appointed its director. In 1929 it was tellingly renamed the Kampfbund für Deutsche Kultur (KFDK, Combat League for German Culture).[9] The KFDK was Rosenberg's attempt to insinuate himself into the Nazi organizational and bureaucratic hierarchy; as such, he often came into conflict with Joseph Goebbels and the Ministry for Propaganda and Popular Enlightenment. Other, less "enlightened" Nazis could not see the reason for preserving any remnant of Jewish culture. Probably most were of the same mind as the Nazi correspondent who reported on the destruction of the library of the Lublin Yeshiva:

> For us it was a matter of special pride to destroy the Talmudic Academy, which was known as the greatest in Poland. . . . We threw the huge talmudic library out of the building and carried the books to the marketplace where we set fire to them. The fire lasted twenty hours. The Lublin Jews assembled around and wept bitterly, almost silencing us with their cries. We summoned the military band, and with joyful shouts the soldiers drowned out the sounds of the Jewish cries.[10]

The ERR evolved into an efficient and highly coordinated organization for the plunder of art from museums, and books, documents, and manuscripts from libraries, schools, universities, and private citizens. It was placed in the Wehrmacht by an official act of Hitler and had its headquarters in Berlin with branch offices in Amsterdam, Brussels, Paris, Belgrade, Riga, Minsk, and Kiev. Each regional branch (Hauptarbeitsgruppe) had subregional offices (Arbeitsgruppen) and local centers (Sonderkommandos). In Eastern Europe alone there were eleven subregional offices and seven local centers.[11] If a desired object belonged to foreign "Aryans," the owners were compelled to sell it; if it belonged to Jews, it was simply confiscated. The property of Jews who had fled the Nazi onslaught was declared "ownerless," and therefore the ERR had the "obligation" to store it in safe places within the Reich.[12] Rosenberg seems to have been particularly interested in libraries for his pet project, a *Hohe Schule* for the NSDAP.[13] This was to be the Central National Socialist University and dedicated to advanced academic study. To this end, several institutes had already been established by 1943: one in Hamburg for the study of colonial research; another in Halle for religion; one in Kiel dedicated to the study of *Lebensraum;* still another in Stuttgart for biology and race; and a center for the "Jewish question." This last project was given the appropriately impressive name of the Institut der NSDAP zur Erforschung der Judenfrage and was centered in Frankfurt where the mayor had already confiscated the Jewish books from the municipal library. The Judaica Collection in Frankfurt had been a gift from the Rothschild family in 1928. The Institut would be critical in "teaching the spiritual basis and tactics of our ideological adversary." Jewish scholars from the liquidated ghetto at Vilna were employed at the Frankfurt center, which eventually collected—in a perverse twist of irony—over 6 million works.[14]

At the Roman Synagogue that September day in 1943, approximately twenty officials searched the premises, paying particular attention—according to the diary of an office worker—to the two libraries: the Biblioteca Comunale and Biblioteca del Collegio Rabbinico.[15] The libraries of the Roman ghetto—like those of other ghettos in Europe—were centers for both the spiritual and the secular life of the community. The next day, 1 October, two men from the ERR returned to the Synagogue and introduced themselves to Foà as orientalists; one, in the uniform of a captain and identified as a specialist in Hebrew from Berlin,[16] asked permission to examine the community's libraries. The American historian Robert Katz has given us a vivid description:

> The Biblioteca Comunale had a magnificent collection, one of the richest in Europe, not only for the study of Judaica, but also of early Christianity. A heritage of 2,000 years of Jewish presence in Rome, the library contained vast treasures that had not yet been catalogued. . . . Among the known material were the only copies of books and manuscripts dating from before the birth of Christ, from the time of the Caesars, the emperors, and the early popes. There were engravings from the Middle Ages, books from the earliest printers, and papers and documents handed down through the ages.[17]

Beginning before the birth of Jesus, the Jewish community of Rome had accumulated these materials, with significant additions during the medieval period. The collection was substantially enlarged after 1492 with the influx of Jews expelled from Spain and Sicily. By the twentieth century, the collections in both the Collegio Rabbinico and the Comunità were still being cataloged according to their date of acquisition, making research difficult.

The Jews of Rome have been caught between the "benevolence and betrayal" of their city.[18] There was the humiliation of being ordered to march under the Triumphal Arch of Titus which depicted the destruction of Jerusalem, to kiss the ground where the pope's foot had trod, and to listen to sermons demanding their conversion to Christianity. In 1322, on orders of Pope John XXII, copies of the Talmud were destroyed in bonfires,[19] neither the first nor the last time such an event occurred in Rome.

The "golden age" of the Hebrew book in Italy was the sixteenth century when—notwithstanding the censorship of papal and civil authorities—Hebrew publishers crafted beautiful and influential texts. Rome became the center of this trade when Isaac Immanuel de Lattes established a press in the Eternal City in 1546. A relative, Bonet de Lattes, was private physician to Pope Leo X, who allowed a Hebrew press to be established in the house of Giacomo Fagiot da Montecchio in the Piazza Montanara. In 1518 this press printed the *Sefer Haharkabah,* the first Hebrew book printed in Rome. The liberal Leo X was succeeded by Clement VII and then Paul III, who first decreed the establishment of the ghettos in 1556. The Counter-Reformation and the workings of the Roman Inquisition effectively blocked publication of new works in Hebrew, and until 1810 no Hebrew book was published in Rome.[20] None other than Pier Luigi Farnese, illegitimate son of Pope Paul III, petitioned his father for the privilege of establishing a Hebrew press in Rome; his father denied the request.[21] The sixteenth and seventeenth centuries witnessed more bonfires of Hebrew books, including one in the Piazza of Saint Peter's itself.[22] The rationalism of the Enlightenment put an end to this practice; now books were merely confiscated rather than burned. In April 1753 papal authorities entered the Roman ghetto after the gates had been closed for the night and proceeded to fill thirty-eight carts with about 650 books.[23]

In 1893 the books of one synagogue were destroyed by fire. Spurred by the losses incurred by the fire, the community acted to preserve a priceless legacy. In 1895 Angelo Di Capua (Mordekhai Yaakov Yosef) compiled an inventory of the Talmud-Torah confraternity which held the rarest and most important texts.[24] At the beginning of the twentieth century, the various collections of the so-called Five Schools were assembled to form the Biblioteca della Comunità Israelitica.[25]

In 1934 a Jewish scholar, Isaia Sonne, spent eight days examining the contents of the Biblioteca della Comunità Israelitica. Sonne had divided his labors among five groups of texts: (1) manuscripts; (2) incunabula; (3) works of the famous Soncino publishing house, which beginning around 1500 was a prodigious publisher within the pontifical state; (4) oriental texts from the sixteenth century (primarily from Constantinople and Salonika); (5) miscellaneous and peculiar works that fit into no particular category. Sonne's eighty-five-page catalog is preserved today by the Jewish community in Rome and allows us some insight into what the officers of the ERR were looking at.[26]

Most of the manuscripts were from the fourteenth to the nineteenth centuries and represented monuments of the literary and intellectual life of Rome. They reveal Jewish participation in the Spanish philosophical movement of the 1400s, as well as the spiritual crisis of the sixteenth century in which the Kabala came to replace philosophy. Among the manuscripts were works of the rabbi and medical doctor Moses Rieti; manuscripts spirited out of Spain and Sicily during the Jewish expulsion in 1492; a Portuguese incunabulum of 1494; a mathematics text of Elia Mizrahi; and an extremely rare edition of a Hebrew-Italian-Arabic vocabulary published in Naples in 1488. There were also twenty-one talmudic tracts published by Soncino, which had been prohibited by Pope Julius II. Included in this collection was a rare eight-volume edition of the Talmud by the famous sixteenth-century Venetian printer Daniel Bomberg.

The ERR officers informed Foà that in the interest of their studies the catalogs of the libraries were to be handed over to them. A few days later, another officer, this time a lieutenant who claimed to be a paleographer and a specialist in Semitic philology, examined the libraries. As his men rifled through the libraries, an eyewitness noticed the Nazi intellectual:

> the officer, with artful and meticulous hands like fine embroidery, touched softly, caressed, fondled the papyrus and incunabula; he turned the pages of manuscripts and rare editions and leafed through membranaceous codices and palimpsests. The varying attention of his touch, the differing artfulness of his gestures were at once proportionate to the volume's worth. Those works, for the most part, were written in obscure alphabets. But in opening their pages, the officer's eyes would fix on them, widening and brightening, in the same way that some readers who are particularly familiar with a subject know where to find the desired part, the revealing passage. In those elegant hands, as if under keen and bloodless torture, a kind of very subtle sadism, the ancient books had spoken.[27]

In the presence of the Synagogue's secretary, Rosina Sorani (whose diary is preserved at the YIVO Institute in New York), the officer telephoned an international shipping company and made arrangements for the books to be transported out of Rome. Her entry for 11 October 1943 reveals that "they turned to me and told me that they had seen very well how many books there were in the libraries, and in what order; they declared the libraries under sequester, that within a few days they would come to get the books and that all was to be as they left it; if not, I would have to pay with my life."[28] Sorani informed Foà who contacted Dante Almansi, president of the Union of Jewish Communities. Together they drafted a letter[29] and sent four copies to various offices within the Fascist regime: the library division of the Ministry of Education; the Directorate General of Religions; the Directorate General of Public Security; and the Directorate General of Civil Administration. Perhaps they should not have been surprised that no Fascist official offered to intercede, especially since the last three offices were under the direction of the notorious war criminal and rabid anti-Semite Guido Buffarini-

Guidi, who was at that very moment preparing anti-Semitic legislation far more severe than that passed by the regime in 1938.[30]

On the morning of 13 October, two full-sized freight cars from the German national railroad, which had been placed on Rome's trolley lines, pulled up in front of the Synagogue by the Tiber River. Foà and Almansi were now frantic. They were concerned about the priceless gold and silver religious articles and hit upon an ingenious solution: the mikvah were emptied of their water, and an artisan began the laborious process of hiding the religious articles within the walls of the baths. Some of the most important works found refuge in a nearby municipal library, the Biblioteca Vallicelliana. At precisely 8:30 A.M. the next day, 14 October (the first day of the festival of Succoth), officials of the ERR returned with workers from the transport company. They spent the entire day collecting the contents of the two libraries and loading them onto the railroad cars. As they were emptying both libraries, the artisan involved in the mikvah deception arrived unnoticed by the Germans and proceeded to complete his work, thereby saving many of the most precious religious articles. Later, pieces were hidden in gardens and homes all over Rome.[31] After the two railroad cars had been loaded to capacity, they departed. Witnesses noted that the cars had come from Munich.[32] Two months later, on 22 December, the Germans returned to carry away the last remaining books and manuscripts from the Rabbinical College.[33] Perhaps they took special pleasure in the fact that it was the first day of Hanukkah. In all, the Nazis confiscated more than 10,000 volumes from the the Jewish community in Rome.

For the next several days, the Jews of Rome debated among themselves the significance of this latest development. Some insisted that this was the beginning of greater persecution; others noted that a crime against books was not a crime against people.[34] Panic began to seep into the community. A foreign journalist noted at the time that

> the population is half crazy; young men and families look desperately for hiding places, get them, then look for better ones . . . convents and seminaries have become the most sought after hideouts. Another famous one is the Lunatic asylum: scores of people have entered and have filled it to the bursting point. Rome never had so many madmen.[35]

But the fate of the Jews of Rome was much more severe than that in store for the precious books. After the war, some of the books were to be returned from Frankfurt after delicate diplomatic negotiations. Most of Rome's Jews who were deported would not return to the Eternal City. By the fall of 1943, much of the diplomatic corps, military officers, and the Vatican, including Pius XII, were aware that the Germans were preparing to deport the Jews. The German consul in Rome, Friederich Möllhausen, had sent a telegram to Foreign Minister von Ribbentrop on 6 October marked "*very, very urgent!*" in which he repeated that Kappler "had received orders from Berlin to seize the eight thousand Jews resident in Rome and transport them to Northern Italy, where they are to be liquidated" (*wo sie liquidiert werden sollen*).[36] As far as I know, this is the only Nazi document that makes a direct reference to "liquidating" the Jews, rather than using the more traditional *Sonderbehandlung* (special handling) or other euphemisms.

In fact, it was only two days after the confiscation of the libraries that the deportations began. In the early morning hours of the Sabbath (16 October 1943), Kappler's men carried out a highly organized search of the ghetto and seized over 1,000 Roman Jews. (There were over 10,000 Roman and foreign Jews in the city.) They were held over the weekend at the Collegio Militare, a mere hundred yards from the pope's residence in the Vatican; Pius XII decided not to intervene on behalf of "his Jews." During the night, Marcella Di Tivoli Perugia, captured with her two children, gave birth in the courtyard after the Germans refused to permit her release to the hospital. On Monday morning, the Jews—including Tivoli Perugia with her three children—were herded into railroad cars and began their nightmare voyage to Auschwitz. The Germans expended far more consideration for the safety of the books than of the Jews. Of the 1,041 Jews deported that day, only 15 returned to Rome after the war.[37]

The books had a different fate. With the Allied bombings of Frankfurt, the vast holdings of the ERR in the Institut der NSDAP zur Erforschung der Judenfrage were moved to six repositories in the small village of Hungen. After the war, the Rothschild Library in Frankfurt served to house the vast collections. In October of that year, a young officer in the Monuments, Fine Arts, and Archives section of the Allied Military Government was assigned to make a survey of the collections in order to expedite restitution, and he recommended that operations be moved to larger quarters at Offenbach.[38] Ironically located in the abandoned I. G. Farben plant, the United States Archival Depot under the direction of Maj. Seymour J. Pomerenze (a former archivist at the National Archives) at Offenbach eventually processed millions of books. The collection of the Collegio Rabbinico of Rome was returned in March 1947, accomplished through the assistance of Capt. Carlo Rupnik, the Italian officer in charge of the restitution effort: 26,568 items were returned by two railroad cars. Of this amount, 159 crates (6,579 books) belonged to the Collegio Rabbinico, 57 crates (6,112 books) and 6 crates of archives belonged to the Istituto Austriaco di studi storici in Rome, and 24 crates (4,585 books) and 15 crates of archives were returned to the Istituto Italiano di Speleologia-Postumia.[39]

Not all of the rare volumes were lost in 1943. A volume of 1485, the *Nebi'im ri'šonim 'im peruš* with commentary by David Kimhi was saved as was Kimhi's *Sefer ha-Shorashim* (Il libro delle radici [The Book of Roots]) published two decades earlier. In addition, there survived an extremely rare Mishnah with commentary by Maimonides published in Naples in 1492. Several sixteenth-century volumes of *Peruh 'al ha-Torah* (commentaries on the Pentateuch) remained hidden within the Synagogue, as well as Isaac Alfasi's *Sefer ha-Halakhot* (compendium of the Talmud) published by the Venetian Bomberg in 1521–22. A ritual prayer book for holy days of the "Roman" rite published by the Soncino firm around 1500 was saved. In addition, one can today find a 1488 edition of Mose Ben Jacob's *Seger miswot gadol* (Il libro grande dei precetti [The Great Book of Obligations]) and Moses Ben Maimon's Mishneh Torah of the late fifteenth century.[40]

What might we conclude from this all-too-brief study of a small episode buried within the immensity of the Holocaust? The true student and scholar must be prepared to abandon previously held conceptions. I had begun this study assuming that the books of the Roman ghetto had "merely" been sacrificed in a burnt offering to racial hatred, a holocaust enveloped in the Holocaust. But the real fate of the books proved to be in many ways even more disturbing: pseudoscience and corrupted scholarship at the service of a deviant and diabolical ideology. Here is but one small—yet bitterly ironic—example of the immense perversity of the Nazi project: a people whose entire existence was bound and symbolized by the Book were systematically destroyed while their precious works were given lavish and even loving attention from the very people who sought their physical destruction.

POSTSCRIPT

On 21 May 2007, Enrico Letta, Undersecretary of State in the Italian government, signed an agreement with Ekaterina Genieva, Director of the Library of Foreign Literature in Moscow, to investigate the possibility that remnants of the Biblioteca della Comunità Israelitica might have ended up in the former Soviet Union. Dario Tedeschi, a lawyer working at the request of the Italian government, described the search—funded by Unicredit Private Banking—as "trying to unravel a historical mystery."[41]

NOTES

This paper was first presented at an international conference, "The Holocaust and the Book," at Drew University (Madison, N.J.) in November 1996. I wish to thank the director of the conference, Prof. Jonathan Rose of Drew University, for his support; in addition, this paper profited from the suggestions of Leonidas E. Hill, Professor of History Emeritus at the University of British Columbia, and Dr. Sem C. Sutter, Bibliographer for Modern Literatures at the University of Chicago. The essay also benefited from the suggestions of two anonymous reviewers who saved me from several embarrassing errors. Finally, I wish to acknowledge the work of Prof. James T. Mellone of the Axinn Library at Hofstra University for his assistance in tracking down some of the sources and the kindness of Dottoressa Simona Foà, archivist of the Jewish Community of Rome, who graciously permitted me to examine the documents which made this essay possible.

1. David Shavit, *Hunger for the Printed Word: Books and Libraries in the Jewish Ghettos of Nazi-Occupied Europe* (Jefferson, N.C.: McFarland, 1997), 48. On the mystical power

of the book, see Marc Drogin, *Biblioclasm: The Mythical Origin, Magical Power, and Perishability of the Written Word* (Totowa, N.J.: Rowan & Littlefield, 1989).

2. Susan Zuccotti, *The Italians and the Holocaust: Persecution, Rescue, Survival* (New York: Basic, 1987; rpt., Lincoln: University of Nebraska Press, 1996), 156.

3. Robert Katz, *Black Sabbath: A Journey through a Crime against Humanity* (New York: Macmillan, 1969), 68.

4. Ibid., 107–8.

5. For the activities of the ERR, see the essay by Donald E. Collins and Herbert P. Rothfelder, "The Einsatzstab Reichsleiter Rosenberg and the Looting of Jewish and Masonic Libraries during World War II," *Journal of Library History* 18/1 (1983): 21–36. See also Jaqueline Borin, "Embers of the Soul: The Destruction of Jewish Books and Libraries in Poland during World War II," *Libraries & Culture* 28/44 (1993): 445–60; Alan Noel Latimer, "Libraries under the Nazi Occupation," *The Library*, 5th ser., 1 June 1946, 45–46.

6. Fritz Nova, *Alfred Rosenberg: Nazi Theorist of the Holocaust* (New York: Hippocrene, 1986), 204; on the Einsatzstab, see also Leon Poliakov, *Harvest of Hate: The Nazi Program for the Destruction of the Jews of Europe*, rev. ed. (New York: Holocaust Library, 1979), 67–72, 81–82; on Rosenberg, see Robert Cecil, *The Myth of the Master Race: Alfred Rosenberg and Nazi Ideology* (New York: Dodd, Mead, 1972).

7. Reinhard Bollmus, *Das Amt Rosenberg und seine Gegner zum Machtkampf im national sozialistischen Herrschafts-system* (Stuttgart: Deutsche Verlagsanstalt, Studien zur Zeitgeschichte, 1970), 145.

8. Nova, *Rosenberg*, 204.

9. Cecil, *Myth*, 56, 109.

10. Quoted in Shavit, *Hunger*, 48–49.

11. Leslie I. Poste, "Books Go Home from the Wars," *Library Journal* 73 (1 Dec. 1948): 1699. The story had caught the attention of popular and academic writers in the days immediately after the war. See, for example, G. N. Kefauver and C. M. White, "Library Situation in Europe," *Library Journal* 70 (1 May 1945): 385–89, and (15 May 1945): 473–76; E. Greenaway, "Librarian Looks at Central Europe," *Library Journal* 73 (15 Feb. 1948): 277–80, (1 Mar. 1948): 366–67, and (15 Mar. 1948): 437–41; K. R. Shaffer, "Conquest of Books," *Library Journal* 71 (15 Jan. 1946): 82–86. Other accounts appeared by J. S. Evans, "Rosenberg's Den of Thieves Holds Key to Looted Art of Europe," *Newsweek* 25 (28 May 1945): 86+; J. Flanner, "Annals of Crime," *New Yorker* 23 (22 Feb. 1947): 31–36, (1 Mar. 1947): 33–38, and (8 Mar. 1947): 38–42; James S. Plaut, "Hitler's Capital: Loot for the Master Race," *Atlantic Monthly* 178 (Oct. 1946): 73–78, and (Sept. 1948): 57–63.

12. Joseph E. Persico, *Nuremberg: Infamy on Trial* (New York: Viking, 1994), 210, 242.

13. Nova, *Rosenberg*, 204.

14. Katz, *Black Sabbath*, 119 and note.

15. Diary of Rosina Sorani, partially reproduced in *Ottobre 1943: cronaca di un'infamia* (Rome: Comunità Israelitica di Roma, 1961), 36.

16. See the report of Ugo Foà in *Ottobre 1943*, 20.

17. Katz, *Black Sabbath*, 120. A brief synopsis of these events is given in Meir Michaelis, "Rome," *Encyclopedia of the Holocaust*, ed. Israel Gutman (New York: Macmillan, 1990), 1300–1302.

18. I borrow the phrase from Alexander Stille, *Benevolence and Betrayal: Five Italian Jewish Families under Fascism* (New York: Simon & Schuster, 1991).

19. William Popper, *The Censorship of Hebrew Books* (New York: Ktav, n.d.), 17.

20. David Werner Amram, *The Makers of Hebrew Books in Italy* (Philadelphia: Greenstone, 1909), 240, 244.

21. Ibid., 248.

22. Popper, *Censorship*, 97.

23. Ibid., 121.

24. The handwritten manuscript (*Elenco deo libri della Biblioteca del Tamud-Torà secondo l'ordine col quale sono contentuti nei vari armadi*) is now held in the Archives of the Comunità Israelitica, Armadio V, pachetto #1.

25. The Five Schools comprised the Scola Tempio and Scola Nova of the Italian rite; the Scola Catalona-Aragonese and the Scola Castigliana of the Spanish rite; and the Scola Siciliana, which lost its books in the 1893 blaze. On the schools and confraternities, see Attilio Milano, "Le confraternite pie del ghetto di Roma," *La Rassegna Mensile di Israel* 24 (1958): 107–20.

26. Isaia Sonne, *Relazione sulla Biblioteca della Comunità Israelitica di Roma* (Rome, 1934). For a catalog of works present in the collections three decades later, see *Catalogo della Mostra Permanente della Comunità Israelitica di Roma* (Rome: Comunità Israelitica, 1963).

27. Giacomo Debenedetti, "16 ottobre 1943," Mercurio (Rome), Dec. 1944, 81; quoted in Katz, *Black Sabbath*, 123.

28. Sorani diary, in *Ottobre 1943*, 37.

29. Following is the text of the letter written by Almansi and Foà, dated 11 Oct. 1943: "This morning a German official of the SS attached to the local German Embassy presented himself at the offices of the Hebrew Community of Rome located in the Synagogue on Lungotever Cenci; he was accompanied by another German in civilian dress, an expert in library matters. The official, after having visited the Library of the Community and that of the Collegio Rabbinico . . . declared to a worker present that all of the books of the two libraries were to be considered under sequester, that they could not be removed, threatening that if anything were removed, the worker would suffer severe physical punishment; he let it be known that the books would be removed within a few days by the German authorities.

"Consisting of very valuable archival material (manuscripts, incunabula, Soncino texts, publications of the sixteenth century, extremely interesting examples of Hebrew books, etc.), which were cataloged a few years ago by an expert [Sonne, *Relazione*, 1934], and which constitute a complex of notable cultural importance, their removal by German authorities who intend to transport them to Germany would leave Italy bereft of an important cultural patrimony.

"The undersigned, respectively in their capacity as President of the Union of the Collegio Rabbinico and the president of the Hebrew Community of Rome—unable to oppose the request of the German Authorities—feel the obligation to inform the Honorable Minister so that he may take whatever he feels are the necessary measures." (Quoted in *Ottobre 1943*, 22–23.)

30. Katz, *Black Sabbath*, 125, 148 n.

31. Ibid., 149 n.

32. Foà, report, in *Ottobre 1943*, 23.

33. Sorani diary, 22 Dec. 1943, in *Ottobre 1943*, 40.

34. Debenedetti, "16 Ottobre," 82.

35. M. de Wyss, *Rome under the Terror* (London: Hale, 1945), 144.

36. The telegram from Möllhausen to von Ribbentrop, dated 6 Oct. 1943, is in Documents of the German Foreign Ministry, 1920–45, National Archives, Washington, D.C., microcopy T-120, roll 4668; it is quoted in full in Katz, *Black Sabbath*, 136.

37. Katz, *Black Sabbath*, App. 1 and 2, 331–41.

38. Poste, "Books Go Home from the Wars," 1700; see also F. J. Hoogewoud, "The Nazi Looting of Books and Its American 'Antithesis': Selected Pictures from the Offenbach Archival Depot's Photographic History and Its Supplement," *Studia Rosenthalia* 26/1–2 (1992): 158–92. On 10 May 1933, 100,000 people marched in New York City to protest the burning of books by Nazi Germany; see Guy Stern, *Nazi Book Burning and the American Response* (Detroit: Wayne State University Press, 1990).

39. Leslie I. Poste, "The Development of U.S. Protection of Libraries and Archives in Europe during World War II" (Ph.D. diss., Graduate Library School, University of Chicago, 1958), 380.

40. Other volumes included Yosef Albo, *Sefer ha-'iqqarim* (Pesaro: Soncino, 1485); two editions of Bahya Ben 'Asher, *Perush 'al ha-Torah* [Commentary on the Pentateuch] (Pesaro: Soncino, 1517, and Rimini: Soncino, 1526); *Ketubim 'im perushim* (Venice: Bomberg, 1525); Moses Ben Nahman, *Perush 'al ha-Torah* (Pesaro: Soncino, 1514); Mahzor Bene Roma, *'im perush Kimha de-'abishonà* (Bologna, 1540); Natan Ben Yehiel, *Sefer ha-'aruk* (Pesaro: Soncino, 1517); Yishaq Alfasi, *Sefer Rab Alfas* (Venice: Bomberg, 1521–22). For a list of those works that managed to escape being confiscated by the ERR, see Ariel Toaff, "Stampe rare della Biblioteca della Comunità Israelitica di Roma scampate al saccheggio nazista," *La Bibliofilia* 80 (1978): 139–49. Some rescued volumes from eastern Europe even found their way to the United States. The 10 January 1997 issue of the *Chronicle of Higher Education* reported that an anonymous eastern European Jew who had survived the Holocaust had donated a small collection of works to Baltimore Hebrew University. Inside the front covers were a stamped swastika and imperial eagle encircled by the words "Library of the New Germany." The donation included volumes from the eighteenth, nineteenth, and early twentieth centuries in Hebrew, Yiddish, Latin, Aramaic, Hungarian, Polish, French, and German. Among the volumes was a four-volume edition of the *Mishneh Torah* by Maimonides and an encyclopedia of Jewish law printed in Amsterdam in 1708.

41. Sarah Delaney, "Hunt for Jewish Library Stolen by the Nazis Turns to Russia," *Times*, 23 May 2007.

III • THE CONFISCATION OF JEWISH BOOKS IN SALONIKA IN THE HOLOCAUST

Yitzchak Kerem

THE confiscation of books from Salonika by the Nazis during the Second World War was more than a loss in itself. It was the first of numerous German anti-Semitic measures that eventually led to the destruction of this great Sephardic rabbinic community, thus cutting off the main lifeline of Sephardic culture in general.

Hitler had appointed Alfred Rosenberg in 1934 to supervise Nazi intellectual and philosophical education. In 1939 Rosenberg founded the Institute for the Investigation of the Jewish Question, whose function was to pillage the libraries, archives, and art galleries of European Jewry for material that could be used against the Jews. Rosenberg believed that the Jewish question could be solved only when the *Lebensraum,* the living space of a Greater Germany for the German people, was void of Jews.

Since 1934, when the Nazi Party and the German Foreign Ministry began systematic intelligence work on Salonikan Jewry, the city had been targeted as a key Sephardic Jewish community. Rosenberg viewed it as another center of "racial chaos, stemming from metropolitan life and Jewish finance,"[1] which had to be eliminated to pave the way for "Aryanization." German Nazi specialists on Sephardic Jewry and their history, like Hermann Kellenbenz, were utilized to study Sephardic communities and write about them in order to state the Nazi case against the Jews once Germany was victorious and all of the Jews of Europe had been killed. Even after the Nazis were defeated, Kellenbenz, in the guise of a historian, published several studies of Sephardic Jewry, and not until recently was his Nazi identity uncovered.[2]

When the Rosenberg Commission established itself in Salonika in mid-June 1941, it quickly and secretly confiscated an enormous number of books, documents, Torah scrolls, and religious artifacts. At that early stage in the German military occupation of Salonika, this expropriation was not seen as a specifically anti-Semitic act, since many Christians were also targeted for arrest and confiscation.[3]

Directing the confiscation for the Rosenberg Commission was Dr. Johannes Pohl, director of the Hebrew Department of the Nazi Institute for Jewish

Research in Frankfurt. Salonika attracted him because its Jewish community possessed rare old books, incunabula, manuscripts, and documents that could shed light on Jewish culture and increase awareness about Judaism. The Rosenberg Commission established its headquarters at 10 Kalari Street in the plush building of the former American consulate.

Pohl had sufficient knowledge of Hebrew and the Talmud to recognize Sephardic rabbinical exegeses and other Jewish Halachic works. He used that knowledge to direct the pillage of the massive Jewish collections in the city, efficiently instructing his workers on how to locate rare books, documents, Torah scrolls, artistic scrolls, prayer books, mahzorim for Passover, archives, certificates, and communal and educational papers and records. The confiscated materials were sent to Frankfurt where they were checked and sorted. Teams of forgers distorted the contents of texts in order to advance Nazi propaganda against the Jewish religion and race.[4]

The Germans took thousands of books, many of them produced in Salonika where Don Gedalya had founded the first Jewish Hebrew and Ladino printing press in the city around 1513.[5] Hans Heinrich, a poet, together with a policeman and an Armenian translator, led the actual confiscation of collections.[6] These despicable agents of nazism packed the books and documents and labeled them "Geschlossen und versiegelt durch die Feldpolizei der Feldkommandantur" (closed and signed by the Field Police of the Field Command). The crates and boxes were classified and cataloged and given serial numbers.[7]

Mark Mazower has described the function of the Rosenberg Commission and its Salonikan confiscation of Jewish books, ornaments, and documents:

> The information obtained by the Foreign Office was put to use as soon as the occupation began. In 1940 Hitler instructed the regime's chief ideologue, Alfred Rosenberg, to seize "all scientific and archival materials for the ideological foe" for a new institute to be established in Frankfurt to educate the German people about Jews. First Rosenberg plundered the cultural treasures of French Jewry; then came the turn of Greece. On 23 April 1941 Rosenberg informed [Martin] Bormann, Hitler's private secretary, that his team was already in the Balkans, enjoying the full support of the army and the SD [*Sicherheitsdienst*, the SS Security Service]. In Greece, local military commanders issued orders to their troops instructing them to assist the so-called Rosenberg Sonderkommandos. Between May and November a unit of more than thirty officers and German academics scoured the country, visiting no less than forty-nine synagogues, clubs, associations, schools, banks, newspapers, bookshops and hospitals as well as over sixty individual homes. Archives, synagogue ornaments, manuscripts, incunabula and priceless collections of rabbinical judgements were taken. Two years later, the director of Rosenberg's new "Library for Exploration of the Jewish Question" boasted proudly that among his 500,000 volumes was a collection of 10,000 books and manuscripts from Greece. "In the New Order of European Organisation," he predicted, "the library for the Jewish Question, not only for Europe but for the world, will arise in Frankfurt."[8]

From the end of the fifteenth century, when Spanish expellees arrived, until the beginning of the nineteenth century, Salonika was a major publishing center for Jewish religious works. From the mid-nineteenth century until the beginning of German occupation in 1941, Salonika was a center for the publication of Judeo-Spanish novels, historical works, ballads, Complas (special holiday ballads) for Purim, short stories, and newspapers.[9] Rabbis amassed large collections of books and religious responsa, and affluent laymen built up private collections as a sign of status. Local Jews had also collected works printed in major centers of Jewish publication: Livorno, Venice, Amsterdam, Vienna, Krakow, Warsaw, Lvov, and Vilna. Salonikan libraries included Hebrew talmudic and biblical editions, religious and philosophical works, scientific and medical literature, as well as Arabic and Latin volumes. Many works were copied or printed on parchment and bound artistically in leather.

Great fires swept through the city in 1545, 1620, 1734, 1759, 1877, 1890, and 1917, and huge collections were burned. Commonly, any remaining copy of a valuable work would be recopied by hand for safekeeping. But much was irreplaceable: the encyclopedias and historical works burned in the home of the Westernized French-Jewish educational reformer Rabbi Juda Nehama in 1890; the libraries of the Yeshiva La Buena, Rabbis Yaakov Kovo, Shaul Amarillio, and Asher Simha; and the Kadima Library (founded 1899) of 3,000 volumes on Hebrew culture. All of these burned in the fatal fire of 1917: "La Fuego Grande."

In the early nineteenth century, book collectors like Ephraim Reinard and El-kana Adler came to Salonika and bought many incunabula and valuable rare compositions, which were preserved in New York and London.[10] In the 1930s YIVO representatives in Vilna obtained valuable manuscripts from Salonika, as did the National Library in Jerusalem (then on Mount Scopus) and the Library of Congress in Washington.

In 1941 the first collection confiscated by the Rosenberg Commission was that of Joseph Nehama, community leader, banker, historian, director of the Alliance Israelite Universelle school, and son of the aforementioned Juda Nehama. His library had contained many encyclopedias and essays in history, sociology, and philosophy, as well as complete sets of important journals and periodicals.[11] Soon, many other Jewish communal and private book collections were expropriated: the 2,500-volume library of the Beit-Din-Tsedek, the rabbinical court, acquired mostly in Palestine after 1919; the writings of Yosef Caro and local rabbinical responsa; the communal library donated by Juda Nehama, containing post–Moses Mendelssohn Hebrew Haskalah books; schoolteachers' libraries of 600 volumes, including textbooks on language, history, and modern Hebrew literature; the German Judaic library of Chief Rabbi Dr. Zvi Koretz totaling some 1,000 volumes, among them a beautiful set of the Babylonian Talmud as well as his rich collection of medieval Arabic Islamic and Jewish philosophy; the 500-book collection of Rabbi Shaul Amarillio containing important responsa, and Jewish historical and Halachic works which had been expensively replaced after the library was partially destroyed in the 1917 fire; the rare historical book collection of Michael Molho, containing some 100 very rare editions in addition to first editions of prayer books and mahzorim; the collection of the Monastir Synagogue on Syngrou Street holding many valuable Torahs and Jewish law works donated by Yaakov Israel; the famous library of the Haimutcho Yeshiva at 2 Menekse Street, donated by the eminent Chief Rabbi Haimutcho Kovo, which included a wealth of responsa from many historical periods and Jewish communities, Midrashic literature, kabalistic, talmudic, and biblical commentary, historical works, and collections of derashot and eulogies (Torah sermons). One of the greatest losses was the enormous library built over several generations by the revered Rabbi Haim Habib and his ancestors, containing 8,000 Halachic works and commentaries. It was hidden with the Jewish communal archives in the basement of the Jewish community's central office. Unfortunately, this library was not sent to Germany but burned by the Nazis at the Baron Hirsh internment camp in Salonika.

The Rosenberg Commission also confiscated the archives of the Jewish community and those of the Union Bank of Salonika, which was owned by local Jews. The latter collection was to serve the Nazis in defending their theory of the power of international Jewish wealth, purportedly exposing the "mysterious connection" that aligned the "Jewish plutocrats" against Germany. The Rosenberg Commission stole 250 Torah scrolls, of which 150 were sent to Germany on the same train with the Jewish Spanish nationals deported to Bergen-Belsen on 2 August 1943. The other Torahs were burned or defaced in Salonika. Many of the gold and silver Torah rimonim ornaments and the ark curtains, the parochet, had been made in Salonika by Jewish artisans and craftsmen after their arrival at the end of the fifteenth century. Many of the documents and manuscripts had been brought to Salonika by Sephardic refugees from the Iberian Peninsula after the numerous expulsions of the fourteenth, fifteenth, and sixteenth centuries.

Other collections were never detected by the Nazis. They were dispersed in pieces throughout the city, primarily to used-book dealers, or were more profanely used to make bags for grocery stores or to wrap vegetables in the market. Such was the fate of the mobile libraries of the organization Anciens Élèves (the graduates of the popular French-Jewish Alliance Israelite Universelle school system in Salonika) containing some 2,500 books, the B'nai B'rith (2,000 volumes), and the students of the Mission Laïque Française.

Also untouched by the Nazis, but later dispersed by the Greek public, was the renowned collection of the yeshiva on Queen Olga Boulevard, linked to the library of the Yeshiva Haimutcho on Menekse Street. The two libraries complemented each other and together totaled 3,000 volumes. These collections had been further expanded by large donations from local Jews and from other Jewish communities in Thrace, Macedonia, and Thessaly.[12]

Fortunately, a part of the communal archives was hidden and preserved. Today this material is stored in more than 400 files at the Central Archives of the Jewish People at the Givat Ram campus of the Hebrew University. Another part of the archives was recently uncovered in Moscow after the fall of the Communist regime[13] and is currently being microfilmed for the Archive of the Diaspora Research Institute at Tel Aviv University. When I told Prof. Mina Rosen about this collection at a 1992 Ottoman studies conference in Ankara, Turkey, she proceeded in high gear to raise $200,000 from the Salonikan Recanati family of the Israel Discount Bank in Tel Aviv. She also convinced Russian archival directors to permit the microfilming of more than 400 files from the Salonikan Jewish community and three files from the Athenian Jewish community. The archive housing the files was at first known as the "Secret Archive" in 1945; later as the "Osove" archive in 1991–92; and now the name has been changed to the Center for the Preservation of Historical Collections in Moscow.

The collection, under the direction of Prof. Mansour Michaelovitch Muchamedjanov, contains materials invaluable to historians. It includes circumcision, marriage, and death records from 1870 until 1941.[14] One file, on the Eretz-Israel Office, contains requests of Jews wanting to emigrate to Palestine in the 1930s. Another, on the Salonikan-Palestine Corporation, has records of its investors and the property they purchased in Palestine, mainly plots of land in the future Florentine Quarter between southern Tel Aviv and Jaffa.[15]

After the Second World War, many single pages of Jewish books appeared in Salonikan markets. Parts of Torah scrolls and Jewish Hebrew and Ladino exegeses had been made into soles for shoes. No Judeo-Spanish newspaper collections were preserved in the city, but luckily large collections were found in Kavalla, Tel Aviv, Jerusalem, Paris, and Washington after the war. The largest collection of some 70,000 Judeo-Spanish newspapers was in Kavalla, Greece, and belonged to the tobacco merchant Yehuda Perahia.[16] David Benveniste, a Salonikan historian resident in Jerusalem, eventually brought the entire collection to the Ben Zvi Institute Library in Jerusalem.[17] In the 1920s and 1930s newspapers had been collected by the Central Zionist Archives and the National Jewish Library in Jerusalem and the Greek Jewish Immigrants Association of Tel Aviv. In Paris and Washington, the Alliance Israelite Universelle and the Library of Congress (respectively) had collected Judeo-Spanish newspapers from Salonika since the past century. The only collection in the West which did not fare well consisted of numerous Sephardic rabbinical works and was housed at the Jewish Theological Seminary in New York City. It burned in the institution's tragic fire in 1966.

The Nazis confiscated most of the rabbinical and cultural works of the Sephardic Jewish community of Salonika along with its numerous archival collections. The expropriation was more or less thorough and systematic, and most of the confiscated publications were never found again. Salonikans in Israel and local historians like Michael Molho, Joseph Nehama, and Yitzhak Emmanuel, who survived the Holocaust, preserved and recalled the prewar literary and historical traditions of the community as best they could. Molho and Emmanuel[18] copied large samples of gravestones in the decade before the war, before the Nazis ordered the destruction of the 450-year-old cemetery in December 1942.[19]

The rabbinic responsa taken from the community constitute one of the greatest losses of irreplaceable documents. Despite the preservation of old newspapers by the Ben-Zvi Institute, most of the city's active Judeo-Spanish press from 1876 until 1941 has not survived. The artifacts taken are also lost, though some may reappear one day in archives, in German or former Soviet storage houses, or on the commercial market. Because of the enormous pillage of Judaica from Salonika, little Salonikan Jewish art is available for study by art historians. The pillage and destruction of the literary heritage of Salonikan Jewry were one facet of the Nazi plan to annihilate this vital Sephardic community. Unfortunately, the Germans largely succeeded: Salonika was never the same after the war. The Nazis knew that by taking the books of luminary rabbinic figures like Haim Habib, Shaul Amarillio, and Haimutcho Kovo they could destroy the religious spirit of the community. When they killed Haim Habib in Birkenau in front of the community's remaining young men, the Nazis finally crushed their belief in God. Confiscating the community's books and documents was a first step toward destroying the traditional Sephardic culture of Salonikan Jewry.

NOTES

1. Fritz Nova, *Alfred Rosenberg: Nazi Theorist of the Holocaust* (New York: Hippocrene, 1986), 5, 34.

2. Hermann Kellenbenz, "History of the Sephardim in Germany," 26–40, and "The Sephardim in Scandinavia," 41–45, in Richard Barnett and Walter Schwab, eds., *The Sephardi Heritage,* Vol. 2: *The Western Sephardim* (Grendon, Northants.: Gibraltar, 1989).

3. Yosef Ben, *Greek Jewry in the Holocaust and the Resistance, 1941–1944* (Tel Aviv: Institute for the Research of Salonikan Jewry, 1985), 36 [in Hebrew].

4. Michael Molho and Joseph Nehama, *The Destruction of Greek Jewry, 1941–1944* (Jerusalem: Yad Vashem, 1965), 42 [in Hebrew].

5. Alexander Matkovski, *A History of the Jews in Macedonia* (Skopje: Macedonian Review Editions, 1982), 42; and Tracy Harris, *Death of a Language: The History of Judeo-Spanish* (Newark: University of Delaware Press; London and Toronto: Associated University Presses, 1994), 131.

6. Molho and Nehama, *Greek Jewry,* 43. See also Mark Mazower, *Inside Hitler's Greece: The Experience of Occupation, 1941–1944* (New Haven: Yale University Press, 1993), 237–38.

7. Molho and Nehama, *Greek Jewry,* 115.

8. Mazower, *Inside Hitler's Greece,* 237–38.

9. Moshe David Gaon, *A Bibliography of the Judeo-Spanish (Ladino) Press* (Jerusalem: Ben-Zvi Institute, Hebrew University, and National and University Library, 1965) [in Hebrew].

10. Molho and Nehama, *Greek Jewry,* 112–13.

11. Yitzchak Kerem, "Joseph Nehama," *Encyclopaedia Judaica, Decennial Book, 1983–1992: Events of 1982–1992* (Jerusalem: Encyclopaedia Judaica, 1994), 294.

12. Molho and Nehama, *Greek Jewry,* 113–15.

13. Yitzchak Kerem, "Sources on Greek Jewry in the Special Archives of Moscow," *Sharsheret Hadorot* 7 (Apr. 1993): x–xi.

14. Meirav Nesher, "Train Cars of Entire Lives," *Ha'aretz,* 13 Dec. 1994, 2b [in Hebrew].

15. Mansour Michaelovitch Muchmadjanov, lecture, Diaspora Research Institute, Tel Aviv University, Ramat Aviv, 13 Dec. 1994 [in Russian].

16. Miriam Novitch, *Le Passage des Barbares: Contribution à l'histoire de la déportation et de la résistance des Juifs grecs* (Kibbutz Lochamei Getaot: Ghetto Fighters, 1982), 86–88.

17. Yitzchak Kerem, "David Benveniste," *Maguen* (Caracas) 81 (July–Sept. 1991): 26–27.

18. Michael Molho, *Tombstones of the Jews Cemetery of Salonika* (Tel Aviv: Institute for the Research of Salonikan Jewry, 1974) [in Hebrew]. Isaac S. Emmanuel, *Precious Stones of the Jews of Salonika*, 2 vols. (Jerusalem: Kiriyat Sefer, 1963) [in Hebrew].

19. *Saloniki: Ir Ve'em Beyisrael* (Jerusalem and Tel Aviv: Institute for the Research of Salonikan Jewry, 1967), 26.

IV • EMBERS PLUCKED FROM THE FIRE: THE RESCUE OF JEWISH CULTURAL TREASURES IN VILNA

David E. Fishman

THE effort to collect and preserve Jewish historical documents and cultural treasures in Eastern Europe was launched with an impassioned public appeal by Simon Dubnov in 1891; it was institutionalized and broadened into a social movement with the founding of YIVO in 1925, and it reached its heroic culmination with the rescue activities by Abraham Sutzkever, Shmerke Kaczerginski, and others in Vilna between 1942 and 1946. The final reverberations of that movement were felt in 1996, when the surviving remnants of YIVO's Vilna archives were shipped from Lithuania to New York. That shipment was the epilogue to the story of the Vilna Ghetto's "Paper Brigade."

Between Dubnov and Sutzkever

Dubnov issued his appeal to save the Jewish past from oblivion at age twenty-nine, in a Russian-language pamphlet called *Ob izuchenii istorii ruskikh evreev* ["On the study of Russian-Jewish history"], and in an adapted Hebrew version of that pamphlet called *Nahpesa ve-nahkorah* ["Let us search and inquire"]. He opened by citing the words of Cicero that "not to know history means to remain forever a child," and declared that this maxim applied to entire nations as well as to individuals. The measure of a people's spiritual development was its level of historical consciousness; from that perspective, the Jews of Russia and Poland were still immature children—despite the fact that they belonged to one of the most ancient peoples on earth. They had neither knowledge nor consciousness of their 800-year historical experience in Eastern Europe. There was virtually no scholarship on Russian-Jewish history, and its absence posed a serious threat to Jewish continuity since, in the modern era, shared historical consciousness was destined to replace religious faith as the glue of Jewish group cohesion.

Most shameful of all, from Dubnov's perspective, was the neglect of Jewish historical documents, especially of the *pinkasim* of communities (*kehilot*) and voluntary associations (*hevrot*), which he called "the natural resources of our history."

They are lying in attics, in piles of trash, or in equally unpleasant and filthy rooms, among various broken household items and rags. These manuscripts are rotting away, they are being eaten by mice, and are being used by ignorant servants and children who tear off page after page for all sorts of purposes. In one word: year by year they are disappearing and being lost to history.[1]

Dubnov concluded that the collection of such materials required an "archeo-logical expedition," organized preferably by a central institution for the study of Russian-Jewish history. The institution could appoint local representatives to acquire materials and would work on classifying, cataloging, copying, and pub-lishing the documents in its possession.[2]

In the Hebrew version of his essay, Dubnov urged his readers to join him in the great task of documentary collection and preservation and appended detailed instructions on how to go about their work.

> I appeal to all educated readers, regardless of their party: to the pious and to the enlightened, to the old and to the young, to traditional rabbis and to Crown Rab-bis. . . . I call out to all of you: come and join the camp of the builders of history! Not every learned or literate person can be a great writer or historian. But every one of you can be a collector of material, and aid in the building of our history. . . . Let us work, gather our dispersed from their places of exile, arrange them, publish them, and build upon their foundation the temple of our history. Come, let us search and inquire![3]

The ideas expressed in Dubnov's *kol koreh* (appeal) became the credo of three generations of East European Jewish intellectuals, beginning with his contempo-raries Sh. Ansky and Saul Ginsburg, continuing with the generation of Elias Tcherikower and Max Weinreich, and culminating with the young interwar gen-eration of Emanuel Ringelblum and Abraham Sutzkever. A virtual cult of docu-mentary collection existed in Jewish Eastern Europe between 1925 and 1939, with the Vilna YIVO as its temple. Groups of volunteer *zamlers* (collectors), in scores of cities and towns in Poland, Lithuania, Romania, and across the globe, inun-dated YIVO with a mass of historical, literary, artistic, and ethnographic materi-als. Their work became the subject of poetic odes, short stories, and feuilletons; the stuff of folklore and legend.[4]

But with the advent of the Second World War and its aftermath, with the German and Soviet occupations of Eastern Europe, Jewish documents and trea-sures faced a new threat, infinitely more sinister than the one Dubnov had por-trayed in 1891. They were now at the mercies of political regimes which were intent on destroying them or locking them away.

What follows is the story of a group of Jewish intellectuals who, driven by the Dubnovian imperative, risked their lives to rescue Jewish books, documents and artifacts. In recounting it, I will refrain from offering grand insights on Jewish

Vilna, on "spiritual resistance," or on the fate of Judaism in the Soviet Union. My goal is to provide the basic facts, which are scattered across more than a dozen different published sources. In doing so, I am following the approach of Dubnov and Sutzkever, that the best way to affirm one's attachment to the past is, first of all, to document it.

EINSATZSTAB ROSENBERG IN VILNA

It was the task of the Special Detail of Reich-Administrator Alfred Rosenberg (Einsatzstab des Reichsleiter Alfred Rosenberg) to ransack and round up Judaica collections throughout Europe and arrange for their shipment to Germany, to the Institut zur Erforschung der Judenfrage (Institute for the Study of the Jewish Question) in Frankfurt. Rosenberg, Nazi Germany's chief ideologue, was the institute's rector, and titular head of the Einsatzstab. On a day-to-day basis, however, the work of the Special Detail was directed by one of the institute's senior staff members, Dr. Johannes Pohl, who had studied Judaica at the Hebrew University in Jerusalem from 1934 to 1936 at the Nazi Party's behest. Pohl was the author of a book on the Talmud, a regular contributor to *Der Stürmer,* and a spokesman for what he called "Judenforschung ohne Juden" (Jewish Studies without Jews).[5]

A week after the Germans captured Vilna (on 24 June 1941), a representative of the Rosenberg Detail, Dr. Gotthardt, arrived in the city. He began by collecting information—paying visits to various museums, libraries, and synagogues, and asking questions about the state of Jewish collections and the whereabouts of various Jewish scholars. In late July, he instructed the Gestapo to arrest three such scholars: Noyekh Prilutski, the Yiddish folklorist and linguist who had been YIVO's director during the brief period of Soviet rule in Vilna in 1940–41; Eliyohu Yankev Goldschmidt, a veteran Yiddish journalist and director of the Ansky Jewish Ethnographic Museum; and Chaikl Lunski, the legendary head of the Strashun *bibliotek,* Vilna's Jewish communal library. Prilutski and Goldschmidt were transported daily from their cell in the Gestapo prison to the Strashun Library, where they were ordered to compile lists of incunabula and rare books. In late August, Gotthardt left for Germany with lists and materials in hand. Shortly after his departure, Prilutski and Goldschmidt were murdered by the Gestapo. Lunski was released.[6]

The Germans apparently learned from this first attempt to seize Jewish cultural treasures from Vilna that the city housed simply too many rare Jewish books, too many valuable manuscripts and artifacts, to seize all of them in a single raid, using one or two arrested Jewish scholars. This tactic had been employed elsewhere by the Rosenberg squad with success, but in Vilna a long-term work group was needed in order to sift through tens of thousands of items. When Dr. Pohl himself visited the city in February 1942, accompanied by three *Judenforschung* specialists from Berlin, he arranged for the establishment of such a group. He ordered the ghetto to provide him with twelve workers to sort, pack, and ship materials, and put two prominent Jewish intellectuals in charge of the operation:

Herman Kruk, a Bundist refugee from Warsaw who was head of the Vilna Ghetto Library, and Zelig Kalmanovich, a disciple of Dubnov who had been one of the directors of prewar YIVO. Chaikl Lunski was appointed as bibliographic consultant. The group was given spacious work facilities in a building belonging to the Vilna University Library (located at Universitetska 3), an indication of the high priority which Pohl, as head of the Rosenberg squad, assigned to its work.[7]

The entire Strashun library, some 40,000 volumes, was to be transported to Universitetska 3, where it was to undergo a *selektsia* between materials to be shipped to the Frankfurt institute, and materials destined for destruction. The latter were to be shipped to nearby paper mills for recycling. Kruk and Kalmanovich were to describe and catalog the items of greater value. From the very first day, they looked for opportunities to take some of the books back into the ghetto, either legally—by having them reconsigned to the ghetto library—or secretly. At first, Kruk reacted to his job assignment with wistful ambivalence. "Kalmanovich and I don't know whether we are gravediggers or saviors," he wrote in his diary. "If we'll manage to keep these treasures in Vilna, it may be to our great merit. But if the library will be sent out, we will have been accomplices. I'm trying to insure us in either case." By the end of February, the entire Strashun library was on Universitetska 3, as were the *sforim* from various synagogues, including the Vilna Gaon's *kloyz*. The YIVO library was rumored to be on its way.[8]

But instead of transferring YIVO's collections to Universitetska 3, the Germans decided to expand the operation of the Rosenberg squad, and established a second work site in the YIVO building at Wiwulskiego 18. The Jewish work group was expanded to forty people, and its scholarly staff was increased as well. In March 1942, the Yiddish poets Abraham Sutzkever and Shmerke Kaczerginski, who had been leaders of the prewar literary group *Yung-vilne*, and several other members of the Jewish intelligentsia, were recruited by Kruk.[9]

Prior to the Rosenberg squad's taking control of the YIVO building, it had been used by the Germans as a military barracks. When Kruk and others first entered this former cultural shrine, they found it in disarray. In the majestic entry hall, where a Yiddish map of the world had once hung, with an inscription: "Der yivo un zayne farbindungen iber der velt" ["YIVO and its affiliates across the globe"], a German eagle and swastika now hung, with a new inscription: "Deutschland wird leben und deshalb wird Deutschland siegen" ["Germany will live, and therefore Germany will prevail"]. The collections and catalogs were thrown as trash into the basement or were strewn across the floor.[10]

YIVO soon became the depot and processing center for a variety of libraries and collections—Jewish, Polish, and Russian—from Vilna, Kovna, and neighboring towns. Sutzkever noted the parallels between the operations of the Gestapo and the Rosenberg squad. Just as the former raided houses in search of Jews in hiding, the latter conducted aggressive searches for collections of Jewish books. (In the course of the search at the library of Vilna University, the floor of the reading room was torn open to check for Jewish books.) Once books were seized, they were subjected to a process of *selektsia*—between life and death. Just as the

Germans sent many non-Jews to their deaths along with the Jews, the Rosenberg squad destroyed non-Jewish libraries as well. The collections of the Polish Museum, the Society of Friends of Science (Towarzistwo Przyacziol Nauk), the Thomas Zohn Library, the library of the Evangelical Church and others were seized and sent for processing in the YIVO building. And as with the extermination of the Jews, the destruction of Jewish books was meticulously recorded, with biweekly statistical reports on the numbers of books sent to Germany, the number sent to the paper mills, with breakdowns according to language and century of publication.[11]

A quota of 70 percent was set as the proportion of books to be disposed of as trash. Since the German *Judenforschung* officials in charge, Scheffer and Sporket, knew virtually nothing about Jewish culture, they often decided the fate of a book based on the attractiveness of its binding. Books with impressive bindings were sent to Frankfurt, while poorly bound items went to the paper mills. In June, 1942 Kruk wrote: "The Jewish porters occupied with the task are literally in tears; it is heartbreaking to see this happening." In early July he added: "YIVO is dying; its mass grave is the paper mill".[12]

THE PAPER BRIGADE

The members of the work group at YIVO mastered a variety of tactics to save books and documents from destruction. The first, and simplest, was to drag out the work process as much as possible. When the German officers left the building in the hands of a Polish guard, the staff would often turn to other activities, mainly to reading books. Sutzkever would read and recite to others the works of his favorite Yiddish poets: Leivick, Leyeles, Yehoash, and Glatstein. He and Kaczerginski wrote most of their ghetto poetry inside the walls of the YIVO building at Wiwulskiego 18. But there were limits and risks to foot-dragging. Members of the work group soon began smuggling materials into the ghetto, in the belief that they would be safer there.[13]

At the end of the work day, they would stuff materials inside their clothing to prevent their detection by the guards at the ghetto gate. If, when they arrived at the gate, it was manned by the Jewish ghetto police, there would be no problem. The latter would let them pass with only a cursory inspection, knowing full well that all they were carrying was paper. The ghetto police called them mockingly *Di papir-brigade* (the "Paper Brigade"), and the nickname spread throughout the ghetto. But if German SS, Gestapo, or military were stationed at the gate, anxiety rose among the members of the work group. If word reached them ahead of time that Germans were at the gate, they would take a circuitous route back from work and "drop off" the materials temporarily with non-Jewish friends. But there were instances when the group had to pass through German inspection. When books and papers were found on their bodies, they were beaten and warned of severe consequences.[14]

Over the course of a year and a half, between March 1942 and September 1943, thousands of books and tens of thousands of documents made their way back into the Vilna ghetto thanks to the smuggling of the *papir-brigade*. The group of smugglers consisted of Kalmanovich, Kruk, Sutzkever, Kaczerginski, Dr. Daniel Feinshteyn, Dr. Yankev Gordon, Naomi Markeles, Uma Olkenicki, Ruzhka Korczak, and Rokhl Pupko-Krinsky. Kaczerginski later recalled: "Jews looked at us as if we were lunatics. *They* were smuggling foodstuffs into the ghetto, in their clothing and boots—and *we* were smuggling books, pieces of paper, occasionally a *Sefer Torah* or mezuzahs." To those who criticized the group for occupying themselves with the fate of papers in such a time of crisis, Kalmanovich replied emphatically that "books don't grow on trees."[15]

Sutzkever was the most active and ingenious rescuer of materials in the group. He once obtained a written permit from one of the Germans to take some wastepaper into the ghetto for use in household ovens, and then used the permit to take in letters and manuscripts by Tolstoy, Gorky, Sholem Aleichem, Bialik, one of Theodore Herzl's diaries, drawings by Marc Chagall, and a unique manuscript by the Vilna Gaon. With the help of some well-connected friends, he even managed to smuggle sculptures by Antokolsky and paintings by Repin and Levitan out of the YIVO building and into the ghetto.[16]

But once the materials were inside the ghetto, the question was where to hide them. Many were handed over to Kruk for concealment in the building of the ghetto library (located at Strashun 6). Sutzkever divided his materials among ten hiding-places, including the walls and floor of his own apartment (at Strashun 1). The safest of all was a bunker built more than sixty feet underground by a young construction engineer named Gershon Abramovitsh. The bunker, which was brought to Sutzkever's attention by one of the commanders of the ghetto's United Partisan Organization (FPO), featured its own ventilation system, electricity drawn from wires outside the ghetto, and a tunnel leading to a well on the Aryan side. Abramovitsh had constructed it to hide and rescue his paralyzed mother—and agreed to keep the YIVO treasures together with her.[17]

Not all books smuggled into the ghetto were buried in hiding places. Textbooks and children's literature were delivered to the clandestine schools in the Vilna Ghetto, and a Soviet munitions manual, with instructions on how to make Molotov cocktails and land mines, was handed over to the commanders of the FPO. It enabled the ghetto's partisans to produce their very first arsenal. On the other hand, some of the rare books and documents were not smuggled into the ghetto. Sutzkever and Kaczerginski handed them over to Polish and Lithuanian friends, who paid visits to Wiwulskiego 18 during the lunch break, when the German officers were away. The Lithuanian poet Kazis Borutas and journalist Anna Šimaite were among those non-Jews who received packets of materials for safekeeping. Sutzkever also used lunchtime encounters to deliver valuable Polish books and materials to members of the Polish underground, including a document signed by Polish freedom fighter Tadeusz Kosciuszko.[18]

Unknown to Kruk and Kalmanovich, several members of the *papir-brigade*, beginning with Sutzkever and Kaczerginski, were also members of the underground FPO, and one of the lunchtime visitors, Kaczerginski's Lithuanian friend Julian Jankauskas, used their meetings to deliver arms. At first he brought tiny pistols, then larger ones, and then one day Jankauskas appeared unexpectedly with a machine gun inside a viola case. Kaczerginski and the others quickly disassembled its parts, and hid them in different rooms of the YIVO building. A moment later, Willy Scheffer returned with high-ranking visitors from Berlin and began to show off "his" treasures, room by room. Scheffer was about to lift up the Chagall painting which covered the barrel of the machine gun, when a last-second diversion by Rokhl Pupko-Krinsky saved the day. (She ran over to show the Germans a rare book from the seventeenth century.)[19]

As the shipments to the paper mills intensified, it became clear that the *papir-brigade* was winning small battles but losing its war. Only a tiny fraction of the treasures were being rescued.[20] That is when Sutzkever thought of a new tactic—to create a hiding place, a *malina,* inside the YIVO building itself. Upon examining the building's architecture, he found large cavities underneath the beams and girders in the attic. All one needed to do was distract the Polish guard, Virbilis, so that Sutzkever and others could whisk the materials up to the attic. Luckily, Virbilis had ambitions of being more than just a guard some day, and regretted that the war had interrupted his formal education. So two members of the work group, Drs. Feinshteyn and Gordon, offered to teach him mathematics, Latin, and German during the lunch break. As teacher and student were engrossed in study, the transfer of materials to the attic proceeded.[21]

The work at Wiwulskiego 18 continued until shortly before the final liquidation of the Vilna Ghetto, on 23 September 1943. Kalmanovich wrote in one of the last entries in his diary, on 23 August: "Our work is reaching its conclusion. Thousands of books are being dumped as trash, and the Jewish books will be liquidated. Whatever part we can rescue will be saved, with God's help. We will find it when we return as free human beings."[22]

Most of the members of the *papir-brigade* perished at Ponar, the mass-murder site outside of Vilna, or in labor camps in Estonia. Among them were its heads, Kruk and Kalmanovich. But the FPO members in the work group—Sutzkever, Kaczerginski, Rokhl Pupko-Krinsky, and Ruzhka Korczak—managed to flee to the forests before the ghetto's final liquidation and to join up with various partisan units.

AFTER THE WAR—THE JEWISH MUSEUM

Sutzkever and Kaczerginski returned to Vilna in July 1944, along with the Soviet Army, and helped liberate the city as members of the Jewish partisan brigade *Nekome-nemer* (Avengers). Most surviving Jews who emerged from their hiding places or returned from evacuation to Vilna were concerned, first and foremost, with locating friends and relatives, including the children who had been left behind with Christians. But Sutzkever and Kaczerginski had an additional agenda: to dig up the Jewish books, documents, and treasures they had hidden.

Their preliminary survey of the territory yielded painful results: the YIVO building at Wiwulskiego 18 was a pile of rubble, having been hit by artillery shells. Its attic was burnt to a crisp. Kruk's hiding place inside the ghetto library at Straszuna 6 had been discovered just days before the liberation, and all of its materials had been incinerated in the courtyard. On the other hand, Gershon Abramovitsh's underground bunker was intact, as were other hiding places. An organized salvage operation was needed to retrieve the materials.

On 26 July 1944—just thirteen days after the liberation of Vilna—Sutzkever and Kaczerginski established the "Museum of Jewish Art and Culture," affiliated with the Ministry of Culture of the Lithuanian Soviet Socialist Republic. The museum, which was initially located in their private apartment at 15 Gediminas Street, was the first Jewish institution to be established in Vilna after the war. It became *the* Jewish address in the city, the place where Jewish soldiers, partisans, and survivors gathered, where the short-lived Jewish school was founded, and where all letters addressed to surviving Jews in Vilna were forwarded. In mid-August, the museum moved into the only Jewish communal building not yet expropriated by the Soviet authorities—Strashun Street 6, which had been the site of the ghetto library, various administrative offices, and also of the ghetto prison. The only part of the building which was in usable condition was the prison. The staff of the Jewish Museum worked in the prison cells where Jewish inmates had been tortured by the Gestapo.[23]

With Sutzkever serving as director, and an unpaid staff of six (including the commander of the Jewish partisans, Abba Kovner), the salvage work in the hiding places proceeded. Strewn across Gershon Abramovitsh's bunker were the pages to Herman Kruk's ghetto diary, letters by Sholem Aleichem, manuscripts by Bialik, Gorky, and Mendele. Buried in the ground beneath the bunker were the paintings and sculptures—Ilya Ginzburg's bust of Tolstoy, Antokolsky's statue of King David, and others. In digging out the sculptures, Sutzkever uncovered an outstretched arm, and upon grabbing it realized that it was not made of clay but was human. Gershon Abramovitsh explained: One of the Jews who had hidden in the bunker died there shortly before the liberation and was buried alongside Antoklosky's "David."[24]

Meanwhile, unanticipated troves of material surfaced. Twenty tons of YIVO papers were found at a local paper mill, not yet destroyed. Thirty more tons were in the courtyard of the Trash Administration (*soyuzutil*). Various Jews and Christians started delivering potato sacks filled with books and papers to the museum.

But there was virtually no support coming from the Lithuanian Soviet authorities—no furniture or supplies (Kaczerginski rejoiced when someone brought him envelopes and erasers), no vehicles to transport the vast volume of material to the museum, no salaries for the staff. Appeals to Communist Party officials in Lithuania and to Soviet authorities in Moscow were ignored. Some Lithuanian officials responded: Why do the Jews insist upon a separate Jewish museum, a separate Jewish school? Aren't we all Soviet citizens? Henryk Ziman, a Jewish member of the Communist Party leadership in Lithuania, urged patience; Jewish cultural needs would be met once Soviet rule was consolidated. But Sutzkever was unconvinced. He returned to Moscow in September 1944 with Kruk's diary and other materials in his bags. He sensed that Soviet Vilnius, as the city was now called, was not a safe place for Jewish treasures. With the help of a foreign correspondent, he sent off his first package of materials to YIVO in New York.[25]

It took Kaczerginski, who succeeded Sutzkever as director of the museum, almost a year to reach the same conclusion. A leftist and Communist sympathizer before the war, Kaczerginski traveled to Moscow in March 1945 to complain to Soviet officials about the obstructionist and hostile attitude of the Lithuanian authorities toward the museum and other Jewish institutions. After receiving a sympathetic hearing in the offices of the Central Committee of the Communist party, he returned to Vilna and got off the train, only to learn that the Trash Administration had just transported the thirty tons of YIVO materials in its courtyard to the train depot for shipment to a paper mill. He dashed to the shipping platform and started pulling items out of the piles—a script of a Yiddish drama, a *sefer* from Chaikl Lunski's library, an autobiography from the YIVO autobiography competition. He then rushed from one bureau to another to prevent the shipment—first to the Rail Administration, then to the Trash Administration, then to Ziman. But by the time he returned to the train depot the next day, the mountains of paper were gone.[26]

The bad news continued: in mid-1945, the authorities officially registered the museum as "the Jewish Museum of Vilna" but allocated for it a total of three paid staff positions. With a staff of three, the work of collecting and cataloging its vast holdings was effectively doomed. Then agents of the KGB began to pay repeated visits to Kaczerginski at the museum. Among other things, they reminded him that no books were to be made available to the public without their prior review by Soviet censors. But the volumes which were sent to the censors were never returned. Kaczerginski later recalled:

> That is when we, the group of museum activists, had a bizarre realization—we must save our treasures *again,* and get them out of here. Otherwise, they will perish. In the best of cases they will survive, but will never see the light of day in the Jewish world.[27]

One by one, the museum activists began to emigrate and smuggle out parts of its collection, in an operation which was as dangerous as the smuggling of materials into the ghetto under the Nazis. Abba Kovner, Ruzhka Korczak, Dr. Amarant—each of them took what they could.

Meanwhile, Kaczerginski put up a front of being a loyal Communist operative. He published a proud report of the museum's activities in the Moscow Yiddish newspaper *Eynikayt* on 2 October 1945. He surveyed its collections: 25,000 Yiddish and Hebrew books; 10,000 volumes of Judaica in European languages; 600

sacks full of documentary materials from the YIVO archives; the extraordinary archives of the Vilna and Kovna ghettos. The museum's plans for the future were no less impressive: renovation of the museum building, mounting a large permanent exhibit, and erecting a monument in the courtyard for those Jews who fell in battle against the Nazis.[28]

None of this was ever to be, and Kaczerginski himself knew it full well. As he wrote his article, he was already making plans to emigrate and arranging the smuggling of materials abroad. In November 1945, he submitted his resignation. By July 1946 both he and Sutzkever were in Poland, with museum materials in their bags. From there, they proceeded to Paris. From both destinations, they sent packages to Max Weinreich, YIVO's research director in New York.[29]

As Sutzkever and Kaczerginski intuited, the fate which awaited the multitude of materials that remained in Vilnius was not a happy one. In 1948, word reached the West that the Jewish Museum had been liquidated and ransacked by the KGB. One Vilna émigré and former volunteer in the museum, Leyzer Ran, recorded the news in his diary:

> The "visitors" have come to the ghetto again. This time, they came in new Soviet trucks. They dumped all of the museum's materials—artifacts, books, archives—into the trucks and took them to Szniadecki Street, to the Church of St. Yuri, which is now the *Bikher-palate* (Book Chamber). Materials are kept there in excellent condition. Except for the Jewish materials, which were dumped in the basement.[30]

The Jewish documents remained in the inner recesses of the Lithuanian National Book Chamber, a former church, for the next forty years. During the years of Stalinist terror, between 1949 and 1953, they were hidden there by the Book Chamber's director, Dr. Antanas Ulpis, who quietly disobeyed the orders of his superiors to have them destroyed. In the period of de-Stalinization, Ulpis arranged for thousands of the Jewish books in his repository to be cataloged, but the existence of the bundles of Jewish documents remained a secret that Ulpis kept to himself—until his retirement. Their existence first became public knowledge in 1988. A second batch was unexpectedly discovered during a clean-up of the Book Chamber's facilities in 1993. The materials were shipped to YIVO in 1995 and 1996.[31]

Concluding Reflections: "Grains of Wheat"

In his memoirs, written after his emigration to the West, Kaczerginski gave voice to his bitterness and disillusionment about the course of events surrounding the treasures he had rescued. In the final analysis, he wrote, geopolitics had deceived us and defeated us. Who among us in the "Paper Brigade" could have imagined that the free, liberated Vilna after the war would itself turn out to be a Soviet prison camp? Unfortunately, he wrote, much of our labor had been in vain.

But Kaczerginski, thankfully, was wrong. The final word on the subject belongs to Sutzkever. In a poem entitled "Grains of Wheat" (*Kerndlekh veyts*), written in March 1943, he expressed his faith in the ultimate victory of the *papir-brigade* and its enterprise. Running through the streets of the ghetto with "the Jewish word" in his arms and caressing it like a child, the pieces of parchment and poetry cried out to him, "Hide me in your labyrinth." Once, while burying the materials in the ground, he was overcome with despair. He then recalled an ancient parable: One of the Egyptian pharaohs built a pyramid for himself and ordered his servants to place some grains of wheat in his coffin at the time of his burial. Nine thousand years passed, the coffin was opened, the grains were discovered, planted, and a beautiful bed of stalks blossomed forth from them. Someday, Sutzkever wrote, the grains which he was planting in the soil of the Vilna ghetto would also bear fruit.

> Efsher oykh veln di verter
> Dervartn zikh ven af dem likht—
> Veln in sho in basherter
> Tseblien zikh oykh umgerikht.
>
> Un vi der uralter kern
> Vos hot zikh farvandlt in zang—
> Veln di verter oykh nern,
> Veln di verter gehern
> Dem folk, in zayn eybikn gang.[32]

In 1996, YIVO celebrated the victory of Sutzkever's vision and spirit. Now that these materials are at long last reunited with their spiritual home and with the Jewish people, we can proclaim: "di verter *veln* nern, di verter *veln* gehern, dem folk in zayn eybikn gang"—these words will nourish, these words will belong to the people, on its eternal path.

NOTES

I would like to thank Professor Avrom Nowersztern for his comments on an earlier draft of this essay.

1. *Ob izuchenii istorii ruskikh evreev i ob uchrezhdenii istoricheskogo obschestva* (St. Petersburg, 1891), 51.
2. Ibid., 76–77.
3. *Nahpesa venahkora: kol kore el ha-nevonim ba-am, ha-mitnadvim le-esof homer le-binyan toldot bene yisrael be-polin ve-rusiya* (Odessa, 1892), 23–24.
4. On the *zamlers*, see the Jubilee issue of *Yivo-bleter* 46 (1980): 49–57, 321–25. There were 163 registered circles of YIVO collectors in 1929. Literary responses to their work include Abraham Reisen's poem "mir zamlen," first published in the *Forverts* in 1930 (re-

printed in *Der yivo nokh draytsn yor arbet* [Vilna, 1938], 23), and Abraham Karpinowitch's story "Der folklorist," *Baym vilner durkhoyf* (Tel Aviv, 1967), 69–82.

5. "Einsatzstab Rosenberg," *Encyclopedia of the Holocaust* (New York, 1990), 2: 439–41; Max Weinreich, *Hitler's Professors* (New York, 1946), 279; Kruk, *Togbukh fun vilner geto,* ed. Mordecai W. Bernstein (New York, 1961), 240.

6. A. Sutzkever, *Vilner geto,* 2nd ed. (Paris, 1945), 108; S. Kaczerginski, *Partizaner geyen,* 2nd ed. (Bamberg, Germany, 1947), 65–66; and his more expansive *Ikh bin geven a partizan* (Buenos Aires, 1952), passim. In the instances when Sutzkever's and Kaczerginski's accounts conflict regarding historical details, I have followed the former.

7. Kruk, *Togbukh,* 162–63, 178–79; Sutzkever, *Vilner geto,* 109.

8. Kruk, *Togbukh,* 178–79, 188.

9. Ibid., 200, 211; staff figures from Sutzkever, *Vilner geto,* 109, Kaczerginski, *Partizaner geyen,* 66. Work at Universitetska 3 continued at least until May 1942, and the books of the Strashun Library were still kept there a year later, in April 1943. See Zelig Kalmanovich, *Yoman be-geto vilna ve-ketavim min ha-'izavon she-nimtsa ba-harisot* (Tel Aviv, 1977) 101, 103.

10. Kruk, *Togbukh,* 272; Rokhl Poupko-Krinsky, "mayn arbet in yivo unter di daytshn," *Yivo-bleter* 30/2 (Winter 1947): 214–23.

11. Sutzkever, *Vilner geto,* 110–11.

12. Kazcerginski, *Partizaner geyen,* 68; Kruk, *Togbukh,* 282, 300.

13. Pupko-Krinsky, "Mayn arbet," 216–17; Sutzkever, "A vort tsum zekhtsikstn yoyvl fun yivo," *Baym leyenen penimer* (Jerusalem, 1993), 206–7.

14. Pupko-Krinsky, "Mayn arbet," 217–19; Kaczerginski, *Ikh bin geven a partizan,* 53–57. Kalmanovich, *Yoman,* 89, 94, 112.

15. Kaczerginski, *Partizaner geyen,* 69, and similarly in *Ikh bin geven a partizan,* 41–42. Ruzhka Korczak, *Lehavot ba-efer,* 2nd ed. (Tel Aviv, 1946), 110.

16. Sutzkever, *Vilner geto,* 111–12.

17. Ibid., 122–25, 229. Kruk wrote in his diary on 9 July 1942: "During the last two weeks alone I've obtained documents from the Ukrainian Ministry of Jewish Affairs, materials from the archives of Simon Dubnov, Ber Borochov, Noyekh Prilutski, a file of materials about Isaac Meir Dik, a file of Yiddish idioms, letters and manuscripts by Sholem Aleichem; manuscripts by Dovid Einhorn, Dovid Pinski, S. L. Tsitron, materials from Dr. Alfred Landau's dictionary, photographs from YIVO's Yiddish theatre museum, letters by Moishe Kulbak, Sh. Niger, D. Charney, Chaim Zhitlowsky, Joseph Opatoshu, A. Leyeles, Zalman Reyzen, Leon Kobrin, Moishe Nadir, Marc Chagall, H. Leivick, Dr. Nathan Birnbaum, Yakov Fichman, Dr. Isadore Elyashev (*Bal makhshoves*). This is only a fraction of the material handed over. I'm recording it only to give a slight idea of our rescue efforts. The risk undertaken when smuggling out a piece of paper is enormous; every piece of paper can endanger one's life. But nonetheless, there are idealists who do the job skillfully. I'll mention these people at an appropriate time and record their names for future generations." Kruk, *Togbukh,* 300–1. On 24 September 1942, he added: "Smuggling work has recently intensified; the brigade (*gvardye*) of smugglers has grown by several times" (351).

18. Korczak, *Lehavot ba-efer,* 110; Sutzkever, *Vilner geto,* 112.

19. There are three versions of this story, with slight variations: Sutzkever, *Vilner geto,* 220; Kaczerginski, *Partizaner geyen,* 71–72, and more fully in *Ikh bin geven a partizan,* 45–52; Pupko-Krinsky, "Mayn arbet," 220–21. See also Korczak, *Lehavot ba-efer,* 109–11.

20. A first collection of YIVO documents was removed for shipment to Germany on 25 October 1942, and fifty crates of books were shipped to Frankfurt on 17 November

1942 (Kalmanovich, *Yoman,* 73, 78, 85, 91). A second shipment of 9,403 books left for Germany on 13 February 1943 (Kruk, *Togbukh,* 457). These materials were discovered in Frankfurt after the war, and were returned by the U.S. government to YIVO in New York. See Lucy Davidowicz, *From that Place and Time: A Memoir, 1938–1947* (New York, 1989). Kalmanovich's diary includes numerous anguished entries on the destruction of valuable materials and their shipment to the paper mills in 1943, see *Yoman,* 75, 93, 100, 101, 110, 126.

21. Pupko-Krinsky, "Mayn arbet," 219–20.

22. Kalmanovich, *Yoman,* 126.

23. The above is based on Sutzkever, *Vilner geto,* 229–30; Sutzkever's article "Vos mir hobn geratevet in vilne," *Eynikayt* (Moscow), 12 October 1944, 3 (reprinted as "Vi mir hobn geratevet dem yivo in vilne," *Eynikayt* [New York], February 1945, 15–16, 30); and Kaczerginski, *Tsvishn hamer un serp,* 2nd ed. (Buenos Aires, 1950), 37–45.

24. Sutzkever, "vos mir hobn geratevet in vilne"; Kruk, *Togbukh,* xxxviii–xxxix.

25. Kaczerginski, *Tsvishn hamer un serp,* 45–51; Sutzkever, "A vort tsum zekhtsiktsn yoyvl fun yivo", *Baym leyenen penimer,* 208–10.

26. Sutzkever, *Baym leyenen penimer,* 97–102.

27. Ibid., 107–8, 110–12.

28. M. [*sic*] Kaczerginski, "A yor arbet funem yidishn muzey in vilne," *Eynikayt* (Moscow), 2 October 1945, 3. For an earlier survey of the museum's holdings, see A. Ayzen, "Vilniuser yidisher muzey," *Eynikayt,* 22 March 1945, 4.

29. Kaczerginski, *Tsvishn hamer un serp,* 112–13. By the time Leyzer Ran returned to Vilna, in November 1945, the director of the Jewish Museum was Yankl Gutkovicz. See Ran, *Ash fun yerusholayim de-lite* (New York, 1959), 174–75. On Sutzkever's and Kaczerginski's shipments of materials to YIVO, using various intermediaries, see "Briv fun maks vaynraykh tsu arrom sutskever," *Goldene keyt* 95–96 (1978): 171–83. These materials have been preserved as a unit, as the Sutzkever–Kaczerginski collection of the YIVO Archives (RG 223).

30. Ran, *Ash fun yerushalayim de-lite,* 196. The report which Ran recorded was not completely accurate. The Jewish Museum's materials were transferred to various Lithuanian archives and museums. Only the books and a small part of the documentary materials were taken to the Lithuanian National Book Chamber. The final liquidation of the Jewish Museum took place in July 1949. See Aleksander Rindzionski, "Vilna le-ahar ha-milhama (1944–1959)," *Yalkut Moreshet* 39 (May 1985): 55–84, esp. 59, 64–70.

31. On the history of the Jewish collections in the Book Chamber during the Soviet years, see *Yivo-bleter,* n. s. 1 (1991): 293–98.

32. "Kerndlekh veyts," in Sutzkever, *Yidishe gas* (New York, 1947), 32–33.

V • "THE JEWISH QUESTION" AND CENSORSHIP IN THE USSR

Arlen Viktorovich Blium

Introduced, translated, and annotated by George Durman and Donna M. Farina

TRANSLATORS' INTRODUCTION

This essay is a translation of sections from Arlen Blium's book, The Jewish Question *under Soviet Censorship, 1917–1991 [Evreiskii vopros pod Sovetskoi tsenzuroi, 1917–1991] (St. Petersburg: Peterburgskii evreiskii universitet, 1996). These excerpts describe the persecution of Soviet Jews, Jewish culture, and Jewish books during the Stalin era. The plan for the book was born, as Blium notes in his Introduction (p. 23), during the years he spent studying Soviet censorship in the various archives of Moscow and Leningrad, with no hope of publishing his findings. Though he was not allowed to see many crucial materials, he still managed to find traces of censorship activity, carried out by the main Soviet censorship agency, the Central Directorate for Literary and Publishing Activity, usually called Glavlit (Glavnoe upravlenie po delam literatury i izdatel'stv), which was part of the People's Commissariat of Education (Narodnyi komissariat prosveshcheniia). The documents Blium uncovered had, of course, never been published; most of them were classified "Secret" or "Strictly Secret." Blium noticed that the "Jewish Problem" was the subject of a disproportionately large number of these documents.*

The value of these materials is obvious. The censorship agencies who wrote and circulated them were acting under direct oral instructions received from top Party ideologues; they were literally following the "Party line." These documents allow us to reconstruct all the important policy changes toward Jewish culture, Jewish literature, and the Jewish theme in general during the Soviet period. In his book, Arlen Blium cites directives repressing Hebrew and Yiddish books; Jewish writers, poets, and scholars; and Jewish themes in Russian literature and the Russian media.

Although the Jewish theme in the Soviet Union has long attracted the attention of scholars and journalists, sources of information on the subject are extremely limited. For many years Glavlit did its work in secret, behind the scenes. That is why Blium's book was called "innovative" by editor D. A. El'iashevich in his preface (p. 5). It is the source of much of our current knowledge about the censorship of Soviet Jewish life.

For this translation, excerpts were taken from two chapters, "Years of the Great Terror, 1930–1941" and "The 'Fatal Forties,' 1941–1953" ["Gody Bol'shogo terrora, 1930–1941" and "'Sorokovye-rokovye,' 1941–1953"]. They cover periods of time that were par-

ticularly critical for Soviet Jewry. During Stalin's reign Jews were not the only Soviet citizens to suffer, and it is important to understand the context of Jewish repression. The Great Terror or Great Purge usually refers to the period of Stalin's reign after the 1934 assassination of S. M. Kirov. Kirov was the head of the Leningrad Party organization and a full member of the Politburo. After he was elected as a secretary of the Central Committee, he was considered to be Stalin's rival. Between 1934 and 1939, 70 percent of the upper echelons of the Communist Party were executed (including most Jewish members), and there were numerous show trials. About 8 million people were arrested, of which approximately a million were executed. The rest went to prison or to labor camps, where only a fraction survived. Blium believes that state anti-Semitism also began during the Purge, specifically in 1936: the earliest archival documents he found dealing with Jewish issues date to that year. In any case, state-sanctioned anti-Semitism intensified after the Molotov–Ribbentrop Non-Aggression Pact was signed in 1939.

The Terror would probably have continued had it not been interrupted by the Second World War. It is ironic that the early years of the war brought Jews and other Soviet citizens some relief from repression; the demonstration of patriotic sentiment was encouraged, allowing relatively more freedom of expression. After the war, Stalin immediately resumed the attack on his own population.

With respect to the Jews, Blium says that Stalin took up Hitler's baton right after the war's turning point, when the Soviet Army went on the offensive (1943) after the Battle of Stalingrad. Blium uses the title "Fatal Forties" to describe the postwar anti-Semitic campaign that lasted until Stalin's death in 1953. First, it was forbidden to mention in print any facts about the Holocaust. Then the campaign gained momentum in 1948 with the closure of the Jewish Anti-Fascist Committee, established in 1942 to mobilize Jewish support for the war effort. The committee broadcast appeals to Jews around the world for contributions to the Red Army, collected and published information on Nazi atrocities, and opposed anti-Semitism. Its journal was the Yiddish-language Einikayt. The committee was shut down along with other important Jewish institutions in November 1948, and its leading members, representatives of the Jewish intelligentsia, were arrested over the next few months. The committee's chairman, Solomon Mikhoels (Solomon Mikhailovich Vovsi, born 1890 in Minsk), was murdered by the secret police on Stalin's orders in December 1948. Mikhoels was a popular Yiddish actor and the director of the State Jewish Theater in Moscow.

Not long after his assassination, the so-called Theater Critics' Affair began, in January 1949. Critics, most of them Jewish, were denounced in Pravda for their lack of patriotism; they were expelled from the Soviet Writers' Union. The Affair of the Cosmopolitans, which began in the press in the same year, was different in tone: the first open attack on Soviet Jews as Jews. Jews were accused of being "cosmopolitans" without a homeland, of hating the Russian people, of supporting Zionism. The real names of Jews who used (usually Russian) pen names were exposed.

While the open campaign abated by April–May 1949, anti-Jewish policies continued. In 1952 began a secret trial of the Jews arrested following the closure of the Jewish Anti-Fascist Committee. They were accused of conspiring to separate the Crimea from the USSR and convert it into a Jewish republic. All of those tried (except for Lina Shtern)[1] were executed in August of the same year. These events are usually called the Jewish Anti-Fascist Committee Affair in Russia but are better known in the United States as the Crimea Affair.

The next stage in this massive anti-Semitic campaign might well have led to the annihilation of Soviet Jewry. The "Doctors' Plot" involved the "exposure" of some eminent Moscow doctors for supposedly conspiring to assassinate Soviet leaders. In January 1953 Pravda reported that nine doctors, six of them Jews, had been arrested and accused of murdering A. S. Shcherbakov and A. A. Zhdanov. Shcherbakov (1901–45) was a secretary of the Central Committee and candidate member of the Politburo. Zhdanov was a member of the Central Committee, was named head of the Leningrad Party organization to succeed the murdered Kirov, and later became a member of the Politburo. Zhdanov carried out the Leningrad purges during the Great Terror. After the war, he was thought to be Stalin's heir apparent and was put in charge of literary and artistic policies from 1946 until his death in 1948. During this period, called the Zhdanovshchina, he terrorized the intelligentsia, including Jews. His death was probably due to heart failure and alcoholism, though there were rumors that he was murdered, since he had fallen out of favor a few months before he died.

Five years after his murder, Solomon Mikhoels was named as a co-conspirator in the Doctors' Plot, along with his (living) relative Dr. Miron Vovsi. Pravda claimed that the doctors were spies for the American Jewish Joint Distribution Committee (known as the "Joint"). The anti-Semitic rhetoric continued in the press through February 1953. Stalin died on 5 March, and on 4 April Pravda announced that the doctors were not guilty. There is evidence that Stalin intended, following a planned show trial of the accused doctors, the mass deportation of the Jewish population from the European part of the USSR to eastern Siberia. Fortunately, Stalin died before any such plan could be carried out.

Book history is a well-established discipline in Russia,[2] but only since the late 1980s have scholars been able to write about censorship in the Soviet era. There are two obvious reasons for this: first, the topic itself was censored, to some extent even during the late Soviet period of glasnost and perestroika; second, most of the materials relating to the topic were inaccessible, scattered in archives closed to historians and to practically everyone else as well. For both reasons, Blium published on the more acceptable topic of censorship in eighteenth- and nineteenth-century Russia during most of his academic career. This background enriches Blium's work on the Soviet period; he is well equipped to compare censorship techniques of what he calls the Tsarist "police state" with the more extreme methods of the Soviet "totalitarian regime." Today, Russian scholars are trying to seize an opportunity which they could not have imagined less than a decade ago: it is estimated that about 30 percent of the materials in the special archives (containing secret documents) have been made available to them. This even includes some documents marked "Keep secret forever" (khranit' vechno): their previous guardians were so certain that their reign would last eternally.

In spite of this partial opening of the special archives, numerous problems remain for researchers, as Mikhail Kheifetz recently wrote.[3] Back during the Khrushchev era, *many documents on the repression signed by Khrushchev himself were destroyed. While Yuri Andropov was the chief of the KGB (before he became General Secretary of the Communist Party) "unnecessary" documents were liquidated, especially those that could compromise the secret police. During* perestroika *(1986–91) many Soviet bu-reaucrats began worrying about what would happen to archival materials that men-tioned their names and took precautionary measures. Even after the fall of the Soviet Union (1991), as Anatolii Prokopenko notes, "The civilized and complete opening of the archives on the history of the Communist Party and the Soviet government never took place."⁴ Prokopenko, a historian and archivist, formerly headed the top-secret Special Archive of documents seized from twenty countries during World War II; later he was vice-chairman of the Russian Archival Committee. Prokopenko says that after Boris Yeltsin publicly ordered the archives opened in 1991, he then met secretly with the leaders of the intelligence agencies to curtail the process of disclosure.*

This constant state of uncertainty about the future of secret materials drives the approach being taken by many scholars today. They are so busy extracting and publish-ing formerly secret documents that they have little time to devote to analysis and com-mentary. The opportunity for in-depth discussion will come later, when enough has been published.

As his translators, we are very grateful for Arlen Blium's important work, and for the opportunity to make it available to an English-speaking public. In addition to Blium's own notes, we have supplied some further annotation to explain persons and events that may be unfamiliar to Western readers.

THE YEARS OF THE GREAT TERROR

H ISTORIANS disagree as to when exactly officially inspired, state-sanctioned anti-Semitism began in the USSR. (They more or less agree that everyday anti-Semitism always existed, sometimes in mild, latent forms and sometimes—usually in connection with a particular historical event—in quite harsh forms.) They tend to agree that it began at least before 1948, though it was not yet openly proclaimed by the ideological leadership. By 1948 an openly anti-Semitic campaign was in full swing, with the destruction of the Jewish Anti-Fascist Committee, the assassination of Mikhoels, the closing of Jewish theaters and the publishing house Der Emes, the Theater Critics' Affair, the so-called Affair of the Cosmopolitans, and the executions of the most prominent Jewish poets, all of which logically led up to the Doctors' Plot later on. Some historians consider that state anti-Semitism started earlier, in 1943, when a secret instruction appeared in the midst of the Communist Party Central Committee, concerning restrictions on the promotion of Jews to leadership positions. Other historians relate state anti-Semitism to the Ribbentrop–Molotov Non-Aggression Pact of 1939. During the 1930s, members of the Communist Party Central Committee who belonged to non-Russian nationalities [mostly Jews] were removed from the

Central Committee and then executed.[5] We are forced to conclude that such actions could not have taken place without a secret Party policy. During these years, the following riddle was popular: How are Moses and Stalin alike, and how are they different? The answer: Both brought the Jews out, but Moses brought them out of Egypt, and Stalin—out of the Politburo.

For the most part, we can determine when state-sanctioned anti-Semitism began, thanks to secret reports from the Censorship Office discovered in the archives. This office acted under the direct supervision of the top echelons of the Party ideological leadership. The Jewish question is first raised in these secret reports beginning in 1936, at the height of the trials against "double-dealers," "enemies of the people," and "saboteurs."[6]

In 1936 a change occurred in the orientation of Soviet censorship. The Jewish question was declared nonexistent, and the censorship apparatus zealously began to carry out the new position of the Central Committee ideologues. The last work devoted to anti-Semitism in tsarist Russia had been published in two editions, in 1933 and 1934. This important work, *Tsarist Russia and the Beilis Affair* [Tsarskaia Rossiia i delo Beilisa] was written by A. S. Tager, who later perished during the Great Terror.[7] The book had an introduction by A. V. Lunacharskii.[8] After that, any printed references to Jewish "pogroms"—even if they related to "the accursed past" [tsarist, pre-Soviet Russia]—were invariably banned before publication or pulled afterward.

The Jewish pogroms were supposed to have been carried out by the Black Hundred;[9] under no circumstances could "ordinary working people"—workers and peasants—be implicated in print. Moreover, it was forbidden to mention any contemporary manifestations of anti-Semitism, particularly among the proletariat. Thus, in January–February 1937, censors from the Leningrad City Censorship Office [Gorlit], who were in charge of examining large-circulation factory newspapers, cut all anti-Semitic references from articles submitted for preliminary review. Here are only a few excerpts from reports they submitted every ten days, entitled "Summaries, Cuts, and Confiscations of the Leningrad Gorlit," for the period January–February 1937. These reports were forwarded to the Leningrad Regional Party Committee [Obkom].

From the newspaper *Forest Port* [Lesnoi port], No. 2, 8 January 1937. In the article, "What's Going On in the Repair Shop," a statement about anti-Semitism flourishing among the workers was removed, since the article did not cite a single case as proof. The censor deleted the statement as an accusation not substantiated by a single fact.

From the newspaper of a hydraulics plant, *The Factory Fitter* [Montazhnik], 6 February 1937. In the article, "A Disgraceful Event," the editors, demonstrating ideological ignorance, cited some cases of anti-Semitism: "The Comrade's Court, which convened in May of 1936, showed that in this factory there is animosity toward the Jewish and Tatar nationalities. The Court fined Postnikova and Ponomareva ten rubles each." The editors exclaimed: "Do you think that after the Court's decision (a fine of ten rubles) this animosity stopped? No! The opposite happened." The article was redone.[10]

The Zionist movement in the USSR was completely destroyed by the end of the 1920s. At best, Zionists managed to emigrate to Palestine; at worst, they ended up in concentration camps and perished. Long after the movement was crushed, the word "Zionism" itself was used to inspire fear, always in an extremely vague and accusatory fashion.

The censorship apparatus was continuously searching for the slightest indication of "Zionist propaganda" in print. They found evidence even in a book as innocent as *By Your Own Skill and Means: A Methodological Handbook for the Visual Learning of Mathematics,* by S. I. Melamed. The censor explained his intervention thus (1937): "In the table of geometric figures, there was a nationalistic Zionist sign.—Deleted."[11] Probably the censor, in a state of paranoiac "vigilance," imagined that he saw a Star of David in the combination of two triangles.

In 1937 the Leningrad censor D. Chevychelov wrote a detailed denunciation of members of the distinguished Marshak Group in the Leningrad division of the children's publishing house Detizdat. They were T. G. Gabbe, L. K. Chukovskaia, A. I. Liubarskaia, Z. M. Zadunaiskaia, and others.[12] The censor did not fail to mention that the leader himself, S. Ia. Marshak, "wrote Zionist poems" in his youth.[13] Of course, this excellent team of children's writers and editors was completely compromised in the eyes of the authorities, especially since most of them were Jews. The group was disbanded, and many members were arrested.[14] As for Marshak himself, he indeed had been sympathetic to Zionism when he was young. Starting in 1904, Marshak regularly published his poems in *Jewish Life* [Evreiskaia zhizn'], *Jewish World* [Evreiskii mir], and other Russian-language newspapers and magazines; more than forty of these poems treat biblical and typically Jewish themes. Marshak published such poems over a twelve-year period. Until very recently, all but a select few were omitted from Marshak's bibliography and from his collected works. Quite understandably, Marshak himself never advertised this passion of his youth, which helped to perpetuate the story that he, both as a poet and as a man, was "indifferent" to the fate of his people.

Once they had introduced the policy of complete assimilation of Jews and destruction of their national culture, Party ideologues took great pains to hide this. They hypocritically claimed that under socialism "all nationalities began to flourish" and enjoy "complete equality." Below is a remarkable passage deleted from an article, in which the overzealous [Jewish] author comes too close to the truth. In "A Summary of the Most Important Arrests and Confiscations Carried Out by the Branches of Glavlit" in 1937, there is the following:

In the magazine *Outpost* [Forpost], No. 1, in the Jewish [Yiddish] language (Publishing House Der Emes), the following passages were deleted from an article by Brakhman, "The Soviet Jewish Nation": "(a) After it came into power, the Bolshevik

Party carried out Marx's brilliant directives, which were advanced by Lenin and Stalin during the struggle against Jewish nationalism: elimination of Jewry, death of the Jewish 'nation' as a necessary starting point for the flourishing of the Jewish masses . . . ; (b) Bolshevism penetrated even here, it not only destroyed traditional Jewry . . . "[15]

At that time in the USSR, logocracy (the power of words) rather than ideocracy (the power of ideas) reigned and triumphed. An ideological taboo was imposed on certain words; they were to be printed as little as possible—by no means were they to attract attention. This happened with the words "Jew" and "Jewish." A sort of game of silence began that continued for more than four decades. The words simply disappeared from the lexicon; they were not part of the officially approved vocabulary of the mass media. During the campaigns that would begin later, the media used transparent, ideologically charged euphemisms to refer to Jews, such as "cosmopolitans," "agents of the Joint," "Zionists," and so on. What is more, "Jew" and "Jewish" disappeared from the vocabulary of the liberal intelligentsia. Even for the intelligentsia, these words began to sound improper, out of place. If they used them, they would unintentionally muffle their own voices.

The mass repressions during the Great Terror affected not only people but also books. Tens of thousands of books were sent away to special library storage. Books written by repressed writers as well as books that merely mentioned the names of such writers were suppressed. Directives from Glavlit listing these "arrested" books came out every week, or sometimes more often.

Some of the books listed had been published in the late 1920s and very early 1930s, when it was still possible to denounce anti-Semitism in print. One of the last books on the Jewish theme to appear was a collection of articles and short stories entitled *Against Antisemitism* [Protiv antisemitizma] (Moscow: Zhizn' i znanie, 1930). It included articles and essays by Maksim Gor'kii and Larisa Reisner, short stories by Isaak Babel', Boris Pil'niak, and other writers.[16] As in many similar cases, Glavlit solicited approval in 1940 for a ban on this book, from the Department of Agitation and Propaganda of the All-Union Communist Party Central Committee (Bolsheviks).[17] Sadchikov, the head of Glavlit at the time, wrote: "I request your consent to withdraw *Against Antisemitism* from bookselling organizations and public libraries. Along with valuable materials on antisemitism such as Comrade Lenin's speech, there is also an article by B. Pil'niak in this collection."[18]

The main argument for banning the collection was that it contained stories and essays by Pil'niak and Babel', who by then had been executed. Their other books had already been removed, as had all books by "denounced enemies of the people." However, a review of other suppressed books with a Jewish theme included in the Glavlit lists of that period shows that they did not contain any "criminal" names. They were banned solely because of their subject matter, though of course this was carefully disguised in the censors' explanations. During this same period, Lenin's "Speech on the Persecution of Jews" [Rech' o pogromnoi travle evreev], recorded in 1919, was also suppressed. Initially it was released on Gramophone records along with sixteen other speeches from the 1920s. It discussed "the disgrace of accursed Tsarism, which tormented and persecuted the Jews." In later releases, only this speech was removed from the record.

In the novel *The Golden Calf* by I. Il'f and E. Petrov, a Soviet journalist tries to assure an American colleague attending the opening of the Turksib Railroad[19] that anti-Semitism does not exist in the Soviet Union; in other words, there is no Jewish question, since there are no social roots for it. The American was puzzled. "But in Russia you have Jews, don't you? Doesn't that mean there is a Jewish question?" "No," answered the journalist. "We do have Jews, but no Jewish question."[20] The naive American could not understand that under conditions of totalitarianism any "question" could be declared nonexistent. This situation is strikingly reminiscent of activity in the "Ministry of Truth," where the main protagonist in George Orwell's novel *Nineteen Eighty-Four* works. There, history is rewritten every day, following Big Brother's latest directives. A vanishing person is declared an "unperson": "He did not exist; he had never existed."[21] By analogy, we can say that during those years not only individual "unpersons" disappeared and were declared nonexistent in the USSR but also entire "non-nations." The Jews, of course, were no exception: Stalin's imperial policies at the end of the 1930s and his constant pandering to "the great Russian people" resulted in a substantial limitation of the cultural and political rights of many Soviet nationalities. Unfortunately, the most impressive results were obtained by exploiting traditional prejudices toward Jews. Censorship, that tried and true instrument of ideological implementation, played a far from insignificant role.

THE "FATAL FORTIES"

The famous first line of David Samoilov's poem ["The fatal forties . . . "], though it refers to the period of World War II, is applicable to the entire decade of the 1940s.[22] In the first half of the decade, a genocide unprecedented in history was organized by fascism; in the second half, it is as if Stalin picked up the baton. His shameless, unbridled anti-Semitic campaign led to the arrests and executions of the most prominent figures of Jewish culture and almost ended in the mass destruction of Jews at the beginning of the 1950s. Stalin's daughter, Svetlana Allilueva, frequently mentions his natural anti-Semitism in her memoirs.[23] This, however, receded into the background during the years of the "Great Patriotic War," when practical manifestations of anti-Semitism were put aside until a "better time." Soviet resistance to German fascism (which had determined to "resolve the Jewish question once and for all"), Soviet games with the Allies, their terrible defeats at the beginning of the war—all of this forced them to remove to a degree the taboo on the subject of Jews.

On 24 August 1941, for the first time after a long ban, some notable representatives of culture—Il'ia Erenburg, Sergei Eizenshtein, Perets Markish, Samuil Marshak, David Bergel'son,[24] and others—were allowed to declare openly that they were Jews in an appeal to fellow Jews of the world, to tell about the horrors and calamities "which fascism brought to humanity and, with particular intensity, to Jews."[25] In the following year, the Jewish Anti-Fascist Committee was established, with Mikhoels as its head. It included all the major Yiddish poets and prose writers.

Yiddish literature flourished in the USSR during the war years. Numerous books were published; it was possible to include allusions to traditional, heroic, and biblical ideas, to openly express national feelings, and even to discuss the solidarity of all Jews of the world faced with total destruction and the heroism shown by Jews on the fronts.[26] But what is most interesting is that this relative liberalism on the part of the ideological authorities and censors lasted only for the first few years of the war. Immediately after the war's turning point, when the Soviet Army took the offensive (1943), the general tone of publications and the controlling authorities' approach to Jews changed. In this year, the Communist Party Central Committee sent secret "recommendations" around the country, limiting the promotion of Jews to positions of authority. Even earlier, in 1942, in the midst of the Battle of Stalingrad, the authorities in the Central Committee's Department of Agitation and Propaganda apparently had no more pressing business than "The Selection and Promotion of Personnel in the Arts." Again, the same unfortunate national theme was brought to the forefront: the authorities stated that "non-Russian people" (mostly Jews) were disproportionately represented in arts institutions. As a result, a massive ethnic purge started (in theater, music, cinema); there was a "refreshing of personnel" in the publishing houses and large newspapers.[27] The victims of this purge were mostly Jews. References to war heroes with Jewish last names began to disappear from print. The "inconvenient nationality" disappeared from statistical records on the nationalities of decorated soldiers, in spite of the fact that the records of 1943 show Jews ranking fourth among decorated groups—behind Russians, Ukrainians, and Byelorussians.[28] The censorship institutions must have received specific directives at this time; in any case, once again the Jewish theme was gradually suppressed. At first this was done discreetly, but as the final victory of the war approached, censorship became more open and direct.

One of the first cases known to me is the ban on the publication of Klara Blium's article in the magazine *International Literature* [Internatsional'naia literatura]. In August 1943, the head of Glavlit (Sadchikov) wrote a special memorandum to the Central Committee's Department of Agitation and Propaganda. To it was attached a report by one of the censors "about his most important interventions." The report discussed "issue 4 of the magazine *International Literature*":

> I recommend that Klara Blium's article—on the fascists' attempt to destroy the
> Jewish people—be removed. Although the article is short (2 pp.), the author man-

ages to make many unnecessary and incorrect statements. In particular, the author gives the percentage of Jews among Red Army soldiers as larger than the percentage of Jews in the entire population of the USSR. Her article states: " . . . it is indeed because Jews love peace, because with all their beings they are opposed to violence and bloodshed, that they stand in the front lines against fascist brutality. To their great achievements in the fields of philosophy, poetry, music and sociology, they can add equally great achievements in a fifth field, the military."[29]

It is clear why this article was removed. But it is important to remember that the ideological authorities were informed only about cases of "extremely important censorship intervention." The above was obviously considered one of these.

Just as revealing and significant is the "life and fate" of the literary works of Vasilii Grossman.[30] As is well known, the fate of Jews was a constant concern of this writer, starting with his first literary efforts (one of his early short stories was "In the Town of Berdichev") and becoming more and more pronounced with time. During World War II, this theme resounded even more tragically, and immediately the mechanism of suppression went to work.

"The war was still going on," recalls Grossman's friend, the poet Semen Lipkin, "when Grossman's story 'The Ukraine without Jews' [Ukraina bez evreev] stirred up the authorities' anger. It was published with great difficulty in a second-rate publication."[31] Lipkin was probably referring to the Yiddish newspaper Einikayt (25 November and 2 December 1943). Grossman's story was abruptly interrupted halfway through publication, most likely because of his understandably oblique accusations aimed at the local population, without whose knowledge and participation the mass destruction of Jews in the Ukraine could not have been carried out. The full essay was finally published in Russian almost a half century later, in the Riga magazine Century [Vek]. The publishers found a manuscript of the essay in Grossman's archive and wrote that he first submitted it to the magazine Red Warrior [Krasnyi voin] without success: "the last time the word 'Jew' flashed across its pages was in 1928."[32]

With great difficulty, Grossman's essay "Treblinka Hell" [Treblinskii ad] went through the censorship process in 1945 and was nevertheless published in the magazine The Banner [Znamia]. It was based on accounts of prisoners who miraculously survived, peasants from nearby villages, and other witnesses. This essay was never included in any edition of Grossman's collected works.

The theme of the Holocaust became taboo literally the day after the victory. Not that it was completely forbidden to mention it in print (that would come later!), but it was "recommended" that it be discussed as little as possible: the familiar anonymous Communist Party formulaic "there is an opinion . . . " was used to discourage its mention. This taboo also applied to Yiddish literature. One scholar noticed the following interesting phenomenon: writers, trying to find a way out of the situation, moved the geographical settings of their works outside the USSR, usually to Poland: Victims [Korbones] by Der Nister; "War" [Milkhome] by Perets Markish; and S. Galkin's A Question of Life and Death [Af toit un af leben],[33] a dramatic poem devoted to the Warsaw ghetto revolt.[34] Mention of the no less tragic events in the Ukraine and Byelorussia was "not recommended."

The dramatic fate of the famous *Black Book* is very well known. It contained documented evidence of genocide in the USSR and Poland (orders of command, stories of ghetto and concentration camp victims, their diaries, letters written in the last hours of life, photographs, songs, poems, etc.). The editorial board was a committee of scholars and writers from several countries; the USSR was represented by members of the Jewish Anti-Fascist Committee (S. Mikhoels, I. Fefer, D. Bergel'son P. Markish, and others).[35] In 1944–45, the Soviet publishing house Der Emes brought out the first and second parts of the *Black Book* in Yiddish, under the title *Murderers of the People*. In the following year, variants of the *Black Book* came out in Romania and the United States, the latter in English.

The Russian *Black Book* was already prepared for publication and typeset when it was destroyed in 1948; that same year the Jewish Anti-Fascist Committee was shut down. Fortunately, the manuscript was preserved by the archive of Yad Vashem (the Memorial Institute for Victims of the Holocaust and Heroes of the Resistance). In 1968 the Israeli publishing house Tarbut published it in Hebrew. In Russia, the *Black Book* was not published until 1991, when it was prepared by scholars from Yad Vashem.[36]

Things looked more and more ominous for the Jewish theme and Jewish literature as the fatal year of 1948 drew nearer. The subject of Jews' participation in World War II was practically cut from print. However, in 1947–48, two books on this topic were published by Der Emes, clearly through an oversight of the censors: G. D. Smoliar's *Avengers of the Ghetto* and *Partisan Friendship: Memoirs about Jews in Combat during the Great Patriotic War*.[37] Afterward, nothing at all appeared on this subject for a full forty years, until the end of the 1980s.

At the end of 1946, the works of Perets Markish attracted the attention of Party authorities. On 29 December, M. Shcherbakov, head of the Personnel Office in the All-Union Communist Party Central Committee (Bolsheviks), addressed a secret report to A. A. Kuznetsov, Secretary of the Central Committee, even though Shcherbakov's duties did not directly include supervision of literature. At that time in the USSR, it was not so much that "everything depended on the quality of personnel," as Stalin claimed, but more that everything depended on the whim of personnel officers.[38] Here is what Shcherbakov wrote:

The journal *Soviet Books* [Sovetskaia kniga] (Nos. 8–9, 1946) contains a review by a Professor Nusinov of a book of Perets Markish's poetry, published in Russian by Goslitizdat. Many of Markish's works, including the poem "War" mentioned by Nusinov, have nationalistic and religious overtones. We informed you of this previously in our memorandum concerning the situation in Jewish literature.

The poem "War" glorifies biblical themes and nationalistic ideas, and was received enthusiastically by Jews abroad. Professor Nusinov writes in his review: "The extremely popular American Jewish writer J. Glatstein considers Perets Markish's works on the Patriotic War 'a miracle of Jewish poetry.'" Glatstein's words were quoted with full approbation by numerous American Jewish newspapers in their reviews of the poem. J. Glatstein, before whom Nusinov bows and scrapes with such servility, is an ardent reactionary who hates the Soviet Union. For many years he edited the journal *In Zikh* [Inside], which was full of smears and fabrications against our country. . . . [39] We believe that the editorial staff of *Soviet Books* committed a political error when it published Nusinov's review.

Based on this report, Kuznetsov sent the following resolution:

> To Comrade Aleksandrov [Georgii Fedorovich Aleksandrov, head of the Department of Agitation and Propaganda]:
> It is necessary to set the magazine *Soviet Books* straight, and orchestrate a critique of Nusinov and P. Markish through the newspaper *Culture and Life* [Kul'tura i zhizn'].

A. M. Egolin, Aleksandrov's deputy, sent Kuznetsov a detailed response, pre-ambled by the comment that "this report deserves your serious attention." It turns out that the Party ideologues did not agree with the personnel officers and came to the conclusion that

> It is wrong to describe Perets Markish's works as having religious and nationalistic overtones. On the contrary, they vividly illustrate the brotherly friendship of our country's ethnic groups. Addressing the Jewish question, Perets Markish writes:

> Brothers have the same mother and the same motherland.
> Dying, you clutch your faithful sword
> And kiss the Russian soil like a son,
> Ready to lay down your life for Russia.

> Perets Markish is a Jewish poet, and it is natural that some of his works treat the difficult past of the Jewish people and the suffering brought about by Hitler's invasion. But Markish does not idealize the past at all. Themes of Jewish racial exclusivity, which would be grounds for discussing religious and nationalistic biases, are completely absent from the poetry of P. Markish.

The personnel officers made other errors, too: it turned out that

> Jacob Glatstein, who was mentioned in the review, enjoys great authority in the progressive circles of Jewry abroad. Recently, the occasion of his fiftieth birthday was marked by favorable articles about him in the progressive magazine *Jewish Culture.* This is the publication of the World Union of Activists of Jewish Culture, headed by Marmer, a member of the US Communist Party.[40] Jacob Glatstein's article about P. Markish was published in the American magazine *Einikayt,* whose position toward

the USSR is friendly; its editor is B. Goldberg, the Chairman of the American Jewish Anti-Fascist Committee.[41] Glatstein's article ended with the words: "We salute you, Perets Markish!" The editors of *Einikayt* added to this the following comment: "And we salute Comrade Glatstein for his objective evaluation of developments in Soviet literature." At the present time, any statements against Jacob Glatstein in the Soviet press could be damaging.[42]

There are several reasons for this unexpected defense. First, it seems that the personnel officers were a bit ahead of schedule: the command [i.e., to begin an anti-Semitic campaign] had not yet been given. Second, they had invaded the turf of the Central Committee's ideologues. The most important reason is that at this time in the Kremlin there was an ongoing behind-the-scenes battle between two Central Committee Secretaries—Zhdanov and Kuznetsov—which has been documented.[43] The former could not stand any encroachment on his sphere of influence, which was ideology. Almost all the participants and subjects of this "discussion" would later become victims: A. A. Kuznetsov, former First Secretary of the Leningrad Regional Party Committee [Obkom], transferred to the position of Central Committee Secretary at the beginning of 1946 and was executed in 1950 as part of the so-called Leningrad Affair.[44] Two years later, Perets Markish was executed in connection with the Crimea Affair. The reviewer of the Perets Markish book, Prof. Isaak Markovich Nusinov, one of the most prominent historians of Jewish literature, was arrested for the same reason as Markish and perished in prison.[45] During the Jewish Anti-Fascist Committee Affair [Crimea Affair] investigation came a typical and purely Orwellian turning point. Benjamin Goldberg, yesterday's "friend of the Soviet Union" whose authority the ideologues initially cited, was labeled an "American spy" and "agent of the Joint" [see Introduction]. Goldberg was Einstein's associate in anti-Fascist activity and Shalom Aleichem's son-in-law; not long before the trial he had visited the USSR and met with many Jewish writers. As a result, his name appears very often in the investigation papers. There is even a special volume entitled *Documents about the Visit of the American Spy Goldberg (Veif Benjamin) to Moscow* [Dokumenty o prebyvanii v Moskve amerikanskogo shpiona Gol'dberga (on zhe Veif Bendzhamin)]. He was the one incriminated by the Soviets for trying to publish the *Black Book* in America, for having "collected only materials about the atrocities of German fascists toward the Jewish population."

Officials from Lubianka[46] not only accused the compilers of the *Black Book* of insidious "nationalism" and "exaggeration" of the suffering of Jews during the Holocaust but went so far as to call them "propagandists" for nazism, since "they describe Hitler's racist views in suspiciously excessive detail" and "quote the ridiculous plans of Hitler and his associates about the enslavement of the world and the eradication of communism, thus furnishing them with the broadest possible audience."[47]

It is no less typical that, during the pretrial investigation, the prosecution's main motif became Markish's "nationalistic" and "religious" works from the war years: his poem "To a Soldier Jew" and again the poem "War," already denounced in the 1946 report. Not long before Markish's arrest, A. A. Fadeev[48] invited him to the Writers' Union and told him that people had informed on him to the Central Committee, that he was accused "of Zionism and bourgeois nationalism as revealed by his poem 'War,'" and that these were people "whose opinion the Central Committee values."[49]

The ruthless murder of Mikhoels on the night of 13 January 1948 marked the beginning of the terrible anti-Semitic "Five-Year Plan," which was curtailed only at the death of "The Leader of All Nationalities."[50] The State Jewish Theater in Moscow was destroyed as well as Jewish theaters in Minsk and Kiev, the publishing house Der Emes was closed, books were no longer published in Yiddish, and the newspaper *Einikayt* was closed. Those who worked for the newspaper were automatically considered "bourgeois-nationalistic propagandists" by the MGB, the Ministry of State Security; however, it was practically impossible to name any significant Jewish writer who had not worked for the paper. In February, Stalin signed a decree from the Politburo dissolving all associations of Jewish writers in Moscow, Kiev, and Minsk; the only publishers of almanacs in Yiddish were also shut down, Geimland in Moscow and Der Shtern in Kiev. During 1949, all the luminaries of Jewish literature were arrested. Practically all of Jewish culture was destroyed. Isaak Nusinov and Der Nister died in prison; Perets Markish, David Gofshtein, Leib Kvitko, Itsik Fefer, Samuil Persov, and David Bergel'son were executed on 12 August 1952.[51] In the eyes of the MGB investigators and the "experts" who worked for them, often the language which the poets and writers used was the only "evidence" against them. This language was not Hebrew, already forbidden in the 1920s, but Yiddish, once glorified and now considered criminal. The hatred of Hebrew reached such a point that during the campaign a small stock of Old Hebrew printing typefaces was quickly destroyed.

The mass arrests of writers, journalists, theater people, and other "persons of the Jewish nationality" (the authorities always used this phrase) lasted from January through the summer of 1949. The mass arrests were carefully hidden, but a campaign against "rootless cosmopolitanism" was made public: this was yet another euphemism for the same persecuted nation.

On 28 January 1949, the newspaper *Pravda* published the article "Concerning an Anti-Patriotic Group of Theater Critics." For the sake of decorum the list of Jewish names was diluted with one Russian (Leonid Maliugin) and one Armenian (Grigorii Boiadziev) name.[52] Following the suggestion of writers K. Simonov and A. Sofronov,[53] all the critics mentioned were expelled from the Union of Soviet Writers (I. I. Iuzovskii, A. S. Gurvich, A. M. Borshchagovskii, and others).[54] A campaign against "wanderers of mankind without passports" now began. Though it would have been impossible to camouflage its anti-Semitic purpose, the authorities did not even try to do so: they had to prepare "the masses." The mass media gleefully took the initiative: they exposed "secret cosmopolitans," revealed pseudonyms [of Jews], published satirical articles and drawings with an obvious anti-Semitic bent.

This systematic destruction of Jewish culture and unleashing of an anti-Semitic campaign had begun immediately after the war. Already in 1946 the head of Glavlit, K. Omel'chenko, sent a report to the Central Committee's Department of Agitation and Propaganda:

> The publishing house Der Emes is bringing out *Earth*, a Jewish [Yiddish] language novel by Kh. Melamud. The subject of this novel is the migration of Jews from a Ukrainian shtetl to the countryside and their transition to agricultural labor. The action takes place in the 1920s; the novel is based on real events. The author did not show the leading role of the Party in the social transformation of the Jewish masses. Representatives of the Soviet authorities figure as minor characters, and the Party is mentioned only in passing. In Melamud's novel, the distribution of land and collectivization of the Jewish masses took place spontaneously. Glavlit considers it inexpedient to publish this novel in its present form—it has to be redone.[55]

Nevertheless, Khaim Melamud's *Erd* came out in early 1948, though in altered form—the role of the Party was strengthened. That was the last book published by Der Emes until 1959: there was a complete ban on all Yiddish-language books in the USSR. Although this punishment originated in the top echelons, it was put into practice by the ideological and security agencies, with the censorship offices taking their own "appropriate measures." The mass removal and destruction of books by arrested writers began. According to the rules, each list of books subject to removal had to receive the sanction of the Central Committee. A notice such as the following, from the head of Glavlit and dated 13 March 1949, demonstrates this:

> As you requested, we are sending a list of works by D. Bergel'son, S. Galkin, D. Gofshtein, L. Kvitko, P. Markish, I. Nusinov, I. Fefer, L. Shtern. . . . Enclosure of 46 pages.[56]

This list received the necessary "blessing"; all the books on it were removed from public libraries and bookselling organizations. Glavlit went even further in 1949, apparently concerned that not all books of arrested writers and scholars were covered by the list. It sent a directive entitled "Alphabetical list of authors, *all* of whose works must be removed from libraries and bookselling organizations. Included in this list were Samuil Zalmanovich Galkin, Lev Moiseevich Kvitko, Perets Davidovich Markish, and Itsik Fefer (literature); Lina Solomonova Shtern (physiology, medicine); and Isaak Markovich Nusinov (literary criticism.)[57]

But Glavlit did not limit itself only to scholars and writers under investigation. Having most likely received a directive from higher authorities, for the first time Glavlit began the mass removal of hundreds of books with "Zionist content." On 15 June 1949 it sent out "Directive No. 620 about the removal of publications which should not be used in public libraries and bookselling organizations." This directive included a list of about 500 book titles, all of them "Zionist" and Jewish "nationalistic" books in the Russian language. As before, this list was sent to the Central Committee for approval. In the archival copy the following interesting "Notice" was preserved:

> This list was sent to the Central Committee of the All-Union Communist Party (Bolsheviks). Comrade Usov (Department of Propaganda and Agitation) marked the titles in the text which should be removed, and on the instructions of Comrade Ponomarev (Library Sector), asked to include these titles in different lists.[58]

Apparently, the Central Committee considered it "awkward" and "politically incorrect" to attract the attention of people working in libraries who were involved in the removal of books. It was better to "disperse" these titles into different lists—to, so to speak, dilute them with books on other themes in order to make them less noticeable. Of course, this was an open secret, but Glavlit certainly carried out these instructions: they combined various lists, so that the inclusion of books on this [Jewish] theme appeared incidental. These lists contained works brought out by the publishing house Kadimah in 1917–18, works on Jewish history, books by Zionist leaders (T. Herzl, V. Jabotinsky, A. Idel'son, D. Pasmanik, the *Selected Works* of Ahad Ha-am), and bulletins and magazines of the organization Po'alei-Zion.[59] Books and reference works of the 1930s devoted to Jewish themes were also ostracized: *Jews in the USSR* [Evrei v SSSR] (Moscow, 1935), *Jews in Tsarist Russia and in the USSR: A Concise Guide to the Exhibit* [Evrei v tsarskoi Rossii i SSSR: Kratkii putevoditel' po vystavke] (published by the State Museum of Ethnography, 1939). Reference books which mentioned arrested writers were removed, for example the directory *Jewish Writers of the USSR* [Evreiskie pisateli SSSR], published by the Literary Fund (Moscow, 1936). Among new books, many works published by the Jewish Anti-Fascist Committee were removed, for example: *Jewish People against Fascism: Materials from the Third Anti-Fascist Mass Rally of Representatives of the Jewish People and the Third Plenary Session of the Jewish Anti-Fascist Committee* [Evreiskii narod protiv fashizma: Materialy III Antifashistskogo mitinga predstavitelei evreiskogo naroda i III plenuma Antifashistskogo Evreiskogo Komiteta] (Moscow, 1945).

A large number of books on this same theme appeared in the combined *Bibliographic List of Out-of-Date Editions Not to Be Used* [Bibliograficheskii spisok ustarevshikh izdanii, ne podlezhashchikh ispol'zovaniiu] (Moscow, 1952); in particular, all Yiddish books by I. D. Dobrushin on Mikhoels and Zuskin, his plays, his collection *Jewish Folk Tales* [Evreiskie narodnye skazki], and so on.[60] Books from the 1920s on anti-Semitism also were included in this list, for example *The Unconquered Enemy: An Anthology of Fiction against Anti-Semitism* [Sbornik khudozhestvennykh proizvedenii protiv antisemitizma: Neodolennyi vrag] (Moscow: Federatsiia, 1930), compiled by V. Veshnev. It included works by V. G. Korolenko, C. Iushkevich, D. Aizman, the story "Levinson" from *The Rout* [Razgrom] by A. Fadeev, short stories by I. Babel' and other writers.[61]

In 1948–52, part of the work of destroying literature was given to the branches of Glavlit in the Soviet republics and regions [oblast']. The Ukrainian and Byelo-russian branches played the most active role. They sent in extensive lists of books in Yiddish and Hebrew as well as in Ukrainian and Byelorussian. The Birobid-zhan Regional and City Censorship Office [Obgorlit] was instructed to investi-gate local publications; the instruction was carried out.[62] On 17 September 1949, Glavlit "approved an order from the Censorship Office [Oblit] of Jewish Autono-mous Oblast' No. 7 dated 10 August 1949, concerning the removal from public libraries and bookselling organizations of the following literature: the magazine *Birobidzhan* from 1941 to 1948, and all issues of *Outpost* [Forpost] (Birobidzhan, 1939–1941)."[63]

All works included in Glavlit's proscribed lists were destroyed, or at best hidden in the "book Gulag," a special section in a few of the country's major libraries. Despite some abatement in state anti-Semitism during the period of the Thaw, these books were not "rehabilitated" until forty years later, during the *perestroika* years (1986–91).[64]

In the same fatal year 1949, at the height of the anti-Semitic campaign [the Affair of the Cosmopolitans], Vasilii Grossman finished his novel *Stalingrad,* which dur-ing publication was changed to *For a Just Cause* [Za pravoe delo]. Documents from the Central Committee's Department of Agitation and Propaganda show that the fate of the novel was decided at the very top. It was sent for review to the Institute of Marxism-Leninism, where senior researcher T. Zelenov noted a few problems. For example, the author was suspected of an "uncritical attitude" to-ward America; the reviewer added, "The novel does not contain even a shadow of criticism of American imperialism, but repeatedly mentions American trucks, gifts, etc." V. Kruzhkov, head of the Department of Agitation and Propaganda, directly and unequivocally expressed his major concern with the novel in a report sent to Central Committee Secretary Suslov, who had become a watchdog for ideology:

> To the Secretary of the Central Committee of the All-Union Communist Party (Bol-sheviks), Comrade M. A. Suslov:
> Concerning Vas. Grossman's novel *Stalingrad.* . . . Even the Soviet intelligentsia, who energetically assisted on the front through their creative work, was not por-trayed correctly in the novel. As the main character representing the intelligentsia, the professor of physics Shturm is from a non-Russian nationality.[65]

Characters with Jewish last names were removed from novels published serially in magazines. Literary works were completely banned or cut in half if Jewish characters occupied too much space in the narrative. For example, the publica-tion of Iurii German's short novel *Lieutenant Colonel of the Medical Service* [Pod-polkovnik meditsinskoi sluzhby] was interrupted right in the middle.[66] Its main character was a military doctor named Levin. Readers of the magazine *The Star* [Zvezda] were introduced to the beginning of the novel in the first issue of 1949 but did not find the final part in the next issue: it had been destroyed at the typesetter's office. The first half of the novel was subjected to a scathing critique by the newspaper *Leningrad Pravda* at the height of the campaign against cosmopolitanism. On 18 March the newspaper published a "letter from a group of readers to the editor" [*pis'mo v redaktsiiu gruppy chitatelei*] entitled "Libel against the Soviet People" [Paskvil' na sovetskikh liudei], which condemned the publication of the novel and contained clear hints about the nationality of the doctor Levin. The full text of the novel was published seven years later (1956), during the Thaw.

After the beginning of the notorious Doctors' Plot in January 1953, which almost resulted in the genocide of all Soviet Jews, Glavlit immediately took measures to remove books authored by the "assassins in white coats" [ubiitsy v belykh khalatakh]. Already on 15 January, the head of Glavlit released Order No. 78:

> (1) Remove from public libraries and bookselling organizations all works by the following authors: N. I. Vinogradov, M. S. Vovsi, A. M. Grinshtein, P. I. Egorov, B. B. Kogan, M. B. Kogan, G. I. Maiorov, A. I. Fel'dman, Ia. G. Ettinger. (2) Remove . . . the following books: M. Zagorskii, *Mikhoels* (biographical essay), Moscow-Leningrad, Kinoizdat, RSFSR, 1927; E. I. Smirnov, *Soviet Military Doctors during the Patriotic War*, Moscow, 1945.[67]

We can see that Glavlit decided to include in its "roundup" a book on Mikhoels, whom they implicated in both the Crimea Affair and the Doctors' Plot as "the ideological inspirer of Jewish nationalism." E. I. Smirnov's book was included, and not by accident: it contained a portrait of M. S. Vovsi, the chief Red Army general practitioner and major general of the Medical Service, and it described Vovsi's achievements in great detail (see translators' introduction). Other prominent Jewish military doctors mentioned were A. P. Frumkin, V. D. Bershadskii, and V. S. Levit, deputy to the chief Red Army surgeon. The latter three were not implicated in the Doctors' Plot but were obviously candidates for it, if the campaign had not ended in March 1953.

Apparently, not all the heads of Glavlit's regional branches understood the full meaning of Order 78. So on 26 January an explanation directed to the head of the Smolensk Regional and City Censorship Agencies was "circulated secretly" to all the heads of regional and district agencies:

> This is in response to your inquiry as to the handling of published works containing articles by persons mentioned in Glavlit Order 78 of 15 January 1953, if these works are found in public libraries or bookselling organizations:
> (a) All books written by persons mentioned in the order must be removed.
> (b) Libraries must make corrections in all published works containing individual articles by persons mentioned in the order. In cases where it is technically impossible to make corrections, the collections or editions containing such materials may not be lent to readers. (c) In the bookselling organizations, editions containing articles

or other materials relating to persons mentioned in the order must be removed from sale.

You must verify immediately whether bookselling organizations and libraries are violating the above-mentioned order. If a violation is discovered, draw up a report and hold the guilty parties responsible.[68]

The "cleaning out" of this literature from libraries and bookstores also continued during the uncertain period after 5 March [Stalin's death] until April [when *Pravda* announced that the doctors were innocent]. In the major public libraries today, very often one comes across the above-mentioned books with blackened, crossed-out pages, torn-out portraits, and so on. Finally, on 4 April, the order was given to retreat, the investigation ceased, and the doctors were released from prison. One of the arrested doctors, the prominent pathologist Ia. L. Rappoport, recounted that this day was celebrated as a family holiday.[69] On this day, Glavlit Circular No. 331 appeared:

(1) Order No. 78 of 15 January 1953 and the separate Glavlit directives about the documents mentioned are canceled. (2) The literature that was removed is to be transferred from special storage back to the general collection, and the literature detained in the bookselling organizations is authorized for sale.[70]

It must be said that there was practically nothing to return, except for a few books from those large libraries that had special storage. The smaller libraries and bookstores immediately destroyed such literature. In May, Beriia and a few other major officials from the State Security Office were arrested. The censorship authorities, frightened by the possibility of unpredictable developments, decided to cover their tracks. On 6 May Glavlit released another secret circular, addressed to all its branches:

In some copies of the *Bibliographic List of Out-of-Date Editions Not to Be Used*, No. 1 [the list that included the above-mentioned books], through a printer's error at the All-Union Book Chamber [Vsesoiuznaia knizhnaia palata] publishing house, the following books were mistakenly included [an enumeration follows]. We ask that you examine the copies of the bibliographic list which you received. If the above-mentioned books are listed in your copies, it is necessary to black out the titles of these books.[71]

We see that the printer's employees were blamed for "mistakenly" including books in the list. To rectify the situation, the censorship agency ordered a reprint of the "problematic" pages of the bibliography, but understandably it had not been done in all copies that went out. This case is extremely typical of the Ministry of Truth's activity—rewriting history according to Big Brother's latest directives.

Previously, during the Beilis Affair, decent Russian writers voiced their protest.

But now, complete silence reigned. During the Beilis Affair, the false testimony of Vera Cheberiak was exposed by the press; during the Doctors' Affair not a single Soviet writer could risk protesting the libel of the Soviet doctor Lidiia Timashuk, who was awarded the Order of Lenin for her trouble.[72] This is how a totalitarian regime differs from even the most draconian of police states.

NOTES

1. Lina Solomonovna Shtern (Stern, 1878–1968), physiologist and biologist. In 1939 she became the first woman admitted to the USSR Academy of Sciences; she received the Stalin Prize and several Orders of Merit. She was arrested in 1949 in connection with the Crimea Affair and imprisoned in Lubianka until the trial of 1952. She was the only person tried to escape death and was sentenced to a five-year exile.

2. For a brief overview of Soviet book history, see Edward Kasinec with Robert H. Davis, Jr., "The Rise and Decline of Book Studies in the Soviet Union," *Book History* 2 (1999): 251–62.

3. See Mikhail Kheifets, "Two Bullets for Lenin, from Different Guns: The Sailor Protopopov Was the Assassin, Fanni Kaplan Was Only a Decoy" [Dve puli dlia Lenina i obe raznye: Ubiitsa-matros Protopopov, Fanni Kaplan—podsadnaia utka], *Novoe russkoe slovo* (New York), 19 Dec. 1997 (reprinted from the Israeli publication *Vesti*).

4. See Anatolii Prokopenko, "Archival Access Is Again Being Curtailed" [Arkhivy snova zakryvaiutsia], *Novoe russkoe slovo* (New York), 30 Sept. 1997 (reprinted from the Russian newspaper *Izvestiia*). For more discussion in English of Prokopenko's article and of another book by Blium, see the introduction (268–70) by Donna M. Farina to Arlen Viktorovich Blium, "Forbidden Topics: Early Soviet Censorship Directives," *Book History* 1 (1998): 268–82.

5. In the Soviet Union, Jews were designated as members of a nationality or ethnic group rather than a religion; Russians, Ukrainians, etc. were likewise members of nationalities.

6. These terms were all common euphemisms for Jews.

7. The Beilis Affair was named after Menahem Mendel Beilis (1874–1934), who was charged with ritual murder after the mutilated body of a child was discovered near Kiev in 1911. At the child's funeral, the Black Hundred circulated pamphlets about blood libel (cf. n. 9). Though police traced the murder to a gang of thieves, Beilis was nevertheless arrested and imprisoned for two years awaiting trial. The case received wide attention, and Beilis was found not guilty at his trial in 1913. He emigrated to Palestine and later to the United States.

8. Anatolii Vasil'evich Lunacharskii (1875–1933), a revolutionary and Bolshevik, was appointed by Lenin as the first head of the People's Commissariat of Education [Narodnyi komissariat prosveshcheniia] in 1917, to encourage the development of Russian culture. He was removed from this position by Stalin in 1929.

9. The Black Hundred was a reactionary and anti-Semitic organization founded after the Revolution of 1905 to fight revolutionaries and Jews. They were most active from 1906 to 1911.

10. *TsGA IPD*, f. 24, op. 2-v, d. 2295, ll. 137–38. This is the standard citation used in Russian publications for archival material. The archive listed is the Central State Archive

of Historical-Political Documents in St. Petersburg (Tsentral'nyi gosudarstvennyi arkhiv istoriko-politicheskikh dokumentov); f. = *fond* (archive); op. = *opis'* (section); d. = *delo* (file); l. = *list* (page).

11. *TsGA IPD*, f. 24, op. 2-v, d. 2295, l. 40.

12. Samuil Iakovlevich Marshak (1887–1964) was born in Voronezh, Russia. He wrote poetry in Russian-language Jewish journals and translated European poets; in his early career, his poems were Zionist in theme. His friend Maksim Gor'kii called him the founder of Soviet children's literature. Tamara Grigor'evna Gabbe (1903–60) was a writer, critic, and author of children's books and plays. Lidiia K. Chukovskaia (1907–96), critic and memoirist, was the daughter of Kornei I. Chukovskii. Aleksandra Iosifovna Liubarskaia (born 1908) was a writer and folklorist. Marshak, Zoia Moiseevna Zadunaiskaia (1903–83), and Chukovskaia were the only members of the group not arrested. Gabbe was arrested in 1937 and later freed; Liubarskaia was arrested in 1937 and freed in 1939.

13. *TsGA IPD*, f. 24, op. 2-v, d. 2295, ll. 137–38. (See comment to n. 14.)

14. *TsGA IPD*, f. 24, op. 2-v, d. 2494, l. 1. For more information, see Lidiia Chukovskaia, *About Anna Akhmatova: A Diary* [Zapiski ob Anne Akhmatovoi], Bk. 1, 1938–41 (Moscow: Kniga, 1989). (Due to printing errors in the original Russian text, this and the archival citation in n. 13 may not be accurate.)

15. *TsGA IPD*, f. 24, op. 2-v, d. 2296, l. 285.

16. Maksim Gor'kii (1868–1936), the officially designated founder of socialist realism in literature, died under suspicious circumstances; some suspect that Stalin had him killed. Larisa Mikhailovna Reisner (1895–1926), poet, playwright, literary critic, journalist, died of typhus. Isaak Emmanuilovich Babel' (1894–1941) was arrested in 1939 and died during the Great Terror. The writer Boris Pil'niak (Boris Andreevich Vogau, 1894–1937?) was apparently executed shortly after his arrest.

17. Upravlenie agitatsii i propagandy Tsentral'nogo Komiteta Vsesoiuznoi Komunisticheskoi Partii bol'shevikov (TsK VKP[b]).

18. *GARF,* f. 9425, op. 2, d. 19, l. 25. The archive listed is the State Archive of the Russian Federation [Gosudarstvennyi arkhiv Rossiiskoi Federatsii], which contains the archives of Glavlit from 1938 to 1991.

19. The Turkestan-Siberian Railroad.

20. I. Il'f and E. Petrov, *Twelve Chairs* [Dvenadtsat' stul'ev] / *The Golden Calf* [Zolotoi telenok] (Moscow: Khudozhestvennaia literatura, 1986), 429. Il'f and Petrov were the pseudonyms of Il'ia Arnol'dovich Fainzil'berg (1897–1937) and Evgenyi Petrovich Kataev (1903–42), respectively. Il'f died of illness, and Petrov was killed in a plane crash as a war correspondent.

21. George Orwell, *Nineteen Eighty-Four* (New York: Harcourt Brace Jovanovich, 1961), 41.

22. David Samoilov (David Samuilovich Kaufman, 1920–90), poet and translator.

23. Svetlana Iosifovna Allilueva's (born 1925) memoirs are entitled *Twenty Letters to a Friend* (New York: Harper & Row, 1967).

24. Il'ia Grigor'evich Erenburg (Ilya Ehrenburg, 1891–1967) was a writer and journalist, born in Kiev. A loyal apologist of the Stalinist regime, in 1948 he played some role in the withdrawal of Soviet support for Israel. He collaborated with other members of the Jewish Anti-Fascist Committee on the compilation of the *Black Book*. He escaped the fate of his close friends who were executed in 1952 in connection with the Crimea Affair; instead, he was awarded the Stalin Prize in that year. After Stalin's death he became more outspoken in his criticisms of the state. Sergei Mikhailovich Eizenshtein (1898–1948), film director,

was awarded the Order of Lenin for his film *Aleksandr Nevskii* (1938). He died of heart trouble in 1948 and thus escaped the fate of other members of the Jewish Anti-Fascist Committee. Perets Davidovich Markish (1895–1952), a Yiddish poet, novelist, and playwright, was born in the Volynia region. He was awarded the Order of Lenin in 1939, was a member of the Jewish Anti-Fascist Committee and head of the Jewish section of the Soviet Writers' Union. David Bergel'son (1884–1952), considered one of the foremost Yiddish prose writers, was born in Okhrimovo, near Uman', Ukraine. Beginning in 1920, he traveled around the world, settling in Moscow in 1934. Markish and Bergel'son were arrested in 1949 and later executed in connection with the Crimea Affair.

25. For more information, see R. Einshtein [Einstein], "Soviet Jewry during the Second World War" [Sovetskoe evreistvo vo Vtoroi mirovoi voine], in *Jews in Soviet Russia (1917–1967)* [Evrei v Sovetskoi Rossii], trans. from the English by Maria Al'tman (Jerusalem: Biblioteka Aliia, 1975), 9–37.

26. Kh. Shmeruk, "Yiddish Literature in the Soviet Union" [Literatura na idish v Sovetskom Soiuze], in *Jews in Soviet Russia (1917–1967)*, 234–37.

27. G. B. Kostyrchenko, *Captive of the Red Pharaoh: Political Persecutions of Soviet Jews during the Last Decade of Stalin's Rule* [V plenu u krasnogo faraona. Politicheskie presledovaniia evreev v SSSR v poslednee stalinskoe desiatiletie] (Moscow: Mezhdunarodnye otnosheniia, 1994), 9.

28. Ibid., 17.

29. *GARF,* f. 9425, op. 2, d. 50, ll. 19–20.

30. Vasilii Semenovich Grossman (1905–64), born in Berdichev, Ukraine, wrote novels and short stories. Grossman collaborated on the compilation of the *Black Book.* His 1934 short story "In the Town of Berdichev" [V gorode Berdicheve] dealt with the civil war after the Russian Revolution. It was the basis for the film *Commissar* (1967), directed by Aleksandr Askol'dov. On its completion, Askol'dov was fired and his film, considered an indictment of anti-Semitism, was shelved; it was released only in 1988. Blium alludes to the title of one of Grossman's novels, *Life and Fate* [Zhizn' i sud'ba]. The manuscript copies were confiscated by the secret police from Grossman's residence. Fortunately, one copy was hidden by Grossman's friend Semen Lipkin (b. 1911), a poet and translator. With the help of the writer Vladimir Voinovich (b. 1932), the physicist Andrei Sakharov, and his wife Elena Bonner, the manuscript was transferred to the West and published in several languages. An English edition was published by Collins-Harvill in 1985.

31. S. Lipkin, *The Life and Fate of Vasilii Grossman* [Zhizn' i sud'ba Vasiliia Grossmana] / A. Berzer, *Farewell* [Proshchanie] (Moscow: Kniga, 1990), 19.

32. *Vek* 4 (1990): 18.

33. The Yiddish prose writer and translator Der Nister ("The Hidden One," pen name of Pinkhas Kahanovich, 1884–1950), born in Berdichev, Ukraine, was a Zionist in his early career. He was arrested in connection with the Crimea Affair in 1949 and died in Lubianka hospital in 1950. Samuil Zalmanovich Galkin (Shmuel Halkin, 1897–1960), a Yiddish poet and translator, was born in Rogachev, Byelorussia. He was a Zionist until 1924. He was arrested in 1948 along with other members of the Jewish Anti-Fascist Committee and exiled to Siberia. He was released in 1955 due to poor health and rehabilitated in 1958.

34. Shmeruk, "Yiddish Literature," 235–36.

35. The Yiddish poet Itzik Solomonovich Fefer (Feffer, 1900–52) was born in Shpola, south of Kiev. He was a Communist Party member and vice-chairman of the Jewish Anti-Fascist Committee. Most of his poems were propaganda for the Party. He was arrested in 1948 and executed in connection with the Crimea Affair. In *Stalin's War against the Jews:*

The Doctors' Plot and the Soviet Solution (New York: Free Press, 1990), Louis Rapoport discusses the last meeting between Fefer and the American actor and singer Paul Robeson in 1949 (115–16). The discussion is based on Paul Robeson Jr.'s account ("How My Father Last Met Itzik Feffer," *Jewish Currents*, November 1981, 4) as well as his October 1988 interview with Rapoport.

36. Kiev: MIP "Oberig," 1991; this edition also contains a detailed history of the *Black Book* text and its publication fate. After 1991, other editions came out; the most complete (Russian) edition appeared in Vilnius in 1993, published by Iiad.

37. The Russian titles are *Mstiteli getto* and *Partizanskaia druzhba: Vospominaniia o boevykh delakh partizan-evreev, uchastnikov Velikoi Otechestvennoi voiny*. Gersh D. Smoliar (Hersh Smolar) was born in 1905 in Zambrow, Poland. He was active in the underground in Bialystok and in the Minsk ghetto during the war, and worked in Warsaw afterward. He emigrated to Israel in 1971.

38. At that time, the Central Committee's personnel officers often interfered in literary affairs to demonstrate their vigilance. For example, on 12 August 1946, the same Personnel Department sent A. A. Kuznetsov a report on a collection of short stories by M. M. Zoshchenko. It had been published by the magazine *Ogonek* in a special series in 1946. This report attacked an innocent short story "The Stoker" [Kocherga], which "could be published in any foreign newspaper as an example of anti-Soviet propaganda: even a stove fire stoker was a scarce item in the Soviet Union." See A. V. Blium, "Writers and the Authorities: 12 Stories on Censorship" [Khudozhnik i vlast': 12 tsenzurnykh istorii], *Zvezda* 8 (1994): 88.

39. Jacob Glatstein (Gladstone, 1896–1971) was born in Lublin, Poland, and emigrated to the United States in 1914. He wrote poetry, novels, and essays. He was a columnist for the *Day-Morning Journal* (an American Yiddish-language daily) and for the weekly *Der Yiddisher Kemfer*, a publication of the World Union of Po'alei Zion. He served as editor of *Folk un Velt*, a periodical of the World Jewish Congress. The journal *In Zikh* appeared irregularly from 1920 to 1939.

40. Kalman Marmer (Marmor, 1879–1956) was born near Vilnius. He left Russia in 1899. He was a Yiddish writer and literary scholar, a founder of the World Union of Po'alei Zion, and editor of its weekly *Der Yiddisher Kemfer*. He was a member of the American Socialist Party and later the Communist Party.

41. Ben Zion Goldberg (Veif/Waife Benjamin, 1895–1972) was born in Lithuania and emigrated to the United States at age twelve. He became a writer, columnist, and editor (with a pro-Soviet orientation) for the Yiddish-language newspaper *Day-Morning Journal*. He married Marie Rabinowitz, daughter of the writer Shalom Aleichem. He visited the Soviet Union several times to learn about the situation of Jews there.

42. *RTsKhIDNI*, f. 17, op. 125, d. 562, ll. 1–5. The archive listed is the Russian Center for the Preservation and Study of Documents of Recent History (Rossiiskii Tsentr khraneniia i izucheniia dokumentov noveishei istorii), formerly the Central Party Archive (Tsentral'nyi partiinyi arkhiv), located in Moscow.

43. Some relevant material can be found in D. L. Babichenko, *Writers and Censors: Soviet Literature of the 1940s under the Political Control of the Central Committee* [Pisateli i tsenzory: Sovetskaia literatura 1940-kh godov pod politicheskim kontrolem TsK] (Moscow: Rossiia molodaia, 1994).

44. The Leningrad Affair was a purge of the Leningrad Regional and City Party organizations following the death of Zhdanov in 1948. Many but not all of those purged were Zhdanov's supporters.

45. Isaak Markovich Nusinov (1889–1952), literary critic and historian. He taught at

Moscow University and in the Yiddish department of the Moscow Pedagogical Institute. He contributed to Yiddish journals as well as to the *Great Soviet Encyclopedia* [Bolshaia Sovetskaia Entsiklopediia] and the *Literary Encyclopedia* [Literaturnaia Entsiklopediia]. He was arrested in 1948 in connection with the Crimea Affair and was beaten to death in prison in 1952.

46. Lubianka, an eight-story building near in the heart of Moscow, was the headquarters and prison of the Ministry of State Security (Ministerstro Gosudarstvennoi Bezopasnosti), the precursor of the KGB. The name comes from its address, 2 Lubianka Street.

47. A. Borshchagovskii, *Guilty by Blood: A Documentary History* [Obviniaetsia krov'. Dokumental'naia povest'] (Moscow: Izdatel'skaia Gruppa Progress-Kul'tura, 1994), 215, 287.

48. Aleksandr Aleksandrovich Fadeev (1901–56), writer, head of the Soviet Writers' Union (1946–54). Among those Fadeev apparently named as denouncers of Markish was Fefer.

49. Much has been written about this; for example, see Borshchagovskii, *Guilty by Blood,* and *The Unjust Trial: The Last Stalin Execution: Transcript of the Trial of the Members of the Jewish Anti-Fascist Committee* [Nepravednyi sud: Poslednii stalinskii rasstrel: Stenogramma sudebnogo protsessa nad chlenami Antifashistskogo Evreiskogo Komiteta] (Moscow: Nauka, 1994).

50. *Vozhd' vsekh narodov* was one of numerous flattering titles given to Stalin.

51. David Gofshtein (Hofstein, 1889–1952), a Yiddish poet, was born in Ukraine. Lev (Leib) Moiseevich Kvitko (1890–1952) was a Yiddish poet, novelist, editor, and children's writer. He collaborated on the compilation of the *Black Book.* Gofshtein, Kvitko, and Markish made up the Kiev lyric triumvirate. Samuil (Shmuel) Persov (1890–1952) wrote in Russian and Yiddish. Gofshtein, Kvitko, and Persov were arrested in 1949 and executed in connection with the Crimea Affair.

52. A few non-Jewish names were commonly mentioned in articles of this sort to mask their anti-Semitic purpose.

53. Konstantin Mikhailovich Simonov (1915–79) was a poet, writer, and playwright. Anatolii Vladimirovich Sofronov (born 1911) is a playwright and a poet.

54. Borshchagovskii, *Guilty by Blood,* 385.

55. *GARF,* f. 9425, op. 72, d. 119, l. 3.

56. *GARF,* f. 9425, op. 72, d. 131, l. 17.

57. This typewritten list, which was constantly added to and corrected, can be found in the Russia Abroad Sector [Sektor russkogo zarubezh'ia], formerly a division of special storage in the Russian Academy of Sciences. It includes about 800 names of "enemies of the people," all of whose works had to be banned.

58. *GARF,* f. 9425, op. 2, d. 124, l. 50.

59. Abraham Idel'son (1865–1921) was born in Vekshni, Lithuania, and studied at Moscow University. After the first Zionist Congress he joined the Zionist movement. In 1905 he became editor of the Zionist journal *Jewish Life* [Evreiskaia zhizn']. In May 1917 he opened the All-Russian Zionist Conference in Petrograd. In 1919, as the Zionist movement was curtailed in Russia, he traveled to Paris on behalf of Russian Zionists. He died suddenly in Berlin in 1921. Daniel Pasmanik (1869–1930) was born in Gadyach, Ukraine. He joined the Zionist movement in 1900 in Geneva. He returned to Russia in 1905 and worked on the editorial board of *Jewish Life.* He also contributed to *Die Welt,* the non-Zionist *Jewish World* [Evreiskii mir], and the *Jewish Encyclopedia* [Evreiskaia entsiklopediia]. He emigrated to Paris in 1919. Ahad-Ha-Am is the pen name of Asher Hirsch

Ginsberg/Ginzberg (1856–1927), advocate of practical, educational, and cultural Zionism. He was born in Skvira, Russia (Kiev Province), and spent his last years (1922–27) in Tel Aviv. An extremely influential author and thinker, he wrote articles and essays on a variety of Jewish issues.

60. Yehezkel Dobrushin (1883–1953), a Yiddish literary critic and playwright, was born in the Ukraine. He was arrested (1948) when the Jewish Anti-Fascist Committee was shut down and later died in a Siberian prison camp.

61. Vladimir Galaktionovich Korolenko (1853–1921) wrote short stories and tales (in Russian) condemning anti-Semitism; he also wrote numerous articles about the Beilis Affair. Semen Solomonovich Iushkevich (1868–1927), a physician, playwright, and novelist, wrote in Russian and Yiddish. David Iakovlevich Aizman (1869–1922) wrote stories (in Russian) about poor Jewish people, revolutionary-minded Jewish intellectuals, and Jewish persecution by the tsarist police.

62. Also spelled Birobijan. Originally this was a territory in southeast Russia (on the Amur River) set aside by the Soviet government in 1928 for colonization by Jews. It became the Jewish Autonomous Oblast' in 1934; Birobidzhan is also a city in this oblast'. Most of the population is non-Jewish.

63. *GARF,* f. 9425, op. 2, d. 125, l. 10.

64. The Thaw (1953–64) was the period of relative freedom following Stalin's death, corresponding to the Khrushchev years. The name came from the title of Il'ia Erenburg's novel *Ottepel',* published 1954–56.

65. In her memoirs, A. Berzer includes transcripts of the discussions of the novel. Lipkin, *Grossman* / Berzer, *Farewell,* 165–243.

66. Iurii Pavlovich German (1910–67), novelist and journalist.

67. *GARF,* f. 9425, op. 2, d. 204, l. 7.

68. Ibid.

69. Rapoport's valuable contribution is *Straddling Two Epochs: The Doctors' Plot of 1953* [Na rubezhe dvukh epokh: Delo vrachei 1953 g.] (Moscow: Kniga, 1988). This book appeared in English in 1991: *The Doctors' Plot of 1953* (Cambridge: Harvard University Press).

70. *GARF,* f. 9425, op. 2, d. 200, l. 20.

71. *GARF,* f. 9425, op. 2, d. 204, l. 22.

72. Vera Cheberiak was a woman associated with the gang of thieves in the Beilis Affair. Lidiia Timashuk, a radiologist, first raised the suspicions about Zhdanov's death that would develop into the Doctors' Plot. Her Order of Lenin was rescinded when the plot was discredited.

PART TWO

CULTURE AND RESISTANCE

Prisoners at work in the camp library. The photo is from a propaganda album commemorating an official visit to Dachau by Heinrich Himmler and Anton Mussert, the head of the Dutch Nazi Party. (*KZ Gedenkstatte Dachau, courtesy of USHMM Photo Archives*)

VI • THE SECRET VOICE: CLANDESTINE FINE PRINTING IN THE NETHERLANDS, 1940–1945

Sigrid Pohl Perry

THE long tradition of neutrality maintained by the Netherlands since the time of Napoleon ceased on 10 May 1940 when Hitler's invading forces bombed harbors and coastal areas, then dropped incendiary bombs on the city of Rotterdam itself several days later. On 15 May the Netherlands capitulated after Queen Wilhelmina and members of the royal family had escaped across the English Channel. Arthur Seyss-Inquart, the Austrian lawyer who collaborated with Hitler to annex Austria into the Third Reich, was appointed rijkscommissar of the occupation administration on 29 May. The Germans used the rural telephone system and the network of roads, railways, and canals to deploy troops throughout the countryside. Dutch civilians had few weapons and had made no preparations for underground or resistance activities.

Initially the people cooperated with the Nazi government to keep casualties low. But as freedom for Jewish Dutch citizens and protesters was curtailed, demonstrations and strikes by the population escalated, resulting in arrests, deportations to camps, and executions. A new patriotic Dutch political party, Nederlandse Unie, was formed to counter the Dutch Nazi Party (Nationaal-Socialistische Beweging or NSB). The Unie pledged loyalty to the House of Orange, called for economic cooperation in Europe, and enrolled 800,000 members by February 1941, only to be banned the following December.[1]

The first mass protest was organized in Amsterdam on 25 February 1941, with nearly half of the city participating. Two hundred strikers were arrested and locked into the Scheveningen prison which became known as the Orange Hotel because it housed so many members of the resistance. On 13 March eighteen men, who would become a symbol of the resistance, were executed by firing squad on the dunes near Scheveningen.

Freedom of expression was strictly controlled by the Nazi government. Professors were fired, students were banned from campuses unless they signed a loyalty oath, and newspapers expressing views loyal to the legitimate Dutch government were forced into underground operations. All artists faced censorship in November 1941 when the Kultuurkamer was organized for anyone who intended to perform, exhibit, or publish in the Netherlands. A letter of protest was signed by

2,700 artists, and many of the perceived instigators of the petition were arrested and deported to concentration camps. During the following year, the Dutch underground press began to flourish as the need grew for an alternative to literature produced by collaborating writers whose works were boycotted by readers and sellers alike.

This essay will survey several of the major clandestine presses which published literature in the Netherlands between 1940 and 1945. It will be apparent that the Dutch were certainly not "devoid of all literary taste," a Nazi accusation attributing to them a culture based on inferior "Anglo-Saxon society novels and books by Jewish authors."[2] A total of nearly a thousand items published during the occupation testifies to a strong Dutch literary tradition which participated in the international community of authors and readers.

The earliest works produced by clandestine publishers generally served to strengthen the spirit and morale of the Dutch people. Publishers chose poems that inspired patriotism by recalling the history of past sufferings and the triumph of freedom, or that eulogized contemporary martyrs. The first publication by a clandestine press in December 1940 was a broadside poem by Dutch writer Martinus Nijhoff, *Het jaar 1572* [The year 1572], which praised the Dutch seamen, or *watergeuzen* (sea beggars) who fought against Spain. Nijhoff had written it in 1934 for Princess Juliana's twenty-fifth birthday, and as the members of the resistance were also called *geuzen,* it seemed especially appropriate as a symbol of encouragement.

Reformed minister F. R. A. Henkels, teacher Adriana Buning, and chemist A. J. Zuithoff formed De Blauwe Schuit (The Blue Ship) to produce the Nijhoff poem as a New Year's gift to comfort their friends. The name recalled Erasmus's *Ship of Fools* and Hieronymous Bosch's painting *De blau scute,* as well as Jacob van Oostvoorne's poem which invited membership in the "blue boat guild."[3] Henkels liked the idea of creating a secret guild to counter those organized by the Chamber of Culture, one for daredevils and fools.[4] He asked Groningen artist and printer Hendrik Nicolaas Werkman to produce the poem with Jan Wieger's illustration as a single-sheet *rijmprent* (broadside).

Werkman lived and worked in isolation, rarely leaving Groningen, but his artistic vision soared. It was rooted in the dada movement, and he employed collage techniques similar to those independently developed by Kurt Schwitters, or to the photomontages created by Raoul Hausmann and John Heartfield. Werkman perfected a method which transformed printing into an art form. He designed and printed *druksels* (illustrated "printlets"), which demanded multiple impressions to achieve a complex graphic design in several colors; sometimes a single print was run under the press or stamped with an inked stencil, hand roller, or object up to fifty times. This complicated process severely limited the editions of a work and made each piece almost unique. Some *druksels* were independent of text, others complemented the printed word, and all were atypical of contemporary Dutch illustration and typography. All the publications of the Blue Ship except the first were designed, illustrated, and printed by Werkman.

In 1941 Werkman printed Martin Luther's *Sendbrief an die Christen im Nieder-land* [Epistle to the Christians in the Low Country]. Although Luther's letter was written in 1523 after the burning of the first Protestant martyrs in Brussels, its parallels to the events of 1941 were so apt that many believed the attribution to Luther was fabricated.[5] That same year Werkman produced the *Turkenkalender* for 1942, which linked contemporary oppression with the 1455 invasion of the Turks. This anthology of poetry and short prose compositions in calendar format was compiled by Buning from works written during the wars against Spain, including the proclamation of independence by the united Dutch provinces in 1581. Werkman had hoped a 1943 calendar could contain peace texts by contemporary authors.

The Blue Ship also published works that documented the current struggle against oppression. In April 1942 Werkman printed Martinus Nijhoff's memorial verses to the soldiers killed in action in May 1940, *Bij het graf van den Neder-landschen onbekenden soldaat gevallen in de meidagen 1940* [At the grave of the Dutch unknown warrior, killed in action in May 1940]. Werkman's red and blue illustration to the Easter 1943 edition of *Soldat libre* written by nineteenth-century French poet Louis Bouilhet represents the freedom fighter and was distributed to friends who could not celebrate the feast at home.

Werkman also spent much of his time working on a portfolio of prints based on Martin Buber's Hasidic tales; they were so labor-intensive that he needed two and a half years to print only twenty copies of the entire set of *Chassidische Legen-den*. In 1942 he also printed a few psalms which Buber had translated from Hebrew into German.

Werkman printed for other clandestine publishers besides De Blauwe Schuit after the Kultuurkamer crackdown at the end of 1942. In Agris Occupatis [In the Occupied Country] was an imprint used by A. Th. Mooij, W. H. Nagel, and W. H. Overbeek. Nagel and Overbeek were both active in the resistance after their law careers were disrupted by the war. They published two series of books, *Volière-reeks* [Birdcage series] and *Portefeuille,* books small enough to fit into a wallet. Werkman printed a dozen volumes for them in 1944. The first two Birdcage editions consisted of poems about the sea by Nagel himself, *Een suite van de Zee* [A suite of the sea], and poems by Gerrit Achterberg, *Meisje* [Girl]. Werkman printed the slim wallet books without illustration, first *De leerling Alexander* [The pupil Alexander] by Eddy Evenhuis, then Martin Kloostra's poems, *Gedichten, 1930–1944.* In 1944 he published another Nagel poem as well, *Terzinen van de Mei* [Poem of May in triple rhyme], but for publisher De Bezige Bij (The Busy Bee).

De Bezige Bij was founded in January 1943 by Geertjan Lubberhuizen and Charles Eugene Bloomestein, law students at Utrecht University who refused to sign a loyalty oath for the occupation regime. Both had become active in the resistance, and Lubberhuizen earned the nickname "Busy Bee" because of his efforts to hide Jewish children with Christian families. To raise money for this effort, the two men decided to publish Jan Campert's poem, *De achttien dooden* [The eighteen dead] as a *rijmprent* to be passed out in return for donations to the

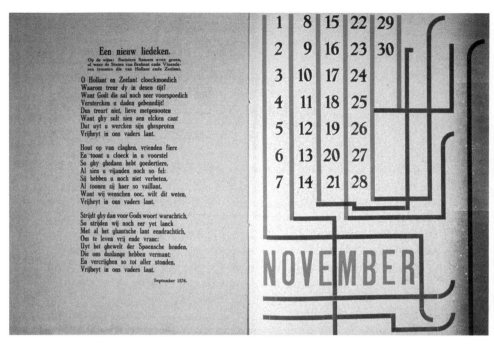

Fig. 1. Pages from the Blue Ship's *Turkenkalender 1942*.

Fig. 2. Colophon from *Turkenkalender 1942*, with Blue Ship logo.

Jewish children's fund. Stenciled copies of the poem memorializing the executions after the Amsterdam strike in 1941 had already been circulating. Within a week 500 copies illustrated by Fedde Weidema under the pseudonym Coen van Hart and printed on a mixed batch of papers were sold out. By the end of the war 15,000 copies from six editions had circulated throughout Holland. Utrecht printer Jan Hendriks was employed for fourteen months printing almost nothing but editions of *De achttien dooden*.[6] People taped the poem to the inside of their kitchen cupboards so it could be read daily yet remain hidden from random searches and Nazi sympathizers. Surplus proceeds from the sale of the broadside were donated to the resistance.

The Busy Bee's second publication in 1943 was *De zeven hoofdzonden* [The seven deadly sins] by Jewish poet Maurits Mok who lost his family during the occupation. Mok used the name Hector Mantinga, and Willem Jacob Rozendaal illustrated the edition as G. J. Machin. This was the first in the Busy Bee *Quousque tandem* [How much longer?] series, to which authors and artists donated their work to help generate funds for the victims of persecution.

The Busy Bee's close ties to the resistance are reflected in other editions as well. The sonnets in *Het wachtwoord* [The watchword] published in 1944 were written while the author Pieter Geyl was interned in Buchenwald; some were smuggled into Holland on tiny scraps of paper hidden in an empty tube of toothpaste; others had been memorized by a repatriated prisoner.[7] *WA-man* published in 1944 by De Doezende Dar, the Dizzy Drone variation of the Busy Bee imprint used only for this book, concerns a Dutchman who joins the Nazi-controlled police. Theun de Vries wrote the story under the pseudonym M. Swaertreger, and Fedde Weidema illustrated the antihero on the frontispiece and the Dizzy Drone logo. According to the colophon, proceeds of this book were only loaned to the resistance, not donated as usual, so that after liberation the publishers would have some working capital. Fokke Tamminga of The Hague printed 1,150 copies "in secret."

By 1945 the Busy Bee decided to acquire its own press. Sjoerd Leiker's *Drie getuigen* was selected as the first new Dutch novel to be published by a clandestine press, with its proceeds to be used for the purchase of the Busy Bee's own printing press. P. Den Boer of Utrecht printed 525 copies. In 1946 it was translated into English and published in the United States as *Three Witnesses*. The first production on the new press was the medieval Dutch lament, *Egidius, waar bestu bleven?* [Egidius, where have you gone?]. A woodcut illustrating the small group of mourners was designed by Tjomme de Vries, printed from a block, and colored by hand.

Some of the publications of the Busy Bee reveal the response of the Dutch spirit to the occupation. The press published poems and stories which sang of the struggle for dignity and freedom against oppression. *Het vrij Nederlandsch liedboek* [The free Netherlands songbook] appeared on 1 April 1944. This edition of resistance poems was compiled by Jan Hendrik de Groot, Han Hoekstra, and Halbo Christiaan Kool and illustrated by Fedde Weidema. It includes an entire

DE ACHTTIEN DOODEN

Een cel is maar twee meter lang
en nauw twee meter breed,
wel kleiner nog is het stuk grond
dat ik nu nog niet weet,
maar waar ik naamloos rusten zal,
mijn makkers bovendien,
wij waren achttien in getal,
geen zal den avond zien.

O, lieflijkheid van lucht en land
van Hollands vrije kust -
eens door den vijand overmand,
vond ik geen uur meer rust;
wat kan een man, oprecht en trouw,
nog doen in zulk een tijd?
Hij kust zijn kind, hij kust zijn vrouw
en strijdt den ijdelen strijd.

Ik wist de taak die ik begon
een taak van moeiten zwaar,
maar 't hart dat het niet laten kon
schuwt nimmer het gevaar;
het weet hoe eenmaal in dit land
de vrijheid werd geëerd,
voordat een vloekb're schennershand
het anders heeft begeerd.

voordat die eeden breekt en bralt
het misselijk stuk bestond
en Hollands landen binnenvalt
en brandschat zijnen grond,
voordat die aanspraak maakt op eer
en zulk germaansch gerief,
een land dwong onder zijn beheer
en plunderde als een dief

De rattenvanger van Berlijn
pijpt nu zijn melodie;
zoowaar als ik straks dood zal zijn,
de liefste niet meer zie
en niet meer breken zal het brood
noch slapen mag met haar -
verwerp al wat hij biedt of bood,
de sluwe vogelaar.

Gedenkt, die deze woorden leest,
mijn makkers in den nood,
en die hen nastaan 't allermeest
in hunnen rampspoed groot,
zooals ook wij hebben gedacht
aan eigen land en volk,
er komt een dag na elke nacht,
voorbij trekt ied're wolk.

Ik zie hoe 't eerste morgenlicht
door 't hooge venster draalt -
mijn God, maak mij het sterven licht,
en zoo ik heb gefaald,
gelijk een elk wel falen kan,
schenk mij dan Uw genâ,
opdat ik heenga als een man
als ik voor de loopen sta.

JAN CAMPERT †

Fig. 3. *De achttien dooden* [The eighteen dead], first publication of the Busy Bee.

Fig. 4. *De zeven hoofdzonden* [The seven deadly sins], second publication of the Busy Bee.

Fig. 5. Frontispiece and title page of *WA-man* with Dizzy Drone imprint.

section of poems in honor of Jan Campert and others who died in concentration camps. Jan Hendriks printed 1,900 copies whose proceeds were donated to the resistance. Fedde Schurer's broadside, *Lied op den verrader Frans Vergonet* [Song of the traitor Frans Vergonet] with music by Margit Leiker relates the murder of a collaborator and informer. An illustration by Chris Zeylstra depicts the traitor's watery grave; Hennie Berkemeier constructed the notes in the score from swastikas and fashioned each treble cleff as a saluting Gestapo officer.

Busy Bee books were not always solemn, traditional, or dignified. A clever series of caricatures satirizes the occupying forces and depicts the stresses of deprivation in an ironic if not humorous vein. Some of these publications enlisted the creativity of artist Karel Leendert Links. The *Vrijheidskalendar 1945* [Freedom calendar 1945], with a photograph of Queen Wilhelmina on the cover, includes illustrations of soldiers searching for *onderduikers* who had "dived" into hiding yet produced clandestine newspapers and operated short-wave transmitters. *Moffenspiegel: Een boekje over Adolf de eerste—en de laatste—en zijn trawanten* [Huns' mirror: a booklet on Adolf the First—and the Last—and his henchmen] lampoons the occupiers, especially Hitler, Himmler, and the SS. Gestapo buffoons fail to find the underground press, and even the device of the Busy Bee is drawn as a caricature. *Het is niet waar . . . Dat hebben we niet gewild!* [It isn't true . . . We never wanted this!] contains twelve postcard cartoons about life during the occupation, depicting scenes such as the confiscation of clothing and bicycles, sumptuous German feasts amid Dutch rationing, and the haunting subjects of devastation and death camps. The colophon offers the proceeds of the 5,000 copies for the "benefit of the victims of today's tyranny."

Besides publishing new Dutch literature, the Busy Bee provided its readers with translations of foreign works which linked their bleak environment with the international literary community. How John Steinbeck's novel *The Moon Is Down*, published in New York in 1942, came to Holland at all remains a mystery. But by 1944 actor Ferdinand Sterneberg had translated it for the Busy Bee edition, *De vliegenvanger* [The flytrap], under the pseudonym Tjebbo Hemelrijk. Sariochmin Salim, using the name Michael Gurney, illustrated the volume which was printed by Fokke Tamminga in an edition of 1,025 copies. The Bezet Nederland (Occupied Netherlands) imprint designated all proceeds for a special relief fund for unemployed actors who had refused to join the Kultuurkamer.[8]

The Busy Bee also managed to obtain the resistance novel of a French author known throughout the war only as "Vercors." Jean Bruller's story about occupied France, *Le silence de la mer* [The silence of the sea], was first published clandestinely in France in 1941. It became an underground international best seller, published in Denmark, Switzerland, and England as well as the Netherlands. The English version was entitled *Put Out the Light*. The Busy Bee published *De stilte der zee* in 1944 as a joint venture with the Amsterdam printing house De Algemeene Vrije Illegale Drukkerij, known as DAVID. Disguised as the Marten Toonder Film Studio, the printers Dick van Veen and Jo Pellicaan printed anything from armbands to newspapers for the resistance.[9] Together with the Busy Bee, they printed the series known as "DAVID-reeks." Near the familiar bee, they added their own device, a rotary press pierced by arrows above the phrase *Door drucken aenvallen* (press to attack). According to the colophon, proceeds from the 325 copies were donated to the families of printer G. J. Willemse and typographer P. Zuiderdorp who were arrested and executed by the Gestapo for printing a previous edition of the book, all of which was confiscated. Other foreign authors published by De Bezige Bij include Edgar Allan Poe, John Gay, André Gide, and Guy de Maupassant.

In order to continue providing his patrons with literature, especially by foreign authors, Amsterdam bookseller A. A. Balkema became his own publisher. He issued fine books either under his own imprint, AAB, or with writer Adriaan Morriën and printer F. E. A. Batten, as the Black Sheep, styled Het Zwarte Schaap for Dutch authors and La Bête Noire for French ones. Dick Ellfers designed a sheep's head for both imprints. Some of the texts published between 1943 and 1944 include Menno ter Braak's travel essays *Reinaert op reis* [Reynard's travels], originally published in Dutch newspapers before he committed suicide after the German invasion rather than risk arrest; a short story by Adriaan Morriën, *Afscheid van Lida* [Farewell to Lida]; and Rudie van Lier's *Praehistorie* poems. French selections included a novel by Paul Léautaud, *Le petit ami,* and reprints of *Réflexions* by Frédérick Paulhan and *Trois jeunes filles* by Stendhal. Various printers were employed for these editions.

Together with printer Jan van Krimpen and Dutch professor W. G. Hellinga, Balkema also published as Vijf Ponden Pers, or Five Pound Press, named for the 2.5 kg. maximum paper weight allowed for unofficial printing. Despite this Nazi edict and an increasing paper shortage, Balkema arranged for the production of over fifty fine editions, including international authors in his booklist such as Rimbaud, Mallarmé, Degas, Baudelaire, Emily Dickinson, Franz Kafka, Omar Khayyam, Pushkin, Emily Brontë, Dante Gabriel Rossetti, and William Blake. He printed only enough copies for a subscribers' list of fifty to fifty-five names.

Balkema also published occupation texts like *Zehn kleine Meckerlein* [Ten little grumblers], which was probably smuggled out of Oranienburg concentration camp and printed by Balkema himself in an edition of forty copies. The short satirical rhymes about the grumblers who vanish one by one share each page with large block numbers decreasing from 10 to 1 and stencils of objects including a wine bottle, a piano, prison bars, and a spade. The stamping technique used is reminiscent of Werkman's but more crudely, or perhaps hastily, executed.[10]

Most clandestine publishers approved of their printers' use of classic Dutch fonts, like Hollandsch Mediaeval, Erasmus, Lutetia, Egmont, and Romulus. Not only were these considered patriotic, but they had the advantage of being common and so popular that the Nazi type registry lists could not trace clandestine works to a particular printer.[11] Of course, as the occupation progressed and type was confiscated and melted down, printers used whatever was available.

Painter and graphic designer Willem Jacob Henri Berend Sandberg, curator of the Stedelijk Museum in Amsterdam since 1937, helped hide the museum's

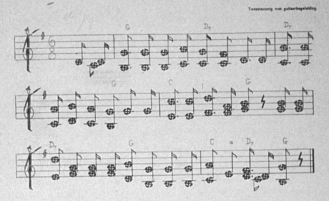

Fig. 6. Fedde Schurer's broadside, *Lied op den verrader Frans Vergonet* [Song of the traitor Frans Vergonet].

Fig. 7. Pages from the Busy Bee's *Vrijheidskalendar 1945* [Freedom calendar 1945].

collections from the Nazis and encouraged contemporary Dutch artists, including Werkman. He and printer Frans Duwaer also used their skills to manufacture
false identity papers, ration cards, and passport stamps so realistic the German
authorities couldn't detect the difference, even in the "rampant lion" watermark.
He considered this accomplishment the highest compliment his typographic
work could receive.[12] After he helped destroy the population registry in Amsterdam in March 1943, making it harder for the Nazis to identify Jews and members
of the resistance, Sandberg was forced into hiding. From December 1943 to April
1945 he traveled across Holland under the name Henri Willem van den Bosch,
planning a series of nineteen booklets with innovative typographic interpretations of quotations and reflections on his experiences. A. A. Balkema published
the first of these, printed by Sandberg's friend Duwaer in 1944 in an edition of
200, as *Lectura sub aqua: Experimenta typographica* [Underwater readings: typographical experiments]. It begins:

> Part of the Dutch nation lives under water / another part just manages to keep its
> head above water / a very small part is for the time being still living with its head in
> the clouds . . . the last group reads little but writes a lot . . . the first group reads

Fig. 8. Pages from *Zehn kleine Meckerlein* [Ten little grumblers], illustrating A. A. Balkema's stamping technique.

a lot / writes too perhaps / but is seldom printed / one of them has copied . . . something of what he's read . . . and for every fragment he's sought a shape / he found a printer.[13]

Sandberg selected texts by Dutch poets or foreign authors such as Nietzsche and Ortega y Gasset and quoted them in Dutch, French, or English using some twenty different typefaces. He enhanced texts by incorporating typographic objects, varying typefaces, and adding color for effect. In so doing he intentionally conveyed significance through the design itself, for example a text about fish forms a visual mold. Duwaer set type for another volume but was arrested and executed in 1944 before it could be printed. Vijf Ponden Pers issued it after the war, but only three more of his typographical experiments have been published since, the last in 1968.[14]

Alexander Alphonse Marius Stols, born into a Maastricht printing family, was perhaps the most secretive publisher of the occupation. Besides his own imprint from The Hague, he published fictitious imprints, both Dutch and foreign, which led a false trail across the Netherlands to Denmark, France, and England. None were published before 1943, yet some bore dates as early as 1927. He issued

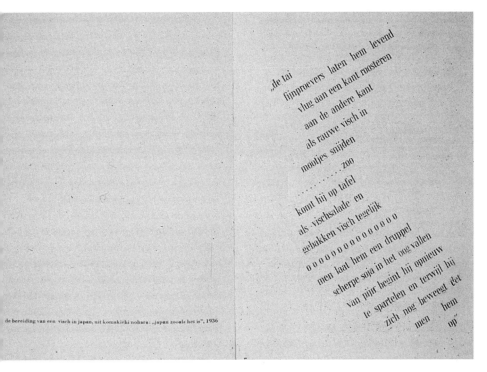

de bereiding van een visch in japan, uit komakichi nohara : „japan zooals het is", 1936

Fig. 9. Typographic design from Willem Sandberg's *Lectura sub aqua* [Lectures under the water].

a series of six letters written to him by Rainer Maria Rilke in 1926 as if they were published in 1927, not in 1943. *Perpetual Treason,* poems by Robert van Eyck, purports to be printed in 1939 by the Somerset Press in Sidcot, England. *Les Poésies de A. O. Barnabooth; Dévotions particulières; Poésies diverses* by Valéry Larbaud was certainly not published in Copenhagen by "Pour les amis danois de Maxime Claremoris" in 1941. Both were published by Stols in 1944. He also used the French imprint of Pierre Mangart, Rosières, Picardie, for *Hommage à Marivaux* by Jean Giraudoux, *Conseils aux jeunes littérateurs* by Baudelaire, and a reprint of a French translation of Oscar Wilde's *Ballad of Reading Gaol (Ballade de la Geôle de Reading).* Stols kept his secrets through the occupation. Even a French friend was struck by the unusual similarity of Mangart's French imprints to Stols's own publications but considered them genuine.[15] When he published multiple editions of the same book, Roland Holst's *Helena's inkeer* [Helen's return] in 1944 and 1945, he still created separate imprints; Gerard Leeu of Gouda and Gerard Leempt of 's-Hertogenbosch were really fifteenth-century printers of incunabula, not modern publishers.

Instead of just omitting their names, Stols invented pseudonyms for his various printers. Even when The Hague printer Fokke Tamminga became his partner in publishing Halewyn Pers imprints, Tamminga was disguised as Dirk Voskens. They published Elisabeth van Maasdijk's poems *Bloedkoralen* [Red coral] in 1944 and Anthonie Donker's resistance poems *In Holland staat ein huis* [In Holland there's a house] in 1945.

Fokke Tamminga, mentioned throughout this survey, was one of the most determined and successful clandestine printers. Although his printing business was officially closed by the Germans, he nevertheless printed underground newspapers and clandestine books behind shuttered windows. He distributed newspapers without charge but earned his living from finely printed books. Besides contracting with various clandestine publishers, he formed the Mansarde Pers, or Attic Press, with Bert Bakker and C. A. B. Bantzinger. They printed selections by Dutch poets, often with illustrations by Bantzinger. In 1944, as the Allies began to advance into Belgium and the southern parts of the Netherlands, they changed their imprint to Final Stage Press in the hope that liberation was not far away. Under this imprint they published a selection of Jan Engelman's poems, *Hart en lied* [Heart and song], and an essay on painting by art historian Abraham Hammacher, *Het leben bloeit op de ruines* [Life blooms within the ruins], with reproductions of paintings by Charley Toorop and Henk Chabot and decorative initials by Bantzinger.

By the beginning of 1945 the number of Dutch citizens living in hiding exceeded 300,000; they included the Dutch army, members of the resistance, many from the intellectual and artistic community, railway employees who had participated in the September 1944 national strike, those avoiding deportation to work camps in Germany, and Jews who had escaped detection.[16] Faced with the Allied advance, the Germans flooded the countryside by destroying dykes, sabotaged railway lines, confiscated possessions for their own use or shipment to Germany, and blocked food distribution into the northwestern coastal areas which resulted in 18,000 deaths from starvation during the winter of 1944–45.[17]

But publishers and printers provided their secret patrons with words of hope. As traditional paper became unavailable, printers used brown wrapping paper, pages torn from household account books, and anything else they could find. Presses were dismantled and reassembled on other sites to avoid detection; type corrections were never made if raids were imminent. As thread and staples became scarce, publishers printed *rijmprents* or issued pamphlets in simple folded sheafs. Colophons testified not only to typefaces and paper quality but to the lack of electricity, heat, and even food as rations sank to one pound of bread and two pounds of potatoes per week.

Werkman almost ceased printing after the middle of 1944 because half of his type had been confiscated, electricity was cut off, and the lack of heat congealed his ink. He finished a few paintings and cut firewood and took long walks to keep warm. In March 1945 Henkels, who had been forced into hiding, managed a visit to Groningen to see Werkman, but on 13 March both were arrested by the security police. On 10 April 1945, Werkman and nine other prisoners were exe-

IN MEMORIAM

Felix P. Abrahamson, Verleger	Joh. M. Duinker, Drucker	A. J. van Leeuwen, Drucker	J. E. W. H. Somer, Drucker
A. F. Adler, Drucker	F. Duwaer, Drucker-Verleger	M. Lindenbaum, Drucker	Melis Stoke, Schriftsteller
D. Allegro, Drucker	M. van Dijk, Drucker	D. v. d. List Sr., Drucker	B. H. van Straaten, Drucker
Lex Althoff, Schriftsteller	Henk Eikeboom, Schriftsteller	Gebrüder Loewenberg, Drucker	C. J. Terwee, Buchhändler
W. J. C. Arondéus, Schriftsteller	P. F. v. d. Ende, Drucker	J. Marcus, Drucker	J. W. Timmer, Buchhändler
S. J. P. Bakker, Drucker	Leo Frijda, Schriftsteller	H. Marsman, Schriftsteller	A. E. van der Veer, Drucker
B. Barend, Drucker	P. Gans, Drucker	J. H. A. Mathot, Drucker	J. A. van der Veer, Drucker
B. de Beaufort, Schriftsteller	W. F. Gerrese, Drucker	P. v. d. Meulen Jr., Drucker	G. Vergeer, Drucker
Ir. H. Belinfante, Drucker	W. J. Gertenbach, Drucker	H. Mok, Drucker	J. Vergeer, Drucker
D. J. Beumer, Drucker	W. Genze, Drucker	E. Th. Mooihroek, Drucker	R. Verseveldt, Drucker
A. van Bienen, Drucker	J. de Groot, Drucker	J. C. Morks, Buchhändler	A. Vlieger, Buchhändler
Andr. Blitz, Verleger	H. Habraken, Drucker	J. F. Otten, Schriftsteller	W. v. d. Voet, Buchhändler
M. Bolk, Drucker	H. Halberstadt, Schriftsteller	E. Overeem, Drucker	A. de Vries, Drucker
J. Boom, Drucker	H. Handgraaf, Drucker	J. W. Pel, Drucker	H. P. de Vries, Buchhändler
H. A. v. d. Boom, Drucker	F. Heinekamp, Drucker	Charles Edgar du Perron, Schriftsteller	A. D. de Vroom, Buchhändler
Emile van der Borch, Schriftsteller	H. P. Heinen, Drucker	C. Pieron, Buchhändler	H. J. G. Waanders, Drucker
J. Bos, Drucker	Jacob Hiegentlich, Schriftsteller	L. Pimontel, Drucker	K. G. Walter, Buchhändler
Menno ter Braak, Schriftsteller	Etty Hillesum, Schriftstellerin	S. Pinkhof, Schriftsteller	H. Wegeling, Drucker
L. Bramson, Drucker	A. J. Honing, Drucker	Em. Querido, Verleger	A. G. v. d. Wel, Drucker
Walter Brandligt, Schriftsteller	C. Hoogeboom, Drucker	Jan Remeo, Schriftsteller	D. Werkman, Buchhändler
Titus Brandsma, Schriftsteller	Hoogendoorn Sr., Drucker	J. F. van Royen, Drucker	H. N. Werkman, Drucker
W. Brinkman, Buchhändler	S. Hijman Jzn, Verleger	A. H. F. de Ridder, Drucker	G. J. Willemse, Drucker
Johan Brouwer, Schriftsteller	William Jakma, Buchhändler	C. Riezchos, Drucker	A. v. d. Woude, Drucker
Tom de Bruin, Schriftsteller	A. M. de Jong, Schriftsteller	C. J. C. Rooda, Drucker	P. B. J. Yzerman, Drucker
Fr. de Bruyn, Drucker	P. H. de Jong, Drucker	Gebrüder Schelvis (Didot), Drucker	S. Zante, Drucker
L. v. d. Burght, Buchhändler	Gebrüder Kessner, Drucker	J. J. Schmidt, Drucker	J. B. van Zomeren, Drucker
Jan Th. Campert, Schriftsteller	L. Kerkmeester, Drucker	Gert Schreiner, Schriftsteller	P. Zuyderdorp, Drucker
J.H.la Chapelle-van Straaten, Buchhändlerin	Dr. J.H. van Klooster, Verlegerin	Jaap Sickenga, Schriftsteller	Ant. Zwiers, Buchhändler
Hendrik Cramer, Schriftsteller	G. H. Laverman, Drucker	M. J. Simons, Drucker	
A. A. van Deutekom, Buchhändler	H. van der Leek, Schriftsteller	Adolf Snijders, Schriftsteller	

IM FREIHEITSKAMPF GEFALLEN

Fig. 10. Memorial tribute to the authors, illustrators, printers, publishers, and booksellers who died during the occupation (from *Drucker gegen Unterdrücker, Unterirdische Druckertätigkeit in Holland wahrend der deutschen Besetzung,* 1946).

cuted in the woods near Bakkeveen. All of Werkman's work which had been confiscated upon his arrest as "cultural bolshevism" and "surrealistic trash" was destroyed during the fighting that liberated Groningen three days later.[18] The Dutch had a special place in their hearts for the printers and publishers who lost their lives. In 1945 Amsterdam established annual prizes in memory of two exceptional printers who had died during the war, Hendrik Nicolaas Werkman and Frans Duwaer. Werkman himself was posthumously awarded one for his *Turkenkalendar,* and Jan van Krimpen received the first Duwaer prize. An exhibition mounted by the Stedelijk Museum in June 1945 displayed many of the books and *rijmprents* clandestinely printed in the Netherlands during the occupation. *Het vrije boek in onvrije tijd* [The free book in an unfree time] prompted the publication of an extensive bibliography with the same title. In his foreword Prof. H. De la Fontaine Verwey writes:

One can say that literature was one of the forces that awakened the people and drove them to resist. Not in a direct sense; only a small portion of the books listed here could be called seditious and directly tied to the resistance. . . . However, never before has literature been so defiant, so national and so topical as during the years of the resistance; the power of poetry as human expression was seldom so strongly felt as in these years.[19]

The Dutch were especially isolated during the war, cut off from the rest of free Europe by occupied Belgium and France, Germany itself, the heavily guarded coastal areas, and the sea. Few escaped; hundreds of thousands lived in precarious hiding places by the end of the war. The literature that was published provided them with a secret voice which rose beyond whispers in cellars and attic rooms and denounced persecution and oppression, spoke of trial and heroism, sang of strength and courage in the face of tyranny, and shouted of freedom to come.

NOTES

1. Gerhard Hirschfeld, *Nazi Rule and Dutch Collaboration: The Netherlands under German Occupation, 1940–1945,* trans. Louise Willmot (Oxford, New York, Hamburg: Berg, 1988), 66–72.

2. *Mein Kampf in Holland; or, Straight from the Horse's Mouth* (New York: Netherlands Information Bureau, 1943), translation quoting from *Volk en Vaderland,* March 1942, 22.

3. Alston W. Purvis, *Dutch Graphic Design, 1918–1945* (New York: Van Nostrand Reinhold, 1992), 189; Dick Dooijes, *Hendrik Werkman,* trans. Roy Edwards (Amsterdam: Meulenhoff, 1970), 15.

4. Dooijes, *Hendrik Werkman,* 15.

5. A. E. C. Simoni, comp., *Publish and Be Free* (The Hague: Nijhoff, 1975; for the British Library, London), 124; hereafter cited as *PBF.*

6. Harry Stone, *Writing in the Shadow: Resistance Publications in Occupied Europe* (London and Portland, Ore: Cass, 1996), 148.

7. *PBF,* 70.

8. Ibid., 187.

9. Ibid., 239.

10. *Zehn kleine Meckerlein* (Amsterdam: Balkema, 1943). The final verse places all the grumblers in Oranienburg concentration camp: "Ein kleines Meckerlein/liesz dies Gedichten sehn/Da kam er nach Oranienburg/Da waren's wider zehn."

11. Kees Broos and Paul Hefting, *Dutch Graphic Design: A Century* (Cambridge: MIT Press, 1993), 135, 181.

12. Willem Jacob Henri Berend Sandberg, *Experimenta typographica, 1943–1968* (Nijmegen: Thieme, 1969), 8.

13. Ibid., 13.

14. Purvis, *Dutch Graphic Design,* 187.

15. *PBF,* 263.

16. Henri A. van der Zee, *The Hunger Winter: Occupied Holland, 1944–1945* (London: Norman & Hobhouse, 1982).

17. Ibid., 305.

18. *H. N. Werkman,* comp. Fridolin Müller, introduction by Peter F. Althaus, and bio-

graphical sketch by Jan Martinet; text in German, French, and English (Teufen: Niggli, 1967), 102.

19. H. de la Fontaine Verwey, foreward to *Het vrije boek in onvrije tijd*, ed. Dirk de Jong (Leiden: Sijthoff, 1958), 2–3; quoted in translation in Purvis, *Dutch Graphic Design*, 179.

BIBLIOGRAPHY

Primary Sources, 1940–1945, Arranged by Publisher

All of the following clandestine editions except *Het jaar 1572* can be found in the Charles Deering McCormick Library of Special Collections, Northwestern University, Evanston, Illinois.

DE BLAUWE SCHUIT: F. R. A. HENKELS, ADRIANA BUNING, A. J. ZUITHOFF; H. N. WERKMAN, PRINTER

Bouilhet, L. H. *Soldat libre.* [Heerenveen:] De Blauwe Schuit, 1943. 75 copies printed and illustrated by Werkman.
Buber, Martin. *Chassidische Legenden.* Facsimile ed. of Werkman's original of 1942/43. Haarlem: J. H. Henkes Grafische Bedrijven, 1967.
Luther, Martin. *Sendbrief an die Christen im Niederland.* [Heerenveen:] De Blauwe Schuit, 1941. 90 copies printed and illustrated by Werkman.
Nijhoff, Martinus. *Het jaar 1572.* [Heerenveen: De Blauwe Schuit,] 1940. Illustrated by Jan Wiegers. 100 copies printed by Werkman.
———. *Bij het graf van den Nederlandschen onbekenden soldaat gevallen in de meidagen 1940.* [Heerenveen:] De Blauwe Schuit, 1942. 150 copies printed and illustrated by Werkman.
Turkenkalendar 1942. [Heerenveen:] De Blauwe Schuit, 1941. 120 copies printed and illustrated by Werkman.

IN AGRIS OCCUPATIS: A TH. MOOIJ, W. H. NAGEL, W. H. OVERBEEK; H. N. WERKMAN, PRINTER

Achterberg, Gerrit. *Meisje.* [Groningen:] In Agris Occupatis, 1944. Volière-reeks, no. 2. 110 copies printed and illustrated by Werkman.
Evenhuis, Eddy. *De leerling Alexander.* [Groningen:] In Agris Occupatis, 1944. Portefeuille, no. 1. 200 copies printed by Werkman.
Leopold, Martin [Martin Kloostra]. *Gedichten 1930–1944.* [Groningen:] In Agris Occupatis, 1944. Portefeuille, no. 2. 200 copies printed by Werkman.
W. H. Nagel. *Een suite van de zee.* [Groningen:] In Agris Occupatis, 1944. Volière-reeks, no. 1. 75 copies printed and illustrated by Werkman.

DE BEZIGE BIJ: GEERTJAN LUBBERHUIZEN, CHARLES EUGENE BLOOMESTEIN; ALSO INCLUDES THE SERIES *QUOUSQUE TANDEM;* VARIOUS PRINTERS

Campert, Jan. *De achttien dooden.* [Utrecht:] De Bezige Bij, 1943. Illustrated by Fedde Weidema [Coen van Hart]. Printed by Jan Hendriks; 15,000 copies total in all six editions printed during the occupation.

Egidius, waar bestu bleven? [Utrecht:] De Bezige Bij, 1945. Illustrated by Tjomme de Vries. 125 copies printed by De Bezige Bij on its own press.

Geyl, Pieter [A. v. d. Merwe]. *Het wachtwoord.* [Utrecht:] De Bezige Bij, 1944. "Quousque tandem," no. 8. 500 copies printed by J. van Boekhoven, Utrecht.

Leiker, Sjoerd [Meeno van Haarsma]. *Drie getuigen.* [Utrecht:] De Bezige Bij, 1944. "Quousque tandem," no. 10. 525 copies printed by P. den Boer, Utrecht.

Links, Karel Leendert. *Het is niet waar . . . Dat hebben we niet gewild!* [Utrecht:] De Bezige Bij, 1945. Set of illustrated postcards printed in an edition of 5,000 copies by H. de Koningh, The Hague.

———. *Moffenspiegel: Een boekje over Adolf de eerste—en de laatste—en zijn trawanten.* [Utrecht:] De Bezige Bij, 1944. 2,000 copies printed by H. de Koningh, The Hague.

———. *Vrijheidskalender 1945.* [Utrecht: De Bezige Bij], 1944. 800 copies printed by H. de Koningh, The Hague.

Mok, Maurits [Hector Mantinga]. *De zeven hoofdzonden.* [Utrecht:] De Bezige Bij, [1943.] Illustrations by Willem Jacob Rozendaal [G. J. Machin]. "Quousque tandem," no. 1. 525 copies printed by Utrechtse Typografen Associatie, Utrecht.

Nagel, W. H. *Terzinen van de Mei.* [Utrecht:] De Bezige Bij, 1944. 200 copies printed and illustrated by H. N. Werkman, Groningen.

Schurer, Fedde. *Lied op den verrader Frans Vergonet.* [Utrecht:] De Bezige Bij, 1944. Music by Margit Leiker, illustrated by Chris Zeylstra, special notation designed by Hennie Berkemeier. 525 copies printed by De Bezige Bij on its own press.

Steinbeck, John. *De vliegenvanger.* [Utrecht: De Bezige Bij] In bezet Nederland, 1944. Translation of *The Moon Is Down* by Ferdinand Sterneberg [Tjebbo Hemelrijk] and illustrated by Sariochmin Salim [Michael Gurney]. 1,025 copies printed by Fokke Tamminga, The Hague.

Vercors [Jean Bruller]. *De stilte der zee.* [Utrecht:] De Bezige Bij with DAVID, De Algemeene Vrije Illegale Drukkerij, 1944. Translated by A. V. Marken [A. Wijkmark]. 325 copies printed by DAVID, Amsterdam.

Vries, Theun de [M. Swaertreger]. *WA-man.* Utrecht: De Doezende Dar, 1944. Illustrated by Fedde Weidema. 1,150 copies printed by Fokke Tamminga, The Hague.

Het vrij Nederlandsch liedboek. In bezet Nederland: [De Bezige Bij], 1 Apr. 1944. Compiled by Jan Hendrik de Groot, Han Hoekstra, and Halbo Christiaan Kool; illustrated by Fedde Weidema. 1,900 copies printed by Jan Hendriks, Utrecht.

A.A.B.: A. A. BALKEMA, AMSTERDAM; HET ZWARTE SCHAPP, LA BÊTE NOIRE: A. A. BALKEMA, ADRIAAN MORRIËN, F. E. A. BATTEN; ALSO INCLUDES SERIES, VIJF PONDEN PERS: A. A. BALKEMA, JAN VAN KRIMPEN, W. G. HELLINGA; VARIOUS PRINTERS

Braak, Menno ter. *Reinaert op reis: Essays.* [Amsterdam:] Het Zwarte Schaap, [1944.] Introduction by Adriaan Morriën and portrait of the author by Emile Brumsteede. 110 copies printed by De Globe, Amsterdam.

Léautaud, Paul. *Le Petit Ami; roman.* [Amsterdam:] La Bête Noire, [1943.] Portrait illustration by Marie Laurencin. 100 copies printed by Meijer's Boek- en Handelsdrukkerij, Wormerveer.

Lier, Rudolf van. *Praehistorie; verzamelde gedichten.* [Amsterdam:] Het Zwarte Schaap, [1944.] 100 copies printed by De Globe, Amsterdam.

Morriën, Adriaan. *Afscheid van Lida.* [Amsterdam:] Het Zwarte Schaap, [1944.] 100 copies printed by Meijer's Boek- en Handelsdrukkerij, Wormerveer.

Paulhan, Frédéric. *Réflexions.* [Amsterdam:] La Bête Noire, [1944.] 100 copies printed by Drukkerij Ed. IJdo, Leiden.

Sandberg, Willem Jacob Henri Berend [Servus Fidei]. *Lectura sub aqua: Experimenta typografica.* [Amsterdam: A. A. Balkema,] 1943. Series Vijf Ponden Pers. 200 copies printed by J. F. Duwaer & Zonen, Amsterdam.

[Stendhal]. *Trois jeunes filles de Stendhal.* [Amsterdam:] La Bête Noire, [1944.] 100 copies printed by Drukkerij Ed. IJdo, Leiden.

Zehn kleine Meckerlein. [Amsterdam: A. A. Balkema, 1943.] 40 copies printed.

A. A. M. STOLS, THE HAGUE: PUBLISHED UNDER VARIOUS FALSE IMPRINTS; VARIOUS PRINTERS. JOINED WITH THE HAGUE PRINTER FOKKE TAMMINGA TO PUBLISH *HALEWYN PERS* IMPRINTS.

Baudelaire, Charles. *Conseils aux jeunes Littérateurs.* Rosières, Picardie: Pierre Mangart, 1944. 150 copies printed by Drukkerij Trio, The Hague.

Donker, Anthonie [Siem de Maat]. *In Holland staat een huis.* [The Hague:] Halewyn Pers, 1945. 750 copies printed by Fokke Tamminga [Dirk Voskens].

Eyck, Robert van. *Perpetual Treason.* Sidcot: Somerset Press, 1939 [1944.] 210 copies printed by Boosten & Stols, Maastricht.

Giraudoux, Jean. *Hommage à Marivaux.* Rosières, Picardie: P. Mangart, 1943. 50 copies printed by Drukkerij Trio, The Hague.

Larbaud, Valéry. *Les Poésies de A. O. Barnabooth; Dévotions Particulières; Poésies Diverses.* Copenhagen: Pour les amis danois de Maxime Claremoris, 1941 [1944.] 99 copies printed by Boosten & Stols, Maastricht.

Maasdijk, Elisabeth van. *Bloedkoralen; gedichten.* [The Hague:] Halewyn Pers, 1944. 525 copies printed by Fokke Tamminga, [Dirk Voskens].

Roland Holst, Adrianus. *Helena's inkeer.* 3rd ed. Gouda: Gerard Leeu, 1944. 1,000 copies printed by Van Marken's Drukkerij, Delft.

———. *Helena's inkeer.* 4th ed. 's-Hertogenbosch: G. van Leempt, 1945. 950 copies printed by Van Marken's Drukkerij, Delft.

Wilde, Oscar. *Ballade de la Geôle de Reading.* Trans. Henry-D. Davray. Rosières, Picardie: Pierre Mangart, 1944. 150 copies printed by Drukerij Trio, The Hague.

MANSARDE PERS, FINAL STAGE PRESS: FOKKE TAMMINGA, BERT BAKKER, C. A. B. BANTZINGER, THE HAGUE; FOKKE TAMMINGA, PRINTER.

Engelman, Jan. *Hart en lied.* [The Hague:] Final Stage Press, 1944. Illustrated by C. A. B. Bantzinger. 400 copies printed by Fokke Tamminga, The Hague.

Hammacher, Abraham. *Het leven bloeit op de ruines.* [The Hague:] Final Stage Press, 1944. Decorative initials by C. A. B. Bantzinger. Reproductions of paintings by Charley Toorop and Henk Chabot. 400 copies printed by Fokke Tamminga, The Hague.

General Bibliography

Broos, Kees, and Hefting, Paul. *Dutch Graphic Design: A Century.* Cambridge: MIT Press, 1993.

Clandestine drukken op letterkundig gebied tijdens de Duitse bezetting in Nederland gedrukt. Catalogus samengest. door E. W. Theissen; inl. van H. de la Fontaine Verwey. Amsterdam: Universiteitsbibliotheek van Amsterdam, 1967.

Dooijes, Dick. *Hendrik Werkman.* Trans. Roy Edwards. Amsterdam: Meulenhoff, 1970.

Drucker gegen Unterdrucker: Unterirdische Druckertatigkeit in Holland wahrend der deutschen Besetzung. Bern: Im Auftrage der Press-Abteilung der Kgl. Niederländischen Gesamtschaft, 1946.

Duke, A. C., and Tamse, C. A., eds. *Too Mighty to Be Free: Censorship and the Press in Britain and the Netherlands.* Zutphen: De Walburg Pers, 1987.

Foot, M. R. D., ed. *Holland at War against Hitler: Anglo-Dutch Relations, 1940–1945.* Foreword by HRH Prince Bernhard. London: Cass, 1990.

's-Gravesande, G. H. *Onze letterkunde in bezettingstijd.* 's-Gravenhage: Dijkhoffz, 1945.

Haestrup, Jorgen. *European Resistance Movements, 1939–1945: A Complete History.* Westport, Conn., and London: Meckler, 1981.

Hirschfeld, Gerhard. *Nazi Rule and Dutch Collaboration: The Netherlands under German Occupation, 1940–1945.* Trans. Louise Willmot. Oxford, New York, Hamburg: Berg, 1988.

Jong, Dirk de, ed. *Het vrije boek in onvrije tijd: bibliografie van illegale en clandestiene bellettrie.* Foreword by H. de la Fontaine Verwey and Gerrit Kamphuis. Leiden: Sijthoff, 1958.

Jong, L. de, and Stoppelman, Joseph W. F. *The Lion Rampant: The Story of Holland's Resistance to the Nazis.* New York: Querido, 1943.

Jong, Louis de. *The Netherlands and Nazi Germany.* Foreword by Simon Schama. Cambridge: Harvard University Press, 1990.

Mein Kampf in Holland; or, Straight from the Horse's Mouth. New York: Netherlands Information Bureau, 1943.

Purvis, Alston W. *Dutch Graphic Design, 1918–1945.* New York: Van Nostrand Reinhold, 1992.

Sandberg, W. J. H. B. *Experimenta typographica, 1943–1968.* Nijmegen: Thieme, 1969.

[Sandberg, Willem Jacob Henri Berend]. *Sandberg: een documentaire = a documentary.* Comp. Ad. Petersen and Pieter Brattinga. Amsterdam: Kosmos, 1975.

Simoni, Anna E. C., comp. *Publish and Be Free: A Catalogue of Clandestine Books in the Netherlands, 1940–1945, in the British Library.* The Hague: Nijhoff, 1975.

Stein, Andre. *Quiet Heroes: True Stories of the Rescue of Jews by Christians in Nazi-Occupied Holland.* Toronto: Lester & Orpen Dennys, 1988.

Stone, Harry. *Writing in the Shadow: Resistance Publications in Occupied Europe.* London and Portland, Ore.: Cass, 1996.

Het vrije boek in onvrije tijd: Tentoonstelling van letterkunde, die in Nederland gedurende de bezetting in het verborgene is gedrukt en verspreid. Amsterdam: Stedelijk Museum, 1945.

[Werkman, Hendrik Nicolaas], *Hot Printing: Catalogue of the "Druksel" Prints and Interim Catalogues of General Printed Matter, Lithographs, Etchings, Woodcuts, Typewriter Compositions, and Paintings.* Ed. Jan Martinet; introduction by W. Sandberg; English translation by James Brockway. Amsterdam: H. N. Werkman Foundation in cooperation with the Stedelijk Museum, 1963.

———. *Werkman.* New York: Museum Books, [1949?].

———. *Hendrik Nicolaas Werkman.* Baden-Baden: Staatliche Kunsthalle, 1962.

————. *H. N. Werkman.* Comp. Fridolin Müller; introduction by Peter F. Althaus; biographical sketch by Jan Martinet; English translation by Mary Lou Mettler, French by Madeleine Joho. Teufen: Niggli, 1967.

Woodruff, John H. *Relations between the Netherlands Government-in-Exile and Occupied Holland during World War II.* Boston: Boston University Press, 1964.

Zee, Henri A. van der. *The Hunger Winter: Occupied Holland, 1944–1945.* London: Norman & Hobhouse, 1982.

VII • READING AND WRITING DURING THE HOLOCAUST AS DESCRIBED IN *YISKER* BOOKS

Rosemary Horowitz

THROUGHOUT World War II, in the ghettos, in the camps, on the Aryan side, in the woods, and in hiding, Jews were keeping diaries, chronicling events, composing poems, running illegal presses, publishing newspapers, writing letters, keeping records, among other activities. Remarkably, these were occurring even in the midst of Nazi-occupied Europe. Later, using these source materials written during the war, along with materials written before and afterward, hundreds of immigrant associations, known as *landsmanshaftn,* prepared *yisker* (memorial) books to commemorate their respective hometowns.

These hundreds of books constitute an interesting, but relatively unknown, collection of Holocaust literature. Their primary readers and writers were *landslayt,* people from the same Eastern European town, who survived the Holocaust and used their affiliation in the immigrant associations to collectively compile a book about their birthplace. In general, each book is a compilation of historical essays, lists, memoirs, biographies, chronologies, poems, letters, newspaper articles, photographs, drawings, maps, and other items. Although their stylistic and editorial features vary, the books tend to be organized along similar thematic and chronological lines, covering the town and its people before, during, and after the Holocaust. As a set, the books contain much information about prewar Eastern European Jewish life. To date, most scholars have studied the contents of the books (e.g., Dobroszycki 1984; Glicksman 1976; Kugelmass & Boyarin 1983). Some have looked at the manner in which the books were written (e.g., Hoffman 1983, 1991; Kugelmass & Boyarin 1989) or the role of the books in *landsmanshaftn* activities (e.g., Kliger 1990). In an earlier work, I examined the books for information about literacy and cultural transmission after the Holocaust (Horowitz 1998). That work suggested the books could also yield information about reading and writing during the Holocaust.

This essay presents findings from a sampling of selected books in order to illustrate the types of reading and writing activities that took place during the Holocaust. I argue that in addition to augmenting what is already known about the Holocaust, the books reflect an ongoing interpretation of the Holocaust by the survivors themselves.

Although *yisker* books are not traditional source documents, nonetheless the material contained in them, despite its fragmentary nature, provides a compelling picture of the need of people in crisis to chronicle their situation. Moreover, it is clear from this picture that a shift in the way people write about the Holocaust and wrestle with the nature of evil is taking place within the survivor community.

Augmenting the Body of Knowledge about the Holocaust

Chief among the documents written during the Holocaust are the diaries. Besides the works of diarists such as Mary Berg, Anne Frank, Chaim Kaplan, Abraham Lewin, Etty Hillesum, and Emanuel Ringelblum, there are scores of others whose diaries are less well known and many more whose works appear only in their town's *yisker* book. *Der Bialystoker Yisker Bukh* yields an example. In that book, several excerpts from Pejsach Kaplan's ghetto diaries appear as a Yiddish article, "Dos lebn un gerangl in geto." Portions also appear in English under the title "Pejsach Kaplan's Ghetto Diary." Kaplan was a prominent journalist for a daily newspaper in Bialystok before the war and a ghetto archivist in Bialystok during it. Although he did not survive the war, his diary did. It was found in the ruins of the ghetto. From what remained, the editor of the Bialystoker *yisker* book picked several passages of the diary to include in the book. Editors of other *yisker* books, for instance *Antopol (Antepolie) Seyfer Yisker, Sefer Drohiczn, Sefer Staszow,* and *Sefer Zikaron Le-kehilat Rozan,* also used selections from the wartime diaries of *landslayt*.

Besides appearing separately, portions from diaries are inserted into other material, as illustrated by *Antopol (Antepolie) Seyfer Yisker.* In that book Professor Czerniak, an Antoloper doctor and partisan who survived the war, includes in his article portions from the diary he kept in the Antopoler ghetto and in the woods after he fled the ghetto. In the Yiddish section of the book, there are two more articles that contain selections from his diary. There are also English translations of these diary excerpts, appearing under the heading "War Years in Antopol (1939–1944): Notes from a Diary." But there is no indication of how he kept the diary with him, the extent of the diary, or what happened to it after his liberation.

Finally, although relatively uncommon, a *yisker* book may contain the complete text of a diary. *Khurban Sharkoystseyney, Dunilavitsch, Postov, Globok, Droyie, un Kazan* stands out as an example. It contains a 178-page diary written by two brothers who survived the Holocaust. They begin:

> First of all, this work was written after fleeing from Gluboke at the time of the great slaughter on the 19th of the month of Av in 1943, at the time of our wandering— wandering in various forests, fields, swamps, etc., where we had to hide from the Germans and their local helpers. And there where we wrote on one side of the page of the happenings, we were not able to write on the second side, meaning that we were constantly forced to change our "dwelling place," migrating from one mire to another, from one forest to another. (Suskovich 1956, 1)

This, the first entry in the diary, is addressed to "a reader," who is told that the diary was written in the woods after the brothers fled from the Gluboke ghetto. Moreover, they note the conditions under which they kept the diary. Because the diary ends with the liberation of the brothers, it is not clear if the work was published elsewhere or what happened to the original.

In addition to containing material from diaries, *yisker* books make references to them. This may be the case if the diary did not survive the war. Examples are found in *Shidlovtser Yizker Bukh* and in its English version, *Szydlowiec Memorial Book*. Mordechai Strigler writes about himself:

> Among the various concentration camps in Nazi-occupied Poland and Germany, this writer lived for 15 months in the "Hasag" factory at Skarzyski-Kamienne near Radom. Here he wrote a lot in secret and collected any and all material that could later be used for writing a precise history of this vale of tears. Unfortunately, all these materials were lost. (Kagan 1989, 241–42)

Although in this article Strigler described the conditions of the camp, he provided no details about his diary other than this passing remark.

Overall, although *yisker* books contain only fragments from or references to diaries and diary writing, the number of fragments and references underscores the importance of that type of writing during the Holocaust. Although each fragment or reference is an incomplete account, the sum of these narratives adds to the weight of testimony about the Holocaust. Besides their sheer number, these fragments and references also give readers an internal perspective on daily life in Nazi-occupied Europe. Readers get a glimpse into the manner in which their *landslayt*, on the verge of annihilation, were recording observations in hopes that their words would survive even if the writers perished.

In addition to the diarists, there are the archivists. The chronicling of events under the direction of Ringelblum in the Warsaw ghetto, as well as under the archivists in Vilna, Lodz, Lublin, Bialystok, and elsewhere, resulted in a collection of information about the fate of Eastern European Jewry written in the immediacy of the moment. Because much of this material is unpublished, *yisker* books generally contain only fragments from and minimal references to ghetto archives. In some cases, editors preparing a book from a city that had an archive selected portions of it for their books. *Pinkes Varshe*, one of the books dedicated to Warsaw, yields an example. By 1955, when *Pinkes Varshe* was printed, two parts of the Warsaw ghetto archive had been unearthed, and some of its contents had been published. Having access to these documents, the editors of the Warsaw *yisker* book included four excerpts from the archives for a total of forty-seven pages from the original work.

Additionally, because archivists also collected materials from refugees who came into the ghettos from outlying towns, *yisker* book editors who were preparing one town's book could use excerpts from an archive that was kept in another.

An example is found in *A Tale of One City,* the English-language *yisker* book dedicated to Piotrkow Trybunalski. It contains passages from Huberband's *Kiddush HaShem,* part of his work for the Warsaw ghetto archives. The editor of the Piotrkow Trybunalski *yisker* book introduces these passages as follows:

> Among the numerous pages that truthfully depict the events in various towns and villages, portraying Jewish people and their struggle for survival, we also find poignant episodes about life in war-torn Piotrkow Trybunalski. With pangs of nostalgia and tears in our eyes for the world dissipated in ashes, we present excerpts from the book, *Kiddush HaShem.* (Giladi 1991, 261)

Interestingly, *Piotrkow Trybunalski Ve Ha Seviva,* the Yiddish-Hebrew Piotrkow Trybunalski *yisker* book published in 1965, does not contain reference to *Kiddush HaShem,* as that first *yisker* book predates the English-language publication of Huberband's book.

Another example of the use of archival material is found in *Pinkas Nowy-Dwor.* According to the book's editor, Jews from Nowy-Dwor who sought refuge in Warsaw after the Germans bombed their town were interviewed by the ghetto archivists. These early accounts of the attack became part of the archives. The editor of *Pinkas Nowy-Dwor* reprinted an extract from the archives based on the accounts of the Nowy-Dwor refugees under the title "Di ershte eydes." This piece is an actual portion of the archive that was published by the Jewish Historical Institute in Poland after the war.

Besides including fragments from archives, *yisker* books refer to them. *Der Bialystoker Yisker Bukh* provides a case in point. Szymon Datner, the Bialystok historian who was commissioned to edit the book, wrote an article about Mordecai Tenenbaum-Tamarof and Hersz Mesik, the chroniclers of the Bialystok ghetto:

> Tamarof needed a safe place to hide the archive should the ghetto be liquidated. He felt that concealing the archive outside the ghetto in a secure place would ensure its ultimate retrieval. Two days before the first liquidation campaign in the Bialystok ghetto in February 1943, Tamarof made plans to transfer the archive outside the ghetto into the hands of Bronja Winicka, one of his contacts. (Shmulewitz 1982, 80)

The article contains no material from the archive; rather, it tells how the archive was established, hidden, and retrieved.

Given the fragmentary nature of the archival material in the books, it is clear that the writers and editors did not intend to give a complete account of the archives. Texts such as Fishman's *Embers Plucked from the Fire: The Rescue of Jewish Cultural Treasures in Vilna* and Web's *Documents of the Lodz Ghetto: An Inventory of the Nachman Zonabend Collection* can provide that level of documentation. But *yisker* books provide readers with a sample of the data collected under the precarious conditions in the ghetto and a glimpse of what it took to collect such data.

Readers may infer that these efforts went on even in the most hopeless times because the imperative to record was paramount. The ghetto chroniclers persevered in spite of the seeming impossibility of their task.

Sometimes in cooperation with the ghetto archivists and sometimes in opposition to them was the Judenrat, the Jewish council that carried out the directives of the Nazis. Like all Nazi administrative organizations, the Judenrat generated a great deal of paperwork, portions of which appear in *yisker* books. In the case of Bialystok, Mordecai Tenenbaum-Tamarof, one of the ghetto archivists, gave copies of the Judenrat archives to the Bialystok resistance organization. These eventually were retrieved and became available to the editor of *Der Bialystoker Yisker Bukh,* who reprinted a number of Judenrat orders such as Order No. 126 (Meldung numer 126), dated 15 October 1941:

> Loyt der farardung fun der deytsher mach, muzn ale mener fun geto, fun 18 biz 55 yor zeyn bashefikt mit arbet. Mir fadern oyf ale mener, az oysnam fun 18 biz 55 yor velche zeynen biz heynt nisht bashefikt, zey zoln morgn dem 16tn oktober, 6 azeyger in der fri, zich shteln in hoyf fun juden-rat. Mir varenen, az oyb men vet zich ophaltn fun meldn zich, kenen kumen zeyer shvere rezultatn, un di nit bashefiktke, vos veln zich nit tsushteln, veln bakumen harbe shtropn, biz evakuirt vern fun Bialystok. (Shmulewitz 1982, 159)

> [According to German decree, all men in the ghetto who are between 18 and 55 years old must be working. We demand that all those not currently working report to the Judenrat office tomorrow, October 16th, at 6:00 A.M. Be warned that if you do not show up, there will be harsh consequences. The unemployed who do not show up will receive severe punishment until they are evacuated from Bialystok.]

This announcement serves as an example of a wartime document for the modern reader.

Although relatively few Judenrat documents appear in *yisker* books, there are many references to them, including descriptions of lists, handbills, orders, and other publications. One from *Antopol (Antepolie) Seyfer Yiskor* illustrates.

> Then came a new decree: there would be two ghettos now, Ghetto A and Ghetto B. The one for skilled workers, useful Jews, the other for the useless. No one wished to be counted among the useless. The Judenrat, along with the Labor Office, had to make up lists. There began the bargaining for places on the useful list, which was believed to involve the difference between life and death. (Ayalon 1972, 88)

As this writer recalls in his memoirs, reading one's name on the wrong list meant death. Unfortunately, in reality, reading one's name on the right list was sometimes only a temporary reprieve. Readers of this account gain an insight into what it meant to see one's name on a death list. They also gain an insight into how a list could determine one's fate. The uncertainty of life in the ghetto is revealed as the writer describes the arbitrary nature of the lists and the presumption of safety. What appears in *yisker* books is a series of personal accounts detailing the effects of the Judenrat on specific individuals. Given that fuller accounts of Judenrat activities may be found in publications of *Vad Vashem*, Dobroszycki's *Chronicles of the Lodz Ghetto*, and elsewhere, the documents and references in *yisker* books are useful for giving readers an overview of the ways in which the Judenrat used print to control life in a particular ghetto. Linking all the personal narratives conveys a unified picture of the overall influence of the Judenrat on the populace.

Letter writing during the Holocaust was another extremely vital activity because the postal system allowed people in the ghettos, in hiding, and in the camps to send information, warnings, parcels, greetings, and requests. *Yisker* books contain portions of this type of correspondence. Examples are found in *Kamenets-Podolsk U-Sevivata* and its English translation *Kaminits-Podolsk: Excerpts from Kamenets-Podolsk U-Sevivata; a Memorial Book*. An author recalls a letter he wrote:

> On the verso of the piece of paper with the address of the German officer, I wrote in German, in Gothic script, a note as follows: "Dear Sir, as promised, I am sending you the man you requested, and he will do his job faithfully to your satisfaction. Respectfully yours." I signed it in an illegible hand and dated it. . . . Close to the border . . . I fell into the hands of two Germans. I showed them the letter I had forged, and they let me through the border. . . . In *Lyublinets*, the militia detained me, the letter in my hand notwithstanding and led me to the German command headquarters on the Polish-Hungarian border. They saw no reason to detain me, and an officer led me to the Hungarian border. (Rosen, Sharig, & Bernstein, 1990, 102)

Within the larger account of his wartime experience, this author provides the text of his note. His description shows readers how taking a chance by forging the letter, in this case, saved his life.

Because letter writing was such a crucial activity, numerous references to it appear in survivor accounts. *Gombin: Dos Lebn un Umkum fun a Yidish Shtetl in Poylin* illustrates:

> I knew that my sister, Rozia, was on the "Aryan" side, in the small town of Sierpien, where she lived as a Christian and I began writing to her. We had made up that she answer my letters on Chabor's address, the only person in the village who knew I was Jewish. Chabor thus became the intermediary between my sister and me. But soon it became apparent that the enterprise was fraught with danger. The letters, it appeared, instead of going directly to Chabor, arrived at the Town Hall, where the old Graboreck, father of the peasant with whom I was staying, became suspicious. . . . I wrote to my sister, instructing her to stop writing to me at Chabor's address and to send the letters directly to me, addressed to one of the old Poles. (Zicklin 1969, 60)

In this passage, the author recalls how he and his sister, he in hiding and she passing as a Christian, corresponded. He goes on to describe the benefits and risks of writing letters. From *Zvoliner Yizkor Bukh* comes another example.

> Eyn mol hot ich geshikt a briv durchn forshtier fun rodemer yudenrat vos flegt brengn di shpeypekler. In briv hot ich ongevunken az ich un hershl muzn vos gicher arum fun gehenum. Meyn foter hot farshtanen dem vant. (Kagan 1982, 270)

> [Once I sent a letter by a member of the Judenrat in Radom who used to transport packages. In the letter, I hinted that Hershel and I needed to get away from our hell. My father understood what I meant.]

This writer explains how he delivered a letter to his father by using a member of the Judenrat as a courier. He further explains that he coded his request in a way that his father would understand. This is another example of the way in which sending and receiving mail could potentially be lifesaving. By including descriptions of letters and letter writing, *yisker* book writers and editors point out the importance of the mail in relaying information and reveal some of the ways that people used letter writing as a survival strategy. Insofar as letter writing during the Holocaust is an underexplored topic, the variety of individual accounts of letter writing can form the basis of research into the functions of the postal system during the war.

The reading of literature also played a vital role during the Holocaust. As Roskies (1989) points out, songs and poems were used to transmit information publicly in the ghettos and camps. Literature served private functions too. *Yisker* books contain accounts of reading novels or poems. An instance is found in *Mezritsh: Zamlbukh.*

> I sat on my straw sack, from beneath which I had just pulled out the few books which I had managed to rescue from my library and hidden here from the wild eyes of our torturers. A bad end awaited anyone caught carrying anything printed, especially in Yiddish; for such a crime the sentence was a bullet in the head. The only possessions I still had were the following books: *The Psalm Jew* [by Sholem Asch]; *In Polish Woods* by Joseph Opatashu; a volume of Ansky's *Collected Works;* and the *Parables* of E. Shtaynberg. Looking into these books allowed me to forget my troubles for a while and remember a not too distant past. (Kugelmass & Boyarin 1983, 168)

In this passage, the author describes how he was able to save a few books and read them. His description of the punishment for reading gives insight into the dangers he faced for possessing any books. Albeit temporarily, some people were able to keep their personal possessions, including books, and gain comfort from them.

Literature was also written during the Holocaust, and works such as *Bearing the Unbearable: Yiddish and Polish Poetry in Ghettoes and Concentration Camps* and *Burnt Pearls: Ghetto Poems of Abraham Sutzkever* attest to the creativity of ghetto poets. To illustrate this, editors reprinted Holocaust poems in their *yisker* books. The editors of *Pinkas Nowy-Dwor,* for instance, reprinted two stanzas from Yitzhak Katzenelson's work, *Dos lid fun oysgehargetn yidishm folk.* In those stanzas, the poet does not mention *Nowy-Dwor* per se; rather, he commands all Jews to cry out about their destruction. Although there is no mention of where and when the poem was written, by including it in the *yisker* book the editors have created an intertextual link to the body of Holocaust literature. Additionally, since the role played by literature during the Holocaust has not been fully examined, the accounts in the books may yield insights into the functions of literature in the camps and ghettos.

Another important vehicle for distributing news during the Holocaust was the underground press. To a degree, *yisker* book writers and editors had access to actual documents, including appeals, reports, and letters, produced by the underground. *Der Bialystoker Yisker Bukh,* for example, reproduces a text of a call to arms to the ghetto population from the Bialystok resistance organization. Readers who want further information about the resistance movement may turn to a number of book-length accounts, such as Chaika Grossman's *Underground Army: Fighters of the Bialystok Ghetto.* But the accounts in the *yisker* book give readers an indication of the mood in the ghetto on the day before the uprising.

Descriptions of illegal publishing activities are also found in *yisker* books. The following passage about Joseph Kaplan, a resistance fighter and organizer from Kalish, found in that town's *yisker* book, is an illustration.

> He devoted all his efforts to the issue of newspapers, first for the Movement and afterwards as an underground press. Only in these papers was it possible to find military reports with expositions of war and political developments. It was extremely difficult to get the paper out of Warsaw, and he therefore decided to publish special issues for other towns. These took the form of three books, each 160–180 pages. They were given a special cover bearing in Polish the name: "Agricultural Calendar for 1942." They contained a selection of the Warsaw press, news from Eretz Israel and the smaller branches, and were distributed by special underground methods. (Lask 1968, 298)

The author stresses Kaplan's resourcefulness in publishing the magazine with its false cover. This description indicates the ways in which information was transmitted despite the dangers inherent in running an illegal press. It adds to documentation found in books such as Kowalski's *A Secret Press in Nazi Germany: The Story of a Jewish United Partisan Organization,* which describes the underground press in Vilna. From the site-specific narratives in the *yisker* books, differences and similarities in partisan activity emerge, adding details to the overall picture of resistance activity. Like the portraits of the partisans, the descriptions of the underground press portray *landslayt* in a heroic way. Analyzing these portraits and descriptions deepens current understanding about the nature of resistance to the Nazis.

Other clandestine activities, such as religious services and academic studies, also took place during the war. Thus, accounts of reading and writing for study and prayer are also found in *yisker* books. *Lask: Sefer Zikaron* provides an illustration.

> Among the Hungarian girls, who had been brought to Aushwiz, it was a pious girl who had a sidurel which was given to her by her father before leaving home. . . . When we were sure that the "Capos" and the "Shtubaves" were disappeared, or were sleeping, the girl brought out the sidurel and read for us with a special tone one of the chapters of the Psalms. . . . Such holy minutes gave us that sidurel, in the night hours, when we were lying on the shelfs, covered with a blanket of suffering, thinking about tomorrow with its new troubles. (Tzurnamal 1968, 113–14)

This author recalls how listening to passages from the Book of Psalms helped her to endure her incarceration in Auschwitz. Her account gives us an indication of the value that was placed on the book. Information from this memoir corroborates what is known about underground religious and educational practices, adding specific details to the general picture of life in the ghettos and camps. It personalizes the accounts and gives insights into the nature of passive resistance among the Jews.

Finally, the books contain reproductions of newsletters, manuscripts, announcements, permits, lists, and other items from the war. Editors and writers culled these items from published and unpublished materials. *Pinkes Varshe* offers an example. Included in 1951 article by Ber Mark is a photograph of several handwritten pages with the caption "Bleter fun D'r E. Ringelblum." It is not clear if these pages are from the Warsaw archives or from Ringelblum's personal diary; nonetheless, they show readers samples of Holocaust writing. Similarly, accompanying an article in *Seyfer Yisker Le Kehilat Luboml* is a photocopy of a fake identification card. And an article in *Antopol (Antepolie) Seyfer Yiskor* includes a reproduction of a permit that allowed the writer to travel out of the ghetto. Readers who want to complete sets of Holocaust documents may turn to Raul Hilberg's *Destruction of the European Jews*. But those who want to see actual items from *landslayt* may find them in their town's book; and for those readers who have no relics from home these documents serve as artifacts from their ancestral town. Furthermore, for those readers who are trying to understand the destruction of Eastern European Jewry without material evidence, *yisker* books themselves serve as a representation of a particular place.

Taken individually, the information in each *yisker* book adds to the overall knowledge of reading and writing during the Holocaust by presenting accounts from places less well known than Warsaw, Vilna, Lodz, and Bialystok. In this way, the books are useful for providing "local details on general phenomena" (Kugelmass & Boyarin 1989, 532). Indeed, the books may be the only sources of localized data from the hundreds of small towns and villages inhabited by Eastern European Jewry. Taken together, what emerges from the books is an amplification of what is known about reading and writing during the Holocaust.

In addition to this, the material in the books may be used for exploring themes related to Eastern European Jewry. The fragmentary nature of the documents and narratives in the books underscores the manner in which editors tried to balance concerns with history and memory. Whereas they wanted to meet professional standards in matters of grammar and printing, they did not want to compromise the personal narratives of the writers. In fact, valuing memory was consistent with the multiple functions of the *yisker* book. Unlike scholars who may be supported by academic or research institutions and who are held accountable to the standards of the academic community, the editors and writers of the *yisker* books were accountable to the *landsmanshaft* and to the related economic necessities and political alliances within their organization. Given these multiple influences, the books are useful for exploring themes related to Eastern European Jewry, a conclusion also reached by Kugelmass and Boyarin (1989). With respect to the theme of reading and writing during the Holocaust, it has been pointed out that the books may be useful for studying topics such as the uses of letter writing, the role of diary writing, the circulation of songs, or the role of the poets.

Finally, of theoretical interest is the way that the books juxtapose documents and narratives written during and after the Holocaust. The juxtaposition of this material suggests an ongoing interpretation of the Holocaust by the survivors themselves because it calls attention to the changing function of reading and writing about the Holocaust.

Reflecting an Ongoing Interpretation of the Holocaust

Influenced by an earlier YIVO mandate to document the life of Eastern European Jewry (Fishman 1996), ghetto archivists were collecting material during the war in order to record what was happening to the Jews of Eastern Europe. As long as they could, the archivists followed this mandate because they wanted to create a record that would be a testimony to the fate of Eastern European Jewry. They hoped the record would remain even if the people should perish. The diarists were guided by similar motivations. They were the witnesses and the chroniclers of events. In general, both archivists and diarists had two related purposes: to document the atrocities perpetrated in Nazi-occupied Europe and to testify about the destruction of Eastern European Jewry. These documentary and testamentary tasks had an immediacy that was related to the uncertain fate of the Jews in Eastern Europe. The extreme living conditions added to the sense of urgency. Besides the dual function of documentation and testimony, reading and writing were important for survival and communication. This was the case for the underground printers, letter writers, and poets, for instance.

After the war, when *landslayt* gathered to prepare their *yisker* books, the need to document, testify, communicate, and survive did not have the same immediacy. Instead, survivors enlisted writing in the service of postwar needs. They still wanted to testify about the destruction and document the atrocities, but they also wanted to memorialize the dead, commemorate their birthplace, record its history, tell the story of their own lives and the lives of ancestors, friends, relatives, and others who died in the Holocaust, as well as guard against future acts of anti-Semitism. Most survivors were young adults at the war's end, who had lost their youth when they were forced from their hometowns. Their writing suggests an eviction from paradise and with it the desire to idealize their towns. For these writers and editors, the books were a tangible representation of their hometowns, which they could give to their children. As time passed, it became clear that Israeli descendants of Holocaust survivors could read the Hebrew sections but not necessarily the Yiddish ones; American descendants of Holocaust survivors might be unable to read sections in either language. This situation prompted some *landsmanshaftn* and individuals in the United States to translate their books into English.

Thus the transmission of information about the war emerged as a major concern in the postwar era. Toward that end, the documentary, testamentary, communication, and survival functions were blended into an overarching one: the transmission of information about the life and death of Eastern European Jewry. Others (e.g., Wieviorka 1994) have also noticed this shift in Holocaust writing. We can see evidence for this shift in the commentary inserted in *yisker*-book articles by editors and writers. This commentary signals to readers that the Holocaust material is embedded in a post-Holocaust book. In some cases, editors assumed that readers would be unfamiliar with the events described in an article and explained the events by inserting a parenthetical note. In this way, a document from the Holocaust is set in its historical context. In other cases, writers merged past and present as they wrote their memoirs for *yisker* books.

The post-Holocaust perspective on Holocaust writing is evident in this note from *Der Bialystoker Yisker Bukh*.

> Der doziker oyfruf fun der yidisher kamps-organizatsye in bialystok iz aroysgeben gevorn dem 15tn oygust 1943, bes di natsishe ritschim hobn likvidirt di bialystoker geto. (Shmulewitz 1982, 205)

> [This call to arms from Jewish resistance organizations in Bialystock was issued on 15 August 1943, before the Nazis liquidated the Bialystock ghetto.]

Following this note from the editor, the text of the appeal to the ghetto populace is given. The comment serves to place the call to arms in its historical context by assigning a date to the document. In actuality, the appeal is not fully contextualized since readers still do not learn that this call to arms was made one day before the Bialystoker ghetto uprising. Neither the significance of the date of this source document nor the history of the uprising is clear. What is significant is that the editor decided to attach the note to the call to arms. In this way, his post-Holocaust comment becomes part of the Holocaust document.

Antopol (Antepolie) Seyfer Yiskor also contains an example of the manner in which *yisker* books merge past and present. In his article about the war, Professor Czerniak writes: "I leaf through the diary of my ghetto days and I come up with the following" (Ayalon 1972, 72). At this point, Czerniak inserts entries from his wartime diary into his text. Then he returns to writing his memoirs. This mingling of past and present, diary and memoir, calls attention to Czerniak's position as a writer using Holocaust material in a post-Holocaust text.

Yet another example of the intermingling of Holocaust and post-Holocaust writing is taken from *Pinkes Varshe*.

> Der document vos mir gich do, iz gefunen gevorn vi an anonimer ksav-yad in tsveytn teyl fun ringelblum arkhiv. Er iz tsum ershten mol farefentlecht gevorn an keyn shum shprachleche oder ortographie enderungen in "bleter far geshickte" fun "yidishn historishn institut" in polyn. Shpeter iz festgeshtelt gevorn az der mekhaber fun "khurbn varshe" iz der bakente yidishe shrayber yehoshue perle. Mir drukn dem document loyt undzer oysleyg. (Katz 1955, 1069)

> [The document given here was found as an anonymous text in the second part of the Ringelblum archive. Its first printing in the journal "Bleter far Geshickte" by the Jewish Historical Institute in Poland was without changes to words or spelling. Later it was discovered that the author of this piece, "Hurban Varshe" was the well-known Yiddish writer Yehoshue Perle. We are printing the document according to our spelling.]

This embedding of Holocaust documents within postwar texts suggests an ongoing interpretation of the Holocaust by the survivors themselves by pointing out a shift in reading and writing about the Holocaust. This may be understood as part of a larger historical shift. Friedlander (1993) has suggested that a group may interpret a major catastrophe by ritualizing or historicizing it. The former involves the manner in which a group interprets a catastrophe in mythological terms; the latter involves the ways in which the group interprets the catastrophe in historical terms. Friedlander posited that both types of interpretation of the Holocaust are occurring within the Jewish community as a means of understanding it. To interpret an event there must be a way to represent it. To Friedlander, no comprehensive representation of the Holocaust has emerged for American Jews as a whole. Part of the problem is the nature of the event itself. Questions about evil are unanswerable in general, and questions raised by the Holocaust are too unsettling to be resolved only fifty years after the defeat of the Nazis. For him, neither mythological nor historical terms are sufficient to encompass the tragedy of the Holocaust. Ultimately it may prove impossible to find an all-encompassing narrative of the Holocaust. The Holocaust may be too different to grasp in simplistic terms. Yet people have a need to understand it. In this light, *yisker* books are an attempt to find meaning in the tragedy. By blending Holocaust documents and post-Holocaust accounts into their memorial books, writers and editors contribute to the process of interpretation insofar as their narratives represent a partial understanding. This is necessary because the interpretation will always be incomplete.

Conclusion

Although *yisker* books include a number of documents from the war period, most of the information in the books was written later. In this way, the books corroborate what is already known about reading and writing during the Holocaust. By juxtaposing source material from the Holocaust period and later descriptions of reading and writing, the books reflect an ongoing interpretation of the Holocaust by the survivors themselves. Ultimately this will yield insights into the relation between history and memory.

BIBLIOGRAPHY

Ayalon, B. H., ed. 1972. *Antopol (Antepolie) Sefer Yiskor.* Tel Aviv: Antopol Societies in Israel and America.
Dobroszycki, L. 1984. *The Chronicles of the Lodz Ghetto.* New Haven: Yale University Press.
Erlich, E., ed. 1962. *Sefer Staszow.* Tel Aviv: Former Residents of Staszow in Israel . . . and the Diaspora.
Fishman, D. E. 1996. *Embers Plucked from the Fire: The Rescue of Jewish Cultural Treasures in Vilna.* New York: YIVO Institute for Jewish Research.
Friedlander, S. 1993. *Memory, History, and the Extermination of the Jews of Europe.* Bloomington and Indianapolis: Indiana University Press.
Funkenstein, A. 1993. *Perceptions of Jewish History.* Berkeley: University of California Press.
Giladi, B., ed. 1991. *A Tale of One City.* New York: Shengold.
Glicksman, W. M. 1976. *Jewish Social Welfare Institutions in Poland as Described in the Memorial (Yizkor) Books.* Philadelphia: M. E. Kalish Folkshul.
Halevy, B., ed. 1977. *Sefer Zikaron Le-Kehilat Rozan.* Tel Aviv: Rozhan Societies of Israel and the U.S.A.
Hoffman, M. 1983. "Memory and Memorial: An Investigation into the Making of the Zwolen Memorial Book." Master's thesis, Columbia University.
———. (1991). "Denkmol un Zikhron: An Oysforshung Funem Tsunoyfshtel fun Zvoliner Yisker Bukh." *YIVO Bleter* 1: 257–72.
Horowitz, R. 1998. *Literacy and Cultural Transmission in the Reading, Writing, and Rewriting of Jewish Memorial Books.* Bethesda, Md.: Austin & Winfield.

Kagan, B., ed. 1974. *Shidlovtser Yizkor-Bukh.* New York: Shidlowtzer Benevolent Association.

———, ed. 1974. *Seyfer Yisker Le Kehilat Luboml.* Tel Aviv: Luboml Landsmanshaft.

———, ed. 1982. *Zvoliner Yizkor-Bukh.* New York: New York Independent Zvoliner Benevolent Society.

———, ed. 1989. *Szydlowiec Memorial Book.* Trans. Max Rosenfeld. New York: Shidlowtzer Benevolent Association.

Katz, P., ed. 1955. *Pinkes Varshe.* Buenos Aires: Former Residents of Warsaw and Surroundings in Argentina.

Kliger, H. 1990. "In Support of Their Society: The Organizational Dynamics of Immigrant Life in the United States and Israel." In K. M. Olitsky, ed., *We Are Leaving Mother Russia: Chapters in the Russian-Jewish Experience* (33–54). Cincinnati: American Jewish Archives.

Kowalski, I. 1976. *A Secret Press in Nazi Germany: The Story of a Jewish United Partisan Organization.* New York: Shengold.

Kugelmass, J., and Boyarin, J., eds. and trans. 1983. *From a Ruined Garden: The Memorial Books of Polish Jewry.* New York: Schocken.

Kugelmass, J., and Boyarin, J. 1989. "*Yizker Bikher* and the Problem of Historical Veracity: An Anthropoligical Approach." In Y. Gutman, E. Mendelsohn, J. Reinharz, and C. Shmeruk, eds., *The Jews of Poland between the Two World Wars* (519–35). Hanover, N.H.: University Press of New England.

Lask, I. M. 1968. *The Kalish Book.* Tel Aviv: Societies of Former Residents of Kalish and the Vicinity in Israel and the U.S.A.

Malz, Y., and Lau, N., eds. 1965. *Piotrkow Trybunalski Ve Ha Seviva.* Tel Aviv: Former Residents of Piotrkow Trybunalski in Israel.

Rosen, A., Sharig, Ch., and Bernstein, Y., eds. 1965. *Kamenets-Podolsk U-Sevivata.* Tel Aviv: Association of Former Residents of Kamenets-Podolsk and Its Surroundings in Israel.

Rosen, A., Sharig, Ch., and Bernstein, Y., eds. (1990). *Kaminits-Podolsk: Excerpts from Kamenets-Podolsk U-Sevivata, a Memorial Book.* Trans. B. S. Sohn. Washington, D.C.

Roskies, D., ed. 1989. *The Literature of Destruction: Jewish Response to Catastrophe.* Philadelphia: Jewish Publication Society.

Shamri, A., and First, D., eds. 1965. *Pinkas Nowy-Dwor.* Tel Aviv: Organizations of Former Novy-Dvor Jews in Israel, the U.S., Canada, Argentina, Uruguay, and France.

Shmulewitz, I., ed. 1982. *Der Bialystoker Yisker Bukh.* New York: Bialystoker Center.

Shtokfish, D., ed. 1969. *Sefer Drohiczn.* Tel Aviv: Drohiczn Landsmanshaft.

Suskovich, S., ed. 1956. *Khurban Sharkoystseyney, Dunilavitsch, Postov, Globok, Droyie, un Kazan.* Buenos Aires: Landslayt Association of Sharkoystseyney, Dunilavitsch, Postov, Globok, and the Surrounding Areas in Argentina.

Tzurnamal, Z., ed. 1968. *Lask: Sefer Zikaron.* Tel Aviv: Association of Former Residents of Lask in Israel.

Web, M., ed. 1988. *The Documents of the Lodz Ghetto: An Inventory of the Nachman Zonabend Collection.* New York: YIVO Institute for Jewish Research.

Wein, A. 1979. "'Memorial Books' as a Source for Research into the History of Jewish Communities in Europe." *Yad Vashem Studies on the Eastern European Catastrophe and Resistance* 9: 255–72.

Weinryb, B. D. 1950. *Texts and Studies in the Communal History of Polish Jewry.* New York: Ha-Akademyah Ha-Amerikait Le-Madae Ha-Yahadut.

Wieviorka, A. 1994. "On Testimony." In G. H. Hartman, ed., *Holocaust Remembrance: The Shapes of Memory* (23–32). Oxford: Blackwell.

Young, J. 1982. *Writing and Rewriting the Holocaust.* Bloomington and Indianapolis: Indiana University Press.

Zicklin, J., ed. 1969. *Gombin: Dos Lebn un Umkum fun a Yidish Shtetl in Poylin.* New York: Gombin Society in America.

VIII • POLISH BOOKS IN EXILE: CULTURAL BOOTY ACROSS TWO CONTINENTS, THROUGH TWO WARS

Sem C. Sutter

INTRODUCTION

MANUSCRIPTS and books have always been fundamental transmitters of human culture, taking their place beside older visual and oral media in bearing the thoughts, discoveries, and aspirations of one generation to those that succeed it. Indeed, the permanence and portability of the word on clay, parchment, and paper have made it the most powerful cultural medium of all. As Horace wrote, "Littera scripta manet" ("The written word remains").

In normal times we may not appreciate the extent to which books are symbols of national identity as well. But when war, revolution, or other forms of unrest disrupt the otherwise orderly world of libraries, we can see concretely how very much books matter and to whom and why. The lengths to which conquerors go to seize or destroy books, the perils that conservators courageously face to safeguard them, the efforts of rival political factions to possess them in order to gain the legitimacy that they can confer: all illustrate the powerful symbolism of the written word.

During World War II a highly select group of priceless Polish books and manuscripts was successfully evacuated first from Poland and then from France, illustrating the extent to which they were national icons as well as cultural documents. Their rescue also calls attention to the story of the millions of books that remained behind in Europe where Nazi conquerors applied their full force to expunging Jewish culture while exterminating the Jewish people, to crushing the book heritage vital to the national identity of the Polish people whom they subjugated, and to seizing cultural treasures for their own institutions. As the war ended, the tale of the exiled books became entwined in the cold war and, quite improbably, in Quebec nationalism as well, offering further proofs of the potency of books as national cultural and political symbols. *Et sua fata habent libelli;* truly, "books too have their fates," and they can mirror the fortunes of nations and peoples.

THE TREASURES OF PELPLIN

On 1 August 1939, one month before German troops invaded the Polish Corridor, the librarian of the Diocesan Seminary of Pelplin, Poland, set out on a carefully planned mission to save its most precious holdings. Dr. Antoni Liedtke had good reason for worry. If war came, little Pelplin lay in the path of its destruction, whether Germany invaded Poland from West and East Prussia or provoked a Polish attack on nearby Danzig. The town of some 4,000 inhabitants was the site of a thirteenth-century cathedral and the diocesan seminary and library whose core collection came from a Cistercian monastery established in the 1274. By 1927 it contained some 30,000 volumes including a collection of manuscripts and 316 incunabula.[1]

Early in the summer the librarian had begun to help parish churches and institutions throughout the diocese protect their valuable artifacts, photographing and describing liturgical objects and finding places to hide them.[2] In the case of his own library, it wasn't difficult for Father Liedtke to decide what was most essential to preserve: a beautiful little vellum-bound psalter manuscript with illuminations of the early-sixteenth-century Czech school, and (dwarfing it in size and fame) Poland's only Gutenberg Bible in two massive volumes together weighing about forty pounds.

The seminary's Bible had a rich history. It had been in Poland since the fifteenth century. Among the forty-seven surviving copies of the Gutenberg Bible, the Pelplin copy was one of only nine in fifteenth-century bindings. A piece of overturned type had left an oblong mark in the lower margin of one page, apparently unique to this copy, enabling book historians to deduce the size and shape of Gutenberg's type.[3] During the 1920s well-publicized sales of three Bibles had spread a kind of worldwide Gutenberg fever. Philadelphia dealer Dr. A. S. W. Rosenbach sold Carl Pforzheimer of New York the earl of Carysfort's Gutenberg for $60,000 in 1923 and in 1926 bought the Melk Abbey copy from Austria for $106,000 on behalf of Mary Stillman Harkness who donated it to Yale. Later that year, with the British dealer E. P. Goldschmidt as intermediary, Rosenbach attempted to acquire the superb example on vellum from St. Paul's Abbey east of Klagenfurt, Austria, only to lose it to German collector and rare-book entrepreneur Dr. Otto H. F. Vollbehr who paid a dizzying $275,000 plus 10 percent for an export license. Vollbehr's copy came to the Library of Congress in 1930 as part of his 3,000-volume collection of incunabula purchased by act of Congress for $1,500,000.[4] In this speculative climate it is not surprising that in 1929 rumors spread that the Pelplin seminary might consider selling its Gutenberg. Foreign libraries, collectors, and rare-book dealers tendered offers reputedly as high as $100,000, but newspaper stories and publicity from Polish bibliophilic associations rallied public opinion against any sale.[5] Ten years later, on the eve of the war, its character as a national treasure remained strong. Having chosen the Bible and the little psalter, Father Liedtke made careful plans to convey them to the underground bank vault in Warsaw where the National Library had already deposited valuable manuscripts. He commissioned Gutkowski, a local saddler, to fashion a leather valise with snug compartments for each volume. On 1 August, when the case was ready, Liedtke packed it and then traveled by taxi and express train to Warsaw.[6] Nearly twenty years were to elapse before he held these volumes in his hands again.

A Nation's Pride

The National Library in Warsaw was a young institution, established in 1928. But circumstances of its founding, righting ancient wrongs at the hands of foreign invaders, made it the pride of the new nation of Poland. And its holdings, especially the precious manuscripts in the bank vault, were venerable bearers of Poland's linguistic and cultural heritage and symbols of its independence regained in the Treaty of Versailles. The earliest antecedent of the National Library was the Załuski Library, founded in 1747 as the country's first public library. But after the third and final partition of Poland among Russia, Prussia, and Austria in 1795, the Russians removed it to St. Petersburg to become a cornerstone of the Imperial Public Library.[7]

Through the century and a quarter that followed, as Polish nationalists longed for the rebirth of their independence, they cherished the idea of reestablishing a national library. Groups of Poles unsuccessfully demanded the return of the Załuski Library and other collections at the Congress of Vienna (1815). In the course of the nineteenth century, exiles founded cultural institutions and libraries abroad with the express hope of someday transferring them to Polish soil. In Paris the Bibliothèque Polonaise and the library of the École Polonaise de Batignolles assumed to some extent the character of national libraries in the scope and ambition of their collecting. In 1870 at Rapperswil Castle in Switzerland, a group of émigrés established a museum as well as a superb collection of books and manuscripts documenting nineteenth-century Polish history, including revolutionary movements and the great Polish emigration of 1830.

As soon as Poland regained its independence at the end of World War I, planning began for a new National Library. Established in 1928, it moved into a new building in 1930. Collections founded in exile arrived from Switzerland and France to become part of the new institution. And the treaty ending the Soviet-Polish war in 1921 provided that the Soviet Union restore cultural property confiscated by the tsars. Binational commissions of experts negotiated to determine which books, manuscripts, and artifacts would return to Poland. Beginning in 1923 the Soviets returned thousands of books and manuscripts to Warsaw where they became part of the new National Library and a source of national pride.[8]

Among the most significant manuscripts returned from the Soviet Union was the oldest extant collection of Polish prose, the *Holy Cross Sermons*, a fourteenth-century copy of thirteenth-century texts discovered in the binding of a Bible. The University of Warsaw Library had acquired the Bible from a monastery in 1819, only to lose it to Russian confiscation in 1833. In 1890 a young Polish philologist on a research visit to the Imperial Public Library in St. Petersburg discovered the ancient sermon fragments. Beyond their inherent iconic character, these medieval texts carried significant linguistic forms and literary content.[9]

In the repatriation process the Poles attached understandable importance to recovering the manuscripts of the oldest Latin chronicles of Polish history. The earliest among them was the so-called *Holy Cross Annal,* a twelfth-century manuscript covering the years 948–1136. It had formerly belonged to the same Benedictine monastery from which the binding fragments containing the *Holy Cross Sermons* had come.[10] Another chronicle, the popular and sometimes fanciful thirteenth-century *Kronika Polska* dated the Polish state from before the time of Christ. It asserted that Poles fought against Alexander the Great and claimed that Julius Caesar's brother had married a Polish princess. The Soviets returned a fourteenth-century vellum manuscript of this chronicle and a fifteenth-century copy on paper, bound for the Załuski Library at the expense of the king.[11]

Important illuminated manuscripts of Polish, French, and Italian origin were also among the treasures that the Leningrad library returned to Warsaw. Notable in this category was an elegantly illustrated late-fourteenth-century manuscript of the *Roman de la Rose.*[12] From the Library of the Friends of the Sciences in Warsaw the Russians had removed an important early manuscript of the *Revelations of Saint Birgitta,* copied and illuminated in Italy shortly after the saint's death in 1373 and bound in the fifteenth century in Poland.[13] And a typical example of the repatriated Załuski illuminated manuscripts was a missal prepared in Cracow about 1515. Giving prominence to saints venerated in Poland (Florian, Stanislaus, Wenceslas), it featured illustrations influenced by the style of Dürer.[14]

But this was just one aspect of the effort to build the National Library. It embarked on an aggressive program to purchase stellar materials, paying about $70,000 to an Austrian abbey for the *Florian Psalter,* an exceptional late-fourteenth-century illuminated manuscript from the royal court in Cracow containing the earliest Polish translation of the Psalms. It was richly decorated with biblical and astrological motifs.[15]

Another significant purchase was a collection of Frédéric Chopin's music. While some may disagree about the Polishness of his compositions, he is a strong national symbol and hero. So when Breitkopf and Härtel, his German publisher, deaccessioned his manuscripts from its archives in 1936, the Polish government was swift to buy them. The collection comprised forty-nine manuscript scores— some in Chopin's own hand, others with his corrections and annotations.[16] Among them were nineteen mazurkas, one third of the corpus of these dances that Chopin had established as an art form and, according to one musicologist, "invested . . . with his personal sense of being Polish."[17] And there were three examples of the polonaise, the processional dance that Chopin idealized as a kind of national epic: the two of Opus 40, said to depict the rise and fall of Poland, and his last extended work for solo piano, the *Polonaise-fantasie* (op. 61).

But in the midst of expanding and organizing its collections, the new library faced mounting concern for their safety. In the summer of 1939 librarians carefully packed the most valuable manuscripts in two trunks and placed them in the bank vault where the Pelplin books soon came to join them.[18]

THE LONG JOURNEY TO SAFETY

When war broke out with a ruthless speed and efficiency, *Blitzkrieg,* that few had anticipated, it became clear that this was sadly inadequate protection. Warsaw managed to hold out until 28 September before capitulating, but by then the Bible and manuscripts had crossed safely into Romania, as had the Polish government, its gold reserves, and tens of thousands of Poles. Two bank officers removed the books from the vault to take them to safety. They crossed the border into Romania the day before Soviet troops invaded Poland from the east. Ten days later they arrived in Paris, where the Polish government-in-exile was soon to form, and deposited the library treasures safely in the Bibliothèque Polonaise.[19]

Their fate was about to converge with that of rich artifacts on their way to France by another route. The Royal Castle on Cracow's Wawel Hill had been a residence of Polish kings since the end of the tenth century. In modern times it became a museum housing national collections. Its most prized historical object was Szczerbiec, the notched and richly embellished sword that had been part of every coronation ritual since the fourteenth century. The most outstanding art works were 136 Flemish tapestries commissioned by King Sigismund II in the sixteenth century. Removed to St. Petersburg in 1795, they returned to Poland in 1921 to grace the castle's walls.[20]

As the war began Dr. Stanisław Świerz-Zaleski, one of the castle's curators, and Józef Polkowski, a restoration engineer, accepted responsibility for evacuating these treasures. Traveling by camouflaged coal barge and then by truck, bus, and horse-drawn wagon, they escaped to Romania. They declined an offer to store the treasures in the royal palace in Bucharest and asked the papal nuncio for safekeeping in the Vatican. He refused, saying that the church could not protect objects that were not ecclesiastical. At this point it seemed wisest to take them to France, so late in October 1939 the curators and the Wawel treasures sailed aboard a grain freighter to Marseilles, going on to the Gobelin factory where conservators could repair water damage that five pieces had sustained en route.[21]

But safety in France was short-lived: as German forces swept across the Low Countries and into France in May 1940, the Polish government and the Polish treasures took to the road and the sea again. On 21 May when Amiens fell, the government-in-exile reached a decision to evacuate the Bible and manuscripts from Paris. Karol Estreicher, a Polish cultural official who went to the Bibliothèque Polonaise and found the National Library manuscripts and the Gutenberg carefully housed in its valise, overcame the reluctance of the library's director to surrender them.

The next day Estreicher moved the books to Angers, depositing them in the Polish Treasury Ministry. He immediately began organizing truck transport to move the tapestries from Aubusson. On 8 June the Polish government reached a

firm decision to evacuate all of the cultural treasures from France, advancing Estreicher 150,000 francs and authorizing him to make further decisions on his
own. On the fourteenth he left Angers in a small car with the books, driving all
night to reach Aubusson where he met the curators of the Wawel treasures. To
the tapestry and regalia packing lists he carefully added the Pelplin and Warsaw
library items and the group proceeded to Bordeaux with their precious charges.

In the Polish consul's office in Bordeaux, Estreicher met the captain of a small
Polish ship who agreed to transport the treasures and their caretakers to England.
As the ship prepared to sail on 18 June, a last-minute complication arose: despite
the fact that the first German attack on the port was only hours away, French
customs officials balked at allowing so many boxes to be loaded without a detailed
declaration of their contents. Fortunately, good French wines and some bank
notes streamlined the process. That night when the attack began, the little ship,
with important Polish civilian officials, soldiers, the poet Antoni Słonimski, and
the cream of Poland's cultural heritage aboard, was safely out to sea. The captain
made a risky, but ultimately wise, decision not to sail in convoy, calculating that
his craft was too small to attract U-boat attacks. The ship sailed in absolute silence at night and rescued sailors from two sunken French vessels before reaching
Falmouth on 22 June.[22]

For a few days these cultural refugees crowded the offices of the Polish embassy in London where the government-in-exile was busily resituating itself. The
ambassador, Count Edward Raczynski, recorded in his diary under date of
18 August:

> Besides human beings, we have had an invasion of cases and packages, including one
> remarkable consignment consisting of the famous Jagiellonian tapestries, the twelfth-
> century Coronation sword and other precious articles from the Wawel Castle in Cra-
> cow. They arrived at the Embassy one day in a lorry and were stowed in the larger
> part of the first-floor drawing-room. There were seventy items altogether, consisting
> either of tin boxes or of bundles sewn up in cloth. . . . Here [they] remained for a
> time, encroaching on the "living space" of officials and secretaries who continued to
> carry out their duties behind screens and a barrage of packages.[23]

But British museums and libraries were already evacuating their valuable holdings
to castles, country houses, and underground slate quarries,[24] so the Poles decided
to send their treasures to Canada. Accompanied by Świerz-Zaleski and Polkowski
from the Wawel, they crossed the North Atlantic in a convoy of merchant marine
ships, arriving safely in Halifax in July 1940.[25]

The treasures entered Canada free of customs inspection. When Poland asked
for space to unpack and store them, the Department of Public Works offered a
room in the Records Storage Building at Ottawa's Central Experimental Farm.
Canada explicitly accepted no responsibility for the treasures, which would remain under Polish government control. The Polish consul general in Ottawa
wrote gratefully to the Department of Public Works:

These objects include, besides some very rare books and documents, a certain number of tapestries of the former Kings of Poland. All of these objects have gone
through many evacuations, across a number of countries, and have not been unpacked for ten months. Two expert custodians have accompanied that precious
cargo, and are now in Ottawa. They are most anxious to unpack the contents of the
cases and bales in order to examine the articles and effect the necessary repairs. . . .
[Our] national treasures have been saved, and—thanks to the Canadian Government—placed, at last, in complete safety.[26]

PLUNDER AND DESTRUCTION

Meanwhile, events in Europe proved the wisdom of the librarians and curators
who had sent their charges so far away. The quiet sanctuary of the treasures in
Canada stands in stark contrast to the fate of the libraries and museums from
which they had come. Just as the war and occupation brought both chaos and
systematically planned death to the people of Poland, they brought random destruction as well as carefully organized plunder to libraries.

A few days into the war Germans appeared at Pelplin seminary to confiscate
the Bible they knew was there. They found only the second key to the valise and
an inventory of evacuated collections. Infuriated, they interrogated the staff
about the librarian's "theft" of this book. Expanding their search into surrounding
towns and parishes, they heard fantastic stories: the bishop had taken it to Portu-
gal and died there, or he had fled to Romania where Americans offered him a
million dollars.[27]

German forces turned the seminary library into a recreation hall,[28] burned
some books and archives in furnaces of a sugar factory,[29] and removed others to
a central collection depot in an old church in Poznań.[30] There German librarians
ultimately gathered two to three million volumes from school, synagogue, and
private libraries throughout Poland, skimming the best books for German libraries (for example, 2,000 incunabula for their new state library in the city) while
destroying others. They sent over 350 libraries directly for pulping—it was more
efficient than trucking them to the depot, and in their view it took dangerous
Polish, Jewish, and Marxist books out of circulation.[31] Of the books trucked to
Poznań, a million volumes were destroyed late in the war when Allied bombs
struck the church. This is the bibliographical hell into which parts of the Pelplin
library tumbled, but the Gutenberg and the psalter, resting safely in Ottawa,
escaped these perils.

Lovers of the endangered written word attempted to conceal and protect it. In
Vilna, for example, the Einsatzstab Reichsleiter Rosenberg forced a team of Jewish workers to sort books and documents in the YIVO building for transport to
Germany. Yiddish poet Abraham Sutzkever and other members of this group
managed to hide books as well as precious manuscripts of Peretz and Sholem
Aleichem, diaries of Herzl, and letters of Tolstoy. Sutzkever wrote a moving poem
about their efforts, describing planting manuscripts like grains of wheat that

would one day grow to nourish people. Miraculously, this actually happened to some of the Vilna books and manuscripts after the war.[32]

The National Library in Warsaw experienced its own trials. The battle for Warsaw damaged many of the city's libraries and destroyed collections: some 500 of the manuscripts from Rapperswil burned. German librarians undertook a radical reorganization of Warsaw libraries, moving large collections from one institution to another in open trucks in the dead of winter and leading to utter chaos.[33] And they confiscated illuminated manuscripts and music scores to take to Berlin.[34] Surely the manuscripts in Canada would have met this fate.

The Bibliothèque Polonaise in Paris would not have been a safe refuge either: in June 1940, less than a month after the treasures left, the Germans sealed the library and their institutions began squabbling over custody of its 100,000 books. The Prussian State Library in Berlin, the German governor of Poland, and the Ministry for Foreign Affairs all demanded the collections, but Nazi ideologue Alfred Rosenberg claimed them for the party educational center. Since his Einsatzstab Reichsleiter Rosenberg was becoming responsible for German theft of cultural property throughout Europe, his muscle carried the day.[35] Rosenberg's staff mistakenly believed they would find Chopin's piano at the Bibliothèque Polonaise but discovered and seized it in September when they confiscated harpsichordist Wanda Landowska's collection of scores and historic keyboard instruments from the home of "the Polish Jewess" in suburban St.-Leu-la-Fôret.[36]

The tapestries were just as fortunate in their evacuation from Cracow. Soon after troops entered the city, thousands of looted artworks were jammed into makeshift storage in the Wawel.[37] The German governor of Poland published a lavish catalog illustrating the finest works that cultural officers had "secured." But one missing prize tempered the boasting:

> In six months it has been possible for the Special Commission for Registration and Safeguarding of Art and Cultural Treasures to collect almost all the art objects in the country with a single exception: the Flemish tapestries from Cracow. According to latest reports, they are now in France, so it will be possible to secure them later.[38]

Wawel castle itself became the seat of the occupation government and the governor's official residence. When Baedeker published a tourist guide for occupied Poland in 1943, an audacious and remarkable volume, the compilers described beautiful portals, coffered ceilings, frescoes by Hans Dürer and Hans von Breslau, and leather wall hangings gracing the castle's interior, accessible to sightseers only with special permission. But there is no mention of the treasured and coveted tapestries.[39]

GREENE, WAUGH, OR WODEHOUSE?

Far from the scenes of death and destruction, the treasures rested safely in the pedestrian quietness of the Experimental Farm. Świerz-Zaleski and Polkowski controlled access to the room. They continued some restoration work on the hangings and monitored the condition of the Bible and manuscripts. Wacław Babiński, the Polish minister to Canada, gave them jobs in the legation to ease their financial strain. Polkowski recalled later that the admiration expressed by occasional high-ranking Canadian visitors to the storeroom helped to assuage the unhappiness of his exile.[40] In 1945 as the war wound down, the librarians and curators in Poland must have begun anticipating the return of their evacuated collections. Little did they suspect that the manuscripts and tapestries would soon become the center of an international imbroglio. As a Canadian journalist put it, it was a story "that could have been written by Graham Greene as melodrama, Waugh as satire or Wodehouse as farce."[41]

But for the Polish government in London and its Canadian supporters, it was deadly earnest. As German control of Poland evaporated, Soviet influence grew rapidly and the government-in-exile was powerless to stem it. A Communist group called the Lublin Committee soon declared itself the provisional government with Soviet backing. The exile government began to fear losing the nation's cultural icons and the political legitimacy that possessing them implied. They could even imagine the new government yielding to Soviet pressure and returning the treasures to libraries and museums in Leningrad and Moscow.

Minister Babiński, a strong anti-Communist, took swift preemptive action. He instructed Świerz-Zaleski and Polkowski to begin dispersing the objects to other sites he was arranging. They deposited two steamer trunks containing the Bible, manuscripts, and sword at the Bank of Montreal's Ottawa branch. They signed papers jointly and were told both would need to sign to retrieve the trunks. The minister arranged to deposit eight cases at the Convent of the Precious Blood in Ottawa and twenty-three trunks of tapestries at a monastery near the shrine of Ste.-Anne-de-Beaupré northeast of Quebec.[42]

By 16 July 1945 when Canada officially recognized the new Warsaw government in place of the exiles, little of value remained at the Experimental Farm. The new Polish minister to Canada, Dr. Alfred Fiderkiewicz, arrived in the spring of 1946 to find only twenty minor objects still there.[43] He did not notify the Canadian government at the time but began quiet efforts to find the missing treasures. Świerz-Zaleski and Polkowski refused to tell him what they knew, at least initially, but by May Świerz-Zaleski revealed the new locations. The legation then informed the Canadian government, asking it to contact the institutions to prevent further transfers. Bank officials responded that their vaults contained two locked trunks, but both religious communities replied that they no longer held any Polish deposits! The Department of External Affairs conveyed this alarming news to Poland in a formal note with a reminder that Canada had never assumed responsibility for security.[44]

But by now Fiderkiewicz and Świerz-Zaleski had made the same discovery. Persons loyal to the London government had followed Świerz-Zaleski and, knowing that he had revealed the hiding places, they had quickly moved the treasures again. When the Warsaw Poles visited the convent and the monastery, they were shown receipts for boxes collected several days earlier by Polkowski who used the proper password. The London Poles failed only in their attempt to take possession of the Gutenberg and the manuscripts: the bank had allowed inspection of the trunks in its vault but insisted that both original depositors must agree to removal.[45]

Despite the frantic activity, Canadians remained unaware of the intrigue in their midst. But in November 1946, convinced that publicity might smoke out the tapestries, the legation broke the story to the press which splashed it across the front pages. "Polish Treasure Gone: Men Use Right Word to Trick Shrine & Convent," proclaimed the *Toronto Globe and Mail*. The press fed the public appetite for information, with accuracy varying wildly from one story to another. The *Globe and Mail* published a cartoon showing an open storage trunk, empty except for a note: "Kilroyski Was Here."[46] The London Poles wasted no time in airing their side of the story. Both Babiński and Polkowski publicly denied any knowledge of the affair, but an anonymous source asserted that most of the objects were not state property. "These are sacred treasures, cared for by and presented to the church centuries ago," he told the *Globe and Mail*. "Our boys just got the treasures in time. . . . The Russians will never get them." And a "former Polish officer" claimed to know that "high Vatican authorities" had directed the removal and hinted that patriots were prepared to ship the tapestries to Rome.[47]

Fiderkiewicz proceeded simultaneously on both public and diplomatic fronts. With photographers in tow, he inspected the bank deposit, hoisting the sword for their benefit.[48] He also met with Lester Pearson, then undersecretary of state for external affairs, who agreed to consider what help Canada could offer.[49] A lawyer representing the London Poles soon contacted him, offering to turn the treasures over to the Canadian government which would protect them and exhibit them throughout the country for five years. If the Polish government were stable then, it could reclaim its property, with any church or private possessions returning to their owners. Pearson agreed to study the proposal and to convey it to the Polish legation. But to no one's surprise, Poland rejected it outright as an inappropriate agreement with persons hostile to it.[50] In the months and years that followed, Canada repeatedly urged Poland to seek redress in the courts, while the Poles insisted that Canada could and should act directly on their behalf.

Poland saw the UNESCO General Conference in Mexico City in November 1947 as an opportunity to raise its grievance in an international forum. But the conference's General Committee ruled that the situation lay outside UNESCO's purview.[51] Despite this setback for Warsaw, the international attention seems to have spurred action in Ottawa. The Department of External Affairs soon asked the Royal Canadian Mounted Police to seek the missing objects and, if successful, to keep them under surveillance.[52] Intervention by the Mounties, those officers in scarlet who "always get their man," precipitated another startling turn of events. In January 1948 the Mounties learned that the tapestries were now in the custody of the Sisters of Hôtel Dieu, a seventeenth-century cloistered convent in the old Haute-Ville in Quebec City. Two senior officers visited the convent to interview the mother superior who confirmed that a very respectable gentleman had asked her to store valuable art objects. The Mounties did not demand to see the treasures, but they accepted the sister's offer to show them the trunks in the basement. They suggested using an outside door rather than passing through the cloister, but she insisted on escorting them through the cloister to the storeroom where they counted twenty-three trunks and one wooden box. The Mounties reported their discovery and stationed a detachment nearby to prevent any unauthorized removal.[53]

External Affairs notified the Polish chargé d'affaires that the police had found the treasures.[54] But rather than starting legal proceedings as Canada hoped, he took a direct approach. He wrote to the mother superior, demanding she turn the deposit over to him as the legal representative of Poland and claiming (falsely) that the Mounties would intervene if she failed to comply within four days. Troubled by the conflicting claims and worried by the threats, she contacted Quebec premier Maurice Duplessis for guidance.[55]

A strong leader, colorful character, and consummate politician who came to be known as "Le Chef," Duplessis was near the peak of his career as leader of Quebec's Conservative Party. As premier from 1936 to 1939, and again from 1944 until his death in 1959, he brought Quebec to unprecedented strength vis-à-vis the federal government.[56] Because Duplessis wasted few opportunities to tweak the nose of Canada's English-speaking majority and had established himself as a fervent anti-Communist, the nun's appeal for advice was irresistible. Its timing made it a political godsend: he was about to call provincial elections and his opponents, the Liberal Party, were ready to choose a new national leader. The heir apparent was a Québecois, Louis St. Laurent, secretary for external affairs and the very man who had sent Mounties to the convent door.[57] Duplessis leapt to the reverend mother's assistance!

The premier directed his chief bodyguard to organize secret transfer of the tapestries to the provincial museum. Within days a detachment of provincial police in plain clothes boldly removed the twenty-four large parcels in public works trucks under the very noses of the Mounties, locked them in the museum vault, and delivered the combination to Duplessis, who soon broke the story to the press.[58] He said the church was the true owner of the treasures, whose removal he had ordered to prevent Communist sabotage or theft, and he went on to needle his opponents.

> We are much grieved that the Federal authorities of our country, particularly the Ministers representing the Province of Québec . . . , made themselves collaborators of Stalin and his Polish Government to the point that they ordered their police to ignore the laws and to violate the cloister of the noble order of the Sisters of the Hôtel Dieu. Conscientiously, the government of Québec could not remain indifferent to this attack against our dearest traditions.[59]

Political reaction was immediate.[60] Duplessis could gloat while St. Laurent squirmed and sputtered, complaining of clumsy smear tactics as he insisted the Mounties had entered at the nun's invitation and not as enforcers for Poland. The opposition asked what measures the government had taken to protect the treasures of another nation and questioned the Mounties' involvement in a noncriminal matter. One House member fulminated that the federal government was playing "the odious part of a gestapo for Poland's impostor and communist government which outdoes in injustice, usurpation, and cruelty, the arrogance of Hitler, . . . to locate priceless sacred vases, church vestments and frescoes—the property of the Polish church."[61] Such characterizations were ironic, given the Vatican's 1939 refusal to help on grounds that the treasures were not ecclesiastical. But wildly inaccurate descriptions mattered little—the affair reinforced Duplessis's image as defender of the faith and helped to bolster his political strength. In the provincial elections, Quebec voters swept him to his greatest victory: his party won eighty-two of ninety seats. But nationally, the incident did St. Laurent and the Liberal Party no lasting harm in the longer run. He accepted the leadership in August, became prime minister in November when Mackenzie King retired, and in June 1949 led the party to a record majority of 190 of 260 seats in the national election.[62]

Duplessis's action turned a difficult situation into a nearly impossible one. He drew clear political advantage from continuing to thumb his nose at Communists and embarrassing the federal government which was constitutionally hamstrung. For the Poles, the repeated suggestion of going to court to claim what was manifestly theirs seemed an affront to national sovereignty. For the increasingly marginalized government-in-exile, maintaining the status quo provided a claim on world attention. And even Warsaw, while aggressively campaigning to get the treasures back, could use a stalemate as grist for propaganda. Except for occasional, futile sorties by one side or the other, the deadlock continued for the next decade. Unless new events shifted the equilibrium or outside parties could nudge the sides closer together, a resolution was unlikely. In fact a combination of these elements between 1956 and 1958 succeeded where both propaganda and official diplomacy had failed, although both churned on.

Let me note here a sad irony, one of many in the history of cultural properties displaced by the war. In 1941 the Prussian State Library in Berlin had begun evacuating precious holdings to castles and monasteries. A remarkable cache of some fifty boxes of rare music scores spent the rest of the war in a monastery at Grüssau in Silesia, territory that was to become Polish. These manuscripts included Mozart's *Magic Flute*, all of Beethoven's Ninth Symphony except the choral finale, Mendelssohn's *Elijah* and the incidental music to *A Midsummer Night's Dream*. In 1946 experts combing the area for Polish property taken there by the Germans found the music and took it to Cracow, first to Wawel Hill, then to the university library. Until 1977 authorities stoutly denied they were on Polish soil, rebuffing German librarians, American musicologists, and even a party-to-party query from East German Communists.[63] The government that castigated Canada for dragging its feet was even less forthcoming with the musical property of a sister socialist state! Some of these manuscripts remain in Cracow today.

POLONAISE-FANTAISIE

By 1956 new events were making it easier for Polish-Canadians to imagine returning the treasures. The political thaw that followed Stalin's death in 1953 and Khrushchev's denunciation of him at the 1956 Party Congress set off reverberations throughout Eastern Europe. That October the Polish Communist Party chose as secretary Władysław Gomułka, who had been imprisoned as a dissident in 1951. Khrushchev headed a delegation that rushed to Warsaw, attempting to halt the liberalization, but after tense discussions he backed down, agreeing to more internal autonomy for Poland in exchange for reining in forces headed toward open revolt. Gomułka soon sent two leading Communists to the monastery where the primate of Poland, Cardinal Wyszyński, had sat in detention since 1953 and brought him back to Warsaw in triumph.[64] It suddenly seemed less credible that the government was the bitter enemy of the church and that it might send the nation's cultural heritage back to Russia. Canada's Polish newspapers, regardless of their political bent, began advocating an early return. Meanwhile, Józef Polkowski (now working as a delicatessen clerk) was growing increasingly concerned. He publicly doubted that the museum could control temperature and humidity and he feared that insects might be feeding on the books in the bank vault. He too began favoring return.[65]

With barriers to a settlement softening, the final impetus came, appropriately, from Chopin's music and one of its most popular interpreters. Pianist Witold Małcużyński, one of Paderewski's last pupils, had left Poland in 1937 and after the war lived in Switzerland, concertizing widely.[66] In the spring of 1958 when Małcużyński returned to Poland for the first time, a tumultuous welcome followed him everywhere. He considered himself apolitical, but the visit moved him deeply, especially his impressions of Polish youth.[67] Old friends and new admirers laid before him the plight of the Chopin manuscripts and the other treasures, and he began active personal diplomacy to secure their release in time for the Chopin sesquicentennial in 1960. He canceled a month of concerts to speak to Polish groups in Canada, strengthening the consensus that the treasures should go home, and he served as an intermediary between Polish curators and scholars and the government-in-exile.

His efforts bore fruit just before Christmas 1958 when he brought a Polish curatorial delegation to Ottawa to meet with Polkowski and London Pole representatives, to open the two steamer trunks, and to seek terms under which the treasures might return home. Most conspicuous by their absence were the Canadian and Polish politicians and diplomats who had failed to resolve the crisis for twelve years.[68] As the group slowly unpacked the trunks at the bank, they examined the objects for signs of deterioration. They found dead insects in some of the manuscripts and beetle eggs in wooden bindings, they noted spots from dampness and mold on the edges of pages, and they detected loss of elasticity in leather and parchment. All present signed a protocol stating that further storage would endanger the objects and violate basic principles of conservation. The treasures in the bank would return to Poland.[69]

It must have been with enormous relief that the Department of External Affairs announced the settlement, the first good news for Canada since the story had broken in 1946.[70] The government took no chances now: the trunks traveled in a railroad sleeping car rented by Poland and guarded by Mounties, determined not to look inept again. The train circled its way to New York via Toronto and Buffalo rather than taking the more direct route through the province of Quebec.[71]

When the manuscripts and Bible arrived in Warsaw in the early hours of 3 February 1959 in the same trunks in which they had left twenty years before, an excited crowd awaited them. On exhibit for five days, they demonstrated their potency as national symbols by attracting over 82,000 visitors before traveling on to Cracow, which expressed its gratitude to Małcużyński with a gold medal; although suffering from a fever, he played a concert—Chopin, of course.[72]

Within a few days the manuscripts were on their way back to the rebuilt National Library. The coronation sword returned to its place of honor in Wawel. And on 25 February the head of the delegation presided at a ceremony returning the Gutenberg and psalter to Dr. Liedtke. He recounted the saga of the Bible and the other treasures over two decades and across two continents. The priest took one of the heavy volumes in his hand, then gently laid it on the table. His voice choked as he told what this meant to his library and to him. And when the ceremony was over, he carefully packed the large Bible and the little psalter as he had in 1939—this time to take them home.[73]

In the course of their peregrinations the Gutenberg and the manuscripts had symbolized the identities, hopes, and fears of a remarkable variety of people. Some of them possessed the precious works, while others sought in vain to secure them: Polish resistance patriots, Nazi invaders, Polish Communists, exiled anti-Communists, and Québecois nationalists. When the story of the books and documents came to world attention in 1946 they captured the popular imagination as cultural objects endangered by high intrigue. But when returned at last to the institutions which had sent them away to safety, they became once more texts for scholarly consultation, more prized than ever because of the perils through which they had come.

POSTSCRIPT

Naturally, the return of the Bible and manuscripts intensified pressure for release of the tapestries. Duplessis's death in September 1959 made this easier. In April 1960 Cardinal Wyszyński wrote to the new premier, declaring that the hangings must return to Wawel and not to the church, which Duplessis had always insisted was their true owner. Quebec soon invited a delegation of Polish curators to effect the transfer, thus avoiding the appearance that the Polish government had won a victory.[74] The tapestries arrived in Poland in January 1961 and, after a month-long exhibit in Warsaw, they returned to the castle for which King Sigismund had commissioned them 400 years earlier.[75]

NOTES

I gratefully acknowledge the support of Martinus Nijhoff International, whose Western European Studies Specialist Grant for 1997 made possible my visits to archives in Berlin and Paris, and the assistance of Prof. Peter Dembowski and James Barron in reading Polish sources.

1. Karol Estreicher, ed., *Cultural Losses of Poland: Index of Polish Cultural Losses during the German Occupation, 1939–1944* (London, 1944), 217.

2. Antoni Liedtke, *Saga Pelplinskiej Biblii Gutenberga* (Gdańsk: Kuria Biskupia Pelplin, 1983), 39–40.

3. Liedtke, *Biblja Gutenberga w Pelplinie* (Toruń: Towarzystwo Bibljofilów im. Lelewela, 1936); Don Cleveland Norman, *The 500th Anniversary Pictorial Census of the Gutenberg Bible* (Chicago: Coverdale, 1961), 5, 108–10.

4. Edwin Wolf 2nd with John F. Fleming, *Rosenbach: A Biography* (Cleveland and New York: World Publishing, 1960), 185, 239–42; *Exhibit of Books Printed during the XVth Century and Known as Incunabula, Selected from the Vollbehr Collection Purchased by Act of Congress, 1930* (Washington, D.C.: U.S. Government Printing Office, 1930), 1.

5. "$100,000 for Gutenberg Bible Said to Be Collectors' Offer," *New York Times,* 16 Nov. 1929, 5.

6. Liedtke, *Saga,* 49–50.

7. Andrzej Kłossowski, *The National Library in Warsaw: Collections and Programmes* (Warsaw: Biblioteka Narodowa, 1991), 9–10; Werner von Grimm, "Studien zur älteren Geschichte der Kaiserlichen Öffentlichen Bibliothek in St. Petersburg (Leningrad) 1794–1861," *Zentralblatt für Bibliothekswesen* 50 (Apr. 1933): 304–6.

8. Zofia Gaca-Dabrowska, "Revindication of Polish Library Collections from Russia in the Years of the Second Republic," *Roczniki Biblioteczne* 33 (1989): 179–81.

9. Józef Korzeniowski, *Zapiski z Rekopisów Cesarskiej Biblioteki Publicznej w Petersburgu i Innych Bibliotek Petersburskich* (Cracow: Nakładem Akademii Umiejetności, 1910), no. 48: 44–45; "Bericht des Prof. A. Brückner über seine von der Königlichen Akademie subventionirte Reise 1889/1890," *Sitzungsberichte der Königlich Preussischen Akademie der Wissenschaften zu Berlin* (1890), 1335; Manfred Kridl, *A Survey of Polish Literature and Culture,* trans. Olga Scherer-Virski (New York: Columbia University Press, 1967), 16.

10. *Annales Poloniae ex Recensione Arndtii et Roepellii,* ed. Georg Heinrich Pertz (Hannover: Hahn, 1866), 1–2; Kridl, *Survey,* 12–13.

11. Heinrich Zeissberg, "Vincentius Kadłubek, Bischof von Krakau (1208–1218; †1223), und seine Chronik Polens," *Archiv für österreichische Geschichte* 42 (1870): 188; Korzeniowski, *Zapiski,* no. 179: 147–48; Kridl, *Survey,* 13–14.

12. Stanisława Sawicka, *Les principaux manuscrits a peintures de la Bibliothèque Nationale*

de Varsovie, du Chateau Royale, et des Bibliothèques: de Zamoyski a Varsovie, du Séminaire de Płock, et du Chaiptre de Gniezo, Bulletin de la Sociétié Française de Reproduction de Manuscrits a Peintures, 19° année (Paris: La Société, 1938), 66–81 and plates IX–X.

13. Ibid., 86–96 and plate XII.

14. Ibid., 169–78 and plates XXV–XXVI.

15. Ewa Śniezyńska-Stolot, *Tajemnice Dekoracji Psałterza Florianskiego: Dziejów Średnio-wiecznej Koncepeji Uniwersum* (Warsaw: Wydawnictwo Naukowe PWN, 1992), 152–55; Kridl, *Survey,* 21.

16. Krystyna Kobylańska, *Rekopisy utworów Chopina: Katalog / Manuscripts of Chopin's Works: Catalogue* (Cracow: Polskie Wydawnictwo Muzyczne, 1977), 1: 119–20, including a complete inventory of the scores in the Breitkopf & Härtel collection, keyed to individual entries with detailed descriptions of each.

17. Adrian Thomas, "Beyond the Dance," in *The Cambridge Chopin Companion,* ed. Jim Samson (Cambridge: Cambridge University Press, 1992), 153.

18. Alodia Kawecka-Gryczowa, "Ochrona Zbiorów Biblioteki Narodowej," in *Walka o Dobra Kultury Warsawa, 1939–1945,* ed. Stanisław Lorentz (Warsaw: Pań stowy Instytut Wydawniczy, 1970), 1: 185–86.

19. Ibid., 186; Liedtke, *Saga,* 57, 60.

20. George Wingfield Digby, "Tapestries from the Polish State Collections," *Connoisseur* 138 (Sept. 1956): 1–9. The best reproductions of the tapestries and an extensive history and artistic analysis may be found in *Les tapisseries flamandes au chateau du Wawel a Cracovie,* ed. Jerzy Szablowski (Anvers: Fonds Mercator, 1972).

21. Norman, *500th Anniversary,* 244; Charles R. Beard, "The Polish Art Treasures," *Connoisseur* 136 (Sept. 1955): 3; Sharon Anne Williams, "The Polish Art Treasures in Canada: Legal Problems and Political Realities" (Master's thesis, York University, 1974), 4. Aloysius Balawyder, *The Odyssey of the Polish Treasures* (Antigonish, Nova Scotia: St. Francis Xavier University Press, 1978), a popular treatment of the subject, includes an unfootnoted account of the rescue (7–28). Unfortunately, it contains numerous factual errors, for example repeatedly asserting that the Bible and manuscripts came from Wawel castle (8, 26–27), and relies heavily on interviews with Polkowski, who tended to minimize Świerz-Zaleski's role in the story and elevate his own.

22. Liedtke, *Saga,* 58–63; Klemens Keplicz, *Miercz i Kobierce* (Czytelnik: Spółdzielnia Wydawnicza, 1955), 55–57.

23. Edward Raczynski, *In Allied London* (London: Weidenfeld & Nicolson, 1962), 66–67.

24. "London Notes," *Library Journal* 68 (15 Dec. 1943): 1041–42; and W. C. Berwick Sayers, "Britain's Libraries and the War," *Library Quarterly* 14 (Apr. 1944): 95–99.

25. Liedtke, *Saga,* 63; Stanisław Lorenz, *Canada Refuses to Return Polish Cultural Treasures* (Warsaw: National Museum, [1950?]), 9.

26. Letters of Consul General Victor Podoski to J. B. Hunter, 27 July 1940; Podoski to Gustave Lanctot, Deputy Minister and Archivist, 1 Aug. 1940; and Lanctot to Podoski, 2 Aug. 1940. All in Canadian Department of External Affairs file 837–40 and transcribed in full in Williams, "Polish Art Treasures," 152–54.

27. Liedtke, *Saga,* 47, 51–54.

28. Norman, *500th Anniversary,* 248.

29. Estreicher, *Cultural Losses,* 215–17; and as evidence in the Nuremberg trials in document USSR-93 in the published proceedings: *Trial of the Major War Criminals before the International Military Tribunal, Nuremberg, 14 November 1945–1 October 1946* (Nuremberg: International Military Tribunal, 1947), 8:69 (hereafter cited as *IMT*).

30. Feliks Lenort, "Biblioteka Wyzszego Seminarium Duchownego w Poznaniu," in Stanisław Kubiak, ed., *Biblioteki Wielkopolski* (Poznań: Politechnika Poznańska, 1983), 201.

31. "Bericht über die Sammlung und Sicherstellung von Bibliotheken und Bücherbeständen aus nichtdeutschen Besitz im Reichsgau Wartheland vom 12. 1939 bis zum 31. 10. 1940," R 21/10589, fol. 38–50, Bundesarchiv (Berlin-Lichterfelde).

32. David Shavit, *Hunger for the Printed Word: Books and Libraries in the Jewish Ghettos of Nazi-Occupied Europe* (Jefferson, N. C., and London: McFarland, 1997), 95–97; Abraham Sutzkever, *A. Sutzkever: Selected Poetry and Prose*, trans. Barbara and Benjamin Harshaw (Berkeley: University of California Press, 1991), 17–21, 156–57.

33. Maria Danilewicz, *The Libraries of Poland* (St. Andrews: University of St. Andrews, 1943), 60–61; Helena Wieckowska, "The Rebirth of the National Library of Warsaw," *Library Association Record* 48 (Oct. 1946): 245; Hanna J. Bednarski, "Warsaw University Library: A History of Wartime Survival," *Canadian Library Journal* 32 (Feb. 1975): 36; and Manfred Komorowski, "Die wissenschaftliche Bibliotheken im Generalgouvernement Polen (1940–1945)," *Bibliotek: Forschung und Praxis* 7, no. 1 (1983): 70–72.

34. Estreicher, *Cultural Losses,* 357.

35. "La Bibliotheque Polonaise de Paris sous l'occupation allemande," [16 February 1945], 208–18, file AMG 248, Box 326, RG 331 (Records of Allied Operational and Occupation Headquarters, World War II), and "The Polish Library in Paris," report dated 10 Oct. 1944, included in Lt. Col. Robert P. Hamilton's 18 Oct. 1944 report to Monument, Fine Arts and Archives Section, Supreme Headquarters Allied Expeditionary Force, 84–85, file AMG 300, Box 323, National Archives, Washington, D.C.; "Zum nationalsozialistischen Kunstraub in Frankreich: Der 'Bargatzky-Bericht,'" ed. by Wilhelm Treue, *Vierteljahrshefte für Zeitgeschichte* 18 (July 1965): 303–4.

36. "Bericht. Betr.: Beschlagnahme der Sammlung alter Musikinstrumente der polnischen Jüdin Wanda Landowska," 8 January 1941, document CCXXXI-22, pp. 11–13, Archives du Centre de Documentation Juive Contemporaine, Paris.

37. Lynn Nicholas, *The Rape of Europa: The Fate of Europe's Treasures in the Third Reich and the Second World War* (New York: Knopf, 1994), 66–67.

38. *Sichergestellte Kunstwerke im Generalgouvernement* (Breslau: Korn, [1940]), 3. Prosecutors introduced the catalog as evidence in the Nuremberg trials, and the transcribed title page and preface appear as document 1233-PS in the published proceedings: *IMT,* 23:74–75.

39. *Das Generalgouvernement: Reisehandbuch* (Leipzig: Baedeker, 1943), 46–48.

40. Norman, *500th Anniversary,* 245; Balawyder, *Odyssey,* 32.

41. McKenzie Porter, "Who's Going to Get the Polish Art Treasures," *Maclean's Magazine,* 15 July 1953, 7.

42. Balawyder, *Odyssey,* 38–41; Williams, "Polish Art Treasures," 10, 13; Porter, "Who's Going to Get Treasures," 42.

43. Stanisław E. Nahlik, "Le cas de collections polonaises au Canada: Considerations juridiques," *Annuaire polonais des affaires internationales* (1959–60): 173.

44. Norman, *500th Anniversary,* 246; Williams, "Polish Art Treasures," 7–8, 14; L. S. St. Laurent, Secretary of State for External Affairs, House of Commons, *Debates,* 4 Mar. 1948, 1859–60.

45. Norman, *500th Anniversary,* 246–47; George Ronald, "Disappears in Canada: Polish Treasure Gone," *Toronto Globe and Mail,* 7 Nov. 1946, 1–2.

46. Editorial cartoon, *Toronto Globe and Mail,* 8 Nov. 1946, 6; "Rumors Fly in Polish Relics Theft," *Montreal Daily Star,* 7 Nov. 1946, 1, 5.

47. "Pole Insists Treasure Now in 'Safe Hands,'" *Toronto Globe and Mail*, 8 Nov. 1946, 1–2, and George Ronald, "Canada Not Obliged to Recover Treasures, Reply to London Pole," *Toronto Globe and Mail*, 9 Nov. 1946, 17.

48. "Missing Polish National Art Treasures That Have Raised a Storm—And Those Still Safe," *Montreal Daily Star*, 8 Nov. 1946, 21.

49. Louis St. Laurent, in House of Commons, *Debates*, 4 Mar. 1948, 1860; Williams, "Polish Art Treasures," 11–13.

50. House of Commons, *Debates*, 4 Mar. 1948, 1860–61; Williams, "Polish Art Treasures," 14–17.

51. United Nations Educational Scientific and Cultural Organization, *Records of the General Conference*, 2nd sess., 1947, Proceedings, 258–62, 315–16.

52. Williams, "Polish Art Treasures," 19–20; St. Laurent, in House of Commons, *Debates*, 4 Mar. 1948, 1861.

53. Porter, "Who's Going to Get Treasures," 44; St. Laurent, quoting RCMP press release, in House of Commons, *Debates*, 4 Mar. 1948, 1861.

54. St. Laurent, in House of Commons, *Debates*, 5 Mar. 1948, 1907, and 8 Mar. 1948, 1951.

55. Williams, "Polish Art Treasures," 21–22; Porter, "Who's Going to Get Treasures," 44–45.

56. Conrad M. Black, "Duplessis," *Canadian Encyclopedia* (Edmonton: Hurtig, 1988), 1:636–37.

57. Dale C. Thomson, *Louis St. Laurent: Canadian* (New York: St. Martin's, 1968), 231–40.

58. Robert Rumilly, *Maurice Duplessis et sons temps*, 2 vols. (Montreal: Fides, 1978), 2:216–18; Norman, *500th Anniversary*, 248.

59. *Ottawa Journal*, 3 Mar. 1948.

60. "Smuggled from Convent: Quebec Seizes Polish Art Treasure," *Toronto Globe and Mail*, 3 Mar. 1948, 1; "Quebec Hits Ottawa on Polish Treasures," *New York Times*, 4 Mar. 1948, 3; Balawyder, *Odyssey* 57–58; House of Commons, *Debates*, 3 Mar. 1948, 1837.

61. House of Commons, *Debates*, 4 Mar. 1948, 1862–63 and 1905; 5 Mar. 1948, 1915.

62. Rumilly, *Duplessis* 229.

63. The remarkable story is told most comprehensively in Nigel Lewis, *Paperchase: Mozart, Beethoven, Bach . . . the Search for Their Lost Music* (London: Hamish Hamilton, 1981).

64. Nicholas Bethell, *Gomułka, His Poland and His Communism* (London: Longmans, 1969), 200–224.

65. Balawyder, *The Maple Leaf and the White Eagle: Canadian-Polish Relations, 1918–1978* (Boulder: East European Monographs, 1980), 206.

66. Frank Dawes, "Witold Małcużyński," *The New Grove Dictionary of Music* (London: Macmillan, 1980), 11: 568–69, and "Obituary: Mr. Witold Małcużyński," *Times* (London), 19 July 1977, 18.

67. "A Polish Pianist Goes Home after 20 Years," *Times* (London), 1 May 1958, 3.

68. Norman, *500th Anniversary*, 249–50; Balawyder, *Maple Leaf*, 208.

69. Document in the Wawel archives (Archivum Państwowe Zbiorow Sztukina Wawelu), published in translation in Balawyder, *Odyssey*, 93–96.

70. Tania Long, "Canada to Yield Polish Treasure," *New York Times*, 9 Jan. 1959, 10; "Art Treasures Going Back to Poland: Secret Canadian Talks Succeed," *Times* (London), 10 Jan. 1959, 10.

71. "Polish Treasures Being Taken Home," *New York Times,* 20 Jan. 1959, 25; "Gutenberg Bible Off to Poland after Wartime Stay in Canada," ibid., 22 Jan. 1959, 28.

72. Balawyder, *Maple Leaf,* 209; "Treasures Return to Poland," *New York Times,* 4 Feb. 1959, 20; A. M. Rosenthal, "National Treasures of Poland Return to Old Cracow Castle," ibid., 17 Feb. 1959, 3.

73. Norman, *500th Anniversary,* 252.

74. Balawyder, *Odyssey,* 99–100, and *Maple Leaf,* 213–15.

75. Balawyder, *Maple Leaf,* 215–16; "Quebec Sends Back Poland's Treasures," *New York Times,* 3 Jan. 1961, 1, 26; "Poles Hail Return of National Relics," ibid., 17 Jan. 1961, 9.

PART THREE

THE READER IN THE HOLOCAUST:
DOCUMENTS

Book vendors in the Warsaw ghetto. Among the book titles for sale are *A Pole in Germany, Death of a Poet, Wilhelm II,* and *Sexual Life.* Posted on the wall above the stand are announcements warning about typhus and lice. Photograph by Willy Georg. (*Raphael Scharf, courtesy of USHMM Photo Archives*)

IX • THE LIBRARY IN THE VILNA GHETTO

Dina Abramowicz

I T was very hard for anybody in the Vilna ghetto to get into the "brigades," which had work assignments outside the ghetto. One had a chance, in such a brigade, to bring home a "package," although it was always a risky undertaking. So everyone was trying to "get in." I succeeded in getting into a brigade of railroad workers. The railroad tracks ran through orchards and farms that could use female farmhands. I obtained this work thanks to Nelly Sachs, a granddaughter of Fanya Romanovna Markus, a founder of the first Jewish school for girls, where my mother was a teacher. This was a connection carried over from better times into this incredible ghetto situation. But, unfortunately, its usefulness was of short duration. Rumors began to circulate that our white work certificates were going to be exchanged for yellow ones. Only workers with yellow certificates would be allowed to remain in the ghetto; the others would be "resettled" somewhere else. It became clear to me after a brief conversation with the leader of the brigade that I had no chance to remain as a worker in his unit. The impossibility of obtaining a yellow certificate, the hopelessness of my situation, threw me into a state of deep depression.

But then, quite unexpectedly, came a lucky break. One evening, stepping out from our crowded quarters into the ghetto street, I bumped into Herman Kruk, the head of the former Grosser Library in Warsaw, an important center of Yiddish secular and socialist cultural activities. Kruk had come with the stream of Jewish refugees from Warsaw to Vilna in the first months of Hitler's invasion of Poland. While others moved on to various points still open to emigration, he remained in Vilna in the hope of returning to Warsaw to rescue his wife from the Nazi clutches. He did not succeed and remained stuck in Vilna to share the destiny of Vilna Jews who did not have refugee status and who had no way of escaping the Nazi trap. This part of Kruk's life was known to me from my previous encounters with him when he used to come to the Jewish children's library where I worked during the period 1939–41. He was a frequent visitor to the library, friendly and very articulate. I liked to chat with this man whose intellectual horizon was so much wider than that of the average reader.

At our chance encounter in the ghetto he did not waste any time to inform me about an important development. He had succeeded in getting the Judenrat to recognize the former library "Mefitse Haskalah," located in the present ghetto, as a ghetto institution whose employees would be paid by the ghetto administration. The former head of the library, Krasner, had been killed by the Germans. But one of the former employees, Moshe Abramowicz, survived and was working already. He needed someone to help him, and Kruk was offering me the job.

I looked at Kruk in astonishment. A library in the ghetto where one is deprived of the most elementary living conditions and where we are suspended between life and death every minute of our existence? How can he think of a library under these conditions, and who will come to read books there? But I refrained from asking him these questions. Didn't he know the situation in the ghetto as well as I did? But, perhaps, he was looking ahead, saw further than I could. I accepted the offer.

The remuneration was very modest: 200 rubles, the equivalent of ten pounds of bread, ration cards, and a white work certificate. But Kruk hoped that he would succeed in obtaining yellow certificates for his workers; he was almost sure of it.

The appearance of the library was a pleasant surprise to me—almost no change from the way it looked in normal times: the floor freshly washed, impressive rows of bookshelves, a peacefulness, an atmosphere of intellectual impassivity—a very unusual spot amidst the ghetto turmoil. Between the bookcases filled to capacity one could see the tall, pale Moshe Abramowicz moving slowly, with a sad smile as if fixed to his face. He welcomed me in a friendly manner, explaining the work to be done. But how had he managed? What did he think of it all? I was asking impatiently, astonished by his incredibly cool, matter-of-fact manner. He smiled, and the smile grew even more pronounced and became almost condescending as he gave me his short answer. He was here with his old mother; she was ailing and there was nobody around to cook for her and take care of her needs; this was all he could worry about. I understood what the answer was implying: since there was nothing one could do about this absurd situation, what was the use of talking and wondering? Things would take care of themselves anyhow. I was somewhat embarrassed. This restraint, this lack of complaints, this remarkable dignity in the face of the incredible humiliation to which we were subjected—wasn't that the attitude we should assume?

The windows of the library looked out on Strashun Street, a narrow ghetto alley with cobblestones, broken sidewalks, and houses on the opposite side that you could touch with your outstretched arm. The adjacent little room was Mr. Kruk's office. His secretary, Rachel Mendelssohn, worked there. He dictated his letters and his ghetto chronicle to her. The windows of this little room looked out on the courtyard of the former temporary community council whose members had been executed by a Nazi firing squad before we were driven into the ghetto. The yard was covered with debris and garbage. A door in the lobby on the opposite side of the room led to a big, empty hall. The windows in the hall were broken, and a bitter cold wind blew in from the desolate space. But rumors were circulating that Kruk wanted to convert the space into a reading room and a museum with Haykl Lunski, the historian of Vilna antiquities and an observant Jew, the librarian of the famous talmudic Strashun Library, as its custodian.

Until January 1942 the work in the library was very irregular. This was the period of the liquidation of the Second Ghetto, of two big "actions" (deportations) in the main ghetto, as a result of which the ghetto population was reduced by approximately one third. Kruk did not succeed in getting yellow work certificates for all his workers. The Judenrat obtained considerably fewer certificates than expected. I did not get a yellow certificate, and I escaped death thanks to my uncle, who included me in his family certificate as his daughter. His own daughter, little Luta, was at that time still hiding as a Christian girl with their former maid, Julia. Kruk used his own yellow certificate to save the Bundist (Socialist) matriarch, Pati Kremer. He declared her as his wife, and I remember how courageously he marched through the ghetto gate, arm in arm with Pati, in front of armed Germans and Lithuanian guards. She looked more like his grandmother than his wife, and his deception risked his own life as well as hers. The executioners looked at the couple and sensed that there was something suspicious. The couple was, however, allowed to pass.

January 1942 was the start of a period of relative stability that lasted about a year in the ghetto. There was hunger, filth, freezing cold, darkness (electricity was turned off between the hours of 4:00 and 9:00 P.M. when it was needed most), many other adversities, but mass deportations were temporarily halted. This was the period of peak activity in the library.

We had several categories of readers. The morning visitors were usually "society ladies," women whose husbands went to work outside the ghetto and who were relatively well provided for. Housework no longer required much time, nor did social activities. The empty time had to be filled with something, and these ladies would come for books in order to forget and escape the frightening reality. They usually asked for the endless serializations of Russian sentimental novels issued by the publishing houses in Riga (the Riga publishing houses were the main sources in the interwar period for Russian non-Soviet literature, mostly novels of the soap-opera type). The ladies were usually very disappointed when part of a sequel was missing and complained bitterly that the library was becoming so depleted that they would soon have nothing to read.

Around two or three o'clock in the afternoon an entirely different type of reader would invade the library—children coming from school. Book requests would pour in in rapid succession: *The Children of Captain Grant, Around the World in Eighty Days, The Adventures of Tom Sawyer, The Prince and the Pauper*. I gave out the books and wondered: Yiddish translations of Jules Verne published in New York early in the century with obsolete and difficult orthography, written in stilted, pseudoliterary language, leafed through by so many avid readers that the text was hardly legible on the greasy pages, volumes where dozens of pages were missing at the beginning and at the end, and probably no less in the middle, bound and rebound again and again so that the margin was nonexistent and the beginning of the line disappeared somewhere deep in the spine of the book—in short, real invalids of books that had deserved to be retired a long time ago. But none of this discouraged the children from using them. The need of the youthful imagination to transport itself to the world of fantasy was not suppressed in the ghetto. On the contrary, the need grew even more intense in an environment that was so confined and deprived of play and joy. Books were possibly the only vehicle for reaching out to the world from which the Jewish children were cut off, possibly forever.

Adolescent readers showed great interest in Soviet books. The book by Ostrowski, *How Steel Was Hardened,* was especially popular. We had to be very careful, however, in circulating Soviet books. Although it soon became clear to us that the Germans cared very little about our political and ideological preferences, and were even less interested in our cultural needs and activities, it was imperative to avoid anything that could serve as material for denunciation or provocation.

In the afternoon and especially on Sundays, we would see a third type of reader: people who went to work outside the ghetto. Young people from the Hechalutz Zionist organizations, many of them refugees from Warsaw, were the most active readers. They used to ask for Polish books, mostly translations from world literature, but also books dealing with Jewish issues as well as wider social concerns. The books of Cronin describing the life of mine workers in Great Britain, of Galsworthy on English society, of the Italian Ignazio Silone, whose *Bread and Wine* portrays the life of peasants in Italy, and of the Americans Upton Sinclair and Theodore Dreiser were very much in demand. Among the works of the German-Jewish writers, Feuchtwanger's *The Wars of the Jews* and especially the remarkable book by Franz Werfel, *The Forty Days of Musa Dagh,* were the most popular. Werfel described an infamous episode of World War I, the annihilation by the Turks of an entire Armenian population living in their country. The idea of a total annihilation of a racial group, the method of destruction, the helplessness of the victims, and the futility of diplomatic rescue efforts—this presented such an astonishing similarity to our situation that we read the book with a shudder, perceiving it almost as a prophetic vision, revealing for us our inevitable fate.

During this period the library was enlarged by two new departments. Kruk realized his plan to convert the big empty hall across from the library into a museum and reading room. The broken windowpanes were replaced by new ones; the walls were whitewashed with fresh paint. Glass cabinets placed along the walls displayed Torah scrolls, silver wine cups, candle holders, and embroidered curtains for the Torah arks. In the course of time the number of Torah scrolls owned by the museum increased considerably. They arrived in a mysterious way from the surrounding villages, conspicuous signs of disappearing Jewish communities. It was already becoming inadvisable and even impossible to display them all unless one wanted to show that the museum was turning into a graveyard. The scrolls were wrapped in bedsheets and there they lay, silent and hidden, in the corner of the ghetto archives.

The ghetto archives were the second new department added to the library. A small dark room equipped with one cabinet and a table served as its quarters. The work there was performed by a certain Miss Halperin, from Kovno or some other place in Lithuania. She spoke two languages in which the majority of Vilna Jews were not fluent: Hebrew and Lithuanian. She was a small, thin woman with a worried expression on her face, and she was always running between the Judenrat, the police headquarters, and the archives, collecting public announcements, orders of the day, reports, and other official documents. She also managed the theater archives, including posters of the shows and some theatrical paraphernalia. She was conscientious and patient performing her work, but one could read on her face the nagging question, "How much more time is left to us before it will all be over?"

The visits of the Lithuanian librarian, Anna Šimaite, were rare bright moments in the gray, sad life of our library. Šimaite worked in the library of Vilna University and used her position as an opportunity to establish a contact with the ghetto library. She was of great help to Herman Kruk in his contacts with the outside world. When visiting us, she would look lovingly at the shelves of Yiddish books and say that she wanted to learn Yiddish in order to be able to know Yiddish literature at its very source. These words from the mouth of a member of the Aryan race sounded almost incredible in this sinister period when Jewish people were facing annihilation, as an "inferior race." Anna Šimaite will always be, for those Vilna Jews who knew her, the symbol of spiritual courage and pure love of mankind.

My work at the ghetto library came to an end in August 1943. The liquidation of the ghetto was approaching at a fast pace. The Judenrat tried desperately to save the ghetto. It was feverishly converting office and clerical work in the ghetto into "productive activity," establishing enormous new workshops to sew military uniforms and to weave footwear from straw and ropes. The workers dismissed from the office and clerical jobs were sent to the shoe and dress shops. I was among those who were dismissed, but not knowing dressmaking or weaving, I was assigned to work in a lumber yard on Piwna Street outside the ghetto. Together with another woman, I carried the heavy wooden boards that an automatic saw dispensed. The lumber yard was situated in the city, and this place gave our family the opportunity to arrange meetings between me and the old Schreiber nursemaid, Julia. She used to bring us some slices of bread covered with a thin layer of marmalade, socks and scarves that remained from the family possessions. Rumors were already circulating in town that we would be deported, so we needed warm clothes. It happened that at one of these encounters we embraced as we never knew whether we would ever see each other again. But we did once more, and she told me that a woman passing by who saw us embrace scolded her loudly and publicly for embracing a Jew.

Once, on a late day in August, news spread in the lumber yard that the Lithuanians were encircling the work areas and taking people, without any previous warning, to labor camps in Estonia. We did not finish the day's work. Our leader quickly assembled all of us, and we were on our way to the ghetto. This was the last day of my work. On the following day the ghetto gate was sealed with bolts and locks, including the small adjacent entrance, usually guarded by a policeman and a sentry. The area was hermetically sealed from the world; the trap was closed in preparation for the final act. We still had to wait three weeks before our final "resettlement."

X • LIBRARY AND READING ROOM IN THE VILNA GHETTO, STRASHUN STREET 6

Herman Kruk
Translated by Zachary M. Baker

GHETTO LIBRARY AND GHETTO READERS
September 15, 1941–September 15, 1942

FOREWORD

AFTER the Ghetto Library's first year of existence, we present this compilation as a historical document about a momentous and difficult time.[1] Our
compilation is not only an annual report; it has an additional objective: to cast
the ghetto reader into bibliopsychological relief.

A special type of reader has emerged from the fabric of our surrounding environment—from recent events and experiences. That is what is of greatest interest
to us.

Cultural work requires peace and quiet. Our period of reporting has unfortunately been anything but a peaceful one. Nevertheless, we are not waiting for
historical perspective but are attempting in the heat of the moment to analyze
and outline certain observations and peculiarities and draw some conclusions.

Our publication was produced using primitive means—unfortunately, they
are all that we have at our disposal.

If our objective has at least in a certain measure been achieved, that is thanks
only to the hard work and tireless efforts of all library staff members.

Vilna Ghetto
October 1942

A YEAR'S WORK IN THE VILNA GHETTO LIBRARY

Some Prehistory

In order to analyze more precisely the sequence of problems of readership in the
ghetto, we feel that it is necessary to introduce a bit of prehistory. The present
Ghetto Library, formerly the Mefitse Haskalah Library, was founded in 1910 by

the Society for the Dissemination of Enlightenment among the Jews of Russia [Hevrah Mefitse Haskalah].[2] Over the years, it managed to acquire several large book collections. In 1918, Fayvush Krasner took over the directorship of the library, and thanks to his tireless work Mefitse Haskalah became the largest Jewish library in Vilna, in terms of both the number of volumes in its collections and the quantity of books circulated to readers. From the standpoint of the book collection's significance as a Jewish library, Mefitse Haskalah ranked far from the top—foreign-language books comprised a solid majority. The 45,000 volumes included in the library in September 1939 were as follows: Yiddish, 10,000 volumes; Hebrew, 5,500 volumes; Polish, 10,000 volumes; Russian, 18,000 volumes; Lithuanian, German, French, English, 2,000 volumes; total, 45,500 volumes. (For precise details, see table 1.)

What was being read during the last ten to twelve years?

With the exception of 1940–41,[3] approximately 90,000 volumes were being read annually. Fiction comprised over 90 percent of the books circulated, according to content. By language, the breakdown was as follows: In 1930, 15.9 percent of the books read were in Yiddish; Hebrew, 10.3 percent. By 1934, 8 percent of the books read were in Yiddish, 6.7 percent in Hebrew. And later on, the two languages combined amounted to less than 20 percent of the total number of books circulated.[4]

The library used to serve an average of 2,000 subscribers (with the exception of 1940–41, when the number of readers rose above 4,000). By age, 60 percent of readers were younger than 20; fewer than 15 percent were older than 30. By gender, women comprised a slight majority (by about 2 percent to 3 percent).

It should also be noted that when we came into the ghetto, none of the library's previous staff remained. The first staff member to be seized was the director, Fayvush Krasner (2 September 1941); then Mgr. Balosh was taken away; and the third to depart was Y. Blokh. The rest were scattered among various forced labor sites. At that point, the library resumed its activities with a completely new staff.

Mefitse Haskalah as Ghetto Library

In the first days of September 1941, the Mefitse Haskalah Library lost about 20 percent of its book collections.

The first breach in the library's completeness occurred when the German occupiers took away 1,500 volumes (in French, English, and German).[5] At that time, the main card catalog, with its 40,000 cards, also was removed.

In conjunction with the sad events of that period, some 4,000 of the highest-quality volumes went astray among the readers.[6] Approximately 2,000 volumes were lost during the days when the Jews were driven into the ghetto (5–7 September). The library's quarters were then completely unsupervised, and the newly arrived ghetto residents held sway within it.

Qualitatively speaking, that is how the best and most popular books were lost from the library.

On 8 September, the library was "occupied" and by the fifteenth began its public operations as the Ghetto Library, thereby becoming one of the first public institutions in the ghetto and its first cultural establishment. Thanks only to the voluntary assistance of a group of workers, working intelligentsia, and young people was it possible to bring the library's collections in order. Chaos was transformed into organization and the library began to function.

At that point, the book collections assumed the following composition: fiction, 70 percent; nonfiction, 20 percent; children's literature, 7 percent; periodicals, 3 percent. During the first two weeks (from 15 September to 1 October), the library enrolled 1,500 subscribers, mainly young people. In October, the number of books circulated attained prewar levels. By February 1942, the number of readers doubled, so that by the present, 15 September 1942, over 4,700 subscribers have passed through the Library (see tables 6 and 7), of whom 1,807 active readers now remain. The rest let their subscriptions lapse and turned from active into passsive readers. A major shift of readers took place during the period of the so-called Actions.[7] At that time, a number of library staff were lost, among them the former director of the children's library,[8] Beyle Zakheim, Esther Musnicka, Feyge Draznin, Rashe Faktorowska, Yehime Striakowska, Mire Epstein, and Motl Epstein.

During the winter months of 1941–42, due to the cold conditions, the library's administrative operations had to be suspended. Ongoing work was being carried out often in subfreezing temperatures. Thanks to the "stabilization" of the ghetto, reading patterns became more normal. An adult readership element emerged. The level of reading rose. Higher-quality literature was requested—both scholarly and popular. Gradually, interesting changes in the language composition of reading could be noted (see tables 3 and 4).

In late spring 1942, it was possible to further normalize the library's administrative operations—inventory taking, preparation of catalog cards, shelf reading, book selection, and so on. "Newly acquired" book collections were brought into the library then, which enriched the Ghetto Library. The library, as a result, "swallowed up" the following collections:

1. Part of the library of the Realgymnasium—containing 3,000 vols.
2. A small library belonging to the writer Veynig[9]—60 vols.
3. Some books from the Ivriyah Gymnasium—385 vols.
4. From the YIVO Institute—357 vols.
5. Of unknown provenance—23 vols.
6. Lawyer P. Kon[10] (deposit)—400 vols.
7. Moshe Shalit[11]—50 vols.

The more valuable books from the Realgymnasium unfortunately did not reach us. Someone else managed to remove them. Nevertheless, the small libraries that were "acquired" were a major contribution to the continuing activities of the Ghetto Library. They also provided the possibility of creating small libraries at a number of sites inside and outside of the ghetto. Such libraries were created at the following places:

1. Ghetto prison—200 vols.
2. Keylis fur factory—150 vols.
3. Yeladim transport office—28 vols.
4. Children's home—53 vols.
5. Youth club—150 vols.

The number of books inventoried reached 4,000 volumes for the year. Among them is a special Lithuanica section, a library collection that as such is not only unusual but also a great treasure, including rare and extremely valuable materials. That library collection includes over 600 items. In addition, a separate inventory of books is being done in the newly established Reading Room, which absorbed the most valuable of the newly received books.

Considerable effort and energy have been devoted to the library catalogs. Some of them had to be completely reconstituted; others needed only to be partially reconstructed. At present, the number of catalogs in the library has reached 50, and they are divided into 27 sections. The catalogs are

A. In Yiddish:
1. Fiction
2. Children's literature
3. History and social sciences
4. Other disciplines
    B. In Hebrew:
1. Fiction
2. Children's literature
3. History and social sciences
4. Other disciplines
    C. In Polish:
1. Fiction
2. Children's literature
3. Nonfiction
    D. In Russian:
1. Fiction Catalog A (books published up to 1914)
    Fiction Catalog B (books published after World War I, 1914–18)
2. Children's literature
3. History and social sciences
4. Exact and natural sciences
5. Literary criticism and literary history

6. Judaica

7. Philosophy

   E. In Lithuanian: 1 catalog

   F. In German: 1 catalog

   G. In French: 1 catalog

   H. In English: 1 catalog

   I. Card catalogs for:

1. Bibliography and library science

2. Statistics

3. Lithuanica

Total: 27 catalogs

One catalog remains to be completed: Periodicals.

Due to the loss of some books and the acquisition of others, the book composition of the Ghetto Library has changed during the last year. The proportion of Yiddish and Hebrew books has risen, at the expense of other languages (see table 4).

Similar changes have also occurred among books circulated, with the percentage of Yiddish books twice as high as in 1934.[12] The children's literature category has grown markedly—Yiddish children's literature is utilized to the maximum (see table 3). There is a shortage of this type of book,[13] because previously children were served by the children's library, which had 20,000 volumes of specially selected content at its disposal. That library has been completely destroyed. The sole library in the ghetto must therefore serve not only students from schools and small children but also adult readers. Compared with previous years, the composition of readers also changed according to age and sex. Now more women[14] are reading (see table 9).[15] Readers aged 30 and over now comprise over one third of the total number of active subscribers, which also has some impact upon the language situation. The avidity of reading, in comparison with normal times, has grown. In midweek, books are circulated to about 20 percent of all subscribers; on Sundays, to about 25 percent. The highest level of book circulation is, naturally, among children, who sometimes exchange books daily.[16] The library also serves workers in the labor camps outside of Vilna. There are several dozen such subscriptions outside of the city.[17]

For the year (1 October 1941–1 October 1942), the lending library circulated 88,697 books.

Reading Room

The Mefitse Haskalah Library, as an institution of the Vilna Jewish community—in the absence of subsidies—closed its reading room as long ago as 1925. Paradoxically, it was under ghetto conditions, in September 1941, that it was possible to proceed and clean up the large areas containing the archives and the library's duplicates, and organize a reading room for the ghetto in that space. After sifting through and becoming acquainted with 20,000 volumes that were in the duplicates storage area, the premises were cleaned. Boards for shelves were collected, some furniture was patched together, and with the help of volunteers the Ghetto Reading Room came into existence. The Reading Room commenced its activities in November 1941. Due to the cold, however, it was necessary to close it in December of that year. Its activities were resumed only on 5 May 1942, and now the Reading Room possesses a book collection of 2,895 volumes, of which 1,425 are fiction (49.2 percent), 640 are children's literature (22.1 percent), and 830 items are periodicals (28.7 percent).

The book collection in the Reading Room is divided into fifteen separate classifications, including: Encyclopedias and Lexicons, Dictionaries, Pedagogy and Textbooks, Children's Literature, Philosophy, Economics and Social Sciences, and so on.

The books are located in separate cases, according to their respective classes. The Reading Room's users also have the right to use books from the lending library. During this entire period, the Reading Room's users have requested 20,564 volumes, of which 12,316 volumes were fiction and 8,248 volumes were nonfiction (see table 8)—plus 7,119 periodical items.

Under ghetto conditions, the Reading Room plays a major and significant role. The consultation of reading matter is not all that takes place here; the space affords an opportunity for both reading and mental relaxation.[18]

In order to provide for maximal use of the premises, a seven-day work week has been instituted here (from 10:00 A.M. to 7:00 P.M.), and in the coming weeks the hours of operation will be extended until 9:00 P.M.[19]

VILNA GHETTO LIBRARY
Annual Report, 1941–1942

Table 1
Book collection, by languages
June 1941 – September 1942

Date	Yiddish	Hebrew	Polish	Russian	Other languages	Total
June 1941	10,000	5,500	10,000	18,000	2,000	45,500
September 1942	10,000	5,000	7,000	16,000	1,000	39,000

Time (date)	Yiddish and Hebrew (%)
June 1941	33.3
September 1942	38.3

Note: Typeset tables have been arranged to read from left to right in translation from the original.

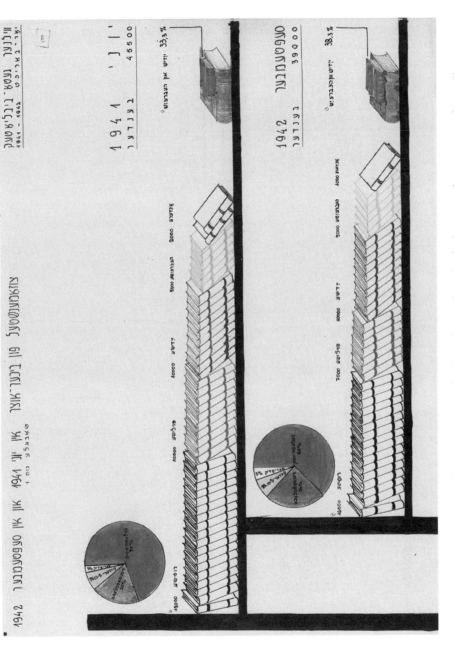

"Table 1. Composition of the book collection in June 1941 and in September 1942."   One book = 1,000 volumes; one cm. spine = 20%

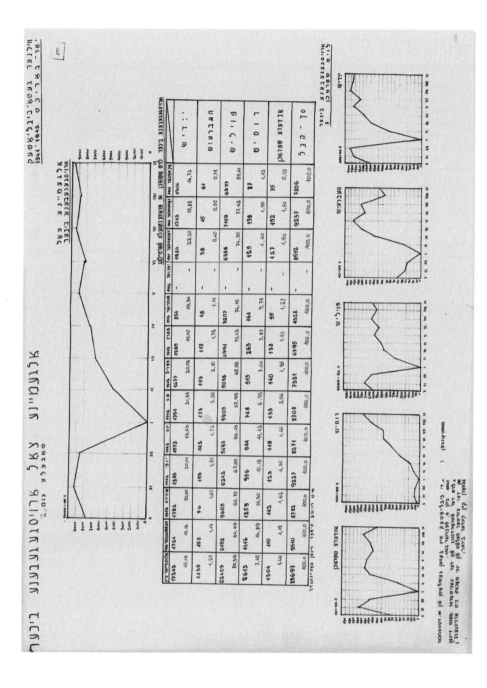

"Table 2. Total number of books lent."

"Note: *(a)* The library was closed from 19 December 1941 until February 1942. *(b)* Pursuant to orders from the sanitation authorities, no children's books were lent during the second half of June."

Top graph shows total number of books lent.

Middle table shows books lent, by language (number and %). Columns from right to left by month: October 1941 – September 1942, Total. Languages from top to bottom: Yiddish, Hebrew, Polish, Russian, Other languages, Total.

Bottom graphs show books lent, by language. From right to left: Yiddish, Hebrew, Polish, Russian, Other languages.

Table 3
Book collection, by languages
15 September 1942

	Yiddish	Hebrew	Polish	Russian
Belle-lettres	59.0	59.0	71.0	52.0
Children's literature	5.0	12.0	16.0	6.0
Nonfiction	30.0	24.0	13.0	30.0
Periodicals	6.0	5.0	–	12.0
Total	100.0	100.0	100.0	100.0

Approximate figures

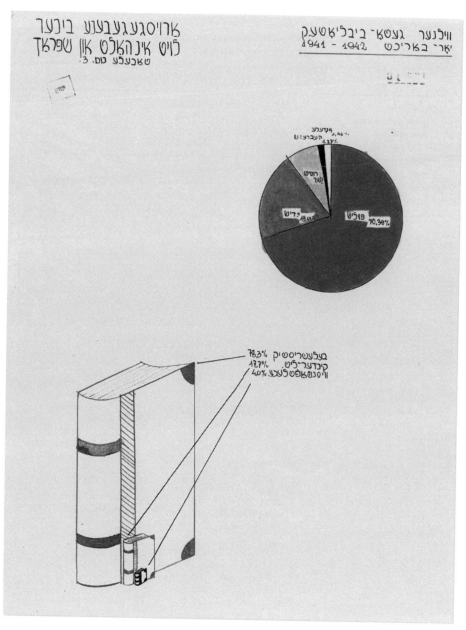

"Table 3. Books lent, by content and language."

Pie chart shows books lent by language (%). Clockwise: Polish (70.39), Yiddish (19.43) Russian (7.46), Hebrew (1.27), Others (1.46).

Book diagram shows books lent, by content (%). Largest to smallest: Belles-lettres (78.3), Children's literature (17.7), Nonfiction (4.0).

Table 4
Books lent, by language and content
September 1941 – September 1942

Books lent (percentages)		Books lent (percentages)	
Belle-lettres	78.3	Yiddish	19.43
Children's literature	17.7	Hebrew	1.27
Nonfiction	4.0	Polish	70.38
		Russian	7.46
Total	100.0	Other languages	1.46
		Total	100.0

Total number of books lent: 88,697 volumes

Precise statistics for children's literature in languages other than Yiddish and Polish are not available.

Table 5
Coefficient[1] of book use
(statistical data for 11 months)

Nonfiction (%)		Children's literature (%)		Belle-lettres, nonfiction, children's literature combined (%)	
Yiddish	15	Yiddish	940	Yiddish	154
Hebrew	–	Hebrew	2	Hebrew	20
Polish	240	Polish	900	Polish	819
				Russian	38
		More precise statistics are lacking; the percentage given is greater than the actual coefficient.		Lithuanian	92
				German	82
				English	130
				French	240

[1] Relation between the number of books lent and the number of volumes held by the library.

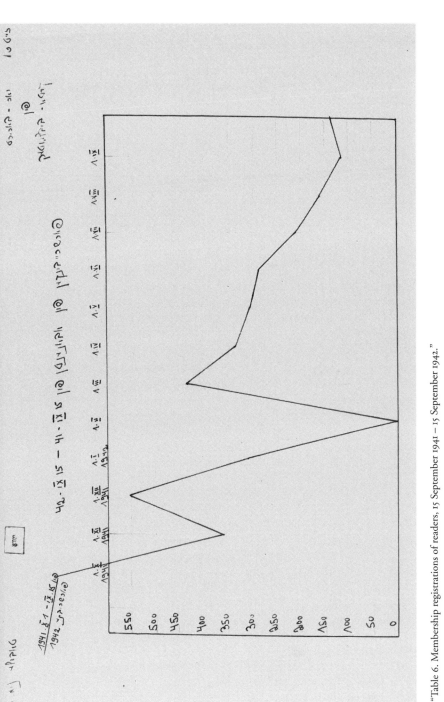

"Table 6. Membership registrations of readers, 15 September 1941 – 15 September 1942."

Left axis: number of registrations; top axis: month and year.
Kühn-Lüdewig: No new registrations took place in January and February 1942, owing to the cessation of work in the library because of the cold weather.

Table 7
Composition of active readers, by age and gender, in 1942

Age (%)	Men (%)	Women (%)	Total (%)
Up to 10	6.9	4.7	5.6
11–14	26.0	17.3	21.1
15–18	16.4	13.0	14.4
19–21	6.9	11.1	9.5
22–30	8.2	15.9	12.7
Over 30	35.6	37.5	36.7
Total	100.0	100.0	100.0

The table includes 1,807 readers.

General total	
59.9%	Women
41.1%	Men
100.0%	

Table 8
Books lent, according to content

	1941	1942						
	December	May	June	July	August	September		Total
Belle-lettres	95	2,235	2,337	2,615	2,693	2,341		12,316
%	31.36	59.56	61.52	55.40	61.78	64.47		59.89
Nonfiction	208	1,517	1,462	2,105	1,666	1,290		8,248
%	68.64	40.44	38.43	44.60	38.22	35.53		40.11
Total	303	3,752	3,799	4,720	4,359	3,631		20,564
%	100.0	100.0	100.0	100.0	100.0	100.0		100.0
Press	444	600	1,201	1,441	1,816	1,557		7,119

During the months of January, February, March, April 1942, the reading room was closed.

Table 9
Number of visitors to the reading room

| | 1941 | | 1942 | | | | | |
	November	December	May	June	July	August	September	Total
Men	–	499	2,192	2,322	2,380	2,129	1,560	11,082
%	–	86.18	83.16	80.82	84.34	85.57	83.92	83.59
Women	–	80	444	551	442	359	299	2,175
%	–	13.82	16.84	19.18	15.66	14.43	16.08	16.41
Total	240	579	2,636	2,873	2,822	2,488	1,859	13,257
%	100.0	100.0	100.0	100.0	100.0	100.0	100.0	100.0

During the months of January, February, March, April 1942, the reading room was closed.

נאָוועמבער ־ 240

דעצעמבער ־ 979

יאַנואַר *

פֿעברואַר

מערץ

אַפּריל

מײַ ־ 2636

יוני ־ 2873

יולי ־ 2822

אויגוסט ־ 2488

סעפּטעמבער ־ 1859

490 80

2192 444

2322 551

2380 442

2129 359

1500 299

*דער לייענזאַל איז געווען געשלאָסן.

פרויען 500   לעזער 500

"Table [9]. Number of visitors to the reading room."
"*The reading room was closed."

Symbols in lower left: Women (gray) = 500 readers; Men (black) = 500 readers.
Months from top: November 1941 – September 1942.

Table 10

Book collection, by content and languages

	Yiddish	Hebrew	Russian	Others	Total	%
Children's literature	460	180	–	–	640	22.1
%	71.88	28.12	–	–	100.0	
Belle-lettres	985	280	110	50	1,425	49.2
%	69.13	19.65	7.72	3.50	100.0	
Periodicals	460	270	70	30	830	28.7
%	55.42	32.53	8.43	3.62	100.0	
Total	1,905	730	180	80	2,895	100.0
%	65.80	25.22	6.22	2.76	100.0	

Table 14

Books lent, by language

Months	Days	Yiddish					Polish					Hebrew	Russian	Lithuanian	German	French	English	Total, all languages
		Belles-lettres	Children's literature	Nonfiction	Total	%	Belles-lettres	Children's literature	Nonfiction	Total	%							
December	1-10	458	552	14	1,024	23.2	2,345	788	73	3,206	72.7	33	65	29	14	11	22	4,404
	11-20	448	407	5	855	20.8	2,318	718	96	3,132	76.3	5	60	21	9	7	14	4,103
	×21-31	—	—	—	—	—	—	—	—	—	—	—	—	—	—	—	—	—
	Total	906	959	19	1,879	22.0	1,663	1,506	169	6,338	74.5	38	125	50	23	18	36	8,507

×During the last third of December the library was closed, by order of the authorities.

Tables 11-13 not present. Table 14 is handwritten and does not include a page number, so its placement in this position does not necessarily correspond to its position in the original typescript.

THE GHETTO AND GHETTO READERS

The Miracle of the Book

It is too early for us to be able to analyze the psychological attributes of the ghetto reader, but we can certainly make an attempt to do so.

Once would have imagined that the notorious events on Glezer Street (2 and 3 September 1941),[20] the move into the ghetto, and the first days of ghetto life could have been harbingers of nothing good—let alone that books might still have any kind of relevance to their harassed and persecuted readers.

Books, which for the overwhelming majority are a medium of entertainment—and an instructional medium only for a minority (a medium for self-reflection, immersion, and self-fulfillment)—for whom could they possibly be of any use now?

Under the prevailing circumstances, the Vilna reader could amuse himself, and absolutely not be entertained. Instruction, self-fulfillment—no one then could appreciate their merits. Vilna was being drowned in Jewish blood. Reading, at that time, could be interpreted only as a form of withdrawal from the surrounding conditions.

Such indeed was the situation, as far as could be imagined. The fact that the initiative to transform the Mefitse Haskalah Library into a ghetto library came so quickly could have been interpreted as a desire to rescue the library as an idea. That books might be read in the ghetto—few could have imagined or believed it. In any case, that was how it appeared on 8 September, when the premises of the library were "seized." But as soon as the library became accessible to the ghetto reader (15 September), it became apparent that these assumptions were far removed from reality. The new ghetto citizens threw themselves at the books like thirsty lambs. Even the terrible events were incapable of restraining not only the children but also a large segment of the adult readership. It became obvious that adult readers could not be parted from the printed word. The book became a narcotic, a means of escape.

A human being can endure hunger, poverty, pain, and suffering, but he cannot tolerate isolation. Then, more than in normal times, the attraction of books and reading is almost indescribable.

In the ghetto, each individual is allotted scarcely 70 square centimeters [approximately 7 square feet]. Everything is heaped onto the floor, without a table or a chair. The house is like a gigantic beehive. Still, you lie down, doubled up on your meager possessions, and you ingest the narcotic—the book. The new ghetto inhabitant thus clings to the little bit of what remained from before. Books carried him away, over the ghetto walls and into the world. A reader could thus tear himself away from his oppressive isolation and in his mind be reunited with life, with his stolen freedom.

On 1 October, Yom Kippur,[21] about 3,000 people were extracted from various hiding places and taken out of the Vilna ghetto, and already on 2 October there were gigantic queues of readers waiting for a book. That same day, 390 books were circulated by the library. On the third and fourth, masses of people were removed from Ghetto No. 2. The tension in Ghetto No. 1 was beyond description, but already on the fifth no fewer than 421 books were circulated. On the twenty-fourth the Action of the "Yellow Certificates" took place;[22] on the twenty-sixth people returned from Ghetto No. 2 to Ghetto No. 1,[23] where aside from the general destruction they encountered doors torn from their hinges and pillaged household goods. And already on the ninth[24] the library circulated 381 books. Thus, from Action to Action, purge to purge.[25]

Each Action, however, left its legacy. Along with the "borrowed" readers, the books that had been lent to them also departed. Fewer people remained in the ghetto, and fewer books in the library.

The more complicated that life becomes, the harder it gets for there to be any kind of intellectual exertion. Not only does the act of reading get more difficult for the reader, but so does the ability to make sense of the artistic details. Readers, first and foremost women, normally devour light fiction, mysteries, and semi-trashy books—and that is the situation that currently prevails. The reading of higher-quality books is rarely encountered. Mostly, as we have already noted, mysteries are requested, for example, [Antoni Stanisław] Marczynski, Nasielski, Romanski, and Błażejewski, in Polish; translations of Courths-Mahler, Wallace, and so on; [Olga] Bebytova, [Nadezhda Aleksandrovna] Lappo-Danilevskaya, Naval, and Wezli [?], in Russian. The middlebrow reader (especially women) devours [Karel] Poláček, [Margaret] Mitchell, [Floyd? Ethel May?] Dell, and Vicki Baum. Among intellectual readers, [Roger Martin] du Gard, [Jakob] Wassermann, [Mark] Aldanov, and [Roman Borisovich] Gul [Yvan Goll?] are popular.[26] In general, though, there is virtually no demand for such authors as [Gustave] Flaubert, [Maksim] Gorki, and so on, and very little demand for [Fyodor] Dostoevsky and [Romain] Rolland.

These are our readers' preferences.

Analogies to the Present

Every social tremor influences the reader's mood and, naturally, his reading. The ghetto reader is psychologically crippled; his highest ideal is to escape from the ghetto. His minimal concern is that at the very least he will survive. In this psychological atmosphere, only two things are possible: reading for the purpose of intoxication—that is, in order to stop thinking—or the contrary, reading in order to ponder, to become interested in comparable fates, to make analogies and reach certain conclusions.[27] If the vast majority of readers fall into the former category, quite the opposite is true of the latter. They are the socially mature readers who endeavor to draw general conclusions from each situation that confronts them.

The reader often likes to use a book as a mirror, as a reflection of his situation and the surrounding conditions. Readers look for analogies in books, which can frequently be quite educational. It is known, for example, that during the World War (1914–18), more sophisticated readers from the civilian population (often also in the hospitals, among the wounded) devoured books about heroism, the history of wars, memoirs about wars, and so on.

Analogies: It was established that a hungry person reads eagerly about hunger, while someone with a full stomach cannot abide that kind of subject matter.

Psychological atmosphere: It is known, for example, that youths of a certain age are adventurous and that at that age the young reader practically drowns himself in adventure literature.

Here, too, similar observations can be made: Here, in ghetto conditions, among a certain stratum of the socially mature intelligentsia, the reading of L. N. Tolstoy (in all available languages)—especially his monumental work *War and Peace*—occupies first place.

The reader, by his very nature, dislikes multivolume works. Experience has demonstrated that the more volumes there are, the more bored the reader gets; the reader loses his patience. This can be especially understood regarding the preoccupied ghetto reader. And yet, there is one fact that speaks to our prewar logic: Tolstoy's *War and Peace* is read with the greatest interest, page by page and volume by volume.

Interestingly enough, during the years 1925–41 (i.e., for approximately 16 years), *War and Peace* was lent by the library a total of 237 times. During the ghetto period (September 1941–September 1942), 86 times—that is, 600 percent more. The same work, in Polish, was lent 150 times during the years 1938–41. In the ghetto period, 69 times—again, 38 times[28] [i.e., percent] more. In Yiddish we are unfortunately unable to render an accounting; the first volumes of the set are missing. All in all, though, the work in Yiddish is read very avidly.

War literature comprises more than just the aforementioned work, however. The library experiences a large number of requests for the following type of war literature: [Erich Maria] Remarque's *All Quiet on the Western Front*, [Jaroslav] Hašek's *The Good Soldier Švejk*, [Emile] Zola's *War*; the Polish translation of [R. C.] Sheriff's *Journey's End* (*Kres wędrówki*), and so on (most of them are banned); requests for war writings by such authors as [Marshal Ferdinand] Foch, [Prime Minister David] Lloyd George; memoirs by [Gen. Anton] Denikin, [Gen. Alexis] Wrangel, Mark Aldanov, and so on. Once again: analogies, analogies, and analogies—people are seeking analogies and exploring them.

The Jewish masses were thrown into the ghetto and a number of readers are delving into Jewish history, especially the history of the Jews during the Middle Ages. They read about and explore the history of the Crusades, the history of the Inquisition, and the demand is strongest above all for such novels as Sholem Asch's *Kidush ha-Shem* or his *Sorceress of Castile*, [Israel] Zangwill's *Dreamers of the Ghetto*,[29] or, in Polish, [Kazimiera] Alberti's *Ghetto Potępione*.

What some are attracted to, the majority runs away from.

The Forty Days of Musa Dagh [by Franz Werfel] is an analogy; *War and Peace*, the Crusades, the Inquisition—all are analogies to the present. Consequently, just now there is a demand for this type of literature. The broad mass of readers does not seek analogies, however. For them, what suffices is reading matter that removes them from reality, carries them off to distant regions, whether via detective stories, suspense, romance, and so forth.

Where one person loses himself through amusement, the other does so by seeking to understand and comprehend.

Languages

It is a mistake to assume that Vilna is experiencing an expansion of Yiddishism. In the historical portion of the annual report we point out that in the former Mefitse Haskalah Library, in 1930, 15.9 percent of books read were in Yiddish; in 1934, 8 percent. In subsequent years Yiddish and Hebrew together reached barely 20 percent, and that also reflected the composition of the book collections: Mefitse Haskalah, the largest Jewish community library in Vilna, possessed 45,000 volumes before the outbreak of the war; of these, Yiddish and Hebrew combined totaled barely 15,000 volumes, and Polish and Russian, 28,000 volumes.

Here in the ghetto, where Yiddish is the language of the street and where it is the official "state" language, the library also reflects this reality poorly. In the ghetto, the reading of Polish accounts for over 70 percent of the average book circulation (see table 2); Yiddish, barely 20 percent; Hebrew, not even 2 percent. The case of Russian is characteristic (see table 2). In the first days of the ghetto, October 1941, the library circulated 87 works in Russian, comprising 1.12 percent of the total number of books circulated. But in September 1942, the library circulated 1,416 works in Russian, comprising 14.89 percent. This can also be explained by the fact that the book collections, for understandable reasons, not only are not growing but, to the contrary, are shrinking. When a Polish book is hard for readers to find, some of them—particularly the older element—return to Russian.

Who Is the Ghetto Reader and How Does He Read?

The first three sections tell us a lot about what and how the ghetto reader reads. Much has been left unstated, however. We recollect our faulty prediction that the ghetto would have no need for reading. We have already seen that people in the ghetto are actually reading avidly—in the first instance, in order to forget themselves; and in the second, because of the quest for analogies, along with immersion and uplift. In both cases, however, this is a means of escape. We have attempted to penetrate the psychological direction of the reader; let us now also attempt to penetrate into his method of reading.

Readers who wish to educate themselves and seek a systematic approach to reading are altogether absent. In the nonfiction category, many biographies and much memoir literature are being read.

As far as fiction is concerned, the quality of the reading matter has fallen significantly. Perhaps this is not entirely the readers' fault; it is most likely a result of the fact that books that might be read with greater enthusiasm are lacking.

From table 4 we learn, for example, that among circulated books, according to language and content, 78 percent of what is being read in the library is fiction; nonfiction, barely 4 percent. Yet a very different picture emerges in the Reading Room: Fiction accounts for almost 60 percent of what is being read; nonfiction is around 40 percent (see table 8).

If the Ghetto Library provides the reader with a book in his home, the Ghetto Reading Room represents a home in and of itself, as well as a study hall for the more sophisticated reader. A reader is often able to conceal his areas of interest by borrowing a book and taking it home; it is difficult for these interests not to be in plain view in the Reading Room.

Our reader tastes the full flavor of the ghetto. We often encounter him taking an interest in the history of the medieval ghetto (analogies once again?). The literature of analogy is not only sought in reference books; histories and works of fiction are also explored. Not only do people read about ghetto history; they also read fiction employing ghetto themes. In the Reading Room we encounter almost the same phenomenon as in the lending library. People study the history of the Jews, Jewish history in the Middle Ages, the Crusades, the period of the Inquisition. Even children are drawn to this type of literature, reading Flavius Josephus's *History of the Jewish Wars*. Sholem Asch's *Kidush ha-Shem* and his *Sorceress of Castile*, and so on, are also being read.

Of visitors to the Reading Room, 13.8 percent are female and 86.2 percent are male.[30] Some are interested almost exclusively in the press. Children often leaf through old illustrated publications. For most readers the Reading Room is a workplace; both reading and writing take place here. Scholarly studies are written here; preparations for public events are also made from here; people study and conduct research here. Thus the Reading Room is the only place for mental relaxation and the only nook for serious intellectual work in the ghetto.

Generally, tired and fatigued adult readers come to the Ghetto Reading Room to relax, not to read. That, for example, is what table 8 demonstrates—that out of 27,683 items circulated during a five-month period, 7,119 were press items. This does not mean (perish the thought!) current press. Most people who come here to relax and sit on a normal chair and at a normal table do not read; they skim. They go through old volumes of the *Literarishe bleter*,[31] the *Tsukunft*[32] (from America), or an illustrated journal and the like. Once again, we note the same thing: People wish to be carried away, over the ghetto walls and into the world of fantasy.

Which segments of the population make up the readers of the ghetto? In previous years (1924–33), as many as 55 percent were women. Later on, the female component declined to 50 percent. Now, in the ghetto, 41 percent of the readers are men, and 59 percent, women. The turnover of books read by women is much more frequent than with men. The reason is clear: men are at work; women work less.

By age: Previously, the largest number of readers was recruited from the 15-to-30-year-old age bracket (in 1920, 50 percent; in 1931, 65 percent; in 1934, 57 percent); today, in the Ghetto Library, the number of readers from 15 to 30 years old amounts to 36.6 percent. Again, the same reason: this element is at work and is more tired out.

Child readers display the most insistent need to exchange their books frequently. All in all, the frequency of turnover is quite high.

There can be no discussion regarding educational work in the library—regarding attempts to elevate the reader and lead him in a particular direction. The situation at hand impedes that, as does the shortage of books. The supply of books is such that we are able to be nourished only by leftovers; nothing new is being, or will be, added. The few books that do remain are virtually swallowed up by the readers. The books are tattered; complete sets are becoming broken sets (e.g., the case of *War and Peace* in Yiddish); and soon the library will be left with empty shelves.[33]

Librarianship can be pursued in the ghetto only to the extent that anything can be achieved here. Just as conditions are difficult in every other area of ghetto life, they are all the more difficult in the library.

Vilna Ghetto
September 1943 [i.e., 1942]

SELECTED BIBLIOGRAPHY

Abramowicz, Dina. "Vilner geto-bibliotek," in *Lite* [Lithuania], ed. Mendel Sudarski et al., cols. 1671–78, New York: Jewish-Lithuanian Cultural Society, 1951. Memoir by a surviving member of the Vilna Ghetto Reading Room staff (later: head librarian [1962–87] of the YIVO Institute for Jewish Research, New York). German translation: "Die Bibliothek im Wilnaer Ghetto," in *Laurentius* 4/5–6 (1987): 37–54.

[Abramowicz, Dina.] "Keeper of a Civilization," by Jeff Sharlet, in *The Book Peddler/Der pakn-treger* 21 (Spring 1996): 9–21.

Arad, Yitzhak. *Ghetto in Flames: The Struggle and Destruction of the Jews in Vilna in the Holocaust*. New York: Holocaust Library, 1982.

Kruk, Herman. *Togbukh fun Vilner Geto* [Diary of the Vilna Ghetto]. Notes and explanations by Mordecai W. Bernstein. New York: YIVO Institute for Jewish Research, 1961. In Yiddish; excerpts were published in English translation under the title "Diary of the Vilna Ghetto," in *YIVO Annual* 13 (1965): 10–78. An expanded English translation has been published: Herman Kruk, *The Last Days of the Jerusalem of Lithuania: Chronicles from the Vilna Ghetto and the Camps*, ed. Benjamin Harshav, trans. Barbara Harshav. New Haven: Yale University Press with YIVO Institute for Jewish Research, 2002.

[Kruk, Herman.] "Erinnerungen an Hermann Kruk," by Dina Abramowicz, in *Laurentius* 6/1 (1989): 51–58. Translated from a Yiddish manuscript.

[Kruk, Herman.] *Herman Kruk: Bibliothekar und Chronist im Ghetto Wilna.* Übersetzt aus dem Jidd[ischen] und herausgegeben von Maria Kühn-Ludewig. Hannover: Laurentius Sonderheft, 1990. The German translation of Kruk's annual report, "Ghetto-Bibliothek und Ghetto-Leser," is found on pp. 48–[74]. This volume also contains an extensive bibliography of Kruk's own writings, works about Kruk, and secondary literature on the Vilna ghetto.
————. "Jewish Libraries in the Polish Ghettos during the Nazi Era." *Library Quarterly* 52/2 (1982): 103–21.
Shavit, David. *Hunger for the Printed Word: Books and Libraries in the Jewish Ghettos of Nazi-Occupied Europe.* Jefferson, N.C.: McFarland, 1997. See the chapter, "Vilna Ghetto" (93–112).

TRANSLATOR'S ACKNOWLEDGMENTS

I would like to express my deepest thanks to my late colleague Dina Abramowicz, Reference Librarian of the YIVO Institute for Jewish Research (New York), for the unique perspective that she brought to bear as the last surviving staff member of the Vilna Ghetto Library and Reading Room. I would also like to express my gratitude to Jonathan Rose, Director of the Center for the History of the Book at Drew University (Madison, N.J.), for his helpful editorial comments, and Maria Kühn-Ludewig (Paris), for her painstaking research on the Vilna Ghetto Library and its librarian, Herman Kruk.

NOTES
by Maria Kühn-Ludewig
(Updated by Zachary M. Baker and Jonathan Rose)

1. Kruk's report was written in 1942 in Yiddish. The original is located in the Archives of the YIVO Institute for Jewish Research, New York (Sutzkever-Katcherginski Collection, R G 223, folder 369/370). The English translation is based on a typed copy of the original.
2. Vilna belonged to Russia until 1915.
3. The Mefitse Haskalah Library, along with other Jewish libraries, was nationalized in November 1940 (i.e., during the Soviet occupation of Vilna) and administered by the Municipal Cultural Affairs Office as Public Library No. 5. With the elimination of subscription fees, usage increased. See Shavit, *Hunger,* 108.
4. Whereas Yiddish and Hebrew titles made up over 30 percent of the holdings, as indicated by the preceding statistics.
5. In the German-occupied Generalgouvernement of Poland as well, the few reopened libraries were not allowed to keep any foreign-language materials; see Hildegard Brenner, *Die Kunstpolitik des Nationalsozialismus* (Hamburg: Rowohlt, 1963), 138. Regarding the library's losses, see Kruk's *Togbukh,* 186 ff. On 25 February 1942, Kruk notes that in addition to restrictions imposed from outside, Jewish librarians also contributed to the destruction of collections, out of fear of German censorship, by setting aside all works that might be politically suspect.
6. Kruk is referring to the shootings, deportations, and forced resettlements that took place in July and August 1941, before the ghetto was established.

7. "Actions" (*Aktionen*) refers to the shootings and deportations that took place from mid-September until 12 December 1941 in the two Vilna ghettos that were originally established, during the course of which 20,000 Jews were murdered.

8. This refers to the Jewish children's library, established in 1909. The names on the typescript are barely legible.

9. Naftali Veynig, pen name of the critic and folklorist Naftali (Norbert) Rose, was active as a teacher in various schools in Vilna. In 1943, he was deported to Estonia and died in a concentration camp there in 1944. See Kruk, *Togbukh*, 81 n. 110.

10. Pinkhas Kon, originally from Lodz, studied law in Vilna. A journalist and staff member of YIVO, he was appointed a member of the German-imposed Jewish Council on 4 July 1941, arrested by the Gestapo on 2 September 1941, and murdered in Ponary. See Kruk, *Togbukh*, 10 n. 20; on p. 82, Kruk mentions the efforts to recover Kon's books for the Ghetto Library.

11. Moshe Shalit was the longtime president of the Jewish writers' association in Vilna. He was deported to Ponary and shot on 29 July 1941. See Kruk, *Togbukh*, 75 n. 103.

12. 1934: 8 percent; 1941/42: 19.43 percent.

13. I.e., a shortage in the Mefitse Haskalah Library.

14. The percentage of women readers rose from 52–53 percent, on average, during the 1930s (Mefitse Haskalah Library), to 59.9 percent during the ghetto year of 1941/42.

15. I.e., table 7 (table 9 deals with use of the Reading Room).

16. See Dina Abramowicz's account of the Ghetto Library in *Lite* (German translation in Laurentius) and in this volume (pp. 167–68), and Jeff Sharlet's article on Dina Abramowicz in *The Book Peddler/Der pakn-treger*.

17. In such camps, forced laborers were used for logging and peat cutting; their "base camp" was the Vilna ghetto. See Kruk, *Togbukh*, 413 (20 Nov. 1942) and 443 (10 Jan. 1943).

18. In a diary entry for 8 May 1942, Kruk notes the great appreciation and pleasure with which the "ghetto intelligentsia" greeted the reopening of the Ghetto Reading Room and their recognition of its role as an important cultural enterprise in the ghetto. Visitors regarded the Reading Room as the "nicest cultural site in the ghetto," thanks to its pleasant atmosphere. See Kruk, *Togbukh*, 262.

19. The lending library was open daily from 11:00 A.M. to 5:30 P.M., beginning on 6 December 1942. See Kruk, *Togbukh*, 419.

20. In the history of Vilna's Jews, this is known as "The Great Provocation." As punishment for an attack against German soldiers that was allegedly committed by Jews, 3,700 Jews were shot during the succeeding days. The Germans were pursuing the objective of "cleaning out" the Jewish quarter of the Old City, in order to establish a ghetto in this district shortly thereafter.

21. The Day of Atonement, the most important Jewish holy day. On that day, the Germans expelled 1,700 Jews from Ghetto No. 2 and 2,200 from Ghetto No. 1. See Arad, *Ghetto in Flames*, 136–39.

22. See ibid., n. 55.

23. On 21 October 1941, Ghetto No. 2 was completely "liquidated"; of the original 9,000 Jews, some 4,000 survived. About 2,000–3,000 were able to take refuge in Ghetto No. 1 or were officially admitted there; see ibid., 141 ff.

24. Kruk does not indicate the month. It could mean either 29 October or 9 November.

25. A similar account is contained in the section "Books and Readers," in Kruk's *Togbukh*, 257 ff. For a contrast, see Kruk's observations after the murder of 4,000 Jews in Ponary on 4 April 1943: "It is quiet in the Library" (503 ff.).

26. Not all of the authors' names can be verified; they are given here with incomplete annotations: e.g., Olga Bebytova, Russian émigrée; Nadezhda Aleksandrovna Lappo-Danilevskaya (born 1876), Russian émigrée; Margaret Mitchell, author of *Gone with the Wind*; either Floyd Dell (born 1887), American author, or Ethel May Dell; Roger Martin du Gard (1881–1958), French short-story writer; Jakob Wassermann (1873–1924), German-Jewish novelist; Mark Aldanov (1886–1957), Russian novelist; either Roman Borisovich Gul (born 1896), Russian émigrée, or Yvan Goll, French author.

27. In a mid-March 1943 diary entry, Kruk deals with problems connected to the drawing of historical parallels to the present. See his *Togbukh*, 471 ff. But there is no historical equivalent to the Germans' extermination policy, which sought to wipe the Jews off the face of the earth.

28. When one calculates that the 150 loans for 1938–41 cover a three-year period, that averages out to 50 loans per year, versus 69 times for 1941/42. If it covers a four-year period, then the average is 37.5 loans per year; thus 1941/42 (69 loans) is 31.5 percent more.

29. The two historical novels by Asch (1880–1957) were published in 1920 and 1921; Israel Zangwill (1864–1918), who was raised in London's East End "ghetto," published his book in 1898; the title of Kazimiera Alberti's book is based upon a 1995 reprint.

30. Kruk, relying on table 9, apparently is referring only to the figures for the month of December 1941. The tables give a cumulative percentage of 16.41 percent females and 83.59 percent males, based on a total of 13,257 Reading Room visitors.

31. This Yiddish weekly, founded by Nakhmen Mayzel (1887–1966), was published in Warsaw from 1924 to 1939.

32. Published (monthly, though lately less frequently) in New York since 1892, this is the oldest surviving Yiddish periodical in the world.

33. A couple of months after concluding the "Annual Report," Kruk noted in his diary (9 Nov. 1942) that 20,000 rubles had been granted by the ghetto leadership for the acquisition of Polish books. See his *Togbukh*, 399.

XI • WHEN THE PRINTED WORD CELEBRATES
THE HUMAN SPIRIT

Charlotte Guthmann Opfermann

To Henny, Sigi, and all the other caregivers-teachers at barrack building L414 in Ghetto Theresienstadt, who gave comfort and meaning to the lives of others in the midst of misery, despair, and death. They live on in the endless memories of those few whom they saved, however briefly, with self-sacrifice, kindness, and love.

A COUPLE of years ago I took part in a seminar at the site of the Theresien-stadt Garrison in Czechoslovakia, which was (from 1941 until our liberation in May 1945) the site of a fierce Nazi concentration camp. One of the breakout sessions during this meeting in 1993, conducted in the former SS Guard club-house, was devoted to the many prominent artists, writers, composers, per-forming artists, and scientists who were imprisoned there at one time or another. Many died in the camp; most were redeported to Auschwitz-Birkenau, Majda-nek, or Sobibor, to their deaths. I was in my teens when I went to Theresienstadt, and I am one of about a hundred children who survived, out of some 15,000 who had been sent to the camp.

A fellow scholar, Frau Kypke from Bonn, was fascinated to learn during the 1993 conference that there were so many famous names among the 65,000 or so inmates who were imprisoned there when I was in the camp—inventors, scien-tists, authors, film stars, and film directors. Word had been spread in Germany at the time, in the early 1940s, that this camp was a privileged "Jewish settlement," intended for World War I veterans, prominent German Jews, and people over the age of sixty-five. Unfortunately, this myth has continued to this day. In reality, it was but a transit point. Many of the arriving trains were never unloaded but sent directly on to the extermination camps and killing fields farther east.

Much to my surprise, Frau Kypke, who was eighty years old or more, spoke freely of the fact that her late husband had been a guard at the Auschwitz concen-tration camp. But she herself had seen the light and now studied the events of the Holocaust. She said she worked for an organization called Für den Frieden (For Peace).

For a while, during my own imprisonment in 1943–45, I had been privileged to know and to enjoy the friendship of some of those prominent prisoners; wonderful and exciting artists who were working alongside the rest of us, doing heavy labor. At the 1993 conference, I was one of the sources of firsthand information. So many artists, so much talent, each with a grand total of 2.5 meters (about 6' × 36") of living space in which to stretch their legs after work for a sleepless, nightmare-burdened night.

During the question-and-answer session, Frau Kypke demanded to know where one could now find the work of these many talented individuals. She was eager to read what they had written about life in the camp. I could not believe my ears. I asked her to repeat the question. Then, trying not to be impolite or to appear condescending, I said: "Frau Kypke, we were brought here to die and to be killed. We had neither paper nor ink nor contact with the outside world. No publisher or printer would have touched any of the output of a Jewish writer even years before we were arrested, 'resettled,' as the euphemistic expression went. They had been famous *before* the Third Reich, not during its reign. In the camp they worked like everybody else at heavy manual labor. Some of the very fortunate ones worked—part-time—for the internal *Freizeitgestaltung* [leisure-time creative organizers]. Their audience was very limited, consisted largely of prominent prisoners such as they themselves were. The rest of us had no time, energy, or leisure to indulge. Good God, we did not have toilet paper, much less paper to write on or to communicate our intellectual output to the free world."

After this outburst, I felt a little guilty. Maybe my SS-guard-widow/colleague-Holocaust-researcher was confused. I told her and some of the other conference-goers that, indeed, many of us had packed a favorite book at the time of our deportation. We were allowed up to 44 pounds of luggage, consisting of warm clothing, sturdy shoes, some nonperishable food, and many of us thought it necessary to pack a book—a prayer book, a Bible, a copy of Goethe's *Faust,* Shakespeare's *Hamlet.* Most of the books then landed on the piles of confiscated luggage upon arrival at the railroad siding in Bauschowitz, where the deportation trains unloaded their sad human cargo for the four-kilometer march along the pot-holed, unpaved road to the gates of Ghetto Theresienstadt, as it was then known.

Toward the end, a lending library was set up in Theresienstadt, its shelves stocked with these confiscated books. But few people could spare the time (we had only one hour of leisure time between the end of our workday and lights-out curfew) or energy to go and search its shelves. The well-intentioned managers of the library, prisoners themselves, organized a rotation program, sending a weekly supply of books to the different barracks. They found that many books would come back with substantial amounts of their pages missing, torn out by prisoners desperate for nonavailable toilet paper.

During the second half of my imprisonment I worked as a caregiver for children. This was a privileged job, and I owe it and the preferred housing in the children's barracks to friends who intervened on my behalf. The children I cared for had to work a regular shift, some ten-hour days. But the internal camp administrators tried to arrange it so that they were assigned easy jobs, working as *Ordon-*

nanzen, running errands for the internal administration, often being the bearers of redeportation schedules (i.e., death notices). Innocent children as angels of death. Most of these children had been imprisoned for three or four years and had not attended any kind of educational institution as long as they could remember.

We tried, in the little time available, to teach them the rudiments of reading, writing, or arithmetic. This was very difficult, since we had neither pencils nor paper nor books to work with. The handsome drawings which are now widely shown as the product of Theresienstadt's child prisoners were produced by Czech children, who were housed in different barracks and lived under slightly different circumstances. The German-Jewish children had no such treats available to them. They suffered the unique distinction of never learning how to love or to hate, to read or to write; they were too busy trying to deal with their growling stomachs, with their grief for lost and redeported parents, siblings, and friends.

Their brief lives were clouded by the knowledge that they were hated and probably destined to die without knowing or understanding the reasons why. We caregivers were not trained or intelligent enough to give them the tools with which they could have dealt with this or with many of their other problems, such as trying to make it until morning, until the next deportation east, to death. In the end, they did not need an education to be marched into the gas chambers at Birkenau.

After the camp's liberation by the Russian army, on 8 May 1945, the internal administrators turned camp liquidators. They set up communication with our hometowns, trying to arrange for our redeportation home. And they also scraped together what was left in the way of confiscated books and clothing from our dead and departed fellow prisoners. Most of the confiscated luggage had been sent back to the Reich earlier. But what was left when the SS guards ran for their lives, trying to escape the wrath of the advancing Russian army and leaving us to our fate, was distributed among the surviving prisoners before we went back to the various cities whence we had come: Berlin, Frankfurt, Cologne, Munich, Hannover, Vienna, and points in between.

Almost every one of the hapless earlier arriving travelers on these Voyages of the Damned had included a book in his or her knapsack. In many cases, probably most, this was a prayer book, as evidenced by the vast accumulation of many editions of well-worn *Gebetbücher* piled up high alongside the railroad tracks, along with family pictures, articles of clothing and toiletry necessities, dolls, and nonperishable food. The owners of these articles perished soon enough, many of them immediately upon landing wherever the train unloaded its cargo. The personal luggage was sometimes shared by the guards with inmate transport helpers. Little was wasted. Clothing was sorted by prisoner workers and returned to the Reich. The books were often destroyed. In Theresienstadt there were huge warehouses, *Kleiderkammer* for the sorting of clothes whose owners were often redeported soon enough. Everything was searched for hidden valuables, every seam tested. The books, too, often held stashes of cash or jewelry—long since forbidden to be owned by us—and vials of poison in their spines.

Recently I assisted with the installation of an electronic antitheft beeper system at the library of Friendswood High School in Texas where I teach. While inserting the little chip in the spine of each book, I could not help but think how many reichsmarks could be secreted in that space between the binding and the pages. How much poison and how many different varieties could be stored here? How much and what kind of jewelry—intended for barter for food later or to bribe camp guards into granting some minor concession or privilege—might fit in this empty space? Gutenberg and early bookbinders never knew what secret caches the design of this new commodity "the book" would provide in the far future, during the twelve dismal years of the "Thousand Year Reich."

The PTA volunteers at Friendswood chatted about soap operas, the latest movies, their children's problems and joys, school football games, proms, student–teacher conflicts, college plans. In my mind, I saw piles of clothing, piles of much-loved books, long dead friends and relatives, while putting on an award-winning performance as a normal neighbor and colleague working to prevent the loss through theft of 8,000 books annually at this school. None of the children I knew in the camp—before they died—would have fathomed such a thing as stealing a book at their school. Most of them had not attended school since the mid-1930s when Nazi laws excluded them from the educational process. They would steal a slice of bread in an effort to fill their aching stomachs. They were not so fascinated with books.

Many books from the incoming transports in Theresienstadt ended up in the library where few prisoners were able to use them for a variety of valid reasons. As noted earlier, such a library did, indeed, exist for a while. It was proudly shown to the International Red Cross inspection committee which came to visit the camp in June 1944. They saw nothing, understood nothing, and returned home to Geneva, persuaded that "The Jewish Settlement of Theresienstadt" was a place where Culture and Literature and Knowledge and Art existed and thrived among happy residents. And their reports and stories still circulate today and are gratefully believed by students and researchers and good people who cannot come to grips with visions of the 30,000 unburied corpses found by the British liberators of Bergen-Belsen, of the sacks full of gold teeth extracted from the dead, of the hair prepared for industrial use, shorn from the heads of the victims of the Auschwitz gas chambers, or with the fact that ashes of our 33,000 Theresienstadt dead were dumped into the nearby Eger River outside the confines of the camp, just before the arrival of the victorious advancing Russian army.

But I had promised myself I would give you an uplifting report, as reflected in the positive title of my essay. The human spirit and the love of literature did triumph, but only after the fact. According to carefully kept records, the Theresienstadt camp took in 15,000 children. When the Russian army stumbled upon our location on 8 May 1945, there were 100 surviving children, most of them late arrivals brought here from the Reich in mid-February 1945, two or three months earlier. They were *Mischlinge,* children of mixed Jewish and Christian unions.

Before we tried to return to our former homes, after the quarantine imposed because of typhus and other diseases which were rampant in our camp in the summer of 1945, the still remaining clothes and the large supply of books were made available to us as part of our return luggage, provided generously by the liquidating team of Red Cross workers and inmate volunteers. We could help ourselves to what our dead comrades and fellow inmates had brought with them when they arrived. I searched through rows upon rows of prayer books, single volumes of luxurious leather-bound editions from the collected works of Shakespeare, Goethe, Schiller, Schopenhauer, Hebbel, Kierkegaard, Freud, but also children's books: *Struwwelpeter, Grimm's Fairy Tales,* Gustav Schwab mythology, Else Ury's *Nesthäkchen* series, Karl May's cowboy and Wild West America stories, Wilhelm Busch's portrayals of *Max und Moritz,* that mischievous team of pranksters—you name it. Our entire cultural heritage was represented there for me to choose from.

An avid reader since early childhood, frustrated over my disrupted education, and a bit of a would-be intellectual snob even then, I selected a slim volume (mindful that we would have to hand-carry our few belongings on the return trip as we had upon arrival) of Schopenhauer's works. It was volume 5 of a complete set of I-know-not-how-many books, printed on lightweight fine-quality paper (the thin pages reminded me of the airmail tissue-weight paper we had earlier used for our desperate but unheeded "please help us emigrate" SOS letters to friends and relatives abroad). I have often wondered who had earlier taken possession of the remaining volumes—usually this personal property was auctioned off for the benefit of the Reich. Friends and neighbors of the deported Jews would acquire priceless collections as well as garden-variety cookbooks for a song. I often wonder how the present owner explains the missing volume 5 to the new generation and whether he or she ever thinks of the fate of the rightful owner.

Truth to tell, this was no triumph of the printed word or the human spirit.

XII • CRYING FOR FREEDOM: THE WRITTEN WORD AS I EXPERIENCED IT DURING WORLD WAR II

Annette Biemond Peck

M Y story is an eyewitness report of the most memorable written materials I read during World War II in my hometown of Amsterdam. I was ten years old when Poland was invaded, and sixteen when my country was finally freed by the Allies after five grueling years.

When it comes to comparing national anthems, I think that the Dutch have one that is more strongly entrenched in their history as a nation than any other. The poem on which it is based, written about 1568, highlights the life of Prince William of Orange (1533–84), known as the Father of the United Netherlands. This poem, the "Wilhelmus," was created in a time of desperation, when the United Provinces were fighting the Spanish with very little chance of winning, and it was a source of great spiritual strength for the distressed Hollanders.

In 1940 the Dutch found themselves again under the tyranny of a foreign power, and this solemn song served to unite them once again in a most compelling way. It had been incorporated for many years in the hymnbooks of most Dutch churches, since it was based partially on the Psalms and portrayed William as a God-fearing man. You can just imagine what it meant to the congregation to be invited to sing the national anthem on a Sunday morning in church during the occupation. The sparks of its electric power flew around the people who had risen from their pews singing and crying at the same time. I was there, and I can only say that the minister took a terrible chance, because spies were everywhere, and it could have meant the end of him.

The war as it unfolded asked for all kinds of responses. Some citizens wrote poetry to contribute to the mental strength now required of all. Their works were often published in the many underground publications that were produced. Many poets were not all that gifted, but some were. One of the most powerful examples of underground poetry written in the Dutch language during this war is titled "Het Lied der Achttien Doden" [The song of the eighteen who died] (1942) by Jan Campert. It was written in a concentration camp in Germany and smuggled back to Holland. Its impact can be felt even now, fifty-three years later. I still cry every time I read it. It is a very powerful piece.

My cell is only two yards long
And barely six feet wide
But smaller still will be the place
Where soon I shall abide. . . .
(Translation by Emile van Loo)

Remarkably, this poem parallels the national anthem so dear to the Dutch heart. It has the same rhythm and length of couplets. It also is written in the first person and proclaims, as does the other, the social responsibility of those who fight for the survival and freedom of their nation against awful odds.

The radio was our last resort for uncensored news from our friends in England. The voices of Churchill and our formidable Queen Wilhelmina were listened to in secret closets. Owning a radio had become illegal, and on top of that the Germans did a good job of jamming.

On 15 May 1940 our country had capitulated to the overwhelming power of the army of the Third Reich. In the seven years that led up to this event, many German Jews had left their country and settled where they thought they would be safe. A great number chose the Netherlands because it had maintained neutrality in the First World War, and it was close by. These German Jews knew better than we what this German occupation was going to mean. With feelings of pain and disbelief I noticed the day after the capitulation that many Jews in our city had come out during the night and thrown their most sacred and beautifully bound books with Hebrew titles in the canal near my home. I saw them there with my own eyes sticking up above the surface of the water! This was undoubtedly done to wipe out any possible implication that the owners were of Jewish extraction. Just think of the heritage that was destroyed this way.

The first illegally printed book that took occupied Western Europe by storm came from France. It was written by Vercors (Jean Bruller) as early as 1941 and was called Le silence de la mer [The silence of the sea]. In 1944 it finally came out in a Dutch translation published by De Bezige Bij, long after we all had read it in French. This poetic short story describes how two incompatible feelings fight with each other in the heart of one woman. One is the silent rejection of the Germans in her country, and the other is the strong love and affection she develops for one German officer who is quartered in her house. She holds on to her national pride and never talks to the officer in question except at the very last moment before he leaves to go to the front. It almost destroys her.

My family had no Jewish roots, but my father was picked up anyway early one morning in 1942 by a German soldier. He kissed us goodbye and he was gone. Later we learned that he was one of 100 Amsterdam leaders who were taken hostage and placed in Amersfoort, a Dutch concentration camp. The wives of many of these men started a friendship group to give each other strength and hope. Once a month my mother was allowed to write a letter addressed to my father at the camp. This letter had to be written on a designated sheet of paper that she had received in the mail from the authorities. She knew of course that each word would be scrutinized by the censors. At irregular times Father was allowed to write back. My mother, who was not a clubwoman, wrote in one of her letters to Dad that the ladies' group was meeting regularly. He understood her perfectly, and when he shared this knowledge with his friends it did wonders for their morale. None of these letters has survived, as far as I know. Father returned home, emaciated but not broken.

The whole world knows about Anne Frank, and I should not take time to elaborate. After the war her diary became the channel through which much of the world began to get some understanding of what so many had gone through. We know from the American Civil War how important diaries can be in such times. Many diaries were written in World War II, by young and old, most not as powerful as Anne Frank's. The need to write is heightened by the circumstances—the need to convey to paper certain issues of fear, of hope, and of everyday life. The person who writes gathers new strength by expressing these thoughts on paper. It is a form of therapy, I am sure. As a fourteen-year-old I also started to participate in this form of release. I am still glad I did.

In the fall of 1944 the situation in Amsterdam looked very bleak. We were at the end of our rope. We were awfully hungry and left with barely any fuel to keep us warm in the approaching winter. The public works of Amsterdam stopped abruptly the delivery of electricity and gas to all city dwellers. My mother found in an antique shop a lamp that could burn with a wick. She put her hand also on a couple of liters of kerosene so that our family of six would at least have one source of light at night. My father concluded that this situation asked for a creative solution. He announced that he would read every evening a chapter or two from a book by Theo Thijssen called *Kees de Jongen* [Kees the boy]. The reading of this now almost forgotten work of Dutch literature became a binding force in our family. My father would sit with the book as close as possible to the tiny lamp placed on the coffee table. We all would sit around in near darkness. The adventures of this boy called Kees from that time on larded our family conversations and gave us a much needed focus away from fear, hunger, and cold.

A month or so later we were able to acquire a better lamp. Its light spread out farther into the room and broadened the circle of people able to read. With curfews in place, and no place to go, a new solution was introduced by the wife of a neighbor. She suggested that we would come together on Thursday night each week to discuss the work of one particular poet. We would decide ahead which Dutch master to read. All of us would make our own selections during the week and read those out loud during our group sessions. Thus a wonderful tradition started in November 1944 in the one heated and lighted room of our home. At first we took a number of famous poets from the time of Shelley and Keats. Then we moved to the early and mid twentieth century up to the living poets of our day. Finally we read together the golden oldies of the seventeenth century and even some of our medieval masters. Evenings like that helped me tremendously to grow in mind and spirit when the rest of my body was stunted in its development.

Underground literature and journalism were very much needed to keep the people informed and to prevent despair. Illegal newsletters gradually reached such proportions that they were bigger than what was left of our regular daily paper. The daily paper had one very uplifting feature in it for us teenagers, and that was the wonderfully creative cartoon by Maarten Toonder called "Ollie B. Bommel." We fought over it, I remember.

In the morning we would sometimes find interesting papers in the street. They were dropped by the Allies over our city to inform us about the war effort and to give us hope. I kept some of these tucked in my diary. One was called "The Flying Dutchman" and was written in Dutch. Another, written in German and dated 26 April 1945, was clearly designed to inform German soldiers about war news that their own leadership did not allow them to know.

The power of the Bible in those times of agony should not be forgotten. There is a wealth of material in there about people struggling under domination of one kind or another. Many men and women who had ended their affiliation with a church were drawn back to it. Not all Christian leaders had the depth of vision needed in this hour of truth for Christianity. Society as a whole was supersaturated with hate for the Germans, and many ministers did not rise above that self-destructive behavior. But there was a small minority of religious people who saw this differently, and who addressed the situation in a very powerful (albeit less popular) way.

People like Corrie ten Boom and her sister Betsy preached the Good News to the people they found themselves with in a concentration camp. What we learn from Corrie through her writing is that they did not fall into the trap of hating the occupiers. Instead, they prayed for them and preached forgiveness. This may seem quite extreme, and it was. But the more I think about it the more I respect their vision and their kind of religiousness.

Another woman who worked in a similar way was Etty Hillesum, a Jewish lady who asked to be allowed to work as a counselor in Westerbork. This was a transit camp in the Netherlands for Jews on their way to extermination in Germany, Poland, or Czechoslovakia. She was exterminated herself, but her writings reveal her religious drive to help ease the pain of so many.

The Lord's Prayer was said more than ever. It may take the length of a whole life to grasp its entire meaning, but it certainly preaches a reaction different from hate: "Forgive us our trespasses, as we forgive those who trespass against us." How hard is that to do? These women did it.

PART FOUR

PRESENT AND PAST

Authors protesting the burning of "un-German" books in Germany picket the German consulate in New York. Among the pickets is the noted writer and artist Rockwell Kent. (*Courtesy of World Wide Photo*)

XIII • ZARATHUSTRA AS EDUCATOR?
THE NIETZSCHE ARCHIVE IN GERMAN HISTORY

John Rodden

God is dead.

Nietzsche

Nietzsche is dead.

God [Gott]

Better dead than read.

MarGott
[Margot Honecker, DDR education minister]

*Grafitti on the western side
of the Berlin Wall, 1988*

Signs and wonders. Greetings from the Phoenix.

Nietzsche to Peter Gast, 1888

I

SILBERBLICK. Bright moment, lucky chance.
A sunny day in Weimar, November 1991. Hedwig, thirty-eight, waits solemnly for me in the town square still known as Karl Marx Platz (formerly Adolf Hitler Platz). A spirited, voluble woman, Hedwig has been eager to show me the cultural splendors of her hometown—the Goethehaus, the Schillerhaus, the Liszthaus, all lining the Frauenplan in the center of old Weimar. But today she is reluctant; today, warm morning rays beaming down upon us, Hedwig seems reserved as we stride along the Schillerstrasse toward the outskirts of town. Today our destination is Humboldtstrasse 36, the Villa Silberblick, home of the Nietzsche Archive, which opened in May to the public for the first time since 1945.

Hedwig hands me a May issue of *Die Zeit*. "The Banished One Is Back!" blazons the headline: the reopening of the Archive has been the cultural event of the year in Weimar. As we walk, I muse on the significance of the return to eastern German life of Friedrich Wilhelm Nietzsche (1844–1900): the author of notorious neologisms and catchphrases such as the Will to Power, the *Übermensch* (Superman), the Antichrist, master and slave morality, the blond beast, the free spirit, the last man, eternal recurrence, "God is dead," "Live dangerously!" "Become hard!" "philosophize with a hammer," and "beyond good and evil"; the writer who inspired thinkers such as Heidegger, artists such as Thomas Mann, and men of action such as Mussolini; the philosopher exalted by the Nazis and reviled by the Communists.

No discussion of eastern German education "after the Wall"—and the ongoing political reeducation of eastern Germans—would be complete without reference to the return of the writer regarded as the most important educator in Germany during the first half of this century. Indeed, *Nietzsche als Erzieher* [Nietzsche as Educator] was the title of a popular book in Wilhelmine Germany written by Walter Hammer, a leader of the Wandervogel (birds of passage) youth movement. And as Nietzsche returns to a powerful, reunited Germany, so too do the questions return about the controversial teachings of the author of *Thus Spake Zarathustra*, about his spectacular and worrisome influence on impressionable youth, about his ghastly fate in Wilhelmine and Nazi Germany, and about the lessons to draw from his repression in Communist East Germany.

I am going to the Nietzsche Archive to explore these questions, concerned not only to learn who Nietzsche once represented for Germans but also to discover who he is for them once again, especially for eastern Germans. What does Nietzsche as Educator mean to them in the last decade of the twentieth century? What might they learn from the example of his history of reception? *Ecce Homo* [Behold the man], Nietzsche titled his autobiography—yet that has been impossible in his home state of Saxony since 1945. Nietzsche has been an unperson without a country.

II

> We have no way of preventing people from *darkening* us: the time in which we live throws into us what is most time-bound. . . . But we shall do what we have always done: whatever one casts into us, we take down into our depth—for we are deep, we do not forget—*and become bright again*!
>
> Nietzsche, *The Joyful Wisdom*

The Villa Silberblick: a stately three-story chateau overlooking Weimar. Here Nietzsche resided, shielded from the public on the second floor, during the last three years of his decade of mental illness. Silberblick literally means "silver view," from which derives the figurative meaning of an auspicious chance. Hedwig points out, however, that "Silberblick" possesses other meanings too. The word pertains to the gleaming residue of silver in the refining process and, in colloquial German, refers to a squint or cross-eye.

Vision, destiny, cosmology, purgation, pathology: Did Nietzsche—the philosopher of "radical perspectivism," the "mad genius" of modern German thought, the peerless aphorist and supreme prose stylist of German letters, the half-blind intellectual seer, the ill-fated posthumous victim of Nazi appropriation—appreciate the resonant irony of this overdetermined name? A previous owner christened the villa; we, if not Nietzsche himself, can appreciate the fitness of the residence's name. For *Amor fati!* (love of fate!) was Nietzsche's clarion call. And Providence has indeed proven no kinder to him in his afterlife than during his life.

Might the reopening of the Nietzsche Archive, however, suggest a turn of fortune? Nietzsche is indeed becoming bright again. Yet, at the same time, the "Heil Hitler!" salutes of young neo-Nazis are also on the ascent. Young *faschos* aren't quoting Nietzsche—yet. No right-wing intellectuals have cited Nietzsche to exculpate skinhead street terror—yet. Still, the militant gospel rhythms of Zarathustra's phrases march through my head: "A good war hallows every cause." "This world is the Will to Power and nothing besides." "What is evil?—Whatever springs from weakness." "Be hard and show no mercy, for evil is man's best force." "There are no facts, only interpretations." "Man is a rope over an abyss." "The oldest and healthiest of instincts: One must want to *have* more in order to *become* more!" "Nothing is true, so everything is permitted!"

It is bracing and incendiary language. In the present climate of political unrest in Germany, and given the availability of a potent arsenal of slogans already battle-certified through a century of ideological warfare, can the remilitarization and neonazification of Nietzsche be far off?

The questions unsettle Hedwig. Yes, for just as The Banished One is now back, so too are the old fanaticisms and the newer warnings; so too is the dithyrambic furor that accompanied Nietzsche's reign as national philosopher in Wilhelmine and Nazi Germany—and the unavoidable fact of his burdensome legacy for Germans. Only recently have the citizens of the former DDR (German Democratic Republic) begun to grapple with his ambiguous bequest, only since abandoning the pretense that East Germans had resisted Hitler all along, that the task of *Vergangenheitsbewaeltigung* (overcoming the past) was not their task at all because East Germans had no guilty past to overcome.

For these reasons, the return of Nietzsche means also the return of countless memories that eastern Germans have repressed since 1945. Now that the Nietzsche Archive is open, the question is finally also open as to whether and how eastern Germans will confront their nazification of Nietzsche. For readmitting Nietzsche to cultural life in eastern Germany means admitting what had always lain behind East Germans' efforts to exorcise him: their reluctance to acknowledge that Communist East Germany had also once been Nazi Germany. It means delving into their own secret archives: The newly opened Villa Silberblick is eastern Germany's intellectual counterpart of the newly opened *Stasi* files.

Might eastern Germans begin to face the past by facing Nietzsche? It will be hard indeed to confront the last century of German intellectual history without addressing him. And it will be impossible to face him by effacing the past: without confronting the gap between what *he* said and what was said *of* him, both before and after 1945, that is, without seeing him whole, not just gobbling snippets out of context and swallowing the Nazi or Communist lines on him.

As neo-Nazi youth once again rule the night in some cities in eastern Germany, the task of *Vergangenheitsbewaeltigung* has hardly begun. It must begin somewhere, and perhaps the most appropriate, if most painful, place to begin is with Nietzsche and the Villa Silberblick. Here in February 1932, Elisabeth Forster-Nietzsche, the dead philosopher's socially ambitious eighty-six-year-old sister, received a rose bouquet from Hitler during the German premiere of *100 Days,* Mussolini's melodrama of Napoleon's final campaign. Here in July 1934, Hitler and reigning Nazi ideologue Alfred Rosenberg visited Elisabeth and presented her with a wreath for her brother's grave bearing the words "To a Great Fighter." Here in October 1934, on the occasion of the philosopher's ninetieth birthday—as Hitler posed for a now famous photograph next to a white marble bust of Nietzsche—the Führer locked eyes with the creator of the Antichrist and received from Elisabeth her beloved Fritz's walking stick (along with a copy of the anti-Semitic petition that her late husband had presented to Bismarck). Here in November 1935, the Führer solemnly placed a wreath on Elisabeth's own grave, as the *Völkischer Beobachter,* the official Nazi organ, eulogized Weimar's grand dowager as "the First Lady of Europe." Here—next door—in April 1936, Albert Speer, Hitler's architect, began work on the Nietzsche Memorial (now a radio station), whose ninety-meter-high central hall would boast portraits of Hitler and Mussolini and bear the inscription "From Adolf Hitler, 1938, in the sixth year of the Third Reich."

And near here in 1937/38—a ten-minute ride from the august Villa Silberblick—workmen completed construction of what would become the other "memorial" in the Weimar environs, on Etters Hill at Buchenwald: one of the first concentration camps in Germany.

Yes, all in Weimar. Weimar, the cradle of German culture, birthplace of the Weimar Republic, crematorium of German humanism—by 1930, it was already residence of the first Nazi minister and city council in Germany. "Believe me," wrote Elisabeth to a friend in 1935, "Fritz would be *enchanted* by Hitler."

The reverberations overwhelm. Yes, a trip to the Nietzsche Archive is a journey through modern German history, and it is but a short ride from the Humboldtstrasse to the camp on Etters Hill. Hence the whispered questions on the lips of visitors to the Villa Silberblick:

With Zarathustra unbound, what repressed energies from the East German past will finally also be released? With the resurrection of the Antichrist, are the droves of disciples soon to follow? Will the philosopher of the Will to Power, the creator of the *Übermensch,* the trailblazer of modernism and postmodernism, soon return to German classrooms? Already Nietzsche is back in eastern German bookstores, but will he become a major presence in the region's intellectual life?

Can Nietzsche possibly be discussed and taught without fixating on his history of reception in Wilhelmine and Nazi Germany? And might it not indeed be irresponsible and hazardous to teach his work *apart* from this context? (Even in western Germany, universities—let alone *Gymnasien*—have only recently and sporadically reintroduced Nietzsche into the curriculum.)[1] In short, now that East Germans can finally "behold the man," can they look him—and themselves—in the face?

And what of Nietzsche's critique of education? "I have no higher goal," declared the twenty-nine-year-old professor in an 1874 letter, "as somehow to become, in a great sense, an 'educator.'" Eight decades later, young Walter Kaufmann, a refugee from the Nazis soon to become the leading English-language postwar scholar of Nietzsche, could conclude in his landmark *Nietzsche: Philosopher, Psychologist, Antichrist:* "It is above all as an 'educator' that Nietzsche seems to us to confront posterity."[2]

Can one teach Nietzsche without taking seriously his views on education and self-development? "To educate educators!" proclaimed Nietzsche in his *Untimely Meditations.* "But the first ones must educate themselves. And for these I write!" He railed that German education was merely "imported knowledge" and had "nothing to do with Life!"

The last time German intellectuals took Nietzsche seriously, his teachings quickly contributed to the generation of both educational reform and youth movements. By the turn of the century, intellectually minded teachers and *Gymnasium* students were reading and taking positions on Nietzsche's writings, sometimes even as part of class assignments. Nietzsche's hatred of the deadening scholarship of his philological colleagues (*On the Future of Our Educational Institutions,* 1872) and his call to reinvigorate the classical humanistic tradition (*On the Advantage and Disadvantage of History for Life,* 1873) had a major influence on proponents and opponents of the so-called Pedagogical Movement of the Wilhelmine era. Advocates of pedagogical reform sought to separate church and school, promote free thinking, adapt the humanistic *Gymnasium* to the needs of the modern industrial world, and increase German competitiveness in international trade. Pedagogical reformers such as Ellen Key and Ludwig Gurlitt (who was known among educators as "Nietzsche's executor") urged liberal, *völkisch* school reforms designed to transform learning into a creative, democratic activity: the free unfolding of the personality, the attainment of *fröhliche Wissenschaft* (joyful wisdom). Their policy proposals included combining the humanistic *Gymnasium* with the more technically oriented *Realschule,* thereby to confront "history" with "Life" and elevate Germany into the front rank of European powers. Following Nietzsche—who, in addition to his lectures at the University of Basel, had taught six hours in a local Swiss *Gymnasium*[3]—they railed against the intellectual poverty of a Wilhelminian *Gymnasium* that was filled with churchmen and scholars who utterly divorced education from Life; German schooling of the future should abolish arid rationalism and academicism and thereby prepare Germany for its leading place in the twentieth century. But critics of pedagogical reform such as

Gustav Wyneken and the young Walter Benjamin rejected superficial institutional reforms and collectivist schemes, denouncing proposals that claimed "advantages" for "Life" in Nietzsche's name. "Youth for Itself Alone!" was Wyneken's slogan. Nietzsche addressed himself to the single individual and sought to create an international aristocracy of intellect, reform critics insisted, not to turn the humanistic *Gymnasium* into a highbrow finishing school, using a classical curriculum to dress up German provincialism with a little Latin and less Greek.[4]

In the early decades of the century, Nietzsche also influenced the so-called Youth Movement in Germany. "The Prophet of the German Youth Movement," one observer of the 1920s called him.[5] Nietzsche was taken up by the two chief youth associations of Wilhelmine Germany, the Wandervogel and the Freideutsche Jugend (Free German Youth), concrete expressions of the two positions on pedagogical reform: Gurlitt was the first chair of the Wandervogel's advisory council, and Wyneken was the leading voice of the Freideutsche Jugend. The Wandervogel promoted *Lebensreform* (life reform), a back-to-nature movement opposed to everything artificial and corrupt in society. In *Nietzsche als Erzieher,* Walter Hammer wrote of Wandervogel boys thrilling to Nietzsche's "summons to the arena of struggle," and how they "stormed forward in the direction that Nietzsche pointed." The Wandervogel movement had "achieved Nietzsche's educational ideals"—which, in Hammer's view, were nationalistic, collectivist, and of pure German origin, and included practicing vegetarianism and abstaining from tobacco and alcohol. By contrast, the Freideutsche Jugend, a more intellectual and cosmopolitan organization, hearkened to Nietzsche's cultural sophistication, his internationalism, and his embodiment of the adventuresome "free spirit."[6] The latter organization considered the romanticism of the Wandervogel escapist and immature; given its intellectual orientation, it ultimately accorded Nietzsche a far more important place than did the Wandervogel. Without question, however, the enthusiasm of Wilhelmine educationists and youth leaders for Nietzsche—especially the reformers' and Freideutsche Jugend's image of a nationalist, *völkisch* Nietzsche—helped set the stage for his state institutionalization by the Nazis in the 1930s, through the schools and the Hitler Youth (HJ).

All this may seem far in the past, but for intellectually minded eastern German youth of today, Nietzsche represents *their* past—in all of its excruciating anguish—and not just since May 1945 but rather since January 1933. "What fails to kill me only makes me stronger": the Ordensburg Vogelsang, training center for Hitler Youth leaders, chose that line from *Thus Spake Zarathustra* as its motto. *Wille und Macht*—an obvious allusion to Nietzsche's *Wille zur Macht* (will to power)— was the title of the main HJ journal. But the Nazis ignored many other aphorisms of Nietzsche, for example, "The surest way to corrupt a youth is to instruct him to hold in higher esteem those who think alike than those who think differently."

The challenge of coming to terms with Nietzsche isn't eased for Germans by his frequent expressions of contempt for his countrymen. From his self-imposed exile in Switzerland and Italy in the 1880s, Nietzsche showered reprobation on Germany and the Germans. Indeed, Nietzsche claimed (with no strong evidence) descent from Polish nobility—a little point about him that irks Hedwig, since her parents, caught in the wave of vengeance against the Germans that swept Eastern Europe at the war's close, were forcibly expelled by the Poles in 1945 from Silesia, now part of Poland. Declared Nietzsche: "The Teutonic *Deutschland über alles* is the stupidest slogan ever devised in the world." "Every great crime against culture during the last four centuries lies on the conscience of the Germans." "[T]his irresponsible race . . . has on its own conscience all the great disasters of civilization in all decisive moments in history." One shudders to imagine what thundering denunciations he would have rained down on German heads had he lived to witness the cataclysms of 1918 and 1945.

So Nietzsche is part of the long-overdue challenge in eastern Germany of *Vergangenheitsbewaeltigung*. His very name evokes the overpowering, numbing *shame* of being a German—an emotion long familiar to western Germans but new to eastern Germans, since (in this rare instance) DDR citizens had welcomed the message their leaders had told them to believe: "We are guiltless of nazism and the Holocaust." Because travel abroad was severely restricted and resident aliens scarce and near-invisible—the DDR was less than 1 percent non-German—East Germans led a sequestered, provincial life, rarely coming into contact with foreigners who would have punctured the fragile myth.[7] With Nietzsche back, everything that had been buried in the private records of the Communist soul has been dusted off, ready for display.

Thus Nietzsche's reappearance attracts all kinds of interpreters inclined to force timely concerns on him. He reminds eastern Germans of the intellectual and psychological wall between them and westerners, of the superiority and "sophistication" of "Western" ideas, of the intellectual backwardness of the DDR's socialist realist fantasies and the naivete of its Marxist illusions: Nietzsche is part of the eastern German *Nachholbedarf* (need to catch up). Indeed, no person, with the single exception of Marx, has had such a powerful impact on the minds of western *and* eastern Germany as Nietzsche. And no other individual, including Marx, is so controversial and so variously understood—and misunderstood. While events in Europe since 1989 have rendered Marx hopelessly out of date for most Germans, Nietzsche remains contemporary—or even "postcontemporary," as the current phrase has it.

Today, eastern Germans suddenly find themselves divorced from six decades of ideological banalities traded between the Right and the Left and cast into the brave new postideological world that Nietzsche envisioned. Nietzsche's main epistemological claims—that there is no coherent self, no stable identity between word and thing, and no fundamental continuity between temporal events—are central to both modernism and postmodernism and have launched intellectual movements that have dominated the postwar West, among them phenomenology and existentialism (Martin Heidegger), French psychoanalysis (Jacques Lacan), linguistic philosophy and criticism (Jacques Derrida, Paul de Man), and poststructuralist historiography and cultural criticism (Michel Foucault, Jean Lyotard, Gilles Deleuze, Felix Guattari). Partly because of their repression of

Nietzsche, easterners are playing catch-up in the task of understanding the history of ideas in our century. For unlike Marx, Nietzsche is a thinker intimately relevant to the world today. Indeed, our fin-de-siècle has been no more imaginable without him than was that of the nineteenth century. It is not, therefore, simply a case of D-marks *über* Marx but of Nietzsche *über* Marx.

"*Ja, Marx ist* out, *und Nietzsche ist wieder* in!" Hedwig fumes.

In January 1889, the forty-four-year-old Nietzsche suffered a mental breakdown in Turin, Italy, from which he never recovered, though he lived on for eleven years, in a vegetative state during the last eight. Throughout the spring of 1989, West German newspapers were announcing the 100th anniversary of Nietzsche's "intellectual death." Then—suddenly and unforeseen—impulsive Fate intervened, ushering a chaotic rush of events intertwining Germany and Nietzsche yet again: the fall of the Berlin Wall, the collapse of the DDR, the return of Nietzsche to eastern German headlines, the reopening of the Nietzsche Archive.

1989: *Is* it merely an uncanny coincidence that the year of Nietzsche's outbreak of insanity coincided with Adolf Hitler's birth? And that their converging centennial anniversaries became the moment of the self-immolation of the DDR and of Nietzsche's phoenixlike rise from the ashes of Hitler's bunker? Is it just a quirk of history that the Villa Silberblick, last home of the Good European, reopened as the European Union moved closer toward monetary unification? ("What I anticipate—and I see it gathering slowly and hesitatingly—is a United Europe," wrote Nietzsche in *The Genealogy of Morals*.) Finally, more darkly, is it also just an accident that Nietzsche is "in" again, just as the first serious outbreaks of neo-Nazi violence convulse eastern Germany?

"I am and ever will be a misunderstanding among the Germans," wrote Nietzsche in *Ecce Homo*. And in a June 1884 letter to Elisabeth: "I tremble when I think of all those who without justification, without being ready for my ideas, will yet invoke my authority."

"No philosopher is a prophet in his own country," I say to myself, as we turn into the Humboldtstrasse.

Pause.

Then, a whisper: "At least not *twice.*"

And now: the era of newly reunified Germany. Nietzsche: More timely—or untimely?—than ever.

His star brightening once again? His long-awaited, second "lucky chance"? Perhaps.

III

The injustice that has been done to him can never be repaired.
Camus, "Nietzsche," *The Rebel*

"Prussian acid!" a friend of mine once called Nietzsche—only half jokingly. Hedwig chuckles grimly as I explain the pun, with its touch of black comedy. Nietzsche grew up in the Prussian province of Saxony. His father, a Lutheran minister, christened him Friedrich Wilhelm after King Friedrich Wilhelm IV of Prussia, on whose birthday Nietzsche was born. The king went insane a few years later; Nietzsche's father suffered from a brain tumor and died. Nietzsche later dropped his middle name, along with his family's Prussian patriotism and strong Lutheran faith, but he did not escape the forenamed fate.

Amor fati! As we stand outside the Villa Silberblick, Hedwig jests darkly that my long-term scholarly contact with Nietzsche could lead to an end similar to Nietzsche's own. Nietzsche as spiritual cyanide? Is this visit my own "Prussian acid test"? Hedwig chides me for my keen interest in the philosopher. A German teacher in an East Berlin *Gymnasium* and an intense admirer of German classicism, she is less than enthusiastic about the reopening of the Nietzsche Archive. No, as happy as she is to introduce me to Weimar, the Villa Silberblick is not high on her sightseeing list. Why don't I go back for another visit to the Goethehaus? Or visit the Schillerhaus or Liszthaus again, *um Gottes Willen!* Unlike her older brother, who has joined a Nietzsche reading group, Hedwig has no intention of joining the Nietzsche parade. No, she would prefer to spend her Weimar visit around the Frauenplan, where the Goethehaus and Schillerhaus lie within sight of each other.

"What *do* you see in him?" she asks in exasperation.

I want to answer by unshrouding the Nietzsche whose prose soars and singes and sings, the Nietzsche who summons the seeker to "become who you are," the Nietzsche who transports his reader to exhilarating intellectual adventures through the superhuman energy of his formulations and the limpid clarity of his voice—the very same Nietzsche whose vitalistic *Lebensphilosophie* (life philosophy) inspired generations before 1933. Mine is the existential Nietzsche of "joyful wisdom"—and doubtless also the foreigner's Nietzsche: a figure little stained by association with his more questionable German admirers.

But no, it does no good to tell Hedwig what she has already heard from countless other Nietzsche "apologists": that the Nazis blatantly distorted him for their own ends; that he is regarded in the West as the most significant philosopher of the last century, equal in importance to Kant and Hegel; that his chief influence was antiauthoritarian until the 1930s, exerted not only on liberal educators but also on progressive movements including feminists, anarchists, and dissident Social Democrats; that most German nationalists and militarists, especially the jingoistic Pan-German League, were wary of Nietzsche before World War I and dismissed him as a nihilist, immoralist, and friend of the Jews. No, before I can formulate an answer, Hedwig adds—with some nostalgia—that, until 1990, scholars needed a *Giftschein* (poison certificate) to gain admittance to the Archive. One man's pleasure is, quite evidently, another woman's poison.

"And now it's becoming fashionable to read him again!" Hedwig sniffs disapprovingly. Nietzsche is "die neuste geistige Modeerscheinung [the newest intellectual fad]!" Despite her rejection of so much DDR propaganda, Hedwig obviously lays the sins of the sons and daughters at Nietzsche's feet, granting the validity of the Nazi and SED claims that Nietzsche was Hitler's spiritual father. Admitting that she has never read Nietzsche, she says she feels no temptation to take up any bad habits.

Why does Hedwig insist on keeping Nietzsche a closed book? Her parents were both NSDAP (Nazi Party) members, she says; her older brother joined the SED (Communist Party). She herself wanted nothing to do with political parties or ideologies. Of course, this was a dangerous attitude in the DDR, where it was somewhat uncommon, at least in East Berlin, to teach German in a respected school without SED membership. And even more uncommon to gain admission to a DDR Ph.D. program in *Germanistik*. Hedwig's Ph.D. thesis dealt with the influence of the 1848 revolution on the work of pianist and composer Franz Liszt (1811–66) in Weimar; her special expertise in music and German literature won her a position in a Berlin school.

I mention that Nietzsche is now being widely taught in eastern German classes in ethics, especially for his "God is dead" theology. But to Hedwig, "Nietzsche" is an expletive to be deleted. She calls him a "degenerate"; since reunification, she says, many Weimar residents equate his name with the outbreaks of neonazism, hatred of foreigners, German jingoism, and juvenile delinquency.

Hedwig's intransigence sets me back. It is hard for me to accept her formidable block against Nietzsche. In today's America, Nietzsche is associated with popular culture, with alternative lifestyles, and with campus debates on political correctness and multiculturalism. Can this be the same Nietzsche whom Arnold Schwarzenegger—our cyborg *Übermensch,* our incarnation of the Will to Power—quotes ("What doesn't kill me only makes me stronger!") in the opening frames of *Conan the Barbarian?* The same Nietzsche whom Allan Bloom blames in *Closing of the American Mind* for student leftist dandyism and the trendy "lifestyle" revolution on campus—for casual sex, rock music, and the blurring of sex roles? The same Nietzsche whom my Texas undergraduates, exhilarated by his philosophy of "perspectivism," cite to defend their preference to "do your own thing"? The same Nietzsche whose face a colleague of mine spotted at a recent academic conference, printed on a T-shirt worn by a woman with purple hair in a punk haircut, under which ran the immortal line: "Nietzsche Is Peachy"?

No, that is not the Nietzsche whom Hedwig knows. She takes Nietzsche seriously. To Hedwig, "Nietzsche" means Brownshirts, not T-shirts.

Can Nietzsche be fully "denazified" in eastern Germany, to become again a philosopher free from the taint of association with fascism?[8] Or is there, for eastern Germans, too much in Nietzsche "that repels, too much 'Hitler,'"[9] too much latent nazism and manifest war rhetoric for any full rehabilitation to be possible, for any reference untrammeled by a slight twinge, any admiration to go untinged by a touch of shame?

History sometimes entwines figures in a strange and unpredictable tradition. Whereas Germans once could hardly avoid hearing the Nietzsche in Hitler, eastern Germans today can hardly avoid hearing the Hitler in Nietzsche. Indeed, after twelve years of pro-Nietzsche Nazi propaganda and forty-five years of anti-

Nietzsche Communist propaganda, Nietzsche's Nazi connection is firm in many eastern German minds: The associations with Hitlerism have raised to an almost insurmountable degree eastern Germans' perception of the "degenerate" in Nietzsche's work—and adulterated the pure, majestic voice that continues to move most non-Germans who encounter it.

Hedwig's indignation reminds me of my correspondence years earlier with West German scholars. Few letters surprised me more during my student days than to receive word that, even in the late 1970s, Nietzsche's work was still too controversial to be taught in *West* Germany's curricula. I knew that Nietzsche was persona non grata under the Communists, but I had no idea that he was still unofficially taboo in the *Bundesrepublik*. This occurred at a time when he was all the rage in Paris and in the American academy, when he was being taken up by literary critics, psychoanalysts, linguists, anthropologists, and postmodern philosophers.

"If you want to study Nietzsche," a prominent West German scholar in *Germanistik* at the University of Konstanz wrote me, "by all means stay right where you are. Don't leave the US. That's where the Nietzsche scholars are." There seemed to be a note of admonition—and perhaps even pride—in his tone, as if to imply that he indeed hoped that I and my Nietzsche scholars *remained* on this side of the Atlantic.[10]

As Hedwig and I overtake two well-dressed elderly ladies to enter the Archive, Hedwig lowers her voice and turns fully toward me. She repeats her verdict on Nietzsche: "*Ja, Marx ist* out, *Nietzsche ist wieder* in!"

As if to say: "*Now then*—are you satisfied?"

IV

The Villa Silberblick is an impressive building. Built in the mid-1800s, it was acquired in 1896 by a Swiss aristocrat as a refuge for Nietzsche and a repository for his papers. It was refurbished according to Elisabeth Forster-Nietzsche's specifications by Belgian architect Henry van der Velde, one of the leaders of the turn-of-the-century *Jugendstil* architecture movement. *Jugendstil* exhibited a high degree of craftsmanship, the use of organic forms, and a decidedly bourgeois sensibility, all of which van der Velde stressed in his redesign of the Nietzsche Archive.

The finished look, however, is one of classical, indeed Attic, elegance. Etched in brownstone is the family name, which rests above intricately carved, solid oak doors and contrasts with the red-brick and white-stone exterior; bronze doorknobs bear the letter "N." A similar restraint prevails inside, where stained-glass windows bathe the public rooms in resplendent light. Particularly beautiful is the library, which exudes refinement and grace. A large golden "N" inscribed on the wall overlooks a green-tiled fireplace, sinuous couches in strawberry upholstery, built-in bookshelves, a grand piano, and glass cases full of Nietzscheana. Within this setting, the mammoth white marble bust of the Master is all the more commanding. Commissioned from the sculptor Hans Klinger, it rests atop a six-foot pedestal between the rear windows, contemplating the scene with Olympian dis-interestedness.

What a spectacle! And all of it, ironically, conceived as a tribute to the simple life of the ascetic philosopher. Completed in 1904, the price tag was RM 50,000—at least $1,000,000 today—all of which Elisabeth had to beg and bor-row. But she held that her brother (who would not live to see the renovations) had suffered a miserable nomadic existence before his breakdown and so de-served, despite his obliviousness to his surroundings, all the comfort that money could buy. A perhaps more telling reason for all the finery, however, was that Elisabeth's own tastes ran toward the luxurious. "Forster" means forest ranger; in later years Elisabeth's pretensions—which extended to riding through the streets with liveried coachmen—earned her the mocking sobriquet among Weimar resi-dents of "Frau *Ober*forster" (head or senior forest ranger).

Even though eastern German intellectuals are finally taking notice of Nietz-sche—and many visitors mill about the Villa Silberblick on this Sunday after-noon—no curator or even guide yet works in the Nietzsche Archive. Due to tight funds and a lack of trained personnel, the Archive has still to be assigned an official guide.

An old gentleman who lives in the Humboldtstrasse, a few doors down from the Archive, collects the admission price. Now in his late eighties, Heinz Koch sits with a little cardboard box filled with change. A few strands of thin white hair, distributed equidistantly in matted rows, stripe his bald head. Herr Koch beams as he accepts my five deutschmarks, his eyes dancing brightly beneath bushy white eyebrows, unconcerned that two of his front teeth are missing.

Hedwig drifts away, leaving Herr Koch and me to chat, and I ask him about the Nietzsche "renaissance." No more than a few thousand people have visited the Archive since May—far less than the Goethehaus admits in a single month, he says. I remark that it seems difficult to find Weimar residents who know very much about Nietzsche at all, that the Weimar *Gymnasium* schoolchildren shrugged their shoulders when I mentioned his name. Herr Koch nods. Hedwig, listening nearby, nods too—with seeming approval. "But my generation knows all about him and his family," Herr Koch adds.

Has he read Nietzsche? I ask. *Ja*, a wartime edition of *Thus Spake Zarathustra* as a soldier, and a popular anthology of Nietzsche's work before the war. *Aber nein*, not since then; do I not know? "To have mentioned his name, let alone praised him, would have raised suspicions of Nazi sympathies."

The stigma endures. Herr Koch leads me to a museum table to show me the last Communist-supervised edition of the official Weimar picture guide (1990).[11] The expensively produced book features full-page color photographs and detailed descriptions of the galaxy of intellectual luminaries who once lived and worked in this almost classical city-state of 63,000 residents.

Weimar: "The city of immortal fame," in Thomas Mann's phrase. In the late eighteenth century, under the benevolent patronage of Prince Karl August, Wei-mar became the residence of Germany's greatest literary figures. Featured in the picture book are numerous pictures of Johann Wolfgang von Goethe (1749–1832) and Friedrich von Schiller (1759–1805), their statues shoulder to shoulder in front of the German National Theatre; the philosopher and poet Johann Gottfried von Herder (1744–1803); and the poet and novelist Christoph Martin Wieland (1713–1813). Also depicted are the painter and graphic artist Lucas Cranach the Elder (1472–1553), whose house is on the market square; the young Johann Sebastian Bach (1685–1750), Weimar chapel organist and court composer for nine years; Franz Liszt, the luminary of mid-nineteenth-century Weimar; Henry van der Velde (1856–1924); and Walter Gropius (1896–1957), leader of the Bauhaus school.

Not a single mention or glimpse of Nietzsche.

Herr Koch points to a quotation from the East German novelist Anna Seghers, which opens the picture book: "The best and worst places of German history are here." Seghers didn't need to elaborate. Yes, it is a short ride from the kingdom of Art to the kingdom of Death. To the tune of Beethoven's "Ode to Joy," Aryan guards at Buchenwald marched their prisoners through the camp gatehouse, with its mind-numbing motto in cast-iron letters: To Each His Own. Bathed in Goethe's hymns to the Etters landscape, the camp commandant calculated the human, all too human, body count: 56,545.

Each year the SED had sponsored elaborate ceremonies on the anniversary of the liberation of Buchenwald, 11 April 1945. The ceremonies were designed to underline the regime's legitimacy by propagating an officially ordained "antifascism" that made "monopoly capitalism" in general and West Germany in particular responsible for nazism and its crimes, thus exonerating East Germans of historic responsibility for what happened. The official rhetoric almost made it appear that wartime eastern Germany had been an occupied country with a heroic Communist underground resistance movement—centered partly in Buchenwald itself, where Ernst Thaelmann was executed.

But in 1990 mass graves were unearthed that contained the remains of the inmates of a Soviet concentration camp operating on Etters Hill during 1945–50. The inmates included not only suspected Nazi militants but also Social Democrats and other liberal opponents of the SED. Whispered rumors about these camps had seeped out for decades; publicized by the western Allies, the allegations were dismissed by the SED as antisocialist propaganda. Rediscovery of the camps in the dying days of the DDR triggered a gruesome debate among East Germans about the comparative evils of the Holocaust and the Gulag: Which was worse, Buchenwald under the Nazis or under the Stalinists?

Herr Koch blurts out the question, then immediately retracts it with a shake of his head and a nervous laugh. The question overleaps the realm of the imaginable. He closes the picture book; he looks away.

"That question didn't exist in the DDR," says Herr Koch, turning to look at me squarely. "No more than did the Gulag. In the DDR, Stalin's crimes never happened. They hardly existed, except as half-believed, half-denied rumor and folklore. Nobody knew about them—at least not officially—and that which people knew unofficially was seldom mentioned. *Nein,* nobody knew about them—nor about Nietzsche either."

"Why was Nietzsche the only one banned by the SED?" I ask. I hear myself racing on: Hadn't Schiller and Wagner also been glorified and rewritten by the Nazis? Schiller was proclaimed the Führer's "companion in arms." Wagner's *Die Meistersinger* was Hitler's favorite opera; the posthumous Wagner was court composer to the Third Reich. So why were Schiller and Wagner subsequently accepted, even honored, in the workers' paradise? Goethe and Beethoven had been similarly transformed by the Nazis into Teutonic geniuses, but the SED embraced them as socialist forerunners, or at least as democrats—Goethe's face graced the DDR's near-worthless banknotes; Beethoven's symphonies resounded throughout DDR concert halls. And what about all the others? The poet and monarchist Heinrich Heine had lashed out at communism—he was forgiven; his cordial personal acquaintance with the young Marx was recast as sympathy for revolutionary socialism. Even Hofmannstahl and Rilke, even Freud—even accommodators to or admirers of fascism like Gerhart Hauptmann, Stefan George, and Gottfried Benn!—were eventually admitted, however warily, into socialist intellectual society. Their explicit antisocialism, their aestheticism and elitism, their outright contempt for the worker, were all explained away as symptoms of bourgeois protest or alienation within the capitalist order.

Was the stretch too great in Nietzsche's case? Was the posthumous Nietzsche so utterly enmeshed with Hitlerism that he could not be disentangled and repoliticized? Couldn't he too have proven ideologically malleable? Or is his language so provocative and his outlook so advanced that SED ideologues sensed that they had no choice but to ban him, that efforts to chastise his philosophy as the product of a decaying nineteenth-century imperialism, let alone attempts to convert him for the Left, could only fail?

Herr Koch nods again and points a gnarled finger toward a folder of clippings that the Archive has collected. He stops at a 1985 article from the respected *Frankfurter Rundschau* by Gerhard Zwerenz, who had urged SED leaders to adopt reform proposals in 1956—and fled the Communist Reich in 1957.

If Nietzsche had lived [in the 1930s], he would have been a Nazi Party member, something like an intellectual version of [Alfred] Rosenberg. Perhaps he would have been shot with Ernst Röhm in 1934. . . . To take Nietzsche seriously is to resemble Hitler, who took Nietzsche seriously, albeit in the most naive fashion: he styled himself an *Übermensch.* Many Germans followed him and did the same. Taking a thinker seriously is serious business: Lenin took Marx seriously, just as Hitler took Nietzsche seriously. Thousands of know-it-alls can rise up and criticize the logical errors involved in this kind of "seriousness": but the Lenins and Hitlers have history and reality on their side. Marx discovered the class struggle, out of which Stalin built the Gulag. Nietzsche preached the revaluation of all values, which led to Hitler and ultimately to the Holocaust. . . . Just as Marx led to Lenin and Stalin, Nietzsche led to Hitler.[12]

"*Marx ist* out, *Nietzsche ist wieder* in." Hedwig's words ring in my ears. I quote them to Herr Koch. Wordlessly, he flips to another article, this one from the local newspaper in Nietzsche's hometown of Röcken. Until 1990 the welcome sign on the village's outskirts had read: "Workers and farmers in socialist agriculture! Go forward to great achievements in the stalls and in the fields!" Today the sign reads: "Welcome to Röcken, home of the birthplace of Friedrich Nietzsche!"

Herr Koch cackles. His laugh is infectious; we grin at each other. The repainting of the welcome sign typifies the refurbishing of East German history since 1989. Such revisions are especially easy in Nietzsche's case, says Herr Koch, because even most Weimar residents don't know the basic biographical facts about the man, facts listed within the glass cases throughout the ground floor of the Villa Silberblick.

And now Herr Koch returns to his official duties, leaving me to inspect the exhibits, each of them devoted to a chapter of the philosopher's arduous life—and of the story of the salon that grew out of Elisabeth's efforts to publish and publicize his *Lebensphilosophie.*

V

"A man has to pay dearly for immortality," wrote Nietzsche in *Human, All Too Human.* "He has to die several times while still alive." Nietzsche lived those words: his passionate pilgrimage was plagued by ill health, public indifference to his work, and unceasing devotion to his writing. If self-knowledge comes only at the cost of great suffering, then Nietzsche must have suffered greatly indeed, for in Freud's view Nietzsche manifested "a degree of introspection greater than anyone else ever achieved and which is never likely to be achieved by anyone else again."[13]

Born in 1844 in the village of Röcken in Saxony-Anhalt, Nietzsche was sickly from his youth. After his father's death from a brain tumor in 1849, the family moved thirty miles west to Naumburg in Saxony. At the age of fourteen, Nietzsche won a scholarship to attend Pforta, the famous and exclusive boarding school located just a few miles from Naumburg and regarded in the nineteenth century as the Eton of Germany. In the 1860s, Nietzsche studied classical philology at the University of Bonn and later at the University of Leipzig. When the chair of classical philology became open at Basel in 1869, Nietzsche's Leipzig *Doktorvater* (dissertation director), Friedrich Ritschl, recommended him for the post, avowing that "in 39 years of teaching I have never seen a young man . . . [who is] *so* mature as this Nietzsche."[14]

The decision to appoint the twenty-four-year-old Nietzsche was unprecedented. He had not written a doctoral thesis, let alone the additional dissertation generally required before a Ph.D. becomes a *Privatdozent* (assistant professor), not to mention the advanced scholarly work (*Habilitationsschrift,* second dissertation) required to become an associate professor. Ritschl wrote his Swiss colleagues that such an appointment was unheard of in Germany, but he reassured them that Nietzsche—who had concentrated on the history of Greek philosophy and actually was not highly qualified for a conventional position in philology—"with his great gifts will work in other fields with the best of success. He will simply be able to do anything he wants to do." Ritschl added: "He is like Odysseus, plunged deep in thought before he speaks, but his powerful delivery is at once effective, engaging, convincing."[15] Leipzig conferred the doctorate on Nietzsche in 1869, without thesis or examination. In 1870 Basel promoted him to a *Professor Ordinarius* (full professor). At the age of twenty-five, he had risen to the highest rank in the academic world.

In 1879 Nietzsche resigned from the university, pleading poor health, and was granted a modest pension. The ensuing decade proved to be his great creative period, during which he published at least one book per year, a triumph over his manifold physical agonies. Until 1888, however, his books received virtually no attention in the press or from scholars. Nevertheless, without response, Nietzsche wrote furiously on. Even *Thus Spake Zarathustra* (1884), his literary masterpiece, had to be published at his own expense. Fewer than a dozen copies were sold; only seven of the forty self-printed copies of his private edition of Part IV could even be given away to interested readers. "I found no one ripe for many of my thoughts," lamented Nietzsche in *Ecce Homo*. "The case of *Zarathustra* proves that one can speak with utmost clarity, and yet not be heard by anyone."

From all accounts, Nietzsche lived an ascetic life as an adult. Rumors have long circulated, however, that he contracted syphilis sometime during his student years after a visit to a brothel. (Thomas Mann makes this claim explicit in the portrait of his Nietzschean hero in *Doktor Faustus*.) The matter has been much debated because Nietzsche's mental illness, resulting in insanity, could possibly have been the consequence of the final stage of syphilis, which often begins with acute migraine headaches and gastric pains, advances to severe bouts of mania and depression, and culminates in a progressive paralysis. Because Nietzsche was evidently chaste during his adult years, other historians who concur in the final diagnosis of his illness speculate that he was infected with syphilis while assisting the wounded during the Franco-Prussian War of 1870/71, in which he served as a medical orderly with the Prussian army.

However Nietzsche contracted syphilis—if he did—the disease had not yet affected his mind during his creative years: his writings cannot be dismissed as the products of a madman. His books—all written before his dramatic collapse in 1889—possess a limpid clarity and stylistic power that command the reader's attention. They must be judged on their merits alone.

The outbreak of Nietzsche's mental illness was sudden and irreversible. In the first week of January 1889, in one of the most famous events in intellectual history, Nietzsche saw a cab driver flogging his horse in the Piazza Carlo Alberto in Turin, shrieked in commiseration, flung his arms around the suffering beast's neck, and slumped unconscious in the street. The small crowd that gathered around him attracted his landlord, who carried Nietzsche home.

Nietzsche's last letters, mailed to intellectual and political leaders in Germany, Switzerland, and Italy during the week preceding his collapse, are moving and pathetic, signed by Nietzsche under various aliases, including "Dionysus" and "The Crucified." To one correspondent he wrote: "I have appointed a meeting-day for the monarchs in Rome. I will order the young Kaiser [Wilhelm II] to be shot." And he signed it: "Nietzsche Caesar."

Thereafter Nietzsche's pen fell silent; some of his most famous books, such as *The Antichrist* (1895) and *The Will to Power* (1908), were edited and published by Elisabeth after his intellectual death. (*The Will to Power* was completely assembled by Elisabeth and has no integrity as a Nietzsche work.) *Ecce Homo*, Nietzsche's bitingly sarcastic autobiography, written in October/November 1888, was withheld from the public by his sister until 1908; she feared until then that it would have a negative impact on his reputation and on the Nietzsche Archive. Rich in humor and irony, the book's four chapters are titled: "Why I Am So Wise," "Why I Am So Clever," "Why I Write Such Excellent Books," and "Why I Am a Destiny." Fearing that hostile critics of Nietzsche would discount his oeuvre as the product of a sick mind, Elisabeth attacked all accounts of Nietzsche's syphilis as fabrications. To this day, the evidence remains inconclusive. We will probably never know the truth of Nietzsche's pathology.[16]

Nietzsche spent the last eleven years of his life in a Jena asylum (1889/90), in the care of his mother in Naumburg until her death (1890–97), and finally with Elisabeth in the Villa Silberblick in Weimar (1897–1900). The Nietzsche Archive, however, was actually founded in Naumburg in 1894, when Elisabeth turned the first floor of their mother's home into a tiny museum, by which time Nietzsche's condition had so badly deteriorated that he was no longer capable of conversation or even of feeding himself. And this state of helplessness imbued still another line of the philosopher with ironic, prophetic significance: "Society should have only a profound contempt for the man who survives like a vegetable," wrote Nietzsche in *Twilight of the Idols* (1888), "after he has lost the meaning of his life, the right to live."

But worldwide admiration, not contempt, would soon be forthcoming from all sides, as Nietzsche's books reached a wider audience and his reputation became the new avenue for Elisabeth's social ambitions. Returning from Paraguay in 1890, after her husband Bernard had committed suicide there in apparent despair over his business failures, Frau "Eli" Forster at first turned her energies toward making Forster the national hero of German imperialists, anti-Semites, and Wagnerites. Forster had been an admirer of Wagner and one of the leaders of the German anti-Semitic movement, and the couple had founded a Teutonic colony in Paraguay called Nueva Germania (New Germany). But Elisabeth's attempt to delude uninformed Europeans about the circumstances of her husband's death and the condition of the colony unleashed a torrent of angry replies from outraged benefactors and colonists, who considered themselves defrauded by the Forsters. Meanwhile, her brother's star was beginning—*mirabile dictu!*—its rapid climb. Suddenly, Eli Forster was reborn as Elisabeth Forster-Nietzsche: In 1892, by court order, Elisabeth officially changed her name, all the better to exhibit herself as Zarathustra's Sister.[17]

Elisabeth Forster-Nietzsche: The contradictions within this hyphenated name suggest the tragedy of Nietzsche's fate. But at least she got the order right: Almost everything she promulgated in her brother's name was Forster first and Nietzsche second.

After their mother's death, Elisabeth took Nietzsche to Weimar. The official canonization of Goethe and Schiller had occurred just a few years earlier, with the founding of the Goethe National Museum and the Goethe–Schiller Archive. Already Elisabeth imagined the same for Nietzsche: She sought to burnish her brother's name by association with Germany's cultural immortals. She "dreamed of a third era of Weimar greatness, centered upon herself and the Nietzsche Archive," an era that would exceed even the earlier peaks of the nineteenth century, the Golden Age of Goethe–Schiller and the Silver Age of Liszt.[18] Elisabeth fantasized about turning the Villa Silberblick into a renowned salon attended by Europe's cultural elite, a center the equal of the annual music festivals at Bayreuth presided over by her onetime friend and current rival, Cosima Wagner, Richard Wagner's widow. And soon the Nietzsche Archive would become her second New Germany, an imperialistic venture that would succeed where the first had failed.

The 1890s marked Nietzsche's turn from obscurity to recognition. While he still resided in Naumburg, his name began echoing in drawing rooms and university lecture halls throughout the continent—though he was, of course, oblivious to his rising status. Already in 1892, one German journalist could write that "the whole cultural world is stirred by his importance. . . . Nietzsche is well on his way to becoming *the* fashionable philosopher, the great event of our time."[19] The Nietzsche Legend was beginning.

Elisabeth assiduously cultivated a Nietzsche myth. She dressed her brother in a long white robe, so that he looked like a Brahmin; visitors raved about his "mammoth" head and "penetrating" glance. Some guests compared Nietzsche's appearance to that of the Prophet Zarathustra, minus the latter's beard. Later Elisabeth cut and preserved snippets of Nietzsche's hair in an envelope and even commissioned a sculpture of Nietzsche as Greek god in the company of Zarathustra's symbolic animals: Nietzsche's leonine head on the body of an eagle, with a serpent entwined around them. The Archive also began selling plaster busts, statuettes, and portraits of Nietzsche; other admirers even mass-produced postcards with his picture (and a fitting quotation), exalting him as a champion of causes such as vegetarianism.[20]

By 1895 the outlines of the Nietzsche cult were visible. Count Harry Kessler, a leading benefactor of the Nietzsche Archive, observed that year that no German student "in his 20s or 30s doesn't owe Nietzsche some part of his *Weltanschauung.*"[21] Already by 1897, the sociologist Ferdinand Tönnies could write a pamphlet titled *The Nietzsche Cult.* Fervent student enthusiasts met for ritualistic readings from *Thus Spake Zarathustra* and intoned psalms celebrating the new religion.

By the time the body of the sick philosopher was finally laid to rest in August 1900, Nietzsche was a secular saint. Indeed, in yet another ironic turn of fate, the author of the Antichrist was buried in a traditional Lutheran rite, complete with pealing church bells and hymns intoned by the village church choir. Elisabeth adorned the coffin with a silver cross and interred her brother in Röcken next to the grave of their father, at the corner of the churchyard near the Lutheran parsonage.[22]

Now Elisabeth got down to the business of serious evangelism, building the Nietzsche cult into the Nietzsche movement. In 1900, shortly after Nietzsche's death, one journalist had written that Nietzsche was widely considered in Germany "a saint, martyr, prophet, and scourge," with his doting sister serving him as "high priestess and Madonna" and presiding over a "Church of disciples, apostles, and fanatics."[23] A critical pamphlet, *The Nietzsche Archive in Weimar* (1904), made similar claims about the Nietzsche "orthodox Church."[24] Another of Nietzsche's prophecies in *Ecce Homo* was reaching fruition: "My time has not yet come. Some men are born posthumously."

At last Nietzsche's time *had* come. But he had also voiced a misgiving in *Ecce Homo:* "I *want* no 'believers.' . . . I have a terrible fear that one day I will be pronounced *holy.*" Now this too came to pass. Elisabeth's program of lionization and mystification of her brother lent the Archive an aura of holiness, as if Nietzsche truly had become the son of Dionysus and Zarathustra, a celestial being deliberately practicing Olympian detachment from mundane affairs: an Antichrist and *Übermensch* rolled into one. "Whoever stays just a little while in these rooms," wrote the artist Edvard Munch, who had painted Nietzsche's portrait in the late 1890s, "feels the nearness of this great man, becomes still, and absorbs his teachings, here in this place, where he lived and from which he departed."[25] Elisabeth established herself as her brother's keeper, the sole representative of Nietzsche's philosophy, denouncing all rival interpreters. High priestess of the Nietzsche cult, she ruled its temple, the Archive, with religious zeal, despite her total ignorance of her brother's philosophy.

VI

And what of Nietzsche's *Lebensphilosophie?* Nietzsche the educator addressed the thrilling and unscholarly questions of individual greatness, intellectual heroism, and the pursuit of vocation and destiny. And it is partly on that account that he aroused such intense passions and opened himself to Elisabeth's exploitation. His view of the philosopher was, as he himself put it in his *Untimely Meditations,* "miles distant from any concept that includes even a Kant, not to mention the academic cud chewers and other professors of philosophy."[26]

To understand the nature of the Wilhelmine and Nazi distortions of Nietzsche's work and how they gained such wide currency, one needs to realize both how antipathetic a close reading of his central doctrines proves to such ideologies and yet how his ideas lent themselves to superficial parallels with militarism and racial theory. But one thing must be said in advance about such abuses. No writer can avoid ideological distortion, let alone posthumous confiscation of his name, for no one can prevent observers from seizing on perceived affinities between his work and that of groups whom he opposed, from linking his position on one issue with a range of other allegedly related issues, or from ignoring or disregarding his stated intentions and/or the original context in which he wrote.

But did Nietzsche *intend* such ambiguities? Certainly he regarded the possibility of fatal misinterpretation as a distinguishing trait of the true philosopher: One incapable of dangerous misinterpretation, he said, is likewise incapable of life-transforming influence. "If you misunderstand the singer, what does it matter?" he declared in *The Joyful Wisdom*. Or as he put it more soberly in *Daybreak:* "What I understand by the word 'philosopher': a terrible explosive, in the presence of which everything is in danger."

And Nietzsche was keenly aware that his ideas were dangerous—and had premonitions that his catchphrases would be turned toward questionable ends. He was furious when he discovered that, after Elisabeth's marriage, numerous anti-Semites assumed him to be a Forster ally. "That in every *Anti-Semitic correspondence* sheet the name *Zarathustra* is used," he wrote Elisabeth in December 1887, "has already made me almost sick several times."

He was no imperialist, race supremacist, or anti-Semite.[27] All of Nietzsche's main ideas—the Will to Power, self-overcoming, the *Übermensch,* the codes of master and slave morality, sublimation, the revaluation of all values, and beyond good and evil—are fundamentally contrary to statist and racial theories. Nietzsche did hold that all life evinces a Will to Power. And yet, as if anticipating Nazi race hygiene, he warned against "scholarly oxen" who might portray him as a German Darwin, as a racial eugenicist who had meant that the *Übermensch* referred to a species that might come into being as the next step of evolution—for example, a superior Aryan race.

Nietzsche scholars have long debated Nietzsche's famous—and infamous—concept of the Will to Power. Most postwar interpreters reject the Nazi claims to Nietzsche, that is, the Nazi view that Nietzsche defended the idea that "might makes right"; Nietzsche specifically condemned the Second German Reich of Bismarck for its militarism, its "human, all-too-human" power. Postwar critics (Walter Kaufmann, Karl Löwith, Alexander Nehamas) understand Nietzsche as stressing the will to self-overcoming, that is, the development of power over oneself. Above all, Nietzsche maintained, people seek creative mastery. His admiration of heroic lives—among them Socrates, Christ, Leonardo da Vinci, Goethe, Schopenhauer—makes it clear that he conceived the zenith of power to be exemplified by lordly self-rule, incarnated in supremely autonomous individuals, in "free spirits" possessed of expansive personalities unhobbled by fears or desires. Their power has nothing to do with the capacity to coerce others but rather is the ability to act with godlike awareness and "joyful wisdom." Indeed, the characters alone of these sovereign figures exhibit such charismatic force that, without benefit of office or organization, they transfigure the lives of those around them and even transmit their visions to persons who encounter them only secondhand through their art.

Instead of constructing a Platonic or Christian ideal above the clouds that reinforces human incapacity, urged Nietzsche, we should conceive of a higher type of humanity that admittedly does not exist now but that we may exert ourselves to become. And so the Will to Power pertains not to collective might but rather to individual self-actualization.[28] "*Become who you are!*" he urged in *The Joyful Wisdom*. The *Übermensch* is the passionate person, like Leonardo or Goethe, who can employ his—and Nietzsche did mean "his"—drives creatively instead of having to repress them. (It was also Nietzsche, long before Freud, who gave the terms "repression" and "sublimation" their modern psychological sense.) In *The Joyful Wisdom*, Nietzsche calls "giving style to one's character" the sign of power, for "it is the weak characters without power over themselves who hate the constraint of style." "The secret of the greatest fruitfulness and the greatest enjoyment of existence is: *to live dangerously.*"

Why is resentment of the passions, the body, sexuality, the critical intelligence—namely, this world and everything strong and healthy in it—so deeply rooted in the Western tradition? Christianity, answered Nietzsche. "Christian love" is calculating and utilitarian: the Christian practices charity, said Nietzsche, merely to get to heaven. Thus it was no accident that the poor and downtrodden, including the slaves of antiquity, converted immediately to the Christian church: Christianity, with its self-serving contrast of good and evil, is a "slave morality" designed to elevate and protect the weak and to undermine strong, free spirits. True generosity and nobility of spirit belonged to the "master morality" of the ancient Greeks and Romans, said Nietzsche. He did not, however, simply exalt pagan or non-Christian morality as superior, let alone celebrate brawn and brutality. He praised the courage and integrity that raise one above resentment. He emphasized the healthiness of "forgetting" as a way of letting go of suffering. And he proposed that humankind go "beyond good and evil," that is, beyond envy and the lust for revenge. No single morality is appropriate to all persons, he insisted. All of us must forge our own moral codes.

It requires little imagination to see how such a doctrine can be interpreted as mere relativism—and can be twisted to justify militarism, race ideology, and even the Holocaust. Once again, it deserves emphasis that, at times, Nietzsche did indeed anticipate that his pronouncements would serve the worst atrocities and catastrophes that the human race would ever endure. On display under the glass cases in the Nietzsche Archive are numerous witty yet also megalomaniacal, terrible, uncannily prescient prophecies from Nietzsche's pen, written during the last two years of his sanity. Later I flipped through various Nietzsche volumes and relocated some of the most memorable pronouncements:

From an April 1887 letter: "With me a *catastrophe* is being prepared. I know its name, but I will not pronounce it."

From a February 1888 letter: "It is not inconceivable that I am the foremost philosopher of the era, perhaps even more than that, a bridge between two millennia, decisive and doom-laden."

From a December 1888 letter: "You [Elisabeth] have no conception of what it means to be closely related to the man and the destiny in whom the question of millennia has been resolved. Quite literally, I hold the future of humanity in the palm of my hand."

And, finally, from *Ecce Homo:* "I know my fate. My name will be linked with something terrible, with a crisis, the like of which has never been known before on earth, with the most difficult conflict of conscience, with the passing of a sentence upon all which heretofore has been believed, required, and hallowed. There will be wars such as there have never been on earth. . . . I am not a man. I am dynamite."

Behold the Man: Nietzsche-Dionysus.

But did the philosopher's verbal explosives really spark the crusades conducted in his name? While it is hard to overestimate Nietzsche's cultural importance, it is easy to exaggerate his direct political influence. No one claims that this century would have been spared two world wars had Nietzsche never lived. And yet, even sympathetic Nietzsche scholars, however obliquely they have worded their verdicts, have laid part of the blame for those cataclysms at Nietzsche's feet. Karl Löwith, in his 1956 introduction to a Nietzsche selection, argued that Nietzsche "created a spiritual atmosphere in which certain things became possible."[29] Or, as J. P. Stern wrote two decades later in *Friedrich Nietzsche:* "It cannot be denied that the intellectual superstructure of these political movements is as inconceivable without Nietzsche's ideas as these movements are without their superstructure."[30]

Yet these scholars concentrate too much on Nietzsche's place in the history of ideas. Thus they underplay the *institutional* dimension of Nietzsche's cultural history, especially the propagandistic function that the Nietzsche Archive played in transforming Nietzsche into the intellectual Hun of Wilhelmine militarists, the pseudo-Superman of Nazi racial ideologues, and the Bogeyman Brownshirt of SED hacks.

As I peer down to read the fading print of old letters and newspaper clippings, Nietzsche in the glass case becomes Nietzsche the looking glass of modern Germany.

VII

Above all, do not mistake me for someone else!
Preface, *Ecce Homo*

Nietzsche's posthumous reception belongs both to the history of philosophy and to the history of publicity. His fame owes not only to the brilliance and provocativeness of his writings but also to the superhuman social climbing of Elisabeth, whose phenomenal salesmanship enabled her to sell the Nietzsche Archive successively to European nobles, to Wilhelmine jingoists, and to Nazi ideologues. One may justifiably speak of Elisabeth's own Will to Power, or at least her Will to Popularity. The letter *N* on the doorknobs of the entrance to the Nietzsche Archive could have pertained to the visionary yet petty-bourgeois Elisabeth, for she was "half Nietzsche, half Naumburg," "diabolical and unbelievably strong-willed" and yet also a thoroughly bourgeois *Streberin* (self-seeker), incarnating "the Will to Power minus the Will to Truth."[31] Not without cause had ten-year-old Fritz, after finding a llama in a storybook described as a stubborn animal, nicknamed his eight-year-old sister "Llama"—and called her "das Lama" for the rest of his life.

Indeed, that Weimar lays claim to Nietzsche's legacy has everything to do with Elisabeth. Energetic, diligent, well-organized, and above all ambitious, her own literary and political talents contributed to the spread of Nietzsche's name and the Archive's success. In addition to overseeing the affairs of the Villa Silberblick, she published separate three-volume (1895–1904) and two-volume (1912, 1914) biographies of Nietzsche, along with three monographs and dozens of articles about him and the Archive. In 1921 she was awarded an honorary doctorate by the University of Jena, the first woman ever to receive the honor. By the 1920s, next to Cosima Wagner, she was probably the most famous woman in German literary life, perhaps in all of Europe. "The Antigone of the North," the Italian revolutionary Gabriele D'Annunzio dubbed her. Elisabeth's name was submitted three times—in 1908, 1911, and 1923—to the Swedish Academy for the Nobel Prize in Literature. In 1923 her sponsors included Count Kessler, Oswald Spengler (*The Decline of the West*), Rudolf Eucken (winner of the 1908 Nobel Prize), and Hans Vaihinger (*The Philosophy of As If*). The Swedish Academy acknowledged her merits but instead bestowed that year's prize on an Irish admirer of Nietzsche: William Butler Yeats.

Until the outbreak of World War I, Elisabeth held an open house every Saturday and granted audiences to Nietzschean pilgrims from almost every continent. The guest book of the Villa Silberblick also bears the signatures of the period's leading German intellectuals: Stefan George, Hugo von Hofmannsthal, Richard Dehmel, Detlev von Liliencron, Paul Ernst, Thomas Mann, Gerhart Hauptmann, Graf Hermann Keyserling, and Oswald Spengler. As H. F. Peters, author of a biography of Elisabeth, notes: "In the first decade of the twentieth century, Nietzsche's gospel attracted a larger following and more attention than any other cultural movement. Even English Fabians such as Bernard Shaw and H. G. Wells saw no contradiction between Nietzsche's concept of a master race and their vision of a socialist utopia."[32]

Not that all intellectuals agreed about Nietzsche's message. On the contrary. "I know both sides," wrote Nietzsche in *Ecce Homo,* "because I am both sides." In the first decade of the century, Europe's stellar thinkers took up radically opposed positions on what Nietzsche had meant. While Stefan George and Thomas Mann saw in Nietzsche's aristocratic radicalism an antidote to the decayed democratic ideals of the West, socialist historian Franz Mehring pronounced Nietzsche "the philosopher of finance capitalism." To the Berlin philosopher Wilhelm Dilthey he was the advocate of "irrational individualism." To André Gide, he was "the Immoralist," who eviscerated conventions in morality just as earlier scientists had dissected superstitions like astrology and alchemy. Their differences notwithstanding, however, intellectuals across the political spectrum acknowledged their incalculable debt. The poet Gottfried Benn summed up the consensus, which suggests the cosmos that Nietzsche's shooting star had traversed in two decades: "Everything my generation discussed and worked through—one could say, teased out—all of it had already been expressed and exhausted by Nietzsche; he gave the definitive formulations, all the rest was exegesis."[33]

Soon the most eager of Nietzsche's disciples, believing that the Nietzsche Archive was far too humble a shrine for the Master, began to outdo even Elisabeth in their ardor. Led by Count Kessler, the moving force behind the 1908 establishment of the Nietzsche Endowment, they suggested the erection of a Nietzsche tabernacle on a hillside outside Weimar. According to Kessler's plan, the Weimar environs would thus become a macrocosm of the library of the Nietzsche Archive. A grand Nietzsche memorial temple in the classical style, designed by Henry van de Velde and including statues of Apollo and Dionysus, would survey Weimar and its magnificent intellectual history. Over the initial objections of Elisabeth (who feared that the new project would eclipse the Archive and jeopardize her own fund-raising efforts), Kessler organized an international committee and quickly raised a considerable sum. Soon, however, he decided that his modest aspirations did injustice to Nietzsche's noble example. The Master was not merely a sage who warranted his own sanctuary; he was an Olympian, and his message challenged modern youth to physical as well as intellectual greatness. The model of the perfectly self-possessed Nietzschean hero embraced the ideals not just of Athens but of Sparta; the grandeur and glory of Weimar in the new Nietzschean epoch would symbolize more than erudition, scholarship, or even cultural eminence: Nietzschean Weimar would represent a new civilization responding to the Master's work as a summons to action in the world. Kessler began collecting funds for a massive arena where European youth could display their athletic prowess in the spirit of ancient Greece.[34]

Thus, within a decade of his death, Nietzsche had eclipsed Goethe and Schiller to become the leading cultural attraction of Germany, arguably the dominant intellectual figure in all of Europe. During 1911–14, the biggest topic of conversation in Weimar was the proposed construction of the Nietzsche Stadium, with its temple and surrounding park, all of which would serve as a German counterpart to the Olympic stadia of Athens and Stockholm. With the German chancellor, Prince Bernard von Bülow, serving as honorary president, the International Nietzsche Committee included not only prominent German and Austrian writers (Gerhart Hauptmann, Hugo von Hofmannsthal), composers (Gustav Mahler, Richard Strauss), and politicians (Walther Rathenau) but also the most distinguished non-Germanic intellectuals and academics of Europe, among them Gabriele D'Annunzio, Maurice Barrès, Anatole France, André Gide, Henri Lichtenberger, Gilbert Murray, Romain Rolland, Bernard Shaw, and H. G. Wells. In 1912 it won the support of the German Olympic Committee, secured funding, and scheduled construction plans. The cornerstones for the Nietzsche pantheon and arena were to be laid on 15 October 1914, the seventieth anniversary of Nietzsche's birth, at which time the third era of Weimar greatness would truly begin. Six weeks before that date, however, war broke out; the continent suddenly found itself the arena of battle.

The Good Europeans who had pledged themselves to Nietzschean internationalism were now whipped up to an unholy fury against one another, destroying all hopes of international cultural cooperation. The Nietzsche movement remained a circumscribed, intellectual one. And the voice of the figure whom scholars have since come to call "the gentle Nietzsche"—the Good European, the existentialist, the champion of self-realization—was drowned out in the calls to arms.[35]

The change in Nietzsche's reputation, both in Germany and abroad, was abrupt and dire. For the next three decades, "the tough Nietzsche" would command the world stage. Aggressive German intellectuals linked his name with talk about *Lebensraum* and the strong-willed *Herrenmensch*. While one German critic hostile to this new Nietzsche blamed him for "pushing humanitarian and pacifistic tendencies into the shade," most intellectuals exalted Nietzsche as the great theorist of the Will to Power; many named Bismarck its supreme practitioner. Under Elisabeth's supervision, a special edition of *Thus Spake Zarathustra* was printed for the kaiser's troops in 1914; "Zarathustra in the knapsack" became a war legend. Elisabeth later claimed, in a 1926 letter to President Hindenburg extolling the morale-building qualities of Nietzsche's work while begging for an honorary pension, that "along with the Bible and Goethe's *Faust*, . . . *Zarathustra* was the book most often read at the front by German soldiers." Certainly it was a German best seller: 11,000 copies sold within the first six weeks of the war; 165,000 sold during 1914–19, far more than during the previous twenty-two years of its existence.[36]

Nietzsche's ideas and slogans were often used as war propaganda. Soldiers were urged to "Become hard!" and, following scattered remarks of Nietzsche, the economist Werner Sombart wrote in *Haendler und Helden* [Merchants and heroes] that the war with England was one between businessmen and visionaries. Whereas the commercially minded Englishmen calculated the future by balance sheets and utilitarian principles, said Sombart, the Germans were a prophetic people who fought to usher in a new, glorious age of adventure and greatness. It was thus "Nietzsche's war," declared Sombart, and also the war of Frederick the Great, Goethe, Schiller, Beethoven, Hegel, and Bismarck. Sombart considered Nietzsche a second John the Baptist, announcer of the good news that the Second Coming was at hand, that the Savior, whom Nietzsche called the *Übermensch*, was poised to return.[37]

Unsurprisingly, Nietzsche was castigated in the foreign press as the bloody father of German nationalists and militarists. His Will to Power was taken as the Will to Violence. Thomas Mann noted in 1915 that English newspapers were linking Nietzsche with the nationalist historian Heinrich von Treitschke and with Gen. Friedrich von Bernhardi, author of *Germany and the Next War,* all three said to be responsible for enflaming the Germans' immoral lust for conquest. A great admirer of Nietzsche—and in 1918 the recipient of the annual literary prize awarded by the Nietzsche Archive—Mann called this trio "a grotesque cacophony to the ear of all intellectual Germans." "It is ridiculous," Mann added, "that Nietzsche should be brought in to complete the panorama of German wickedness."[38]

But British and even many American observers insisted on Nietzsche's blameworthiness. In Britain, editorial writers demonized the Germans as "the blond Teuton beast," after a phrase from *The Genealogy of Morals.* "I should think that there is no instance since history began," Thomas Hardy grandly pronounced, "of a country being so demoralized by a single writer." The London *Athenaeum* castigated Nietzsche's jingoist academic colleagues, who had misguidedly catapulted one of their own kind from the seminar to the public square.[39] Plainly endorsing the German image of Nietzsche as a German imperialist, British war pamphlets included titles like *Germany's War Inspirers: Nietzsche and Treitschke.* In the United States, H. L. Mencken, whose first book, published in 1908, had been on Nietzsche, was arrested as an agent "of the German monster, Nietzsky." And after his English-language translation of Nietzsche's collected works appeared in 1917, Oscar Levy, Nietzsche's British translator, noticed a sign in a Piccadilly bookshop: "The Euro-Nietzschean War. Read the Devil in order to fight him better."[40]

VIII

What is important is not what the creator of an idea of genius may mean, but what this idea becomes in the mouth of whoever transmits it.

Adolf Hitler, *Mein Kampf*

The Nietzsche Archive was never an academic institute or a research center dedicated to the production of scholarly editions of Nietzsche's oeuvre. It served Elisabeth rather as a private court, complete with evenings of musical entertainment and society gossip with visiting royalty and dignitaries. Nor was Elisabeth chiefly an ideological fascist; she was a conservative, a royalist, a passionate nationalist—and, above all, a snob and an opportunist. She felt driven to associate with the Nazis to secure financial support for the Archive. She needed a patron. World War I and the hyperinflation of 1922/23 had wiped out the Archive's endowment. Not only was the Villa Silberblick heavily mortgaged, but the copyright to Nietzsche's works was to run out in 1930, after which the Archive could receive no more royalties. Moreover, Elisabeth had incurred steep debts because she entertained lavishly, paid considerable sums to acquire Nietzsche's letters, and hired and fired editors frequently.

Not until the late 1920s, when the Archive was in its most dire financial straits, did Elisabeth steer it in a decidedly fascist direction. Neither in the years immediately before nor after World War I did the governing board of the Nietzsche Endowment include even a single right-wing militant. Like Elisabeth, her cousins Alfred Oehler, president of the board, and Maj. Max Oehler, assistant custodian of the Archive, belonged to the DNVP (*Deutsche Nationale Volkspartei*, German National People's Party) and shared its conservative values and its restoration-monarchical nostalgia. (After German women got the vote, Elisabeth wrote her widely circulated "Letter to German Women," publicly supporting Hindenburg's DNVP candidacy.) Other board members belonged to the more liberal DDP (*Deutsche Demokratische Partei*, German Democratic Party) or to Gustav Stresemann's DVP (*Deutsche Volkspartei*, German People's Party), which at one time entered into a coalition with the Social Democrats.

In 1923 the board gained a leading right-wing sympathizer: Oswald Spengler, recipient of the Nietzsche Archive's literary prize in 1922. Although Spengler's seat was balanced on the left by Count Kessler and Arnold Paulssen, Elisabeth began to side with Spengler virtually as soon as he joined the board. Her reasons were largely social and financial. Of all board members, Spengler possessed the biggest name and the best connections to German industry and finance; he helped organize the Society of the Friends of the Nietzsche Archive in 1926. So Elisabeth and the Oehlers swallowed whole Spengler's nationalistic, Prussian *Weltanschauung* both because of their own monarchist sentiments and for political and economic reasons. Elisabeth became increasingly sympathetic to right-wing nationalist appeals. Like her conservative friends, she was terrified of the rise of the "red menace" in the towns and villages of Thuringia. In a 1923 letter to Spengler, she bemoaned that the trial of Hitler for the failed beer-hall *Putsch* in Munich was "a travesty," since his attempted coup had been merely "a patriotic aspiration."[41]

During the next two decades, the minuet danced by the Nietzsche Archive and national socialism evolved in three phases. In the opening stage (1923–28), the Archive supported Italian fascism rather than German national socialism. Even before Mussolini's March on Rome and capture of power in 1922, Elisabeth had become aware of the Duce's admiration for Nietzsche and had courted his favor. By 1928, when Elisabeth extolled the Duce in her "Speech of Admiration" as the embodiment of the Superman, the Archive's open embrace of fascism was clear. In the intervening years the Italian ambassador had made several pilgrimages to the Archive; Mussolini had sent Elisabeth a personal contribution of 20,000 lira.

Mussolini had wide-ranging cultural interests and considerable intellectual gifts, and as a student Marxist he had admired Nietzsche. In 1903, as a twenty-year-old, he had written that Nietzsche was "the mind most marked by genius of the last quarter century."[42] Thereafter Mussolini declared his pedigree via his motto: "Vivere Pericolosamente!" [Live dangerously!]. (Here one must emphasize that Nietzsche had a *direct* influence on Mussolini. The Nietzsche Archive had little to do with it; Mussolini was a Nietzsche admirer long before *The Will to Power* appeared.) Mussolini exalted Nietzsche as his teacher and even credited

Nietzsche with his conversion from socialism to fascism—and soon Elizabeth, in turn, credited her own column. Elisabeth's rightward turn moved Count Kessler to confide to a friend: "The good old lady speaks of the right-wing radicals as 'we'! . . . Despite her family name, she represents the incarnation of everything that her brother fought against."[43]

During the second stage of the Archive's progress toward nazism (1928–33), it bestowed its imprimatur on several Nazi professors and intellectuals as Nietzsche scholars. National socialism needed a canon to provide it with an intellectual pedigree. Count Arthur Gobineau, Houston Stewart Chamberlain, Treitschke, Spengler, and Rosenberg were all drafted into service. But the unquestioned star in the Nazi firmament was Nietzsche. The biggest change within the Archive itself was the 1928 election of Carl August Emge, constitutional law professor at the University of Jena, to the board of the Nietzsche Endowment. Thereafter, when Emge signed political leaflets supporting Hitler elections, he cited his Nietzsche Endowment connection, implying that the Archive was officially supporting Hitler.[44] (In fact, despite her fascist sympathies, Elisabeth preferred Hindenburg, but the impression was generally accurate.) Max Oehler publicly declared fascism "the ideal form of government" and Mussolini "the realization of Nietzsche's ideas." In 1928 the Archive also sponsored a much-discussed lecture, "Mussolini and Fascism as an Intellectual Movement," after which it began to receive regular and substantial contributions from German industry. (The most significant of these was from Philipp Reemtsma, a wealthy cigarette manufacturer and financial backer of the Nazis, who contributed more than RM 200,000 to the Archive between 1929 and 1945 and was later tried at Nuremberg.)[45]

In January 1930 Wilhelm Frick became the first Nazi minister in a provincial government in Germany, and he and other Weimar Nazis developed close relations with the Nietzsche Archive. In 1931 Nazi Party leader Hans Frank declared Nietzsche "the father of National Socialism"; that year also witnessed the publication of the first "Nazi" study of Nietzsche, Alfred Baeumler's *Nietzsche, Philosopher and Politician.* Baeumler had just been called to the most prestigious professorship in Germany, the newly founded Chair for Political Pedagogy at the University of Berlin.[46] Soon thereafter he also superintended, along with Alfred Rosenberg, the education of NSDAP members. Baeumler hailed Nietzsche as "a Political Educator" whose heroic philosophy anticipated Germany's glorious destiny. Anticipating the poststructuralist readings of Derrida, Baeumler recast Nietzsche's work, calling the published writings a series of strategic "poses," with the "true" Nietzsche appearing only in marginal comments and notes. Thus Baeumler could confidently conclude: "And when we call to our youth, marching under the swastika, *Heil Hitler*—at the same time we are calling to Friedrich Nietzsche!"[47]

It was because the Nietzsche Archive and the leading Nietzsche publicists— especially Elisabeth and the Oehlers—said that Nietzsche was "four-fifths a Nazi," as one biographer puts it, "that the Nazis themselves believed it."[48] No evidence exists that Hitler himself ever read Nietzsche. Nietzsche's name is nowhere in *Mein Kampf,* which makes extensive reference to other Nazi heroes such as Gobineau and Houston Stewart Chamberlain; and in the volumes of Hitler's published table talk, Nietzsche's name appears only once, in a passing reference, along with Schopenhauer and Goethe.

Neither Baeumler nor Richard Oehler, Elisabeth's nephew, who edited the twenty-volume *Complete Works of Friedrich Nietzsche* (1942), was under any illusions that Nietzsche was actually a proto-Nazi or Aryan supremacist. No one in Nazi Germany was allowed to regard Nietzsche as an opponent of anti-Semitism, however, even though he had called it "a mendacious race swindle" and "brazen humbug." Nietzsche the Good European never deemed the French degenerate or the Slavs subhuman; he considered Forster's anti-Semitism vulgar and urged racial cross-breeding; he abominated Bismarck's Reich and indeed the very notion of political parties and the nation-state. He advocated a cultural integration of Europe, the exact opposite of the Nazi program of destroying European culture in order to transform the continent into a German colony.

Nevertheless, Baeumler and Oehler extolled Nietzsche as an early father of the revolutionary Nazi faith. Point for point, they insisted, his teachings coincided with the cardinal doctrines of national socialism: a transvaluation of all values, the sanctity of the Will to Power, the duty of the strong to dominate, the sole right of great states to exist, the rebirth of Germany and therefore Europe, the coming of the *Übermensch,* the idea of the master race, the leader principle (*Führerprinzip*). Like Hitler, Nietzsche was a solitary bachelor devoted to a higher cause; both men were also vegetarians, nonsmokers, and teetotalers; both advocated discipline, hardness, compulsory military training of youth, and a love of solitude in the mountains (*Bergeinsamkeit*); both condemned modern civilization as effete; both celebrated the singular personality, honored the exceptional talent, defended the right of the superior individual to rule the masses, and denounced communism and parliamentary government; both men heralded the advent of a class of "lords of the earth" who would have the will and authority to command and who would be beyond good and evil.[49]

Hitler's appointment to the chancellory in January 1933 ushered in the concluding phase (1933–45) of the Archive's embrace of nazism, during which it completed the process of *Gleichschaltung* and turned itself into a Nazi cultural center. This step coincided with the state adoption of expurgated editions of Nietzsche's work, selected for ideological training in German curricula and youth programs. Nietzsche was touted as "the intellectual *Führer,*" whose work embodied the Nazi goals "of *Erziehung zum Kampf* [education for battle] and *Erziehung zur Einheit* [education for unity] through blood and deed." Rosenberg linked his arguments for race breeding and "functional education" to Nietzsche, placing Nietzschean illiberalism at the heart of Nazi educational philosophy. Numerous German professors delivered lectures on Nietzsche's "Aryan *Weltanschauung,*" and Baeumler devoted entire seminars to aspects of Nietzsche's thought.[50]

"One repays a teacher badly," wrote Nietzsche in *Zarathustra,* "if one remains a pupil only." But Nazi ideological indoctrination repaid Nietzsche horribly precisely by "teaching" his vitalistic philosophy as a vengeful, antihumanistic *Lebensphilosophie*—with the enthusiastic cooperation of Elisabeth and the Archive. Baldur von Schirach, head of the HJ, befriended Elisabeth and the Oehlers; Nietzsche's name appeared incessantly in his journal *Wille und Macht*. Soon *Thus Spake Zarathustra* became a sacred HJ text. In 1934 its place in the National Socialist canon was officially acknowledged when it was given a cherished spot— alongside Hitler's *Mein Kampf* and Rosenberg's *The Myth of the Twentieth Century*—in the vault of the Tannenberg Memorial, which had been built in honor of Germany's victory over Russia in World War I. Hitler himself visited the Archive no less than seven times. In the famous photograph of October 1934, taken during the memorial celebration commemorating the ninetieth anniversary of Nietzsche's birth, the Führer was shown in profile opposite a bust of Nietzsche. But the photographer inadvertently cut Nietzsche's face in half, leaving one stone moustache curving off into nothing: an inadvertent metaphor for the Nazi bisection of his philosophy.

Hitler's final call on Elisabeth was a surprise visit in October 1935 to assure her that he would provide the money for the construction of a Nietzsche memorial auditorium and library adjoining the Villa Silberblick. They would be used, he said, to hold conferences and workshops for German youth, who would be taught Nietzsche's doctrine of the master race. "One cannot but love this great, magnificent man, if only one knows him as well as I do," rejoiced Elisabeth, in one of her last letters. Hitler himself laid the wreath on her grave in November 1935, and the *Völkischer Beobachter* eulogized her as the Mother of the Fatherland, bannering the story of the funeral on its front page.[51]

Elisabeth never joined the NSDAP, but this was a mere formality. The Nazis agreed that it would be better for the international reputation of the Archive if she did not hold a Party card. By 1933 the Oehler family and the board members of the Nietzsche Endowment were all Nazis.

Elisabeth and the Archive sponsored several selectively edited pamphlets to the greater glory of Nazi Germany, the "Nietzsche Anthologies," published by Kroner Verlag. One typical collection of Nietzsche quotations was entitled *The Sword of the Spirit*, addressed to "German soldiers and patriots." In his study *Nietzsche and the German Future* (1935), Richard Oehler wrote: "To wish to give proof regarding Nietzsche's thoughts, in order to establish that they agree with the race views and aims of the National Socialist movement, would be like carrying coals to Newcastle." With the Führer regularly traveling between the Weimar of Nietzsche and the Bayreuth of Wagner, said Oehler, the conflict between the philosophical and musical geniuses of modern Germany—indeed the division in Germany's soul—had been healed. In the Third Reich, Weimar and Bayreuth were no longer opposed—even a *Sternenfreundschaft* was no longer necessary.[52] "Now we are experiencing the astonishing development: the fulfillment of all [Nietzsche's prophecies] is beginning," gushed Richard Oehler. Nietzsche had indeed been a John the Baptist for the messianic Superman, whose name was Adolf Hitler. The

coming of the Teutonic "Dionysus" (Nietzsche) marked the eschatological moment when the revolution effected by "the Crucified" (Jesus) would be reversed:

> The Cross [*Kreuz*] as a sign *against* health, beauty, common sense, bravery, intellect,
> kindliness of soul—*against Life itself.* The swastika [*Hakenkreuz*] as a sign *for* health,
> beauty, sense, bravery, intellect, kindliness of soul—*for Life itself.*[53]

"In fifty years," Nietzsche had written his mother in 1887, "my name will radi-
ate before the world in awe-inspiring glory." And indeed, by 1937, he was right:
the two leaders of fascist Europe, Mussolini and Hitler, had acknowledged him
as their intellectual hero. "Am Nietzschewesen wird die Welt genesen," announced the Nietzsche Archive in 1938, adapting the kaiser's World War I declaration about Germany's destiny to Nietzsche's historic role: "Nietzsche will save
the world."[54]

Just the opposite almost occurred, of course—as many anti-Nietzsche critics
had warned. Condemning Nietzsche in the foreign press as Hitler's spiritual
guide, they did no more than accept the Nazi interpretation promoted by the
Nietzsche Archive. Already in 1936 the left-wing *Contemporary Review* in England
was calling Nietzsche himself "the pre-Hitlerian man," whose "doctrine is the
spiritual fountainhead of concentration camps and mass executions." The *Boston
Transcript* headlined in 1940: "Hitler War Blamed on Insane Philosopher: Nietzsche Is Nazi Chief's Favorite Author." Harvard historian Crane Brinton published a study of Nietzsche the following year, in which he dismissed Nietzsche
as "an ambitious German professor, who may have developed a philosophy 'beyond good and evil,' but not 'beyond Mussolini and Hitler.'"[55] Writing from
exile on the centennial of Nietzsche's birth in 1944, and with the dimensions of
the Holocaust rapidly becoming public knowledge, Karl Löwith mourned: "The
endeavor to discharge Nietzsche from the guilt of his historical influence is as
futile as the opposite attempt to charge him with direct responsibility. . . . Thus
Rousseau prepared the way for the French Revolution, just as Nietzsche prepared
the way for the German counter-revolution against the ideas of the first."[56]

It was symbolically fitting that the entire edition of Richard Blunck's biography
of Nietzsche, the first officially approved Nazi biography, scheduled to appear in
early 1945, was destroyed in a bombing raid shortly after being printed. The biography did not appear until its 1953 publication in West Germany—and only then,
of course, with Nietzsche's Nazi connection utterly effaced.

IX

> I know of no purpose better than being destroyed by what is great and impossible.
> Nietzsche, *On the Advantage and Disadvantage of History for Life*

"I am not a man," Nietzsche had written in *Ecce Homo.* "I am dynamite." As Germany lay in rubble in 1945, that prophecy too seemed fulfilled. At Nuremberg,

the sins of the sister were laid at his feet; Nietzsche was, as it were, tried along with the leading Nazis—and found guilty. "The morality of immorality," one judge pronounced, "the result of Nietzsche's purest teaching."[57]

Soviet authorities in Weimar decided to encase and stash the dynamite, placing the Nietzsche Archive high on their blacklist as a center of Nazi propaganda. Major Oehler, its custodian, was arrested. He fell sick, was confined by the Soviet occupying army to a basement in a house near the Nietzsche Archive, and starved to death in the winter of 1945. For years Elisabeth's personal papers, correspondence, and diaries remained locked up in the newly organized complex of the National Research Center for Classical German Literature in Weimar, founded in 1953.[58] The Archive itself was turned into a guest house for visiting dignitaries and scholars. The Nazis had wanted to emphasize the similarities between Nietzsche and Hitler—and so too did the SED. It served both sides' purposes to do so.

Although Max Horkheimer of the Frankfurt School had attempted in the 1930s to bring Nietzsche into the fold of Critical Theory as a maverick leftist, his arguments never found favor on the left. In the early 1950s, leading eastern European Marxist intellectuals united in their contempt for Nietzsche. Ernst Bloch pronounced Nietzsche "usable only for fascism." Georg Lukács said that Nietzsche was "the sworn enemy of the working class," the chief destroyer of reason, and the trailblazer for national socialism. He would have "regarded Hitler and Himmler, Goebbels and Goering as moral and spiritual allies." Hitler was merely "the executor of Nietzsche's testament."[59] In 1956 Nietzsche's papers were finally made available to DDR and Western scholars; but Lukács's verdict was in effect the nail in the coffin. In the official DDR publication, *German Literary History* (1974), Nietzsche is merely mentioned and dismissed as a "militant reactionary." In the SED's official 909-page history of Weimar (1976), Nietzsche earns a single paragraph, which condemns his "antihumanistic, extreme individualistic, and irrationalist" teachings.[60] Like the Nazis, the Communists took Zarathustra seriously: "Whatever falls—it should be kicked too!"

Nietzsche's works were not to be found in bookstores or in antiquaries. Instead they were relegated to the *Giftschraenke* of libraries, where researchers were required to obtain an IG pass (*Internen Gebrauch,* for internal [scholarly] use only) to read him. Nietzsche entries in library card catalogs bore special stamps, either "Proof of purpose required" or "Limiting borrowing." The books themselves— as in the case of George Orwell and other authors on the DDR "Index"—came affixed with a red circle: the mark of the censor's eye. Even his name vanished from East German periodicals; at most, liberal scholars might slip it past the censors in an essay on Schopenhauer or Thomas Mann. "Whoever thinks, above all whoever thinks a great deal, will never be a Party man," wrote Nietzsche in his *Untimely Meditations.* "He will think past and through the Party." Yet the strict SED Party line on Nietzsche stayed firm for decades; no prominent SED intellectual thought past it.

In the early 1980s, however, DDR intellectuals began to broach tentative reconsiderations of Nietzsche. The unexpected breakthrough came in 1986 in the intellectual journal *Sinn und Form,* the flagship journal of the Academy of the Fine Arts, when Heinz Pepperle, a liberal professor of historical materialism at Humboldt University, drew a sympathetic portrait of Nietzsche that triggered the last major cultural debate in the DDR before the fall of the Berlin Wall. The argument resembled the public debate that would grip West Germany in 1987 about Martin Heidegger, which was set off by the appearance of a biography by a former student, Victor Farias.

But the DDR Nietzsche debate never reached the wider public.[61] Fought in scholarly journals and conferences, it never made the review pages and letter columns of newspapers. That was not, however, due to public apathy. On the contrary: The SED judged that the Nietzsche dynamite was so explosive that the debate about him would have to be controlled and contained.

Pepperle's essay had urged no wholesale rehabilitation of Nietzsche. Indeed, his proposals were mild—which suggests how controversial Nietzsche remained in the DDR, to the very end. Rather, Pepperle called Nietzsche "a philosopher of significance" and "an unquestionably honest character," who wrote "in an expressive, compelling language" and offered "a sharp critique of dying bourgeois culture." But Nietzsche was finally "an ideologue of his class" whose alienation under capitalism had provoked his outbreak of "irrationalism," said Pepperle. Nietzsche represented a symptom of the tortuous transition from capitalism to imperialism in late-nineteenth-century Europe. A familiar line.[62]

But even this stock approach to nonsocialist thinkers was too much for SED ideologues such as Wolfgang Harich. Harich had served eight years in jail for allegedly conspiring to overthrow the SED leadership and emerged from prison in 1964 both a hard-line Stalinist and a vociferous critic of all modernist (and, soon, postmodernist) experimentation—an ideological and aesthetic orientation that turned Nietzsche into the quintessence of all he opposed. Harich pulled no punches: Nietzsche was a "Nazi worshiper," insisted Harich. His work "smells of Zyklon B," the poisonous gas used in the Nazi concentration camps. "He was a passionate war hawk and potential defender of Himmler. . . . A society can hardly sink lower than when it adopts Nietzsche as part of its general education. It should be one of the basic principles of intellectual hygiene that we ban all quoting of Nietzsche." Nietzsche was an "archreactionary," "inhuman through and through." The list of his crimes was long: master-race theorist, pre-Fascist, misogynist, racist, anti-Semite, warmonger. Pepperle's interest in Nietzsche, said Harich, stemmed from a weakness for "Western fashions." Harich wouldn't even let Nietzsche get away with a collapse into madness. Nietzsche "only pretended" to go mad, when it became evident to him that he was incapable of writing a systematic work of philosophy, said Harich. He escaped his failure by feigning mental illness: that was his only way out. He couldn't write a great work—just collections of aphorisms—and so he finally gave up. Nietzsche's legacy, Harich concluded, was "a giant trash bin." The prosecution closed by calling for the same sentence upon Nietzsche that Brecht delivered against the epicurean Roman general Lucullus in *The Trial of Lucullus:* "Into the abyss with him!"[63]

Not everyone agreed with Harich's formulation, but Party intellectuals toed the line. The word came down: "Better dead than read." That line of graffiti—in English—on the western side of the Berlin Wall in 1988 sums up not only the finale of the DDR Nietzsche debate but also Nietzsche's entire history of reception in the DDR. At the Tenth Writers' Congress of the SED in 1987, the verdict on Nietzsche became official, as representatives of the SED writers' organizations and of every relevant academic field entered the fray. Several young intellectuals demurred, and Stephan Hermlin, then president of the DDR Writers' Congress, praised Nietzsche as "one of the most stimulating writers of the last hundred years" and worried about Harich's "reactionary retrogression." But most of the old guard held firm. Manfred Buhr, then director of the Central Institute of Philosophy in East Berlin and known in the DDR as "the philosophy pope," concerned himself not with Nietzsche but with "the phenomenon of Nietzsche." Buhr argued that pro-Fascist writers could never belong to the cultural inheritance of the anti-Fascist DDR. "Serious" scholars could read "questionable" authors like Nietzsche in restricted sections of the library. But there would never be a DDR Nietzsche edition, let alone a DDR revaluation of Nietzsche.[64]

As late as 1987 that papal bull *ex cathedra* would have been the final word. But a series of factors converged in 1988 to thwart the SED inquisition and keep Nietzsche's name in the pages of DDR journals: the infiltration of postmodernism, the popularity of Nietzsche with Italian Communists (Giorgi Colli and Mazzino Montinari had undertaken their Nietzsche edition with the Italian CP's enthusiastic support), and the bicentennial of Schopenhauer's birth (another conservative, latterly rehabilitated German philosopher, who had exerted profound influence on Nietzsche).[65] The old socialist realist arguments against Nietzsche sounded ever more lame. It was pointless, said some scholars, to ban Nietzsche as a "destroyer of reason" when postmodernism had thoroughly undermined the Enlightenment anyway.

But "Nietzsche can't be separated from his reception history," insisted Harich. "Whoever addresses Nietzsche addresses the politics of fascism." Harich suggested that "even to edit Nietzsche," as Colli and Montinari had done, branded one an "intellectual criminal."[66]

Seeking to prevent an erosion of Marxist dogma, Harich and Buhr concentrated their attacks upon Nietzsche's fatal influence on fascism. For them, the real issue was whether fascism was philosophically supportable—and because Nietzsche had been effectively used once before to make that claim, and because his work might conceivably lead again to the answer "yes"—he was *verboten*. The fear in the DDR was that an edition of Nietzsche might have stimulated a revival of fascism. Instead, the Nietzsche taboo helped lead to the demise of the SED itself and to a revival of Western capitalism.[67]

In hindsight, this vain, last-ditch attempt to save Nietzsche by liberals like Pepperle mirrored the scattered SED attempts before 1989 to save the DDR itself from self-detonating. The alternating mood between hesitant expectancy and harsh dismissal toward a Nietzsche rehabilitation disclosed the hopelessly closed-minded character of DDR cultural life. Although no one, of course, could have predicted it at the time, the closing round in the Nietzsche debate was the high-brow tremor of 1988 before the national earthquake of 1989.

"Who's Afraid of Friedrich Nietzsche?" headlined a West German review of a Darmstadt conference on Nietzsche in 1988 sponored by the West German Communist Party. The headline referred to repression of Nietzsche by East and West German Communists. The Nietzsche debate, said critical West German intellectuals, was a debate about censorship, recalling the censorship debates over Heiner Muller's plays, Thomas Mann's essays (including his 1947 essay, "Nietzsche in Our Time"), Heinrich Mann's fiction, and the work of numerous other German and non-German writers, past and present. "The point isn't whether Nietzsche is an important writer or a 'phenomenon,'" declared one reviewer of the conference, "but when, finally, the SED will stop setting up ideological boundaries and walls, when it will stop policing freedom of expression and criminalizing certain books as 'forbidden literature.'"

The events of autumn 1989 provided the answer. Until the fall of the Berlin Wall, Nietzsche remained in the abyss, an unperson. Harich had even suggested that the Goethe–Schiller Archive sell Nietzsche's papers to the West and raze his grave in his hometown of Röcken.

X

"Blessed are the forgetful," wrote Nietzsche in *Beyond Good and Evil,* "for they get the better even of their blunders."

In the newest New Germany of today, as the crimes of violence against foreigners and Jews uneasily evoke the political climate of the 1930s, that statement of the once and perhaps future philosopher-king of Germany also provokes worry, especially in the east. The former East Germany stands at the crossroads of the two great failed experiments of the century, forever captured in the image of Buchenwald: nazism and Stalinism—experiments allegedly fathered by the two great German minds of the nineteenth century, Nietzsche and Marx. Among Germany's fearful neighbors, the consensus has long been that Wagner, Nietzsche, and Hitler stand in the same relationship to one another as Marx, Engels, and Lenin. That East German intellectuals shoulder the almost unimaginable twin burdens of both nazism and Marxism-Leninism (or Stalinism), indeed that Nietzsche and Marx—the men whose work inspired fifty-seven years of totalitarian rule in eastern Germany—both did academic work at the eastern universities of Leipzig and Jena is a historical fact very tempting for eastern Germans to forget.

"If only Marx had come from East Germany and Nietzsche from West Germany," Weimar wags will tell you, "the DDR propaganda program would have been so much easier!" That Marx was born in Trier and not, say, in Karl-Marx

Stadt (now, once again, called Chemnitz), that Nietzsche was born in Röcken and not, say, in Bonn—complicated the SED's exclusive claim to Marx and impassioned disclaimer of Nietzsche.

Is it Marx *or* Nietzsche? Leading German socialist intellectuals—Mehring, Lukács, Hans Gunther, Johannes Becher, even DDR President Grotewohl—voiced that position. You could not have both. Even though Nietzsche the Good European, the "gentle" Nietzsche, resembled the young, "humanistic" Marx of the 1844 *Economic and Philosophical Manuscripts* in his call for an end to nationalism and the birth of world citizenship, SED leaders portrayed the two as rival prophets of the Right and Left. Nietzsche and Marx never met, nor did they ever say anything specifically about each other. That gave the SED a free interpretive hand. According to the SED, Marx and Nietzsche created the ideological alternatives of our century via their contrary utopian visions of a workers' paradise and an aristocracy of Supermen.[68] So, East Germany was East Germany, and West Germany was West Germany—and never the twain would meet. You must choose, and you must never forget the implications of your choice.

The DDR could never admit that, before the Stalinist era, German and even Russian leftists (Maxim Gorki, Lenin's Minister of Culture Anatoly Lunacharsky) had admired Nietzsche as a thinker of the Left—or that, at least since the 1960s, Nietzsche had been known throughout the West as a pioneer of Green politics, the counterculture, and alternative thinking.[69] Nietzsche—or a Nietzschean neo-Marxism—had replaced Marxism-Leninism in the left-wing pantheon. Western leftists had realized that Nietzsche's revolt against liberal democracy was far more radical than Marx's, who remained within the rationalist, metaphysical tradition. Thus skeptical Marxists, contemptuous of all large-scale conventional politics, wound up derationalizing Marx into an anarchistic neo-Marxist or aestheticized post-Marxist and converting Nietzsche into a leftist. By the late 1980s, the SED was fighting internal skirmishes while the real war had long ago moved on to a different intellectual front.

And yet, even while Marx *or* Nietzsche no longer appear mutually exclusive alternatives in eastern Germany, one must admit: It does seem, uncannily, as if their fortunes in Germany rise and fall in opposite directions. Whenever one swoops, the other soars. And now, since 1989, it is again Nietzsche's turn to take wing.

Indeed, Nietzsche *is* a phenomenon—though not quite in the way that SED intellectuals like Manfred Buhr once imagined. He represents the "phenomenon" of Germans'—especially eastern Germans'—ambivalent relation to their fate and their heritage. Nietzsche forces the question: What does it mean to be German— or to have been "East German"? In the former DDR, Nietzsche was a man without a country—but the DDR was a land without a history.

Nietzsche devoted much of his work to the problem of memory and forgetting. What ought we remember? What should we forget? The questions address the burden of the past, the danger of the future. How does a nation cope?

Accept the past and try to build on it? Simply wave it away, conclude that it doesn't matter?[70] According to Nietzsche, in the modern world the first alternative is no longer possible: "God is dead." The present is thrown into the vertiginous agony and euphoria of an unbridgeable break with the past; history has come to an end. All history has become "antiquarian"—you can't build on it, you can only observe it like a museum of memorabilia.

Has German history, in Nietzsche's sense, come to an end? Is the Holocaust its unbridgeable break with the past, after which nothing can be rebuilt? If so, that leaves only the second, postmodern alternative: not to let the past matter at all. Today, it would seem that "Germany" is a story still being told. But is it? Psychologically, "Germany" does not seem to advance beyond the so-called *Stunde Null* (zero hour) of 1945: Germans and their neighbors are forever returning, given the slightest provocation, to the Nazi years and the Holocaust. If "Germany," as it were, "stopped" at zero, if it is "dead," if it can't be revived, if it can't get out from under its own ever-lengthening shadow, if there is no heritage on which to draw—what then? Then the possibility of a truly *new* Germany doesn't exist—and Germans can only rummage through the historical pawnshop, picking and choosing among the relics and discards of their past. As such, Germany is *the* quintessentially postmodern country, a scavenger among personalities and events of the past, none of which serves to build a history, let alone a heritage.

Yes, Nietzsche is a phenomenally problematic figure for Germans, but his name signifies less a *Schreckbild* (vision of horror) than simply that pressure point at which the accumulated anxieties of a people vilified for decades by the entire world have finally converged and concentrated. Nietzsche is merely the most quotable of a long line of extraordinarily ambivalent figures in German history, ranging from Luther and Frederick the Great to Bismarck and Wagner—and even beyond, to Spengler and Heidegger. Like them, Nietzsche signifies the phenomenon of *heritage*—and how one relates to it. And here enter the worries loosed by his example.

For the spiritual health of a nation can only be gained through a judicious *modus vivendi* with its past. In the 1950s, the DDR developed a new attitude toward German history. Trying to build a socialist society, DDR intellectuals had to *create* a presocialist past; they needed ancestors to fit a genealogy leading upward to the DDR itself.

"We push our citizens to read," wrote Anna Seghers in 1961. "We speak of the national heritage [*Erbe*]. But do we guide our people sufficiently? What heritage is available for them to inherit? . . . We still haven't even started to address adequately the issue of *what* past our citizens should read—and how they can relate that past to themselves."[71]

In the 1970s, the SED made a start on that heritage. It constructed a "humanistic" prehistory of socialism. Above all, SED intellectuals distinguished "good" from "bad" bourgeois literature; even though their work suffered from ideological myopia, some presocialist or nonsocialist—or even antisocialist—writers were, if only implicitly, now praised as "critics of capitalism." True, capitalism had alienated them and warped their visions; but their very negativism was precisely a reaction against capitalism. They were humanists who could be integrated into the DDR "heritage."

East German scholars promoted the new view via a theoretical distinction in SED historiography between *Geschichte* or *Tradition* (history, tradition), which might be thought of as the whole of the past as it affects, consciously or unconsciously, the present; and *Erbe* (heritage), which is limited to those works and historical developments that helped create and sustain the DDR and socialism. The difference turns on the concept of *Aneignung* (appropriation), which mediates between the two regions of the past and constitutes the act of transforming a passively held tradition into an actively used heritage.

Luther, Frederick the Great, Bismarck, Wagner—and Nietzsche—had always been recognized in the DDR as part of German *history*. The decision in the 1960s and 1970s to move the first four into the realm of "heritage"—and still to exclude Nietzsche—was not lightly taken. The DDR conception of heritage was political; *Erbe* was a weapon in the continuing struggle with West Germany and the so-called forces of imperialism. The issue came down to which side—West Germany or East Germany—represented the "real," the "good" Germany. "The DDR is today the embodiment of the best traditions in the German heritage," declared Erich Honecker in 1973: "The Farmers' Rebellion of the Middle Ages, the 1848 revolution, the workers' movement founded by Marx and Engels and Bebel and Liebknecht, the heroes of the anti-Nazi resistance."[72] By reclaiming Luther, the SED was choosing to overlook Luther the theologian and defender of princely authority and to lay claim to Luther the champion of freethinking and the peasant. By admitting Frederick the Great and Bismarck, the DDR was opting to downplay their imperialism, or rather approach it as a necessary and productive stage on the way toward socialism. By embracing Wagner, the DDR was willing to look past Wagner the mature anti-Semite and champion of Bismarckian imperialism, back toward Wagner the youthful supporter of the 1848 revolution.

But the SED could see no advantage in rehabilitating Nietzsche; he remained beyond the pale. "Nietzsche isn't our heritage, the heritage of the working class, the heritage of the anti-Fascists," announced one SED intellectual after another. Nietzsche belonged to the *history* of Germany, they insisted, but not to the *heritage* of East Germany.

It needs emphasizing once again, however, that the "problem" of Nietzsche—and the question of cultural heritage—confronts not just easterners but all Germans today. Indeed, for five decades now, Germany has been a land where the burden of history tends to turn any symbolic gesture into a furious national—and even international—debate. Much of it is linked to the problem of Prussia—with which Frederick, Bismarck, and Nietzsche are especially associated. It served the purposes of both Bonn and East Berlin to vilify Prussia. Given the SED's urge to present the Third Reich as a logical heir to capitalism, Prussia had to be condemned—and with Bonn's desire to present the DDR as the totalitarian successor to Nazi Germany, Prussia (located in the heart of East Germany) also served as an attractive target.

Germany: A land of multiple personalities, divided for centuries and schizoid in recent decades—a land of dozens of principalities in the nineteenth century, a quadripartite occupied territory in 1945, a bisected nation in 1949, a reunified nation in 1990—modern Germany is a land with *too much* history. The DDR, a Stalinist creation sculpted from the rubble of the Third Reich, was condemned from the moment of its inception as being a land with a surfeit of history and a scantness of heritage, an endless firestorm of shattering events in its past and no capacity to fit the vestiges of a different, deceased order into its postwar consciousness.

And here again, evoked by the mere signifier "Nietzsche"—which generates the image of *Nietzsche in Trümmern* (Nietzsche in—and rising up from—the rubble)—intrudes the dreaded apprehension that the entire German heritage is tainted and encumbered beyond renewal or redemption, that it cannot be salvaged. And not only the former DDR but also the current *Bundesrepublik* have long felt the impulse to *build* something out of the ruins, to engage in a massive psychological reconstruction. Though the DDR celebrated lavishly the 500th anniversary of Luther's birth in 1983, it yet remained uneasy about converting the princes' paladin into Comrade Martin Luther. Shortly before reunification, in July 1990, West Germans transported Frederick's body from Stuttgart to be reburied in his palatial retreat of Sans Souci near Postdam in East Germany, fulfilling the last wish of Old Fritz in 1740—and officially affirming the legacy of Germany's greatest military monarch and Hitler's idol. In October 1990, a reunited Germany feted Bismarck—the chancellor of "blood and iron," the tactical genius who united Germany in 1871 after maneuvering Europe into three major wars during 1864–70, the figure associated with German imperialism—with a gala exhibit in the Museum of History in Berlin, within a hundred yards of both Hitler's old chancellory and the rubble remains of the Berlin Wall.

Yes, how does a nation cope? Luther, Frederick the Great, Bismarck, Wagner, and Nietzsche *are* problematic figures. But so too is Thomas Jefferson, to name only one controversial American hero, the slaveowner and founder of my alma mater, the University of Virginia, who has been the target of protesters and hunger strikers. American Caucasians have traditionally sought to spotlight the strengths and to downplay the weaknesses of awkward historical figures like Jefferson. In the age of multiculturalism, and now that African Americans are powerful enough no longer to tolerate such selective history, the era of the Thomas Jeffersons remaining national heroes may be over. America's historical whitewashing always ran—and still runs—the risk of complacency, insensitivity, blindness, and self-congratulation; German history demonstrates, however, that the risk in the opposite direction—when a people (or the ethnic majority) can take no pride at all in their history—may also have a poisonous effect on the national spirit.

Germany and the United States have both long held themselves to be "special" nations, with their own special path (*Sonderweg*) and destiny. Amid the ashes of the Third Reich, the United States decisively and permanently dislodged Germany from formal competition for that role, at least in its positive connotation. That both nations have conceived themselves "special" has much to do with their physical and spiritual isolationism, respectively. Geography has undergirded American exceptionalism, which has survived because the Atlantic and Pacific oceans have made us the unrivaled Great Power on our continent; Germany's distinctive intellectual evolution (traceable from Luther and pietism, rather than Catholicism or the Enlightenment) and delayed political development (unification in 1871) likewise set it on its own different course.

For Germany had never followed the model of France and England toward humanism and political integration. And so it was shockingly easy for the Nazis to invest the notion of the German *Sonderweg* with a new and sinister meaning, portraying their authoritarian government (*Obrigkeitsstaat*) as the fitting conclusion of Luther's insistence on obedience to the medieval prince. During World War II and after, the world adopted the same reasoning; the title of one American scholar's influential political history of Germany bore the much-quoted indictment: *From Luther to Hitler*. Finally, everyone simply accepted the line that German chauvinists had promoted since Bismarck: the Germans' self-interpretation that they were special. So the years 1933–45 became not an aberration or interregnum, not a product of contemporary circumstances, but part of a deep Teutonic past, stretching back a millennium. The seemingly short-lived Third Reich really had, after all, survived for a thousand years.

XI

Hedwig and I return down the long and winding path of the Humboldtstrasse, back to the Frauenplan, into the center of Weimar. As we peek in at the Goethe-haus, I remark on how much more excited the visitors in the Nietzsche Archive seemed, especially the younger patrons.

"They want to 'live dangerously,'" Hedwig replies. Her voice lowers: "Germany has already seen twice where that leads."

Hedwig admits that Goethe exerts no shuddering fascination like Nietzsche; she is glad of it. What begins again with Nietzsche could end again with something much worse.

In the 1950s, Karl Löwith wrote that Nietzsche "is not as current as he was 20, let alone 50, years ago" and that "his teachings are not so tempting and powerful today." In 1968, shortly before the student protests, Jürgen Habermas commented that, while Nietzsche had once exerted "a peculiar fascination" upon leading "revolutionaries of the Right," "[a]ll that lies behind us now and has become almost incomprehensible. There is nothing contagious [about Nietzsche's influence] anymore."[73]

Those assessments have proven premature. In the 1980s, Nietzsche's most recent West German biographer could see past the amalgam of national guilt and wish-fulfillment that had inspired Löwith's and Habermas's vain hopes, observing that it was "uncanny" that Nietzsche is "more current today than ever."[74] The latter judgment still holds, even more so now than a decade ago. In the wake of the *Wende* of 1989, eastern Germany is the scene of the most recent round of Nietzsche's eternal German return. And perhaps this time Germans, easterners and westerners alike, will heed the call of Nietzsche the Educator, the Good European, the "gentle" Nietzsche of Zarathustra's Great Commandment:

My doctrine is: Love that thou mayest desire to live again—for in any case thou *will* live again!

XII

October 1994: The resurrection of the Antichrist is on the horizon.

I don't want to miss Nietzsche's full rehabilitation during this second week of October, which is called "Nietzsche Week" throughout eastern Germany. And so, like hundreds of other curiosity seekers, I race from one Nietzsche event to another, all of them commemorating the sesquicentennial of Nietzsche's birth on 15 October. In Naumburg, an international conference of linguists meets in his honor. In Jena and Erfurt, writers hold public readings from Nietzsche's work. In Berlin, an orchestra ensemble devotes an evening to performing Nietzsche's musical compositions.

But the major events are hosted in Weimar and Röcken.

Or nonevents: in Weimar, the week gets off to a bad start. The symposium that was to be a major cultural attraction of Nietzsche Week—an international conference on Nietzsche and his Jewish critics and admirers—is suddenly canceled, just three days before it is scheduled to begin. The topic "Nietzsche and Nazism" is again headline news in Germany—and Israel. Last week, Ernst Nolte, Germany's leading right-wing historian, made equivocal remarks about the Holocaust revisionists in *Der Spiegel* that provoked a storm of outrage in the Israeli media. Several Israeli participants, who had, at first, welcomed Nolte's participation, responded by saying that they would not attend the conference unless Nolte's invitation was withdrawn. Andreas Schirmer, who organized the conference, tells me that the Weimar Endowment for Classical Culture was torn between disapproving Nolte's views and defending his free-speech rights.

And so, rather than rescind Professor Nolte's invitation, Schirmer and his colleagues finally decided to cancel the conference altogether. When we meet at the Weimar Endowment, across town from the Nietzsche Archive, Schirmer tells me that, given both the rise of German neonazism and the ongoing debates about the fairness or unfairness of the Nazi appropriation of Nietzsche, a topic such as "Nietzsche and the Jews" was bound to be controversial. But he laments that Nietzsche's controversial reception history has again become an occasion for sowing distrust between the Right and Left, and also between Germans and Jews.

"The acrimony [among the invited scholars] runs so deep," Schirmer says rue-fully, expressing dismay that the would-be participants even refused to submit papers intended to appear together in a published volume on Nietzsche.

Just a few blocks away in Weimar, however, another Nietzsche event goes off better—even though its speaker cautions his audience against reelevating Nietz-sche to the status of state philosopher. The occasion is the 12 October restoration by the Friedrich Schiller Gymnasium of its famous stained-glass "Nietzsche win-dow." The window is a ten-foot glass portrait of the philosopher located in a wall of the school auditorium that faces out onto a main street in Weimar; it had been installed during the Nazi era. In 1959—by which time the Schiller school had become one of the elite "Red schools" during the DDR years—the Communist principal ordered the Nietzsche window removed.

Prof. Erhard Naake, the guest speaker for the evening—a former Schiller school student, a Schiller schoolteacher for three decades, and later a professor at the Weimar College of Music—told me later that he suspects that he never ob-tained a full professorship during the DDR era on account of his sympathetic stance toward Nietzsche. Asked by an audience member whether the New Ger-many should heed Nietzsche's words or not, Professor Naake smiles. He allows that the best answer would be to quote the philosopher himself. Professor Naake then selects a line from *Thus Spake Zarathustra:* "Thousands shout my name! I tell you: Go away from me and protect yourself from me—you honor me badly when you follow me!"

Nonetheless, at the little shrine of Nietzsche's birthplace, Röcken, we followers, gathering two days later to honor Nietzsche's birthday, pay little heed to this counsel of Zarathustra. On a warm Saturday morning, more than a thousand people crowd into the little Lutheran church in this tiny eastern German hamlet of 130 residents near Weisenfels, about fifteen miles outside Leipzig. Many of the attendees are local residents gathered to honor a native son. The gala event is un-questionably the highlight of Nietzsche Week for the German public.

"I've never seen so many cars in all my life!" a boy exclaims as the ceremony commences. Luminaries throughout eastern Germany are scheduled to speak. But our host, the black-bearded village pastor—who lives in the very rectory where Nietzsche was born—notes that the organizers are "commemorating" rather than "extolling" Nietzsche. Indeed, the program refers to a "memorial event" rather than a "celebration." And the program title—derived from Nietz-sche's clarion call in *The Joyful Wisdom,* "Become who you are!"—also seems cho-sen with deliberately subtle ambiguity: "How one becomes what one is."

No consensus on the vexing question of what Nietzsche "is"—or might "be-come"—emerges at the "commemoration." But virtually every speaker stresses the importance of national memory and moral vigilance. The "past," the memo-rialists caution vaguely, must not be forgotten.

Reinhard Hoppner, minister-president of the state of Saxony-Anhalt, which sponsored the memorial event, greets the audience: "Nietzsche's influence has prompted new questions to be asked. Our questioning is more radical and our thinking is consequently different. Can one say anything more positive about a thinker, even if one voices many questions about his thinking? . . . Nietzsche urged us to remember. Before our reunified Germany falls into another round of smugness and self-forgetting, let us heed his words. Nietzsche can help us to overcome our tendency to self-inflation; he can help us to know ourselves better."

During a break, the crowd mills about in the rectory courtyard, waiting for the 3:00 P.M. inauguration of the new Nietzsche Museum, which has been built next to the rectory. "Are you a Nietzsche fan?" a woman from Austria asks me. She has come with three Cubans and two Frenchmen to the sesquicentennial event. "It's like a prayer meeting," says an elderly gentleman, noting that hundreds of people are carrying various works of Nietzsche and quoting aloud from them to one another. I ask a teenage boy why—like me—he is taking such extensive notes. He says that he is an eighth-grader from the local Röcken school and has volunteered to give the first school report on Nietzsche since 1945.

The boy and I notice that a man is hawking reprints of a 1912 postcard of Nietzsche's second childhood home in Naumburg (with Nietzsche's name misspelled "Nitzsche"—just as in the original, and thus a real collector's item, the man says). He is also pushing his self-designed telephone cards featuring Nietzsche's image, actually worth six deutschmarks in phone calls (which he sells for thirty deutschmarks). Business is slow, however; there are few takers. Suddenly, the crowd's attention is drawn to another man, who sports a top hat and bushy moustache. He is buttonholing bystanders and introducing himself as—Friedrich Wilhelm Nietzsche.

What's going on? I ask. A nearby woman says that the Saxony-Anhalt state TV agency is covering the commemoration and that an actor has come dressed for the evening show, "Who Am I?" The woman grimaces. "It's a sacrilege," she says. She takes in both the postcard/phone card salesman and the pseudo-Nietzsche with a dismissive wave of her hand. "They're turning the commemoration into a circus."

More than that—unfortunately. The wife of the village pastor shows me a small sticker, several of which have been found throughout Röcken today. "Go Right before Left," proclaim the stickers. Members of the far-right Republican party have left their message, she says. They want to claim Nietzsche too. The national election is tomorrow, 16 October, she reminds me. She hasn't seen any neo-Nazis in Röcken, but she worries that Nietzsche's mantle might once again be captured by the German Right. I mention the canceled Weimar conference on "Nietzsche and the Jews"; she nods her head and says simply, "It worries me."

Seeing her husband, the village pastor, near the rectory, I ask to speak to him about his experience of Nietzsche during the DDR years. Ironically, Hans-Jürgen Kant, thirty-five, was one of the few DDR citizens who did read Nietzsche. Pastor Kant says that the DDR's few theology students were encouraged by the state to read Nietzsche's "God is dead" critique in *The Joyful Wisdom* and other works in order to gain sympathy for atheism; Nietzsche also entered discussions about the work of German theologians such as Rudolf Bultmann and Dorothee Solle on

demythologization and secularization. The DDR imposed no "fascist interpretation" on Nietzsche in theology courses; Nietzsche was granted a limited place in
the curriculum as a fierce critic of Christianity.

"But the church under the DDR never really exploited the limited freedom we
had to pursue a radical reinterpretation of Nietzsche," Pastor Kant admits. "We
had other, more serious worries under the Communists!" Pastor Kant does note,
however, that some of the activities of the secret "Nietzsche Circle" were organized under the cover of the Lutheran church, which had copies of Nietzsche's
works.

Does the pastor feel at home in the residence of Germany's famous Antichrist?

"Yes, I do," he says. He pauses and then laughs. "But I must say: Some of my
house guests claim at times to hear Nietzsche's voice in the night! It makes them
very uneasy."

Outside, in the rectory courtyard, the speeches to inaugurate the Nietzsche
Museum are in full swing. A professor of German and representative of the Nietzsche Research Association, founded in 1990, declares: "We wanted to honor him
with something more than a refurbished rectory. We wanted a museum, which
symbolizes the task ahead: to recover what has been left in the past and forgotten.
And this is the only proper course to take. For Nietzsche is the most important
thinker in the entire world. And finally, Germany is honoring him as he deserves
to be honored."

Yes, Nietzsche's reembrace by German officialdom is under way. Another
round of politicians and professors honoring Nietzsche—a few of them, I am
told, the same figures who had blocked his rehabilitation during the DDR era.

Would Zarathustra have snickered or screamed?

Suddenly, however, the crowd's own smugness is rudely upset. The speaker, a
tall, bearded man named Kai Schmidt, is a local politician and a former critic
of the SED regime: "We had a personal relationship to this rectory during the
Communist dictatorship."

The last two words trigger murmured remarks; Schmidt is breaking the un-
written taboo against plainspoken criticism of the Communist era at the "commemoration." Schmidt's "we" is an exclusive one: He is referring to those few
members of the clandestine "Nietzsche Circle," an underground reading group
that passed around copies of Nietzsche's works and was regularly spied upon by
the DDR secret police. Professor Naake had told me about its activities. But
Schmidt's speech marks its first mention in a public forum.

"We prayed here together, and we honored Friedrich Nietzsche's example as a
freethinker," Schmidt continues. "Our first Nietzsche evening occurred in 1980.
But we could only read him and speak about him in secret. Because of his misuse
by the Nazis, the greatest philosopher of Germany was cast aside by the Communists. We laid a wreath on his grave, here in Röcken, year after year; now we open
this museum in his memory."

Then the mayor throws open the museum front door; the rechristening of the
Antichrist is now official. Inside, the museum exhibits resemble those in Weimar;

they too tell the story of Nietzsche's life, though they concentrate on his boyhood in Röcken. One exhibit, titled simply "F. W. Nietzsche," features the current work of eighth-grade students from Röcken's junior high school, who have written poems and reports for the sesquicentennial celebration that offer tribute to Nietzsche.

The area around the little church is now deserted. As I enter the church, lines of Nietzsche dance in my head. "I *want* no 'believers.' I have a terrible fear that one day I will be pronounced *holy.*"

I muse once again on Nietzsche's extraordinarily complicated return to German politics and letters. Here in this church is where it all began. Here in these pews, Fritz spent countless hours as a small boy, listening to his father playing hymns on the organ and preaching the word of God. I look up at the biblical passage etched in stone on the church's left-side wall:

I live and you should also live (John 14.19).

And whether the echoes be ironic or fated, I am once again reminded of Zarathustra's own gospel of love:

My doctrine is: Love that thou mayest desire to live again—for in any case thou *will* live again!

NOTES

I would like to thank Beth Macom for her meticulous and often inspired editing of this essay. I am also grateful to Andreas Schimmer, Rosawith Wellkopf, and Prof. Erhard Naake for their conversation and support.

1. See, for instance, the special issue of *Zeitschrift fuer Didaktik der Philosophie* 6 (1984), devoted to teaching Nietzsche in West German *Gymnasium* and university courses such as "Introduction to Philosophy" and "Introduction to Ethics." In 1983 one *Gymnasium* teacher assigned Nietzsche's work in a thirteenth-grade course entitled "Philosophical Aspects of War and Peace." Most of his students were strong supporters of the European peace movement, but Nietzsche "provoked the students to a remarkable militancy." The teacher concluded: "Nietzsche mobilizes thinking—however double-edged his sword may be. . . . Nietzsche was and remains a provocation to thinking, whom we philosophy teachers should present—not in the sense of a duel, but of a promise: Nietzsche helps one think freely" (169–70).

2. Kaufmann, *Nietzsche,* 345.

3. On Nietzsche's classroom duties and manner, see the chapter "Nietzsche als Erzieher" in Ross, *Der ängstliche Adler,* 345–69.

4. For an overview of the response to Nietzsche among Wilhelmine-era German educators, see Canĉik, "Der Einfluss Friedrich Nietzsches." Many of the leading educators of the day visited the Archive and even befriended—and, sometimes, became disenchanted with—Elisabeth Forster-Nietzsche. For instance, Ellen Key frequented and lectured at the Archive in the early 1900s. Ludwig Gurlitt was a leading member of the Society for German Education, which held its annual meeting in Weimar. He became acquainted

with Elisabeth in 1904, corresponded with her regularly, and was the only philologist invited to speak in the Nietzsche Archive on the gala occasion of her sixty-fifth birthday in 1921 (69).

Walter Benjamin is an especially interesting example of a young intellectual interested in the pedagogical dimension of Nietzsche's work. A student of Wyneken, Benjamin was a great admirer of Nietzsche's "aristocratic radicalism." Before his Marxist turn, the twenty-year-old Jewish banker's son, who had recently graduated from an experimental Berlin "reform school" that combined *Gymnasium* and *Realschule,* even wrote a treatise against the reform movement in 1912. Benjamin urged educators to resist modernizing and "industrializing" the school and instead to revive the aristocratic spirit of Greece, as Nietzsche urged. In 1914 Benjamin presented similar ideas in a lecture at the Nietzsche Archive, titled "The Life of Students." His enthusiasm for Elisabeth and the Archive cooled in the 1920s, however, especially after her embrace of fascism and the scattered reports of her fabrications of Nietzsche's letters. In his hostile pamphlet, *Nietzsche and the Archive of His Sister* (1932), Benjamin attacked Elisabeth for betraying Nietzsche (56–58).

5. Aschheim, *Nietzsche Legacy,* 114.

6. See Thomas, *Nietzsche,* 102–3.

7. In the eyes of the SED (the DDR's Communist Party), Nietzsche was not only the hated Nazi idol but also the champion of the Good European—a threatening cosmopolitan intellectual—and "der Kosmopolitismus" was an early postwar code word in Communist jargon for "Western," "anti-Socialist," and therefore "subversive."

8. See Penzo, "Zur Frage."

9. The phrase is Thomas Mann's, applied to Wagner. Quoted in Ross, *Der ängstliche Adler,* 246.

10. Walter Kaufmann's portrait of a liberal, humanistic Nietzsche effectively started the process of "denazification" in the Anglophone world, but no comparably significant revaluation occurred in the *Bundesrepublik.* The following passage in a BRD history of philosophy text of the 1950s typified the attitude toward Nietzsche for much of the postwar era: "It's time that our flirtation with the nonsense, the insanity, and the so-called depth of Nietzsche's world of thought came to an end. Nietzsche has already caused enough trouble. Germany ruined culture, he said. It would be more correct to say: Nietzsche ruined philosophy. A young person who has his first contact with philosophy through Nietzsche's work will never learn to think clearly, critically, soberly, and above all plainly. Rather, he will begin to lapse into one-sidedness and a subjectivity, make aphorisms, and fire off edicts." Quoted in Janssen, "Behandlung," 467.

Educator's misgivings about Nietzsche's work persisted into the 1980s. In the 1984 special issue of *Zeitschrift für Didaktik der Philosophie,* one *Gymnasium* teacher admitted that her inclusion of Nietzsche in a twelfth-grade course "may be received by some with astonishment" (156). Two other *Gymnasium* teachers related the reservations of colleagues about their decision to teach Nietzsche: If we teach Nietzsche, the colleagues objected, "isn't relativism, nihilism, and even cynicism just around the corner?" (151). Still another teacher declared: "A spectre is haunting the German *Gymnasium,* years ago and now once again: Nietzsche" (167).

11. *Weimar: Bilder einer traditionsreichen Stadt* (Berlin: Aufbau, 1990).

12. Zwerenz, "Ein Partisan," 3.

13. Minutes of the Vienna Psychoanalytic Society, vol. 2, 1908–10, cited in Hayman, *Nietzsche,* 1.

14. Janz, *Friedrich Nietzsche,* 1:254.

15. Ibid., 254–55.

16. Franz Overbeck, Nietzsche's closest colleague at the University of Basel, thought Nietzsche had been "living his way" toward the final breakdown for years. Nietzsche himself wrote in a May 1884 letter: "I want to make things as hard for myself as they have ever been for anybody: only under this pressure do I have a clear enough conscience to possess something few men have or have ever had—*wings*, so to speak." Did Nietzsche anticipate and even promote his breakdown? One biographer writes: "He planned the finale like an artwork." Overbeck, and later Peter Gast, Nietzsche's student and editorial assistant, had independent impressions on separate visits to Nietzsche—more than a year after his collapse—that he was simply feigning his madness, for whatever reason.

These observations have given rise to speculations by postmodern intellectuals that Nietzsche's madness was a form of "inner emigration." On this view, having written his autobiography, *Ecce Homo*, Nietzsche had effectively settled his earthly affairs. Ceding his fame and public life to Elisabeth in return for the security and freedom to explore his own private realm, he now enacted in Nietzschean fashion his philosophy. Indifferent to human events, he took leave of his readers, exploded the naive bourgeois dualism of sanity/insanity, and joined Zarathustra in an otherworldly vocational quest far beyond the realm of the all-too-human. Perhaps all that is what Nietzsche meant when, in December 1888 shortly before his collapse, he wrote to Gast, his single disciple and dearest friend, that he had "crossed the Rubicon."

17. See Peters's book, titled *Zarathustra's Sister*, esp. 122–26. My discussion of the Nietzsche Archive's fortunes between the 1890s and World War I is greatly indebted to Peters.

18. Peters, *Zarathustra's Sister*, 109.

19. Thomas, *Nietzsche*, 2.

20. Aschheim, *Nietzsche Legacy*, 33.

21. Cancîk, "Der Nietzsche-Kult," 406.

22. Peters, *Zarathustra's Sister*, 173.

23. Cancîk, "Der Nietzsche-Kult," 407.

24. Ibid.

25. Ibid., 412.

26. Or as he wrote in his assault on the conventional scholar in his Schopenhauer essay: "How can they be great . . . and have never yet disturbed anybody? The epitaph of university philosophy: it disturbed nobody." Nietzsche was also thinking of the intellectual/academic "herd" when he wrote in *The Will to Power*: "It is not a matter of going ahead . . . , but of being able to *go it alone,* of being able *to be different!*"

27. See Duff and Mittelman, "Nietzsche's Attitude," 301–17. Quoting Nietzsche's numerous admiring statements about preprophetic Judaism and modern Jewry, the authors argue persuasively that he felt antipathy toward Jews of only one historical period: the ancient prophetic and early Christian era. This critical focus evinces that Nietzsche's real animosity was reserved for Christianity, since he only attacked that phase of Jewish history—prophetic Judaism—directly responsible for the rise of Christianity, i.e., the part within the "Judeo-Christian" tradition. Nietzsche, who condemned Wagner's anti-Semitism and deplored his turn toward the church in *Parsifal,* was "strongly and consistently anti-anti-Semitic," conclude the authors (317).

28. This aestheticizing of politics—Nietzsche's first champion, the Danish Jew Georg Brandes, referred to Nietzsche's "aristocratic radicalism"—does, it must be said, carry its perils. As Max Weber, another admirer of Nietzsche, later stressed, charisma is commonly the tool not only of heroes but also of demagogues.

29. Löwith, *Sämtliche Schriften*, xi.

30. Quoted in Hayman, *Nietzsche*, 359.

31. "Elisabeths Wille zur Macht," *Neue Deutsche Hefte*, Jan.–June 1957, 248. Nietzsche scholar and devotee Rudolf Pannwitz first used the phrase "half-Nietzsche, half-Naumburg" to characterize Elisabeth. Elisabeth's compromises with the truth extended to wholesale misrepresentations of Nietzsche's life in her biographical studies of him and the forging at least thirty of "his" letters. Usually she sought to burnish her relationship to Fritz and smooth over any rough spots. If she found a particularly complimentary passage in a letter written by Nietzsche to someone else, she would burn off the addressee's name and readdress it to herself. Or she would produce "copies" of letters for which the originals had been lost or misplaced. But her greatest act of misrepresentation was her publication of *The Will to Power*, which she presented as Nietzsche's masterwork. It was the work most often cited by the Nazis as "the true Nietzsche." Nietzsche had certainly planned such a work (with the tentative title *Transvaluation of Values*), but he had never organized his thousands of jottings and had apparently abandoned it before 1889.

32. Peters, *Zarathustra's Sister*, 113.

33. Friedrich Wodtke, *Gottfried Benn*, quoted in Ross, *Der ängstliche Adler*, 89.

34. For the architectural design of the temple and stadium, see Canĉik, "Der Nietzsche-Kult," 413–17.

35. Peters, *Zarathustra's Sister*, 199–201; Canĉik, "Der Nietzsche-Kult," 418. The distinction between the "tough" and "gentle" Nietzsches—which derives from William James's psychology—was first applied by Craine Brinton his *Nietzsche* (1941), 184–99.

36. Peters, *Zarathustra's Sister*, 212–13.

37. Thomas, *Nietzsche*, 114–16.

38. Ibid., 119.

39. Hardy is quoted in Aschheim, *Nietzsche's Legacy*, 130. The *Athenaeum* editorialized: "We find the principles of Nietzsche at work in the life of the German nation, in the teachings of her professors and schoolmasters, more starting than this, we find them embodied in the texts of the German [Military] Staff College. . . . This deadly seriousness, which can drag a professor from his lecture room and bear him in triumph through the land—for this may be said of Nietzsche—cannot but end in explosion."

40. Ibid., 130–31; Brinton, *Nietzsche*, 202.

41. Wollkopf, "Die Gremien," 235.

42. Kashyap, 165.

43. Canĉik, "Der Nietzsche-Kult," 425.

44. Board members of the Nietzsche Endowment were elected to seven-year terms. Spengler and Emge left the board in 1935 and were replaced by the philosophers Martin Heidegger and Hans Heyse.

45. Wollkopf, "Die Gremien," 233, 237–41. See also Wollkopf, "Das Nietzsche-Archiv."

46. Baeumler's appointment signified the near-fulfillment of yet another Nietzsche prophecy from *Ecce Homo:* "People will eventually find it necessary," declared Nietzsche in the chapter "Why I Write Such Good Books," "to have institutions in which man lives and teaches as I understand living and teaching; it may even be that they eventually establish university chairs for the interpretation of Zarathustra."

47. Baeumler, *Nietzsche*.

48. Hollingdale, *Nietzsche*, 8. Despite the authority of Baeumler and the Nietzsche Archive, some Nazi scholars considered Nietzsche "degenerate." See Penzo, "Zur Frage," 116.

49. Postwar German scholarship also drew attention to the similarities between Nietzsche and Hitler—in the negative sense, of course. For a detailed discussion of the comparisons in personality and psyche between Nietzsche and Hitler—from a non-Nazi viewpoint—see Ernst Sandvoss, *Hitler und Nietzsche* (Göttingen: Musterschmid Verlag, 1969).

50. Aschheim, *Nietzsche Legacy,* 240–45. Not all Nazi educators agreed, however. In *Erziehung im nationalsozialistischen Staat* (Berlin, 1935), Ernst Krieck, professor of philosophy and pedagogy at the University of Heidelberg, advanced the prewar conservative position on Nietzsche as a "sick" mind. Nietzsche's work opposed the healthy, heroic Nazi spirit; it was a debilitating influence on young minds. Christoph Steding agreed. In his 800-page *Das Reich und die Krankheit der europaeischen Kultur* (Hamburg, 1938) he made Nietzsche the chief villian responsible for the decadent avant-garde. On these views, see Reifenrath, "Die Nietzsche-Rezeption."

51. The year 1935 proved to be an axial moment in Nietzsche scholarship—as if Elisabeth's passing cleared the scene for other images of Nietzsche to emerge. Despite the full embrace of nazism by the Oehlers, new non-Nazi and anti-Nazi interpretations of Nietzsche gained currency among German-speaking intellectuals, exemplified by Karl Löwith's *Philosophie der ewigen Wiederkunft des Gleichen* (1935), Carl Jung's lecture series on *Zarathustra* during 1935–39 (first published in 1988), Karl Jaspers's *Nietzsche* (1936), and the beginning of Heidegger's lectures on Nietzsche (1936).

52. Nietzsche had used this concept of "star friendship" in his farewell letter to Wagner on their parting of the ways over Christianity and Bismarck's Reich. Although lamenting their breakup, Nietzsche maintained that friends in disagreement need not become estranged but can continue to regard each other as companions, occupying the same galaxy and radiating toward each other like distant stars.

53. Oehler, *Nietzsche,* 132–33.

54. Löwith, *Sämtliche Schriften,* 447.

55. Brinton, *Nietzsche,* 145. The news reports quoted are from Brinton, 132–33.

56. Löwith, *Samtliche Schriften,* 399. The centennial celebration itself, held in October 1944, was a decidedly somber affair. Hitler and Goebbels sent wreaths for Nietzsche's grave; Mussolini sent a statue of Dionysus, which barely escaped Allied bombers and was never displayed; Alfred Rosenberg delivered the keynote. The Nietzsche memorial, located next to the Archive, remained unfinished.

57. *Der Spiegel,* 13 Nov. 1981, 24.

58. The Archive was officially closed by the Soviet occupation government in December 1945. In October 1949 the Archive was turned into a workroom of the Goethe and Schiller Archives, whose director had already assumed administrative control of the Nietzsche papers. For a report on the Archive by its administrator from the Goethe–Schiller Archive during the last years of the SED, see Hahn, "Das Nietzsche-Archiv."

59. See Lukacs, *Die Zerstörung.* For an overview of Nietzsche's reception in Eastern Europe and among German socialists, see Behler's articles, "Nietzsche in der marxistischen Kritik Osteuropas" and "Zur fruehen sozialistischen Rezeption Nietzsches in Deutschland." One large difference, however, distinguished prewar and postwar views of Nietzsche among orthodox Marxists. During the 1930s and 1940s Nietzsche was identified with fascism and nazism. After 1950, in response to Western attempts to "denazify" his work, Nietzsche was linked in the DDR to Western imperialism—which signified a return to the theme of Mehring's criticism. The postwar work of Lukács bridged the gap and linked all three views. Lukács argued both that Nietzsche was a spiritual ally of Hitler

and that the postwar West's humanistic reinterpretation of Nietzsche represented "the deepest nadir that we have ever reached, evidence of the downward slide of American imperialism."

60. Gitita Günther and Lothar Wallraf, eds., *Geschichte der Stadt Weimar,* 470–71.

61. Nor are the cases of Heidegger and Nietzsche really comparable. Heidegger lived through the Nazi period and wrote many letters explicitly supporting Nazi doctrine. Whereas Heidegger was the Nazis' hand-picked rector of Freiburg University in 1933, allegations about Nietzsche's "nazism" are speculative and unsupportable.

62. See Pepperle, "Revision," 934–69.

63. See Harich, "Revision," 1018–53. Harich's final allusion was all too fitting. At the SED's insistence, Brecht turned the 1938 play into a Stalinist tract in 1951 and changed its title to *The Condemnation of Lucullus.* (The new play still did not please the DDR cultural censors, who ordered cancellation of the 1951 production after a few performances; soon thereafter it had a successful run in West Berlin.) Other intellectuals besides Harich also had harsh words for Nietzsche in the 1970s and 1980s. But their condemnations were generally reserved for Western attempts to rehabilitate Nietzsche. See, for example, Heller, "Nietzsche," and Malorny, "Tendenzen."

64. "Meinungen zu einem Streit," *Sinn und Form* 40 (1988): 179–220. In addition to the aforementioned participants in the Nietzsche debate, the contributors included: sociology *Dozent* Hans-Georg Eckhardt; the writer Rudolf Schottländer; Aufbau editor Stephan Richter; Gerd Irrlitz, professor of the history of philosophy at Humboldt University; Klaus Kandler, instructor at the Academy of Fine Arts; and poet Thomas Böhme.

65. The result of Colli and Montinari's effort was the 22-volume *Complete Works* and the 16-volume *Letters,* which began appearing in 1967 and 1975, respectively. These works were simultaneously published by Adelphi in Italy, by Gallimard in France, and by de Gruyter in West Germany. Neither work ever appeared in the DDR.

66. Harich, "Revision," 1045. Harich meant what he said. It was not the first time he had stepped in to stem the Nietzsche "infection" in the DDR, which had been been building for more than a decade. The story of Nietzsche's underground life in the DDR is fascinating and complex. Since 1976 a secret circle of DDR authors, including the poet Rolf Schilling, had met every year in Röcken to pay homage to Nietzsche's memory and discuss his work. Their activities remained unknown until 1989. But several years earlier, apparently with initial SED approval, two Halle philosophy professors prepared a carefully selected edition of the *Untimely Meditations* and *The Joyful Wisdom.* They also organized a small Nietzsche colloquium, whose proceedings were to be published. In addition, Karl-Heinz Hahn, director of the Goethe–Schiller Archive, worked with Montinari on an expensive limited edition of the *Ecce Homo* manuscript, primarily designed for export to the West. At the last minute, Buhr and Harich—the latter had returned from the West in 1981 after two years of voluntary exile—stepped in and scotched all these publishing plans. Only a few copies of *Ecce Homo* ever reached DDR bookstores. Still, rumors flew that Harich had seen a copy in one bookstore, raised his voice and cane, and demanded its removal. It was removed. Later, in 1988, Harich supposedly threatened Erich Honecker that he would depart again for the West if the SED lifted the Nietzsche ban. For further details, see Schwik, "Eine Andacht," and Corino, "Abwertung."

67. That Colli and Montinari were members of the Italian Communist Party—and that their Nietzsche editions were partly underwritten by the Italian CP—makes clear that the East German misgivings about Nietzsche had always less to do with his connection to fascism per se and more to do with his links to German militarism and nazism.

Ironically, however, in certain ways Italy is much "closer" to Nietzsche than is Germany. Fascists like Mussolini and Gabriele D'Annunzio were early admirers of Nietzsche; Hitler and most other Nazi leaders probably never read a line of him. But there is no trace of guilt about Nietzsche felt by Italians, probably because Nietzsche was never exalted as Italy's national philosopher. Likewise, despite Fascist interpretations of Nietzsche in Vichy France, the French have always been able to see Nietzsche apart from his Fascist reception history. Already in 1945, Parisian intellectuals founded the Society for Nietzsche Studies; French intellectuals of the Left ranging from Sartre and Camus to Georges Bataille, Jean Granier, Maurice Blanchot, Michel Foucault, Jacques Derrida, Sarah Kofman, and Gilles Deleuze have written hundreds of admiring pages about Nietzsche.

68. For a controversial Western view of Nietzsche and Marx as rival antagonists, see Ernst Nolte, *Nietzsche und der Nietzscheanismus*. Nolte sees Nietzsche and Marx as two great intellectual gladiators who finally confronted each other posthumously, at the turn of the century, in the face-off between their followers on the Right and Left, the champions of Nietzcheanism and Marxism.

69. On Nietzsche and the alternative Left, see the following: Werner Ross, "Nietzsche taucht aus der Versenkung auf"; Magris, "Ich bin der Einsamkeit"; and Augstein, "Wiederkehr eines Philosophen." Augstein's 1981 article ran as *Spiegel*'s cover story. The *Spiegel* cover depicts Hitler rising from the head of Nietzsche-Zeus—and pulling a trigger aimed at the philosopher's head as he emerges.

70. See Stephen A. Erickson, "Nietzsche and Post-Modernity," *Philosophy Today*, 1990.

71. Quoted in Starke, "Stationen," 269.

72. Quoted in Meier and Schmidt, *Erbe und Tradition*, 122.

73. Quoted in Augstein, "Wiederkehr eines Philosophen," 160.

74. Ross, *Der ängstliche Adler*, 8.

BIBLIOGRAPHY

Aschheim, Steven E. *The Nietzsche Legacy in Germany, 1890–1990*. Berkeley: University of California Press, 1992.

Augstein, Rudolf. "Wiederkehr eines Philosophen: Täter Hitler, Denker Nietzsche," *Der Spiegel*, 13 Nov. 1981, 156–84.

Baeumler, Alfred. *Nietzsche, der Philosoph und Politiker*. Leipzig: Reclam, 1931.

Behler, Ernst. "Nietzsche in der marxistischen Kritik Osteuropas," *Nietzsche-Studien* 10/11 (1981/82): 92–123.

———. "Zur fruehen sozialistischen Rezeption Nietzsches in Deutschland," *Nietzsche-Studien* 13 (1984): 503–20.

Brinton, Crane. *Nietzsche*. Cambridge, Mass.: Harper and Row, 1941.

Cancîk, Hubert. "Der Einfluss Friedrich Nietzsches auf der Berliner Schulkritiker der wilhelminischer Ära," *Der altsprachliche Unterricht* 30 (1987): 55–73.

———. "Der Nietzsche-Kult in Weimar: Ein Beitrag zur Religionsgeschichte der wilhelminischen Ara," *Nietzsche-Studien* 16 (1987).

Corino, Karl. "Abwertung aller Werte," *Süddeutsche Zeitung*, 22 Sept. 1990, 49.

Duff, Michael F., and Mittelman, Willard. "Nietzsche's Attitudes toward the Jews," *Journal of the History of Ideas*, 1984, 301–17.

———. "Elisabeths Wille zur Macht," *Neue Deutsche Hefte*, Jan.–June 1957, 248–49.

Gunther, Gitita, and Wallraf, Lothar. *Geschichte der Stadt Weimar.* Weimar: H. Bohlaus Nachfolger, 1977.

Hahn, K. H. "Das Nietzsche-Archiv," *Nietzsche-Studien* 18 (1989): 1–18.

Harich, Wolfgang. *Nietzsche und seine Brüder: Eine Streitschrift.* Schwedt: Kiro-Verlag, 1994.

――――. "Revision des marxistischen Nietzsche-Bildes?" *Sinn und Form* 39 (1987): 1018–53.

Hayman, Ronald. *Nietzsche: A Critical Life.* New York: Oxford University Press, 1980.

Heller, Peter. "Nietzsche," *Nietzsche-Studien* 7 (1978): 27–58.

Hollingdale, R. J. *Nietzsche: The Man and His Philosophy.* Baton Rouge: Louisiana State University Press, 1973.

Janssen, Peter Heinrich. "Behandlung von Friedrich Nietzsches 'Also sprach Zarathustra' im Unterricht," *Die paedagogische Provinz* 13 (1959).

Janz, Curt Paul. *Friedrich Nietzsche: Biographie.* Munich: Hanser, 1978.

Kashyap, Subhash C. *The Unknown Nietzsche: His Socio-Political Thought and Legacy.* Delhi: National, 1970.

Kaufmann, Walter. *Nietzsche: Philosopher, Psychologist, Antichrist.* Princeton: Princeton University Press, 1950.

Love, Nancy S. *Marx, Nietzsche, and Modernity.* New York: Columbia University Press, 1986.

Löwith, Karl. *Sämtliche Schriften: Nietzsche.* Vol. 6. Stuttgart: Metzler, 1987.

Lukács, Georg. *Die Zerstörung der Vernunft: Der Weg des Irrationalismus von Schelling zu Hitler.* Berlin: Aufbau Verlag, 1954.

Maier, Charles S. *The Unmasterable Past: History, Holocaust, and German National Identity.* Cambridge: Harvard University Press, 1988.

Maier, Helmut, and Schmidt, Walter, eds. *Erbe und Tradition: Geschichtsdebatte in der DDR.* Cologne: Pahl-Rugenstein Verlag, 1989.

Magris, Claudio. "'Ich bin der Einsamkeit als Mensch," *Süddeutsche Zeitung am Wochenende,* 3–4 Jan. 1981, 45.

Malorny, Heinz. "Tendenzen der Nietzsche-Rezeption in der BRD," *Deutsche Zeitschrift für Philosophie* 27 (1979): 1493–1500.

Oehler, Richard. *Friedrich Nietzsche und die deutsche Zukunft.* Leipzig: Insel Verlag, 1935.

Penzo, Giorgio. "Zur Frage der 'Entnazifizierung' Friedrich Nietzsches," *Vierteljahrschrift für Zeitgeschichte* 34 (1986): 105–16.

Pepperle, Heinz. "Revision des marxistischen Nietzsche-Bildes?" *Sinn und Form* 38 (1986): 934–69.

Peters, H. F. *Zarathustra's Sister: The Case of Elisabeth and Friedrich Nietzsche.* New York: Crown, 1977.

Reifenrath, Bruno H. "Die Nietzsche-Rezeption der nationalsozialistischen Paedagogik," *Vierteljahrschrift für wissenschaftliche Paedagogik* 56(1980): 245–69.

Ross, Werner. *Der ängstliche Adler: Friedrich Nietzsches Leben.* Darmstadt: Deutsche Verlagsanstalt, 1980.

――――. "Nietzsche taucht aus der Versenkung auf," *Rheinischer Merkur/Christ und Welt,* 19 Sept. 1980.

Schwik, Heimo. "Eine Andacht für den Antichrist," *Rheinischer Merkur/Christ und Welt,* 31 Aug. 1990, 21.

Starke, Manfred, "Stationen der marxistischen Rilke-Rezeption," *Rilke-Studien: Zu Werk und Wirkungsgeschichte.* Berlin: Aufbau, 1976.

Thomas, Hinton. *Nietzsche in German Politics and Society, 1890–1918.* London: Manchester University Press, 1983.

Wollkopf, Rosawith. "Das Nietzsche-Archiv im Spiegel der Beziehungen Elisabeth Forster-Nietzsches zu Harry Graf Kessler," *Jahrbuch der Deutschen Schillergesellschaft,* ed. Wilfried Barner, Walter Muller-Seidel, and Ulbricht Ott, 125–70. Weimar: H. Bohlaus Nachfolger, 1990.

———. "Die Gremien des Nietzsche-Archivs und ihre Beziehungen zum Faschismus." *Im Vorfeld der Literatur,* ed. Karl-Heinz Hahn, 230–50. Weimar: H. Bohlaus Nachfolger, 1991.

Yack, Bernard. *The Longing for Total Revolution: Philosophic Sources of Social Discontent from Rousseau to Marx and Nietzsche.* Princeton: Princeton University Press, 1986.

Zwerenz, Gerhard. "Ein Partisan dichtet sich selbst," *Frankfurter Rundschau,* 16 Sept. 1985, 3.

XIV • *CONVIVENCIA* UNDER FIRE: GENOCIDE AND BOOK BURNING IN BOSNIA

András Riedlmayer

The fire lasted for days. The sun was obscured by the smoke of books, and all over the city sheets of burned paper, fragile pages of grey ashes, floated down like a dirty black snow. Catching a page you could feel its heat, and for a moment read a fragment of text in a strange kind of black and grey negative, until, as the heat dissipated, the page melted to dust in your hand.

> Kemal Bakaršić on the burning of Bosnia's National and University Library, August 25–27, 1992 ("The Libraries of Sarajevo").

All that is written endures, what is committed to memory takes flight.

> Mula Mustafa Ševki Bašeskija (1731–1809),
> diarist and chronicler of eighteenth-century life in Sarajevo.

THE most famous book in Bosnia is a lovely illuminated manuscript known as the Sarajevo Haggadah. Although it found a home in Bosnia in the early 1600s, it was made in another place and time. It is a testimony to the artistic and cultural creativity of those who made it, valued it, and protected it over the ages. It is also a survivor. On at least four occasions in its long history, the Sarajevo Haggadah has survived attempts to destroy multicultural communities. Each of these attempts to eradicate pluralism was also accompanied by the burning of books. This small codex, illustrated with sixty-nine miniatures and containing the readings for the Jewish feast of Passover and a selection of religious poems and prayers, was made around 1350 in the kingdom of Aragon.[1] It is a rare and particularly fine example of the Hebrew manuscript production that flourished amidst the *convivencia* of medieval Spain—a pluralistic society where, despite individual and communal jealousies and tensions, a multiplicity of religions (Christian, Jewish, and Muslim), cultures, and languages (Romance, Hebrew, and Arabic) coexisted and interacted with each other.

In all three of the great monotheistic traditions, Judaism, Christianity, and Islam, the book has a special status as the repository of divine revelation and the law, as the means of binding together the community and of transmitting and elaborating tradition. In the era of *convivencia,* the book also played a central role in the connections made across cultural and religious boundaries, which went beyond the famous translation projects and philosophical debates to the creation of new artistic and literary forms born out of these interactions. These included phenomena such as the emergence of secular Hebrew poetry influenced by Arabic poetic forms, and the flowering of the arts of the book in all three traditions. Even religious manuscripts, such as Bibles and Haggadoth, or the Christian biblical commentaries of Beatus of Liebana, clearly show the cross-cultural influences of Islamic, Jewish, and Christian artistic traditions. Profiat Duran, a fourteenth-century Jewish physician, philosopher, and astrologer at the court of King John I of Aragon, wrote about the importance of fine books:

> Study should always be in beautiful and pleasant books, containing harmonious script written on fine vellum, and with luxurious bindings, and should be carried on in pleasant buildings; for the beholding and study of beautiful forms with delicate drawing and fine painting is one of those things that please the soul, urges on and strengthens its powers. It has therefore been to the perfection of our nation that the wealthy and prominent in every generation have always exerted an effort in the production of beautiful codices.[2]

Many of the "beautiful codices" that delighted Profiat Duran and his pious and learned contemporaries did not survive the second half of the fifteenth century, when the era of *convivencia* came to a tragic end with the mass expulsions of Jews and Muslims from the Iberian Peninsula. The "cleansing" of all non-Christians from the land was accompanied by the ceremonial burning of Jewish and Islamic books. Mass burnings of Jewish books in Valladolid (1461) and Salamanca (1490) preceded the expulsions of 1492, while the triumph of Catholicism over Islam and the forced conversion or expulsion of Muslims from Spain was celebrated in 1499 by a public and festive burning of Islamic books in Granada, by order of the archbishop of Toledo, Francisco Jiménez de Cisneros.[3]

One of the books that escaped the flames was the codex now known as the Sarajevo Haggadah, taken along into exile as a cherished family heirloom when its Jewish owners were expelled from Spain. Of the handful of manuscripts that survive from the golden age of Hebrew bookmaking in Spain not one remains in its country of origin. After a sojourn in northern Italy, sometime in the early 1600s, this Haggadah codex arrived in Bosnia where a community of Spanish Jews had found refuge and a new form of *convivencia* in the city of Sarajevo.

In the course of the sixteenth century Sarajevo had grown from a village at the foot of a medieval fortress into the commercial and administrative center of the Ottoman province of Bosnia. It was a city where Muslim, Jewish, and Christian craftsmen, merchants, scholars, clerics, and laborers lived and worked side by side and where religious and cultural diversity was seen as part of the normal fabric of communal life. As in medieval Spain, *convivencia* in Sarajevo did not imply an absence of hierarchies of status or of periodic friction between individuals and groups, but the fact of pluralism itself was taken as a given.

Among the benefactions of Sarajevo's first native Bosnian Muslim governor, Gazi Husrev Beg, was the city's first public library, established in 1537. Within sight of the great mosque, also founded by Gazi Husrev Beg, stood the city's first Orthodox Christian church, built to attract tradesmen of that faith to the city's newly laid-out bazaars. Another Ottoman governor, Siyavuş Pasha, endowed an Islamic pious foundation (*waqf*) in 1580/81 to erect a large apartment building (*han*) for the poorer members of Sarajevo's Jewish community and gave permission to build the city's first synagogue.[4]

As the city grew and prospered, it became a center of scholarship and literary life and of book production. From the colophons of still-extant manuscripts and from documents, we know the names of hundreds of Bosnian authors and copyists who produced thousands of manuscripts in a variety of languages and alphabets: Arabic, Ottoman Turkish, Persian, Hebrew, Ladino (Judeo-Spanish), and Bosnian Slavic written in *aljamiado* (Arabic script), *bosančica* (the Bosnian variant of Cyrillic script), or *latinica* (Latin script), as well as Church Slavonic and Church Latin. This interaction of cultures in Bosnia, like the *convivencia* of medieval Spain, gave rise to some wonderfully complex forms, such as lyrical poetry written by Muslim Slavs in the classical Islamic literary medium of Arabic and Persian verse but showing the clear influence of Petrarchan sonnets brought in from the Dalmatian coast.[5]

In its new home in Sarajevo, the exquisite little Haggadah codex from Aragon continued in its role as the centerpiece of family Passover observances. Wine and food stains mark some of the pages; on one, there is a child's scrawl. But before the century was over it was once again in danger. In the year 1697, Sarajevo and its version of *convivencia* came under attack as the city was sacked and burned by the army of the Hapsburg emperor, under the command of Prince Eugene of Savoy. Just eleven years previously, the combined Hapsburg and allied armies of the Holy League had stormed the walls of Buda, the capital of Ottoman Hungary. The fall of the city on 2 September 1686 came after a hard-fought three-month siege. When the victorious Christian troops surged through the breaches in the walls they spared neither the city's residents nor their homes and belongings. In the last decade of Ottoman rule, the Jewish community in Buda had numbered about 1,000 people. Barely half of them survived the city's reversion to Christian rule.

In a memoir entitled *Megilat Ofen* [The Book of Buda] and in the marginal notes of a scriptural commentary, Isaac Schulhof, a learned and prosperous member of the city's Jewish community, has left a firsthand account of these events, which took the lives of his wife and son, his home, and all of his possessions. Along with the looting and the slaughter in the streets, Schulhof witnessed the massacre by Hapsburg troops of seventy-two Jews inside a synagogue where they had tried to take shelter. Hundreds more captives were killed by drunken mercenaries on the banks of the Danube. Those who survived the siege and its aftermath, including several hundred Jews and 6,000 Muslims, were taken by the Christian troops as chattel to be sold as slaves or held for ransom. Many of the surviving Jews, including Schulhof himself, were ransomed by Samuel Oppenheimer, the Hapsburg emperor's banker; others were redeemed with money collected from Jewish communities all over Europe.

The "cleansing" of Buda's non-Christian communities was not an isolated event. It was preceded in 1670 by a Hapsburg imperial edict ordering the expulsion of all Jews from Vienna and Lower Austria. Oppenheimer himself and a handful of other Jews whose services were deemed indispensable to the court were allowed to stay but had to pay for this privilege with a substantial annual fee (*Toleranzgeld*).

In Buda and Pest, mosques and minarets were pulled down and the city's three synagogues were burned. That the losses must also have included books may be inferred from one of Isaac Schulhof's marginal notes to his scriptural commentary, recalling the days before the siege:

> About three years ago (i.e. before 1686) some thirty heads of families [in Buda] got together and elected me to study with them. And every week on Wednesday nights I would study through the night until dawn with them, reading the five books of Moses, the Prophets and the Hagiographa, the Mishna, the Haggadah and midrashic works. At the conclusion all would stand and with loud voice and pleasant melody sing songs like "My Soul's Beloved," which are printed in the book *The Gates of Zion*, and then melodiously recite the prayer that is customary following the study of the scriptures. And since learning is enriched by competition among those who thirst for knowledge, others also got together, bachelors and young men who had recently married; there were about twenty of them, who also engaged a scholar to study with them. . . . If only the destruction of the city had not intervened, this institution would have endured forever.[6]

Among the survivors of the fall of Buda was a learned young man named Zevi Hirsch Ashkenazi, who was to become famous as one of the leading religious scholars of the age. His wife and young daughter were killed in the 1686 siege and his parents were taken captive by Prussian soldiers, but he found a safe haven in Sarajevo, where the Jewish community employed him as their *chacham* (rabbi). Four years later, the rabbi left to find his parents in Berlin and thus was spared from seeing scenes of the sack of Buda repeated in Sarajevo.[7]

The burning of Sarajevo is described in an entry in Prince Eugene of Savoy's war diary:

> On 23 October [1697], I placed the troops in a broad front on a height directly overlooking the city. From there, I sent detachments to plunder it. The Turks had already taken the best things to safety, but still a great quantity of all sorts of goods remained behind. Towards evening the city began to burn. The city is very large and quite open; it has 120 fine mosques. On the 24th I remained at Sarajevo. We let the

city and the whole surrounding area go up in flames. Our raiding party, which pursued the enemy, brought back booty and many women and children, after killing many Turks.[8]

In his description of the burning of Sarajevo, the prince does not mention books as such, but the pain of seeing books consumed by the flames figures prominently in a verse lament for the city's destruction written by an anonymous Muslim author:

> They came and burned the beautiful city of Sarajevo down.
> Like cattle they drove the innocent people out,
> They came and burned the beautiful city of Sarajevo down.
> They burned Korans by the thousands and countless [other] books,
> How many mosques they burned, sanctuaries pulled down!
> The whole city, from one end to the other, they ruined and devastated,
> They came and burned the beautiful city of Sarajevo down.[9]

Before Prince Eugene and his expeditionary force withdrew with their loot and captives, the city center, including the synagogue and the houses and shops of Sarajevo's first Jewish quarter around El Cortijo, the great apartment building built from the bequest of Siyavuş, Pasha, had been completely burned and sacked. Many books had perished but, although we have no witness other than the fact of its survival, the Sarajevo Haggadah once again was saved.[10]

Sarajevo, including its old Jewish quarter, was retaken and rebuilt, and Ottoman rule endured for another three centuries until another Hapsburg army took the city in 1878. Fortunately, times had changed, and the Hapsburg empire was now a formally pluralistic enterprise no longer interested in imposing religious uniformity upon its subjects. Instead, Bosnia-Herzegovina's new rulers sought to bring their newly acquired territory into the modern age. Among the civic improvements of the Hapsburg era was the Zemaljski muzej (Landesmuseum, now the National Museum), established in Sarajevo in 1888 as Bosnia's first scientific institution and research library organized on the Western model. In 1894 the codex that is now known as the Sarajevo Haggadah was purchased from a private owner to become one of the new museum's most prized possessions. It was taken to Vienna to be examined by the leading experts and then returned to the custody of the museum in Sarajevo, which has preserved it to this day.

Although Sarajevo gained notoriety in 1914 as the site of the political assassination that sparked the Great War, the city survived that war physically unscathed. At the end of the war in November 1918, Bosnia's last Hapsburg governor, Baron Sarkotić, handed over power in Sarajevo to the Bosnian local authorities. A few days later, Serbian and Montenegrin troops entered the city and Bosnia became part of the newly founded Kingdom of the Serbs, Croats, and Slovenes, which before long was renamed Yugoslavia.

From the outset, the new kingdom was beset by disputes between centralists and local autonomists and by competing Serbian and Croatian nationalist ambitions. From 1929 until the eve of World War II, the country was ruled by decree as a royal dictatorship, which instead of resolving these divisions wound up exacerbating them. Despite the political tensions and the economic depression of the 1930s, cultural and literary life continued to flourish among Sarajevo's diverse ethnic and religious communities. During the interwar years, about half of all Sarajevans were Bosniaks (Muslim Slavs), one seventh were Jews, and the rest included Orthodox Serbs, Catholic Croats, and others. Cultural and literary associations, clubs, religious societies, and labor and business groups published books, almanacs, and journals and maintained dozens of libraries and community reading rooms. Among them was La Benevolencija (est. 1892), Sarajevo's leading Jewish cultural, educational, and charitable society, which in 1933 opened its own research library.[11]

Nazi Germany invaded Yugoslavia in April 1941 and partitioned the country among its allies and local collaborators. Bosnia-Herzegovina, divided into German and Italian occupation zones, was assigned to the so-called Independent State of Croatia, run by a brutal Fascist regime installed by the Germans in Zagreb. As in World War I, Sarajevo once again emerged from the four years of war and occupation with only minor physical damage, but Bosnia and its people had suffered terribly. More than 300,000 Bosnians of all ethnic groups died in concentration camps, reprisals, and massacres, in fighting the Nazis or each other. Hardest hit as a community were Bosnia's Jews—of an estimated 12,000–14,000 Jews in Bosnia-Herzegovina barely 2,000 survived the Holocaust.

In the initial days of the German occupation, anti-Jewish laws were enacted and all of Sarajevo's eight synagogues and its other Jewish community institutions were sacked and vandalized.

> Treasures that were not stolen were burned. Centuries of record books, precious silver, ancient libraries, and illuminated manuscripts—nearly the sum total of Sarajevo's Jewish heritage—was carted off or went up in smoke.[12]

Among the institutions attacked by the Nazis and their local sympathizers were the library of La Benevolencija, the Jewish community reading rooms (*Jevrejske čitaonice*), and other communal and private library collections. Much was lost in the first orgy of looting and destruction, but the Germans took care to pack up some of the more valuable items from La Benevolencija's library and the historical documents of the Sarajevo Jewish community and sent them off to the Einsatzstab Reichsleiter Rosenberg, a central institute set up to collect such cultural loot from all over Europe. A wartime report preserved in the Bosnian state archives makes reference to one such shipment of twelve crates of books from La Benevolencija's library, which was sent off to Berlin on 29 October 1941. After Sarajevo's liberation, the Ministry of Education of Bosnia's new Communist government was informed in July 1945 by a representative of La Benevolencija that the society's library before the war had contained "some 2,000 books" including documents "of great antiquity and historical value . . . which the Ustaša [Croatian quisling regime] took away in 1941 and until now we haven't been able to establish where these books are located."[13]

Among the few survivors of that dark era was the famous Sarajevo Haggadah codex, concealed from the Nazis in the worst days of the occupation by a courageous Bosnian museum curator. More than half a century later, we still don't know exactly how the Haggadah was saved, but the amazing fact that this book—Sarajevo's most famous Jewish cultural artifact—was somehow kept from falling into the hands of the Nazis has given rise to a variety of anecdotes and legends. According to one account,

> In 1941, immediately after the occupation forces entered Sarajevo, a German officer came to the National Museum and ordered the director [Dr. Jozo Petrović] to hand over only the manuscript Haggadah from the rich Museum collection. The director used various excuses to delay the delivery of the valuable leather codex, and managed in the meantime to smuggle it out of the large museum building into a mountain village in the vicinity of Sarajevo. After the city was liberated, this true treasure was returned to the safe of the Museum.

Recent studies, based on documents in the National Museum's archives, have called into question key features of the legends surrounding the rescue of the Haggadah, such as the dramatic story of the manuscript being spirited out of the building under the noses of the Nazis and hidden in a mountain village (buried beneath a peasant's threshold, inside a mosque, or under an apple tree according to some accounts). Although the documentary record is tantalizingly incomplete, it points to the part played by museum curator Derviš Korkut in the preservation of the manuscript during the war. His role presents an example of the intercommunal and interpersonal ties fostered by centuries of *convivencia* in Bosnia.

Korkut, a Bosnian Muslim, was in charge of the National Museum's library. He also had a close and long-standing connection with Sarajevo's Jewish community. In the 1920s, his translation of an Ottoman-era document recording prominent Jewish families in early nineteenth-century Sarajevo was serialized in the local newspaper *Jevrejski glas* [Jewish voice]. On the eve of the war, when the "Jewish question" in Yugoslavia had become a hot political issue (in October 1940 the royal Yugoslav government enacted the first anti-Jewish decrees), Derviš Korkut responded by writing an article entitled "Anti-Semitism Is Foreign to the Muslims of Bosnia and Herzegovina" and having it published in Belgrade.

Following the Nazi invasion, there is evidence that Korkut used his access to museum records to alter labels and catalog entries in order to conceal and protect manuscripts, including several codices personally entrusted to him for safekeeping (*u amanet*) by a Sarajevo Jew, Vito Kajon, in October 1941. Kajon's Jewish manuscripts survived the war in the museum's library, in a box labeled "Archiv der Familie Kapetanović—Türkische Urkunden" (Archives of the Kapetanović family—Turkish documents). As for the museum's famous Haggadah codex, the evidence suggests that Korkut was the last person to sign for the manuscript before the war. Thereafter it disappears from the record and is not mentioned in inventories until the end of 1943, when the museum was closed for the duration of the war and its most valuable collections were evacuated from the building and placed in a vault of the State Bank. The Sarajevo Haggadah is listed in the inventory of items evacuated from the museum on 9 December 1943 by order of the new museum director, Vejsil Ćurčić. Six weeks prior to this, on 29 October, the museum library's inventory book records—after a long silence—Ćurčić's receipt of the Haggadah codex from Derviš Korkut. The complete details of how the Haggadah was preserved from the Nazis are still unknown. However, the fact that this unique manuscript was deliberately concealed for a time during the German occupation and emerged intact after Sarajevo's liberation is not in question.[14]

Half a century after the Nazi invasion, the idea of *convivencia* in Bosnia once again came under attack by the ideologues of ethnic and racial purity. Selected as targets of these attacks were not only people of the "wrong" ethnic or religious heritage but also books, libraries and archives, museums, works of art, houses of worship, and historic architecture. In terms of the deliberate destruction of cultural heritage, the 1992–95 war in Bosnia and Herzegovina far surpassed the material damage inflicted on the country during World War II.[15]

In the summer of 1992, Sarajevo witnessed what may well be the largest single incident of book burning in modern history.[16] The target was Bosnia's National and University Library, housed in a handsome Moorish Revival building erected in the 1890s as Sarajevo's City Hall. Before the fire, the National and University Library held an estimated 1.5 million volumes, including over 155,000 rare books, unique archives, and special collections, 478 manuscript codices, 600 sets of periodicals, a complete set of all the books, newspapers, and journals published in Bosnia since the mid nineteenth century, as well as the main research collections of the University of Sarajevo.[17]

In a three-day inferno (25–27 August) the library building was gutted, the greater part (an estimated 90 percent) of its irreplaceable contents reduced to ashes. Shortly after nightfall on 25 August a barrage of incendiary shells fired by Serb nationalist forces from several positions on the heights overlooking the library burst through the roof and the large stained-glass skylight, setting the bookstacks ablaze. Repeated shelling kept rekindling the fire, while snipers, mortar shells, and antiaircraft guns fired at sidewalk level targeted firefighters and volunteers attempting to save the books. Eyewitness reports describe the scene:

> [The National Library] was blazing out of control Wednesday after the besieged Bosnian capital came under fierce bombardment overnight. Firefighters struggling with low water pressure managed to extinguish the blaze several times during the night but the building . . . kept coming under renewed attack. . . . By mid-morning, the north and central sections of the crenelated four-storey building were completely engulfed by flames. Windows were exploding out into the narrow streets and the building's stone north wall was cracking and collapsing under the heat of the raging

inferno. . . . The fire started shortly after 10 P.M. on Tuesday night and, despite the efforts of the city's fire department, kept reigniting and growing. The slender Moorish columns of the Library's main reading room exploded from the intense heat and portions of the roof came crashing through the ceiling.[18]

Serb fighters in the hills ringing Sarajevo peppered the area around the library with machine-gun fire, trying to prevent firemen from fighting the blaze along the banks of the Miljacka river in the old city. Machine gun bursts ripped chips from the crenelated building and sent firemen scurrying for cover. Mortar rounds landed around the building with deafening crashes, kicking up bricks and plaster and spraying shrapnel. Asked why he was risking his life, fire brigade chief Kenan Slinić, sweaty, soot-covered and two yards from the blaze, said: "Because I was born here and they are burning a part of me."[19]

Braving a hail of sniper fire, librarians and citizen volunteers formed a human chain to pass books out of the burning building to trucks queued outside. Interviewed by a television camera crew, one of them said: "We managed to save just a few, very precious books. Everything else burned down. And a lot of our heritage, national heritage, lay down there in ashes." Among the human casualties was Aida Buturović, a thirty-two-year-old librarian in the National Library's international exchanges section. She was killed by a mortar shell as she tried to make her way home from the library. Amidst the carnage caused by the intense Serb nationalist bombardment of the city, her death went unnoted except by her family and colleagues. Bosnia's Ministry of Health reported on 26 August that 14 people had been killed and 126 had been wounded in Sarajevo during the preceding twenty-four hours.[20]

Three months earlier, the Serbian gunners' target had been Sarajevo's Oriental Institute (est. 1950), home to the region's largest collection of Islamic manuscript texts and Ottoman documents. Targeted with phosphorus shells on 17 May, the Oriental Institute and virtually all of its contents were consumed by the flames. Losses included 5,263 bound manuscripts in Arabic, Persian, Ottoman Turkish, and Bosnian Slavic written in Arabic script; an archive of 200,000 Ottoman documents, primary source material for 500 years of the country's history; a collection of over 100 Ottoman cadastral registers recording land ownership and population structure in Bosnia from the sixteenth through the late nineteenth century; and 300 microfilm reels with copies of Bosnian manuscripts held by private owners or by foreign institutions. The institute's reference collection of 10,000 printed books and 300 sets of periodicals, the most comprehensive special library on its subject in the entire region, was also destroyed, as was its catalog and all work in progress.[21]

In each case, the library alone was targeted; adjacent buildings stand intact to this day. Serb nationalist leader Radovan Karadžić has denied that his forces were responsible for the attacks, claiming the National Library had been set ablaze by the Muslims themselves "because they didn't like its . . . architecture."[22]

Fig. 1. *Convivencia:* Jewish and Islamic books rescued from the burning National and University Library of Bosnia-Herzegovina, August 1992. (*Photograph by Andrea Markov*).

The 200,000-volume library of Bosnia's National Museum (Zemaljski muzej Bosne i Hercegovine) in Sarajevo was evacuated under shelling and sniper fire during the summer of 1992. Among the books successfully rescued from the museum was one of the country's greatest cultural treasures, the Sarajevo Haggadah.[23] We have the word of the Bosnian Serb officer in charge that the shelling of the museum was intentional. In September 1992, BBC reporter Kate Adie went to the siege lines and interviewed the battery commander, asking him why his men had shelled the Holiday Inn, where all the foreign correspondents were known to stay. The officer apologized, explaining that they had been aiming at the roof of the National Museum, across the street from the hotel, and had missed.

The National Museum was badly damaged during the three-and-a-half-year siege. Shells crashed through the roof and the skylights, and all of its 300 windows were shot out; shell holes penetrated the walls of several galleries. Parts of the museum's collection that could not be moved to safe storage remained inside the building, exposed to damage from artillery attacks and to decay from exposure to the elements. Dr. Rizo Sijarić, the museum's director, was killed by a shell burst during Sarajevo's second siege winter (10 December 1993) while trying to arrange for plastic sheeting from UN relief agencies to cover some of the holes in the building.[24]

The libraries of ten of the sixteen faculties of the University of Sarajevo were also wholly or partly destroyed by Serbian shelling, suffering combined losses of 400,000 books and 500 periodical titles. Of the remaining faculty libraries and specialized research institutes affiliated with the university, all suffered some degree of damage to their buildings, equipment, and collections; all the libraries lost members of their staffs. Eight branches of Sarajevo's municipal public library were also shelled and burned.[25]

The catalog of losses does not stop there. One could mention the destroyed and looted monastery, church, and library of the Franciscan Theological Seminary in the Sarajevo suburb of Nedžarići; the shelling and partial destruction of the regional archives of Herzegovina in Mostar; the 50,000 volumes lost when the library of the Roman Catholic bishopric of Mostar was set ablaze by the Serb-led Yugoslav army; the burning and bulldozing of the sixteenth-century Serbian Orthodox monastery of Žitomislić south of Mostar by Croat extremists; and similar acts of destruction in hundreds of other Bosnian communities subjected to "ethnic cleansing" by Serb and Croat nationalist forces.[26]

The fates of two such communities, Janja in eastern Bosnia and Stolac in the country's southern region of Herzegovina, are representative of a widespread pattern of destruction. Before the 1992–95 war, Janja was a small town of 10,000 people, 95 percent of them Bosniaks (Muslim Slavs), located near the Drina River about six miles south of Bijeljina. In 1993–94 Janja was in the news as the scene of a particularly brutal "ethnic cleansing" campaign conducted by nationalist thugs led by a former soccer player named Vojkan Djurković, members of a Serbian paramilitary unit under the command of Željko Ražnatović (known by the *nom de guerre* "Arkan").

According to information received from the State Commission for Investigating War Crimes in Bosnia-Herzegovina, the old mosque in the center of Janja was blown up at 4:00 A.M. on 13 April 1993; a second mosque was demolished in the same way a short time later. Janja's other cultural treasure was the private library of the late Alija Sadiković, a scion of one of town's oldest families. In a survey of Islamic manuscript collections in Bosnia, published in 1992, the Sadiković collection is recorded as having about 100 manuscripts in Ottoman Turkish, Bosnian, Arabic, and Persian. The entire library was burned in the spring of 1993, along with the historic mansion where it was kept. The family graveyard with the tombs of Alija Sadiković and his forebears was also destroyed.[27]

In the months that followed, the "ethnic cleansers" also disposed of the town's Bosnian Muslim population, sending the men to concentration camps and making women, children, and old people pay extortion money for the privilege of being expelled across the confrontation lines. All but a handful of 30,000 Bosniaks living in the Janja–Bijeljina area were "cleansed" by Djurković and his men, reportedly acting on direct orders from Radovan Žaradžić's headquarters in Pale. Most of Janja's surviving inhabitants are now refugees living in temporary housing in the Tuzla area. Vojkan Djurković is alive and well and a prominent man in the nearby town of Bijeljina, which is still controlled by pro-Karadžić hard-liners, as is Janja. Since the end of the war, investigators from the International Criminal Tribunal for the Former Yugoslavia have discovered three mass grave sites near Janja, which are believed to hold the remains of hundreds of massacred Muslim civilians.[28]

The losses in Stolac, a historic small town in Herzegovina, also illustrate the link between the destruction of a community through the killing or expulsion of its members and the destruction of its communal memory by the "ethnic cleansers." On the eve of the recent war, Stolac was inhabited by some 19,000 people, about half of them Bosnian Muslims, one third Bosnian Croats, and one fifth Bosnian Serbs. Considered by the Bosnian government for nomination as a UNESCO world heritage site during the 1980s, Stolac was known for its well-preserved traditional residential architecture, its seventeenth-century market, four ancient mosques, and a baroque Serbian Orthodox church built in the last years of Ottoman rule, all spectacularly arrayed on a hillside beneath imposing Ottoman-era fortifications.

In the summer of 1993, Stolac was "ethnically cleansed" by the Bosnian Croat nationalist militia (HVO). A report by the office of the UN high commissioner for refugees describes what happened:

> In early July [1993], hundreds of draft-age men in Stolac, a predominantly Muslim town, were reportedly rounded up [by the Bosnian Croat authorities] and detained, probably in [the concentration camps at] Dretelj and Gabela. The total number of

detained civilians from Stolac is believed to be about 1,350. . . . On 1 August, four mosques in Stolac were blown up. That night, witnesses said, military trucks carrying soldiers firing their weapons in the air went through the town terrorizing and rounding up all Muslim women, children and elderly. The cries and screams of women and children could be heard throughout the town as the soldiers looted and destroyed Muslim homes. The soldiers, who wore handkerchiefs, stockings or paint to hide their faces, took the civilians to Blagaj, an area of heavy fighting northwest of Stolac.[29]

A memorial book issued in 1996 by the presidency-in-exile of Stolac Municipality lists the following losses of unique original manuscripts, documents, and community records burned by the HVO:

> The Library of the Muslim Community Board of Stolac, including 40 manuscripts from the 17th–19th centuries, valuable printed books and community records going back to the 19th century (burned in mid-July 1993 by HVO militiamen)

> The Library of the Emperor's Mosque in Stolac—tens of manuscripts in Bosnian, Arabic, Turkish and Persian, from the 17th–19th centuries, along with 8 framed *lawhas* (illuminated single-page compositions of Arabic calligraphy) from the 18th and 19th centuries. Burned by the HVO in early August 1993, together with the Emperor's Mosque (Careva džamija, Mosque of Sultan Selim I, built in 1519)

> Library of the Podgradska Mosque (Mosque of Ali Pasha Rizvanbegović) in Stolac— tens of manuscripts and historical documents of the 18th–19th centuries, and 5 *lawhas* (the oeuvre of one local 19th-century calligrapher). The mosque library was burned in the fire set by the HVO to destroy the Podgradska Mosque (built in 1732–33) at 11 P.M. on July 28, 1993; the burned-out building was mined on August 8. The rubble remaining after the explosion was trucked away and the site was leveled.

> Several important private collections of documents, manuscript volumes and rare books belonging to Bosniak (Muslim Slav) families in Stolac were burned by HVO militiamen when the town's Muslims were rounded up and expelled and their houses destroyed in July–August 1993. We have only limited information available on the contents of these collections. There is a published description of 50 bound manuscripts (39 Arabic, 2 Persian, 9 Ottoman Turkish) in the Habiba Mehmedbašić collection; the manuscripts were burned when the Mehmedbašić family home was looted and set ablaze by Croat extremists. The historic mansions, libraries, and family papers of other old Bosniak families in Stolac—Rizvanbegović, Behmen, and Mahmutćehajić—were also burned and destroyed.[30]

Throughout Bosnia, public and private libraries, archives, museums, and other cultural institutions were targeted for destruction in an attempt to eliminate the material evidence—books, documents, and works of art—that could remind future generations that people of different ethnic and religious traditions once shared a common heritage and life in Bosnia. In hundreds of towns and villages, communal records (cadastral registers, parish records, endowment deeds) that documented the historical presence of minority communities were torched by nationalist extremists as part of "ethnic cleansing" campaigns. An estimated 481,100 linear meters of records—the equivalent of a row of document storage boxes more than 300 miles long—were destroyed in attacks on historical archives and local registry offices during the 1992–95 war. Lost in the flames were hundreds of thousands of documents recording people's births, deaths, and marriages, their properties and businesses, their cultural and religious lives, civic and political activities and associations.[31]

While the destruction of a community's institutions and records is, in the first instance, part of a strategy of intimidation aimed at driving out members of the targeted group, it also serves a long-term goal. These records were proof that others once lived in that place, that they had historical roots there. By burning the documents, by razing mosques and churches and bulldozing graveyards, the nationalist forces who took over these towns and villages were trying to insure themselves against any future claims by the people they had expelled and dispossessed.[32]

Underlying these "practical" motives was a structure of ideological justification. Public support for "ethnic cleansing" was promoted by nationalist publications and the electronic media, which presented history as the eternal struggle of the pure Serb (or pure Croat) nation against a racial and religious enemy threatening its very survival. Beginning in 1986, the Serbian public was treated to a deluge of television docudramas, historical novels, essays, and speeches in which Muslims were portrayed as race traitors and Christ-killers.[33]

Patriotic academics were called upon to explain to a credulous public the true depravity of the Muslims, who were alleged to be using books as an instrument to plot genocide against Serbs. Thus in April 1993, at the height of "ethnic cleansing" by Serbian forces in Bosnia, the Serbian scholar Nada Todorov informed readers of a military journal that

> the traditional *Thousand and One Nights* tales, which Muslims are supposed to have read in their childhood, deserves special blame, since these stories have provided "subliminal direction" to the Muslims to torture and kill Christians. As Todorov explains: "Since these stories are full of eroticism, it is certain that they [the Muslims] read them carefully during puberty, so that their effect on the personality of the latter is clearly evident. In committing atrocities in Bosnia-Herzegovina, [their] conscious, sub-conscious, and unconscious levels of personality have been at work."[34]

This theme was also promoted by the psychiatrist Dr. Jovan Rašković, Radovan Karadžić's mentor and cofounder of the nationalist Serbian Democratic Party (SDS), in his book *Luda zemlja* [A mad country], published on the eve of the war. In this book, Dr. Rašković presented his psychoanalytic theories about the ethnic groups of Yugoslavia, which he claimed to have discovered in his clinical practice. He declared that Muslims were plagued by an "anal-erotic fixation" (as evidenced by their practice of frequent ritual ablutions) and by a compulsion for acquiring assets and money. Croats allegedly suffered from "castration anxieties" and were weak and incapable of true leadership, but they had a "genocidal instinct" which made them especially dangerous to Serbs. Serbs, on the other hand, were the only psychologically healthy and vigorous group capable of exerting authority and thus were destined to dominate the other Yugoslav peoples.[35]

Dr. Biljana Plavšić, professor of biology and former dean of the Faculty of Natural Sciences and Mathematics at the University of Sarajevo, took this kind of "racial science" one step further in her role as vice-president in Radovan Karadžić's Bosnian Serb war cabinet. "Ethnic cleansing" was a "natural phenomenon," she assured the Serbian public, made necessary by the "genetic deformity" of Bosnian Muslims. The Muslims' ancestors, she averred, had originally been Serbs,

> but it was genetically deformed material that embraced Islam. And now, of course, with each successive generation this gene simply becomes more concentrated. It gets worse and worse, it simply expresses itself and dictates their style of thinking and behaving, which is rooted in their genes.[36]

Implied in this and similar statements is the idea that by adopting an "oriental" religion the ancestors of Bosnia's Muslim Slavs had crossed not only religious but racial boundaries. Such ideas can have fatal consequences. On 11 July 1995 the UN-protected enclave of Srebrenica in eastern Bosnia was overrun by Serb nationalist forces led by Gen. Ratko Mladić. Bosnian Serb radio, based at Karadžić and Plavšić's headquarters in the ski resort of Pale, broadcast the news that normality had been restored to "free Srebrenica." This announcement was followed by the song: "Die you scum, the Serbs are the champions. Come out onto your balconies and hail the white Serb race."[37]

In April 1996, after the Dayton peace agreement, the first Western journalists were allowed to visit "free" Srebrenica by the Bosnian Serb authorities. Elizabeth Neuffer of the *Boston Globe* reported what she found there:

> Eight months have passed since the Bosnian Serb army overran this United Nations "safe haven" and some 8,500 Muslim men and boys disappeared, many now believed to have been executed and dumped in mass graves nearby. But the memory lives on.
> The tangled remains of Srebrenica's two mosques are still crumpled on the main street. Piles of garbage reveal burned books with Muslim names on the flyleaves.[38]

Despite all that has happened, there are still people in Bosnia and elsewhere who are working to preserve the memory of that country's pluralistic society, its long history, and its multicultural heritage. At the forefront of that struggle are the librarians of the National and University Library of Bosnia and Herzegovina (NULBH) who are determined to rebuild their institution. They have a long-term plan to reconstitute the library's collection of Bosniaca. According to Dr. Enes Kujundžić, the director of the NULBH, the term *Bosniaca* refers to Bosnian imprints (books produced in Bosnia on all subjects), and books about the subject of Bosnia (wherever they were produced). Assembling and preserving this kind of national "collection of record" is the first of the two main functions of any national library. The other function, of course, is its role as the country's major research library.

Since 1995 OCLC Inc., a cataloging consortium based in Dublin, Ohio, and the University of Michigan Library have compiled on-line bibliographies recording holdings of Bosniaca in major American libraries. Closer to home, the national libraries in Slovenia and Croatia are sharing data and expertise with their counterparts in Bosnia. This will help Dr. Kujundžić and his staff at the NULBH in planning the first phase of their project to reassemble a core collection of important Bosnian imprints and books written about Bosnia and Herzegovina. The records in these databases will be part of a master bibliography, from which the Bosnians can select which works they would like to have in the form of microfiche, CD-ROM, or other facsimiles, and which small subset of books they deem important enough to include in a desiderata list of works that the Sarajevo library will seek to acquire in the original form (by purchase, donation, or exchange).

Both the OCLC project and the University of Michigan data will help with efforts to gather information about Bosniaca, by identifying North American libraries that currently own publications that may no longer exist in Bosnian collections. These items can then be given priority in ongoing preservation programs that film or scan rare library materials. Once that is accomplished, arrangements can be made at relatively modest cost to provide additional copies for the Bosnian library.[39]

Another way in which Bosnian publications can be rescued from the ashes is by reissuing them. Since the end of the war, Bosnia's publishing industry has been turning out hundreds of reprint editions of classic works originally published in Bosnia or written about Bosnia, as well as anthologies of Bosnian literature and new studies of Bosnian culture and history. These new editions will help take the place of many of the books that were lost in the burning and pillage of both public and private libraries during the 1992–95 war.[40]

The Bosnian Libraries Project, a program of book donations organized by Jeffrey Spurr, a librarian at Harvard University, helps address the other important function of the National and University Library—its goal to serve once again as a major research library that can support teaching and other academic and professional work in Bosnia-Herzegovina. More than 30,000 books and journals donated by American university presses, other publishers, academic libraries, and learned societies as part of this project are either already in Sarajevo or on their way there. Other book donations have come from Europe and the Middle East.

For obvious reasons, the goal of restoring working academic libraries that can serve the needs of the University of Sarajevo and other educational institutions in Bosnia has taken precedence in terms of the urgency and scale of efforts involved. The quest to recover Bosniaca—including both published works and copies of manuscripts—is a long-term undertaking that is only now beginning to bear fruit. In an effort to resurrect some of Bosnia's lost manuscripts and documents from the ashes, a team of Bosnian and American scholars has established the Bosnian Manuscript Ingathering Project. We were prompted by the realization that although the collections of the Oriental Institute and many other manuscript libraries in Bosnia perished in the war, a number of the destroyed originals probably still exist in the form of microfilms, photocopies, or other facsimiles taken by foreign scholars as part of research projects or sent abroad as part of exchanges between Bosnian libraries and foreign institutions. By setting up a registry of the current locations of these copies, we hope to help our Bosnian colleagues to reconstitute at least part of their collections.

Recently, the Ingathering Project received a packet of about 360 pages of archival photocopies from Eleazar Birnbaum, a retired professor at the University of Toronto. Birnbaum had gone to Sarajevo in 1981 to do research in Bosnian manuscript libraries and had brought back several hundred photocopies of items that interested him. Some of those photocopies reproduce parts or all of a number of manuscript codices in the collection of the Sarajevo Oriental Institute. Eleven years after his visit, the institute was shelled and burned. All of its original manuscripts perished in the flames, but the Canadian scholar still had the stack of photocopies from Sarajevo in his study. When he found out about the Ingathering Project from an announcement in a professional journal, he wrote us a letter, offering to let us make copies of his photocopies, as a contribution toward recovering at least some of the Oriental Institute's lost manuscript collection. What he sent us includes full or partial copies of fourteen works in Ottoman Turkish, two in Persian, and one in Arabic. Several of the recovered items are unique (copies of works not recorded in other collections); among them are texts of considerable philological, literary, historical, and artistic interest. All qualify, in one way or another, as Bosniaca.

Among these resurrected images of lost originals, we found a copy of an intriguing work, Orijentalni institut u Sarajevu MS 4811/II (84 fols.—complete copy), a collection of anecdotes (ḥikāyāt) written in Ottoman Turkish by an anonymous author in 1585 (copy dated 1640). A number of the anecdotes refer to Bosnian topics and to personages of Bosnian origin. Of particular interest is a story recounting the conversion of the Bosnian Muslims to Islam, followed by a satire on the manners and customs of the more rustic Bosnian converts, known as poturs. This unique text is important as a document of cultural history, showing how Bosnians perceived themselves, their neighbors, and their society during an era of social and religious transformation. The recovery of this manuscript is of particular significance, since it is not recorded in Salih Trako and Lejla Gazić's 1997 catalogue of the lost literary MSS of the Sarajevo Oriental Institute.[41]

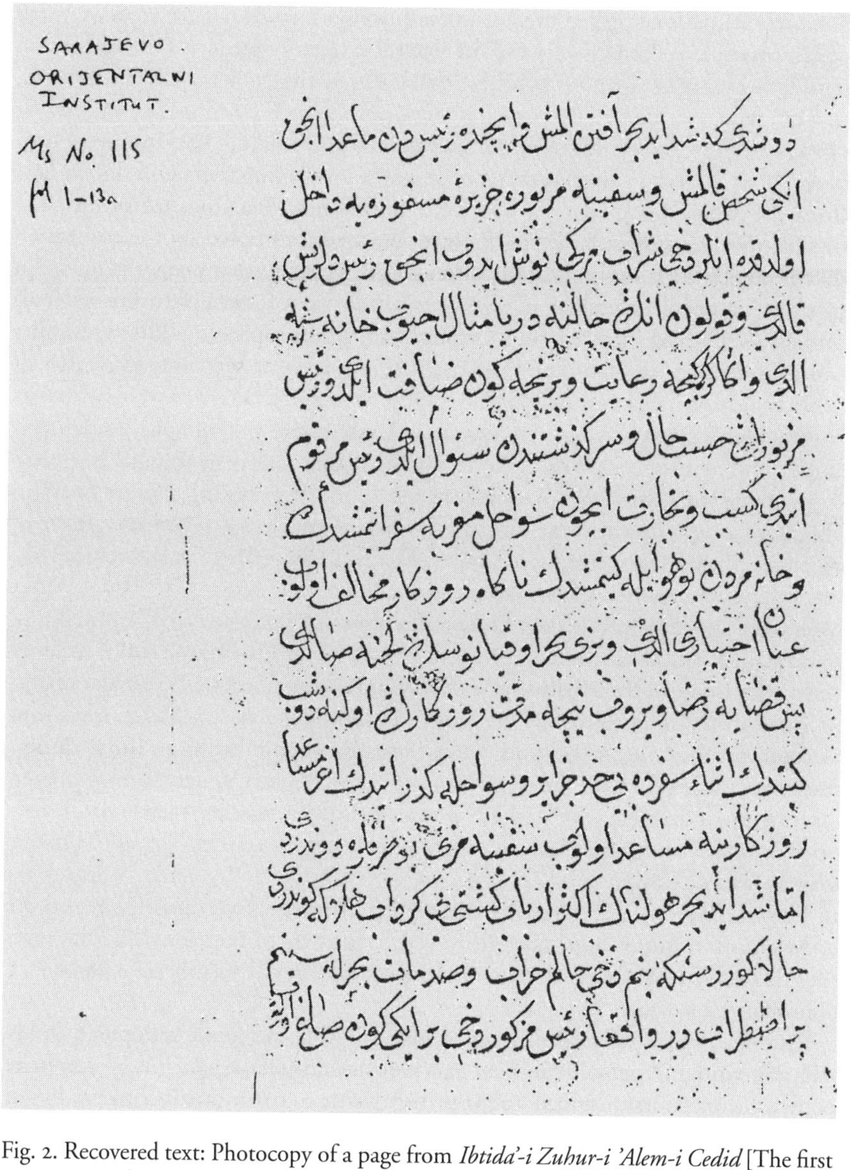

Fig. 2. Recovered text: Photocopy of a page from *Ibtida'-i Zuhur-i 'Alem-i Cedid* [The first appearance of the New World], an early treatise in Ottoman Turkish on the discovery of America. The original manuscript was one of 5,263 codices burned when the Sarajevo Oriental Institute was shelled by Serb nationalist forces on 17 May 1992. Photocopies of this text and of other destroyed codices have been recovered by the Bosnian Manuscripts Ingathering Project.

Another item among our recovered manuscripts turned out to be an example of "Bosnian Americana"—an excerpt from a sixteenth-century Ottoman work on the discovery of the New World: Orijentalni institut u Sarajevu MS 115 (fols. 1b–13a), part of a miscellany copied in Sarajevo the early 1700s. The manuscript opens with a work entitled *Ibtidā'-i Ẓuhūr-i 'Ālem-i Cedīd* [The first appearance of the New World], a sixteenth-century treatise in Ottoman Turkish on the discovery of America and the marvels of the New World (based on texts translated from Latin and Spanish). While the text is recorded elsewhere, the existence of this particular manuscript testifies to the fact that there were people in Sarajevo around 1700 with an intellectual curiosity about the world beyond the confines of the Balkans and the Ottoman Empire, who commissioned such manuscripts and presumably read them and discussed them with their friends (recorded in Salih Trako and Lejla Gazić's 1997 catalog, p. 308, no. 525).

This item came to us separately from two sources: one photocopy was included among the items received from Professor Birnbaum; another, somewhat clearer copy of the same manuscript was donated to the Ingathering Project by Prof. Thomas Goodrich, a specialist on the history of cartography and on Ottoman accounts of the New World. Goodrich, who recently retired from Indiana University of Pennsylvania, is also donating a valuable collection of reference books from his personal library to the Oriental Institute in Sarajevo.

A Bosnian graduate student at the University of Chicago contacted us recently with some vital information—she had worked at the Oriental Institute in Sarajevo before the recent war and remembered the names of several scholars from Germany, Italy, Macedonia, and Turkey who had come to the institute during the 1980s and had taken large numbers of photocopies. We are now trying to locate those individuals (or, in the case of two of them who have since died, their heirs) to see if we can get them to supply us with copies of their copies of the lost manuscripts of Bosnia.

The search continues, as we hope it will for many years to come. Each item we uncover is one bit of light rescued from the darkness of oblivion and one more way to frustrate the aims of those who tried to destroy Bosnia, its people, and their cultural heritage.[42]

Aside from gathering documents, donations of books, equipment, and funds for education and rebuilding, how can and should we respond to these attacks against culture? First, we have to reassert and act on our own belief that there are principles of decency and international legality that are worth defending. This means doing everything in our power to make sure that those who violate international laws are indeed punished and not rewarded for their deeds. It means pressing our governments to provide not only political but serious financial support for the prosecution of such crimes before the International Criminal Tribunal for the Former Yugoslavia (ICTY) and demanding the arrest and extradition of indicted war criminals who are still at large.

The targeting of libraries, archives, and cultural monuments cannot be construed as an expression of one side's views in a political dispute. Nor is it merely one of the many regrettable calamities of war. It is a war crime and a serious violation of international laws and conventions. The latter include the Geneva Conventions of 1949, the 1954 Hague Convention on the Protection of Cultural Property in the Event of Armed Conflict, and the 1977 Protocols I and II Additional to the Geneva Conventions, which add criminal penalties to the terms of the 1954 Hague Conventions.

All of these conventions were ratified by the government of the former Yugoslavia and have been accepted as legally binding by its successor states. Determined to do more than just help remedy the damage, we have gathered eyewitness statements and other evidence that will assist the ICTY prosecutor's office at The Hague in preparing indictments against those responsible for targeting the National and University Library in Sarajevo in August 1992. The successful prosecution of crimes against culture in a court of international law will set an important precedent, and we hope it will serve as a warning to would-be "cultural cleansers" everywhere.

Bosnians of all ethnicities need our help. Faced with the bitter aftermath of war and the difficulties of an imperfect peace, many of them nevertheless remain committed to rebuilding and recovering their multicultural heritage and to keeping not only the memory but the practice of *convivencia* alive. Supporting them in this endeavor will help shape their society's future and ours.

NOTES

1. For a discussion of the origin, importance, and ownership history of this manuscript, see Eugen Verber, *The Sarajevo Haggadah* (Sarajevo: Svjetlost, 1988), 19–22, and Bezalel Narkiss, "Manuscritos iluminados hispanohebreos," in *La Vida judía en Sefarad,* ed. Elena Romero (Madrid: Ministerio de la Cultura, Dirección General de Bellas Artes y Archivos, 1991), 170–96.

2. An excerpt from Profiat Duran's grammatical treatise *Ma'aseh Efod,* trans. and cited by Gabrielle Sed-Rajna in "Hebrew Illuminated Manuscripts from the Iberian Peninsula," in *Convivencia: Jews, Muslims, and Christians in Medieval Spain,* ed. Vivian Mann, Thomas F. Glick, and Jerrilynn Dodds (New York: Braziller, in association with the Jewish Museum, 1992), 134; my statement on the special role of the book in the monotheistic traditions is adapted from Sed-Rajna. For the historiography and varied interpretations of the term *convivencia,* see Thomas F. Glick's introductory essay to the same volume (1–9).

3. On the burning of Jewish books in Valladolid, see Taddäus Zaderecki, *Der Talmud im Feuer der Jahrhunderte,* trans. M. Safier (Vienna: Victoria, 1937), 20; for the 1490 book burning in Salamanca, see Anne Lyon Haight, *Banned Books,* 3rd ed. (New York: Bowker, 1970), 7; the above, as well as the great 1499 *auto da fé* of Islamic books in Granada, are described in H. Rafetseder, *Bücherverbrennungen: Die öffentliche Hinrichtung von Schriften im historischen Wandel* (Vienna: Böhlau, 1988), 142. The forced conversion of Muslims and the expulsion of the unconverted were not concluded until 1502; in 1609–14 the descendants of these forced converts, known as Moriscos, were also expelled from Spain. It was the historical memory of the burning of Islamic scriptures in Granada that inspired

the now-famous line in Heinrich Heine's play *Almansor*, where an Andalusian Muslim named Hassan is heard to say: "That was merely a prelude; where they burn books, in the end they will also burn people" (Rafetseder, *Bücherverbrennungen*, 101).

4. On Bosnian society and culture in the Ottoman era, see Noel Malcolm, *Bosnia: A Short History*, rev. ed. (New York: New York University Press, 1996), chaps. 4–10; for the *waqf* of Siyavuş Pasha and the early history of Sarajevo's Spanish-Jewish community, see Moritz Levy, *Die Sephardim in Bosnien: Ein Beitrag zur Geschichte der Juden auf der Balkanhalbinsel* (Sarajevo, 1911; rpt. Graz: Wieser, 1996), 11–22, 134. Siyavuş Pasha's grant of permission for the building of a synagogue next to the *han* was, technically, a violation of Islamic law—which allows the repair and reconstruction of preexisting non-Muslim houses of worship but not the erection of new ones where none had stood before. What makes this bending of the law all the more remarkable is that the property was entangled with two Islamic pious foundations: the *waqf* of Gazi Husrev Beg, which owned the land underneath the buildings, and that of Siyavuş Pasha. For the history of Siyavuş Pasha's foundation and of the great *han* he built for the Jews of Sarajevo (which they called El Cortijo, the "Great Courtyard," in Judeo-Spanish), see Alija Bejtić, "Sijavuš-pašina daira," *Prilozi za proučavanje istorije Sarajeva* 2 (1966): 61–102.

5. For Arabic-script scriptoria in Bosnia during the sixteenth to nineteenth centuries, see Muhamed Ždralović, *Bosansko-hercegovački prepisivači djela u arabičkim rukopisima* [Bosnian and Herzegovinian copyists of works in Arabic manuscripts], 2 vols. (Sarajevo: Svjetlost, 1988); for Bosnian authors of works in Arabic, Ottoman Turkish, and Persian, see Amir Ljubović, *Logička djela Bošnjaka na arapskom jeziku* [Treatises on logic written in Arabic by Bosnian authors] (Sarajevo: Orijentalni institut, 1996); Lamija Hadžiosmanović, and Minka Memija, *Poezija Bošnjaka na orijentalnim jezicima* [Poetry written by Bosnians in oriental languages] (Sarajevo: Preporod, 1995); Amir Ljubović, and Sulejman Grozdanić, *Prozna književnost Bosne i Hercegovine na orijentalnim jezicima* [Prose literature of Bosnia-Herzegovina in oriental languages] (Sarajevo: Orijentalni institut, 1995); for works in Ladino and Hebrew, see Muhamed Nezirović, *Jevrejsko-španjolska književnost Bosne i Hercegovine* [Judaeo-Spanish literature of Bosnia-Herzegovina] (Sarajevo: Svjetlost, 1992). One of many examples of intertextuality in Bosnian literature is a poem about a failed uprising of Bosnian Muslim notables, written in the Bosnian Slavic vernacular in Hebrew script, found in a nineteenth-century MS on *materia medica* preserved in the collection of the Sarajevo Jewish community; similar poems are found in *aljamiado* manuscripts (Slavic in Arabic script) and in early collections of Bosnian oral folklore: Jasna Šamić, "Qu'estce que 'notre héritage': plus particulièrement sur un manuscrit conservé au siège de la communauté juive (Jevrejska opština) de Sarajevo," *Anali Gazi Husrevbegove biblioteke* 17–18 (1996): 91–96.

6. Isaac Schulhof (1650–ca. 1733), [*Megilat Ofen*] *Budai krónika 1686*, trans. László Jólesz, commentary by Ferenc Szakály (Budapest: Magyar Helikon, 1979), cited passage on 71–72. All three of Buda's synagogues were sacked and burned and eleven of the city's twelve mosques were demolished after the siege; the remaining mosque, on the Danube riverbank, was converted into a saltpeter mill; József Molnór, "Az utolsó budai dzsámi" [The lastmosque in Buda], *Műemlékvédelem* 12/2 (1968): 104–5.

7. Levy, *Die Sephardim*, 28–29, based on Chacham Zevi Ashkenazi's biography by his son Jacob Emden (1697–1776), *Megilat sefer*. For the dates of Chacham Zevi's stay in Sarajevo and the circumstances of his departure for Berlin, see the preface to the French translation of this work, *Mémoires de Jacob Emden; ou, L'anti-Sabbataï Zewi*, trans. Maurice-Ruben Hayoun (Paris: Editions du Cerf, 1992), 13–14, 74–75.

8. Excerpt from Prince Eugene's war diary, cited and translated by Noel Malcolm in *Bosnia*, 84–85.

9. Anonymous poem from 1697; English translation adapted from an excerpt quoted in Miroslav Prstojević, *Sarajevo, ranjeni grad* [Sarajevo, the wounded city] (Sarajevo: Ideja, 1994), 20; for the full text of this poem in Bosnian, see Amina Šiljak-Jesenković, "Motivi u pjesmama o Sarajevu na turskom jeziku" [Motifs in poems about Sarajevo written in Turkish], in *Prilozi historiji Sarajeva: radovi na znanstvenog simpozija Pola milenija Sarajeva, održanog 19. do 21. marta 1993. godine*, ed. Dževad Juzbašić (Sarajevo: Institut za istoriju, Orijentalni institut, 1997), 157–64, esp. 163–64.

10. Levy, *Die Sephardim*, 28, 109–15.

11. On the ethnic politics that broke up the first Yugoslavia, see Ivo Banac, *The National Question in Yugoslavia: Origins, History, Politics* (Ithaca: Cornell University Press, 1984); for the role of libraries in the cultural life of Bosnia between the world wars, see Ljubinka Bašović, *Biblioteke i bibliotekarstvo u Bosni i Hercegovini, 1918–1945* [Libraries and librarianship in Bosnia and Herzegovina, 1918–1945] (Sarajevo: Veselin Masleša, 1986); Samija Sarić, *Jevrejska kulturna i druga društva u Bosni i Hercegovini, 1885–1945: regesta* [Jewish cultural and other associations in Bosnia and Herzegovina, 1885–1945] (Sarajevo: Državni arhiv Bosne i Hercegovine, 1995).

12. Edward Serotta, *Survival in Sarajevo: How a Jewish Community Came to the Aid of Its City* (Vienna: Brandstätter, 1994), 22.

13. For the October 1941 document and the July 1945 report, see Bašović, *Biblioteke i bibliotekarstvo* 181–82, 370–72; for the collecting activities of the Einsatzstab Reichsleiter Rosenberg, see Peter M. Manasse, *Verschleppte Archive und Bibliotheken: Die Tätigkeit des Einsatzstabes Rosenberg während des Zweiten Weltkrieges* (St. Ingbert: Rohrig, 1997).

14. The version of the rescue story cited here is from Verber, *Sarajevo Haggadah*, 20; for a more elaborate variant, see Serotta, *Survival in Sarajevo*, 22–24. These legends are compared with the documentary evidence by Kemal Bakaršić in: "The Story of the Sarajevo Haggada," *Judaica Librarianship* 9 (1994–95): 135–43, and "Gdje se nalazila Sarajevska Haggada u toku drugog svjetskog rata?" [Where was the Sarajevo Haggadah during the Second World War?], in *Sefarad '92: Sarajevo, 11.09–14.09.: zbornik radova*, ed. M. Nezirović, Boris Nilević, and Muhsin Rizvić (Sarajevo: Institut za istoriju; Jevrejska zajednica Bosne i Hercegovine, 1995), 285–303. For the Haggadah rescue tales as folklore, see Vlajko Palavestra, "Pričanja sudbini Sarajevske Haggade" [Stories about the fate of the Sarajevo Haggadah], in *Sefarad '92*, 305–12.

15. Council of Europe, Committee on Culture and Education, *Information Reports on the Destruction by War of the Cultural Heritage in Croatia and Bosnia-Herzegovina* (Strasbourg: Council of Europe, Parliamentary Assembly, 1993–97), vols. 1–10 = Assembly Documents 6756, 6869, 6904, 6989 + addendum, 6999, 7070, 7133, 7308, 7341, 7674, 7740; Vesna Blažina, "Mémoricide ou la purification culturelle: la guerre et les bibliothèques de Croatie et de Bosnie-Herzégovine," *Documentation et bibliothèques* 42 (1996): 149–64; Alain-Charles Lefèvre, "Bosnie et Croatie: un désastre culturel sans précédent," *Archéologia* 328 (Nov. 1996): 26–35.

16. By some estimates, the total number of books destroyed by the Nazis before and during World War II was in excess of 20 million, in about forty-five major and countless smaller book burnings. In no single instance, however, did the destruction reach this scale of magnitude. Another infamous case of library burning occurred in the early days of World War I, when the German army set fire to the library of the Catholic University of Louvain in an act of reprisal that shocked the civilized world. An estimated 600,000

volumes were consumed by the flames when the library was set afire on the night of 25–26 August 1914—seventy-eight years to the day before the attack that destroyed the Sarajevo library; on the burning of the Louvain library, see Wolfgang Schivelbusch, *Eine Ruine im Krieg der Geister: Die Bibliothek von Löwen, August 1914 bis Mai 1940*, rev. ed. (Frankfurt: Fischer Taschenbuch, 1993).

17. The losses are described by the library's director, Enes Kujundžić, in "Memoria Bosniaca—Memoria Mundi," *Bosniaca: časopis Nacionalne i univerzitetske biblioteke Bosne i Hercegovine* 1 (1996): 5–12, and "From Ashes: The Fate of the National and University Library of Bosnia and Herzegovina" (Web site: http://www.geocities.com/CapitolHill/6777/library.htm).

18. Kurt Schork, "Sarajevo's Much-Loved Old Town Hall Ablaze," Reuter Library Report, 26 Aug. 1992.

19. John Pomfret, "Battles for Sarajevo Intensify as Bosnian Peace Conference Opens," Associated Press, 26 Aug. 1992.

20. Manuscripts and books evacuated from the building during the fire and surviving materials salvaged from the library's basement after the foundation had cooled were taken to a former Ashkenazi synagogue, which in 1945 had been donated by Sarajevo's Jewish community for cultural uses: Tatjana Praštalo, "Death of a Library," *Logos* 8/2 (1997): 96–99; Fahrudin Kalender, "In Memoriam: Aida (Fadila) Buturović (1959–1992)," *Bibliotekarstvo: godišnjak Društva bibliotekara Bosne i Hercegovine* 37–41 (1992–96): 37; casualty figures for 25–26 August cited in Phil Davison, "Ancient Treasures Destroyed," *Independent* (London), 27 Aug. 1992, 8.

21. Lejla Gazić, "Stradanje Orijentalnog instituta u Sarajevu" [The Destruction of the Oriental Institute in Sarajevo], *Glasnik arhiva i društva arhivskih radnika Bosne i Hercegovine* 32 (1992–93): 23–25.

22. Statement by Karadžić quoted in D. Firestone, "Peace Rebuff," *Newsday*, 30 Nov. 1992.

23. Once again, the escape of the famous Haggadah from destruction gave rise to legends and speculation; one particularly dramatic but apparently spurious account appears in Marian Wenzel, "Eye Witness in Sarajevo: Our Sister and Brother Curators and Art Historians," *Art Newspaper* (London) 4/32 (Nov. 1993): 7. The evacuation of the National Museum and its collections, including the Haggadah, is described by the museum's librarian, Kemal Bakaršić, in "The Libraries of Sarajevo and the Book That Saved Our Lives," *New Combat: A Journal of Reason and Resistance* 3 (Autumn 1994): 14–15, and "Story of the Sarajevo Haggada," 135, 141–42. As the siege of Sarajevo continued, speculation concerning the famous manuscript culminated in an article by Thom Shanker, "Missing Pages: Sarajevo Postcard," *New Republic* 212/7 (13 Feb. 1995): 14–15, which included the scurrilous charge that the "Muslim government" in Sarajevo—allegedly indifferent to the fate of a Jewish cultural treasure—had already disposed of the manuscript in order to obtain cash for buying weapons. The Bosnian authorities responded by risking a public display of the Haggadah manuscript at Passover observances that spring; see Roger Cohen, "Bosnia's Jews Glimpse Book and Hope," *New York Times*, 16 Apr. 1995.

24. Kate Adie's interview cited in "Bosnia's Written History in Flames? The Major Libraries and Archives Reported Destroyed," *Art Newspaper* (London) 3/21 (Oct. 1992): 1; for damage to the National Museum, see Rizo Sijarić, "Update on the Zemaljski Muzej, Sarajevo," *Museum Management and Curatorship* 12 (1993): 195–99; Marian Wenzel, "Obituary: Dr. Rizo Sijarić, Director of the Zemaljski Muzej, Sarajevo. Killed in Sarajevo, 10 December 1993," *Museum Management and Curatorship* 13 (1994): 79–80.

25. Emir Žuljević, "Die Lage des Bibliothekswesens in Bosnien-Herzegowina: Bücher

teilen das Schicksal der Menschen," *Gutenberg-Jahrbuch*, 1996, 315–21; Kevin Myers, "Blasting Holes in Bosnia's History," *Irish Times*, 14 Aug. 1993.

26. The destruction of the Nedžarići library and of other private and public libraries and art collections in Sarajevo, including his own, is described by the writer Ivan Lovrenović, "The Hatred of Memory," *New York Times*, 28 May 1994; see also *Cultural Institutions and Monuments in Sarajevo*, ed. Aida Čengić and Ferida Duraković (Budapest: Open Society Institute, Open Society Project of Sarajevo, Mar. 1995); András Riedlmayer, "Erasing the Past: The Destruction of Libraries and Archives in Bosnia-Herzegovina," *Middle East Studies Association Bulletin* 29/1 (July 1995): 7–11.

27. Muhamed Ždralović gives a very brief description of the Alija Sadiković collection in "Bosnia-Herzegovina," *World Survey of Islamic Manuscripts*, ed. G. J. Roper (London: Al-Furqan Foundation, 1992); 1: 95; information on the fate of the collection was provided in a personal communicaton (21 May 1998) from Prof. Aiša Sendijarević, who kindly contacted Mr. Sadiković's grandson Fahrudin Sadiković (now living in Tuzla) on my behalf. Data on the destruction of the mosques in Janja were obtained in July 1997 from the State Commission for Investigating War Crimes on the Territory of the Republic of Bosnia-Herzegovina (Državna komisija za prikupljanje činjenica o ratnim zločinima na području Republike Bosne i Hercegovine) in Sarajevo; reporter Robert Block, who visited Janja in May 1993, wrote about the town's ruined mosques and terrified Muslim residents in "Referendum Haunted by Fear," *Independent* (London), 16 May 1993.

28. On the "ethnic cleansing" of Janja, see Charlotte Eagar, "Muslims Pay for Own Ethnic Cleansing," *Observer* (London), 4 Sept. 1994; Robert Block, "Town Moves from 'Limbo to Living Hell': 'Ethnic Cleansing' in Janja Is Being Executed with Businesslike Efficiency," *Independent* (London), 27 Sept. 1994; Roger Thurow, "Reporter's Notebook: Return to Janja Finds the 'Cleansing' Sadly Complete," *Wall Street Journal*, 22 Nov. 1994; Laura Berman, "The Price of Peace," *Detroit News*, 18 Mar. 1996; Roy Gutman, "Albright Team Views Graves: Bones Protrude from Furrows," *Newsday*, 23 Mar. 1996; John Pomfret, "Bosnian Serb Switches from Purges to Politics: Will Elections Legitimize 'Cleansers'?" *International Herald Tribune*, 23 Aug. 1996.

29. UNHCR Press Release REF/1034, 23 Aug. 1993.

30. For a description of the Mehmedbašić collection, see Fehim Nametak, "Rukopisna zbirka Habibe Mehmedbašića iz Stoca" [The manuscript collection of Habiba Mehmedbašić of Stolac], *Anali Gazi Husrev-begove Biblioteke*, 11–12 (1985): 181–82; on the destruction of cultural heritage in Stolac, see Matej Vipotnik, "Searching for Bosnia's Lost Cultural Treasures," *Berserkistan* (on-line newspaper), 30 July 1996, at http://www.linder. com/berserk/culture.html, and the documentation compiled by the presidency-in-exile of the Municipality of Stolac, *Crimes in Stolac Municipality, 1992–1994* (Mostar: Zid, 1996), 45–54; excerpts from the latter are also available as a Web document at http://www. haverford.edu/relg/sells/Stolac/StolacCrimes.html.

31. Before the 1992–95 war Bosnia's state archives at the national and regional level held a combined total of 25,054 linear meters of archival materials. Of this body of material, 1,625 linear meters (6.5 percent of the total) were destroyed, lost, or seriously damaged during the war. However, 155,961 linear meters of archival materials (more than six times the combined holdings of the state archives) were held by 11,997 local registry offices; 85 percent of this material was more than twenty years old, some of it dating from the Austro-Hungarian period (1878–1918) or from the era of Ottoman rule (late 1400s to 1878). More than half of these archival holdings, an estimated 81,000 linear meters (52 percent) were destroyed during the war. Local registry offices additionally held 767,808 linear meters of

active registry materials, of which an estimated 398,500 linear meters (49.8 percent) were destroyed. The Oriental Institute in Sarajevo held more than 200,000 historical documents and cadastral registers from the Ottoman provincial archive as well as the archives of Ottoman-era kadi's courts; the collection was totally destroyed in May 1992. Data cited by permission from an unpublished paper by Azem Kožar, "War Destruction of the Archival Materials in Bosnia and Herzegovina," presented at the International Symposium on the Rehabilitation of the Archive Service in Bosnia-Herzegovina, Public Record Office, London, 7–8 May 1999.

32. The rationale behind this kind of cultural "cleansing" was summed up by a Croat nationalist militiaman, who told a Western reporter in September 1993 why he was trying to destroy the 427-year-old Ottoman bridge at Mostar: "It is not enough to clean Mostar of the Muslims—the relics must also be removed." Robert Block, "Croatian Death Squad Talks Tough around the Pooltable," *Independent* (London), 6 Sept. 1993. Since the end of the war, the stones of the destroyed Old Bridge (Stari Most) have been recovered from the riverbed—it will be rebuilt; Jerrilynn Dodds, "Bridge over the Neretva," *Archaeology* 51/1 (Jan./Feb. 1998): 48–53.

33. Mark Thompson, *Forging War: The Media in Serbia, Croatia, Bosnia and Hercegovina,* rev. ed. (Luton: University of Luton Press; London: Article 19, 1999); Michael A. Sells, *The Bridge Betrayed: Religion and Genocide in Bosnia,* rev. ed. (Berkeley: University of California Press, 1998); Vesna Pešić, *Serbian Nationalism and the Origins of the Yugoslav Crisis* (Washington, D.C.: U.S. Institute of Peace, 1996); *Radicalisation of the Serbian Society: Collection of Documents,* ed. Sonja Biserko and S. Stanojlović (Belgrade: Helsinki Committee for Human Rights in Serbia, Dec. 1997).

34. Nada Todorov, interviewed by Col. Nikola Ostojić in "Genocidne poruke iz '1001 noći'" [The genocidal messages in 'The Thousand and One Nights'], *Vojska,* 8 Apr. 1993, 20, cited in Norman Cigar, *Genocide in Bosnia: The Policy of Ethnic Cleansing* (College Station: Texas A&M University Press, 1995), 70, 221; for other statements of this kind, see N. Cigar, "Serbia's Orientalists and Islam: Making Genocide Intellectually Respectable," *Islamic Quarterly* 38/3 (1994): 147–70.

35. Jovan Rašković, *Luda zemlja* (Belgrade: Akvarijus, 1990); Dennis L. Breo, "Human Rights II: Cherif Bassiouni Condemns 'Psychology' of Balkan War Crimes," *Journal of the American Medical Association* 270 (1993): 643–45. Stevan Weine, *When History Is a Nightmare: Lives and Memories of Ethnic Cleansing in Bosnia-Herzegovina* (New Brunswick, N.J.: Rutgers University Press, 1999), 87–132.

36. Statement by Plavšić, published in September 1993 in the journal *Svet* (Novi Sad), cited by Slobodan Inić in "Biljana Plavšić: Geneticist in the Service of a Great Crime," *Bosnia Report* (London) 19 (June–Aug. 1997): 1; Professor Inić's article first appeared in Serbian in the November 1996 issue of *Helsinska povelja* [Helsinki charter], published in Belgrade by the Helsinki Committee for Human Rights in Serbia.

37. Charlotte Eager, "From Haven into Hell," *Observer* (London), 16 July 1995.

38. Elizabeth Neuffer, "War Crimes Probe Pains Srebrenica: Genocide Charges Stir Range of Emotions in Bosnian City," *Boston Globe,* 2 Apr. 1996.

39. Edward T. O'Neill, Jeffrey A. Young, and Robert Bremer, "The Bosnian National Library: Building a Virtual Collection," *Annual Review of OCLC Research 1996* (http://www.oclc.org/oclc/research/publications/review96/bosnia.htm). Kimberly Sweet, "Volumes of Hope," *University of Chicago Magazine* (October 1998), College Report, viii–x (http://www2.uchicago.edu/alumni/alumni.mag/9810/CollegeReport/volumes.htm).

40. The move to reprint books began almost immediately during the war, with the issue of a facsimile edition of Mehmed-beg Kapetanović Ljubušak's classic work, *Što misle muhamedanci u Bosni,* first published in 1886. Issued in 1992 under the imprint Edicija Memoria Bosniaca, this edition is marked "Reprint izdanja gradje spašene iz Vijećnice— NUB BiH razorene 25./26.08.1992" [reprint (based on a copy) of the original publication rescued from the Town Hall–National and University Library, destroyed on 25–26 August 1992]. This was one of hundreds of books and periodical titles published in besieged Sarajevo and in other Bosnian towns during the war; *Bibliografija monografskih publikacija 1992–1994: popis ratnih izdanja* [Bibliography of monographic publications, 1992–94: a checklist of wartime publications] (Sarajevo: Nacionalna i univerzitetska biblioteka Bosne i Hercegovine, 1995); Enes Kujundžić, *Gutenberg's Legacy in Wartime—Bosnia and Herzegovina: The Publishing of Periodicals, 1992–1994* (Siena: Università degli Studi di Siena, Comitato LI.SA, 1995).

41. *Katalog rukopisa Orijentalnog instituta: lijepa književnost* [Catalog of the manuscripts of the Oriental Institute: Belles-lettres], ed. Salih Trako and Lejla Gazić, Posebna izdanja, 20 (Sarajevo: Orijentalni Institut u Sarajevu, 1997), 410 pp., a descriptive catalog of 564 Arabic, Persian, Turkish, and *aljamiado* (Bosnian Slavic in Arabic script) manuscripts of belles-lettres held by the institute. This was one of several catalogs being prepared for publication by scholars at the Oriental Institute on the eve of the war. After a barrage of Serb incendiary shells had destroyed the institute's collection and all work in progress, a copy of the typescript draft of this catalog was discovered on deposit in the files of Bosnia's Ministry of Culture. Two senior staff members of the institute, Salih Trako and Lejla Gazić, made their way out of the besieged city, taking the manuscript of the catalog with them. They were able to complete the final editing work as houseguests of the great scholar of Islamic manuscripts, Dr. Fuad Sezgin, and his wife, Ursula, in Frankfurt, Germany, where they had access to the necessary reference works, which no longer existed in Sarajevo.

42. The Bosnian Manuscript Ingathering Project was established in 1994 by Amila Buturović (York University), András Riedlmayer (Harvard University), and İrvin Cemil Schick (Harvard University and MIT); for further information readers are urged to consult the project's home page on the World Wide Web: http://www.applicom.com/manu/ ingather.htm. The "more information" page provides lists of Bosnian libraries that have asked for assistance, addresses of other projects to help libraries in Bosnia, information on international law and war crimes prosecutions, and related documents and links: http:// www.openbook.ba/bmss/manu/index.html.

PART FIVE

BIBLIOGRAPHY

Browsing at a street bookstall in the Warsaw ghetto. Photograph by Joe J. Heydecker. (*Courtesy of Bildarchiv Preussischer Kulturbesitz*)

XV · JEWISH PRINT CULTURE AND THE HOLOCAUST: A BIBLIOGRAPHIC SURVEY

Joy A. Kingsolver and Andrew B. Wertheimer

1. INTRODUCTION

THIS essay offers an introduction to research on the impact of the Holocaust on the cultural life of European Jewry. First, it is important to understand what existed prior to the Holocaust, so we include select references to studies of prewar Jewish libraries, booksellers, and publishers. Further sections follow these cultural institutions through the years of the Holocaust, including their suppression by the Einsatzstab Reichsleiter Rosenberg (ERR). This essay briefly explores the postwar repatriation of books by Jewish Cultural Reconstruction (JCR), as well as the emergence of Holocaust documentation centers and the *yisker* books. We also address the question of library acquisitions of Holocaust denial materials. Suggestions for further research will made throughout the essay.

This bibliography is derived from the authors' research for their *Jewish Print Culture: A Bibliography*, which is several years away from publication. We have only begun to explore archives and the vast quantity of material published in Hebrew, so there will inevitably be gaps in our coverage. A number of brief articles from *yisker* books on community libraries also have not been included, and other items may have been overlooked owing to the great scattering of this literature.

We hope that this volume, along with recent writings by David Shavit, Rosemary Horowitz, and others, will encourage further English-language scholarship on print culture in the Holocaust, incorporating an understanding of Jewish and European history with the methodologies of book history.

2. LIBRARIES AND ARCHIVES

A variety of sociolinguistic, religious, and cultural factors, as well as anti-Semitism, led to the growth of a wide range of Jewish libraries in Europe. Synagogue

The authors would like to thank Dan Sharon and Kathy Bloch (Asher Library, Spertus Institute of Jewish Studies) and Michael Terry (Dorot Chief Librarian, New York Public Library) for their assistance, as well as Jonathan Rose for his encouragement.

and yeshiva libraries, Zionist Hebrew collections, socialist popular libraries, Yiddish cultural collections, as well as personal libraries could be found even in small Jewish communities. The ferment of public debate—religious vs. secular, nationalistic vs. assimilationist, diasporaism vs. Zionism—produced an equally vibrant press, which was collected in community libraries. These libraries were special environments where Jews could escape anti-Semitism and immerse themselves in self-improvement, study, or recreation. Indeed, a first step for many political organizations was to assemble enough books and funds for a reading room. These libraries may have been for members only or open to the larger community. Some were licensed (as was required in some communities) while others were underground. Several European research libraries also had assembled significant Judaica collections, such as the Frankfurt Stadt-und-Universität Bibliothek and Amsterdam's Rosenthalia.

Prewar Europe also produced the first modern Jewish archives, most notably that of the YIVO Institute of Vilna. Others were created to document ethnographically the Jewish experience. This historiographical spirit inspired the inhabitants of Eastern Europe's ghettos to later produce significant caches of Holocaust records, such as the *Oneg Shabbes* Archive, which was found after the war in milk containers buried below the remains of the Warsaw Ghetto.

This section focuses on libraries, archives, and librarians before and during the Holocaust. The systematic looting of these collections is mentioned in many of the following articles, although works specifically on the Einsatzstab Reichsleiter Rosenberg are treated separately (see section 4). This section also includes studies of reading and libraries in Theresienstadt and other concentration camps.

Abramowicz, Dina. "Die Bibliothek im Wilnaer Ghetto (1941–1943)." In *Bücher und Bibliotheken in Ghettos und Lagern, 1933–1945*, 119–136. Hannover: Laurentius-Verlag, 1991. A German translation of the author's Yiddish-language essay in the *Lite yisker* book.

———. "Guardians of a Tragic Heritage: Reminiscences and Observations of an Eyewitness." In Proceedings of the 33rd Annual Convention of the Association of Jewish Libraries, 11–19. Ed. Barbara Y. Leff and Laurel S. Wolfson. New York: AJL, 1999.

Arad, Yitzhak. *Ghetto in Flames: The Struggle and Destruction of the Jews in Vilna in the Holocaust.* Jerusalem: Yad Vashem; New York: Anti-Defamation League of B'nai B'rith, 1980. This book uses diaries kept by librarians Herman Kruk and Zelig Kalmanovich in describing the Ghetto Library before its destruction. Its bibliography includes a list of archival material.

Beinfeld, Solon. "The Cultural Life of the Vilna Ghetto." *Simon Wiesenthal Center Annual* 1 (1984): 5–26. This article discusses cultural life in Vilna in general, including library activities.

Bohmuller, Lothar. "Der Salman Schocken Verlag Berlin und die Universitatbibliothek Jena, 1937–1938." In *Bibliotheken während des Nationalsozialismus*, 2: 223–26. Ed. Peter Vodosek and Manfred Komorowski. Wolfenbutteler

Schriften zur Geschichte des Buchwesens, 16. Wiesbaden: Harrassowitz, 1992.

Bry, Ilse. "Reading for Refugees." *Library Journal,* Nov. 1940, 903–6.

Buzás, Ladislaus. *German Library History, 800–1945.* Trans. William D. Boyd. Jefferson, N.C.: McFarland, 1986.

Cohen, Israel. *Vilna.* Philadelphia: Jewish Publication Society, [1943] 1992. A history of the Jewish community in Vilna. Most of the book was written in the 1930s; although the epilog was written in 1943, it does not describe the destruction of the ghetto in detail. The history and founding of the Strashun Library is discussed. There is also a short discussion of YIVO.

Danilewicz, Maria. *The Libraries of Poland.* Trans. Helena Brochocka. St. Andrews: University of St. Andrews, 1943. This book was the result of wartime cooperation between the University of St. Andrews and the Polish university libraries. It details the background and holdings of Polish libraries and includes Judaica collections.

———. "Polish Libraries Must Start Nearly Afresh." *Library Journal* 71 (1946): 257–59. Damage to Polish libraries included extensive destruction in the Biblioteka Narodowa, the National Library, where a large Judaica collection was housed.

———. "Polish Libraries under German Occupation." *Library Association Record,* Apr. 1943, 61–64.

Dawidowicz, Lucy S. *From That Time and Place: A Memoir, 1938–1947.* New York: Bantam, 1991. A moving account of the author's year of study at the YIVO in Vilna. The author also worked at the Offenbach Depot, used for the gathering and sorting of confiscated books, after the war.

Friedman, Philip. "The Fate of the Jewish Book during the Nazi Era." *Jewish Book Annual* 15 (1957–58): 3–13. Reprinted with footnotes in Philip Friedman, *Roads to Extinction: Essays on the Holocaust.* Ed. Ada June Friedman. New York: Jewish Publication Society, 1980. Documentation of the "greatest book pogrom in Jewish history." The author served on the Commission on European Jewish Cultural Reconstruction, which compiled the "Tentative List of Jewish Cultural Treasures in Axis-Occupied Countries" (see section 5). This article summarizes the findings of the commission. Friedman also describes in detail the Nazi looting of Jewish books and libraries and the actions of the ERR.

Gabel, Gernot U. "The Bibliothèque Medem for Yiddish Language and Literature in Paris." *Judaica Librarianship* 5 (1990–91): 228–29.

Heller, Bernard. *Books from Vilna.* Offprint from the *Michigan Alumnus Quarterly,* n.d.

Hyams, Barry. "How YIVO Came Out of the Abyss." *Jewish Digest,* Apr. 1981, 55–60. An interesting but unacademic historical treatment of the YIVO Institution and Library. Abstracted from an article in *Friday.*

Kalmanovitch, Zelig. "A Diary of the Nazi Ghetto in Vilna." *YIVO Annual of Jewish Social Science* 8 (1953): 9–81. The diary was kept by the librarian at

YIVO during 1941, when the ghetto was under Nazi occupation. The diary, originally written in Hebrew, details the struggle to survive in the ghetto and the systematic destruction of the books of the YIVO library. References are made to the *genizah*, the cache of books in YIVO that were hidden for preservation. Kalmanovitch later died in a camp, and his diary was found among the remains of the Ghetto Library in 1945.

Kermish, Joseph, ed. *To Live with Honor and Die with Honor! . . . : Selected Documents from the Warsaw Ghetto Underground Archives "O.S."* Jerusalem: Yad Vashem, 1986. This collection includes remarks by Emanuel Ringelblum on the *Oneg Shabbes* Archive and excerpts from his diary.

Krause, Rolf D. "Lesen-Nachlese: Lektüreverhalten in den nationalsozialistischen Verfolgungsstaätten—Ammerkungen zu Forschungsstand." In *Bücher und Bibliotheken in Ghettos und Lagern, 1933–1945*, 9–28. Hannover: Laurentius-Verlag, 1991.

———. "Vom Kalten Wind: Leseverhalten und Literaturrezeption in den nationalsozialistichen Konzentrationslagern." In *Alltag, Traum und Utopie: Lesegeschichten—Lebensgeschichten*, 124–40. Ed. Rainer Noltenius. Schriften des Fritz-Hüser-Instituts für deutsche und ausländische Arbeitliteratur, 7. Essen: Klartext, 1988.

Kruk, Herman. *Herman Kruk: Bibliothekar und Chronist im Ghetto Wilna* [Herman Kruk: Librarian and chronicler in the Vilna Ghetto]. 2nd expanded ed. Hannover: Laurentius-Verlag, 1988.

———. *Togbukh fun Vilner Geto* [Diary of the Vilna Ghetto]. New York: YIVO Institute for Jewish Research, 1961. Kruk, a librarian in the Vilna ghetto, included information on the Ghetto Library in his diary. The diary has been published only in Yiddish so far, but a more complete English translation is in progress which will go beyond the excerpts in *The YIVO Annual of Jewish Social Science* 13 (1965): 10–78.

———. *Zwischen den Fronten: Zeugnisse aus den Jahren 1940–44* [Between the fronts: Testimonies from the years 1940–44]. Trans. Maria Kühn-Ludewig. Hannover: Laurentius-Verlag, 1990.

Kühlman, Marie. "Les Bibliothèques dans la Tourmente." *Histoires des Bibliothèques Françaises*. Ed. Martine Poulain. Vol. 4: *Les Bibliothèques au XXe Siècle, 1914–1990*, 222–47. Paris: Promodis, 1988. Although Kühlman's focus is not on the Jewish aspects of libraries, she does mention that several Jewish librarians were deported to camps. She also lists the various censorship lists of French libraries, which included banned books by Jews and bibliographies on them.

Kühn-Ludewig, Maria. "Die Bibliothekarin Batia Temkin-Berman und ihre Kinder-Bibliotheken im Warschauer Ghetto" [The librarian Batia Temkin-Berman and her children's libraries in the Warsaw Ghetto]. In *Bücher und Bibliotheken in Ghettos und Lagern, 1933–1945*, 103–18. Hannover: Laurentius-Verlag, 1991.

————. "Hunger nach dem gedrucken Wort: Bücher und Büchereien im Ghetto Lodz, 1940–1944" [Hunger for the printed word: Books and bookstores in the Lodz Ghetto, 1940–1944]. In *Bücher und Bibliotheken in Ghettos und Lagern, 1933–1945*, 83–102. Hannover: Laurentius-Verlag, 1991.

Kuperniminc, Jean-Claude. "La Bibliothèque de l'Alliance Israelite Universelle." *Histoire des Bibliothèques Françaises*. Ed. Martine Poulain. Vol. 4: *Les Bibliothèques au XXe Siècle, 1914–1990*, 238. Paris: Promodis, 1988. Kuperniminc gives a one-page summary of the history of the Alliance Israelite Universelle Library from 1860 to the present, with an emphasis on the Nazi period and later recovery.

Liening, Walter. "Das Schicksal der Juden in Polen Wahrend des Zweiten Weltkrieges" [The fate of Jews in Poland during the Second World War]. *Bücherei und Bildung* 13 (1961): 295–99.

Loewy, Ernst. "Die Judaica-Sammlung der Frankfurter Stadt-und Universitätsbibliothek." *Bulletin des Leo Baeck Institut* 29 (1965): 55–64. This briefly discusses the fate of the collection during the Nazi years, as part of the history of this important collection.

Mallinger, Stephen. ["Historical Study of Jewish Libraries during the Holocaust"]. Manuscript. 1975. Hebrew Union College, Klau Library, Cincinnati, Special Collections. Mallinger describes in detail the dismantling of the YIVO archives and library. He uses valuable primary source material.

Meyer, D. "Bibliotek Vesen." *Bicher-velt: Kritish-Bibliographisher Zhurnal* 1 (1922): 215–18, 331–36, 467–76.

Mishnun, Ruth. "Libraries Abroad." *Wilson Library Bulletin* 14 (1939): 317–18. This was one of the few specific contemporary American mentions of the fate of the Judaica collections in Germany and was taken from "Kurze neue Nachtrichten," *Zentralblatt für Bibliothekwesen* 56 (1939): 506–7.

Muller-Jerina, Alwin. "Zwischen Ausgrenzung und Vernichtung: Judischer Bibliothekare im Dritten Reich." In *Bibliotheken während des Nationalsozialismus*, 2: 227–42. Ed. Peter Vodosek and Manfred Komorowski. Wiesbaden: Harrassowitz, 1992.

Musler, M. "The Nazi Looting of Jewish Books in the Low Countries." *Yad La-Koré* 3/4 (1952/53): 164–65. In Hebrew.

"Nazi Looting of Jewish Books in Kovno Ghetto." *Yad La-Koré* 5/4 (1958–59): 179–80. In Hebrew. An excerpt from a book published by Yad Vashem titled *Kovno Jews in the Holocaust*.

"On Jewish Book Collections Looted by the Germans." Editorial. *Yad La-Koré* 1/5–6 (1946): 125. In Hebrew.

Oshry, Rabbi Ephraim. *The Annihilation of Lithuanian Jewry*. Trans. Y. Leiman. New York: Judaica Press, 1995. Chap. 16 of this English translation of *Churbin Lita*, "How Jews Risked Their Lives for the Jewish Book," is most interesting.

Pinson, Koppel S. "Jewish Life in Liberated Germany: A Study of the Jewish

D.P.s." *Jewish Social Studies* 9 (1947): 101–26. This early study briefly mentions reading and libraries in the displaced-persons camps, which were set up at the end of the war. This is one area which merits further research.

Richards, Pamela Spence. "'Aryan Librarianship': Academic and Research Libraries under Hitler." *Journal of Library History* 19 (1984): 230–58.

Richter, Kornelia. "Bibliotheksarbeit im Ghetto Theresienstadt." *Zentralblatt für Bibliothekwesen* 102 (1988): 97–103.

———. "Lesen im Ghetto Theresienstadt." In *Bücher und Bibliotheken in Ghettos und Lagern, 1933–1945,* 43–56. Hannover: Laurentius-Verlag, 1991.

Roth, Cecil. "The Reconstruction of the Mocatta Library, London." *Journal of Jewish Bibliography* 3/1–2 (1942): 2–4. Roth describes the destruction of the library of the Jewish Historical Society of England in a 1940 bombing raid. The library was rebuilt with donations; the acquisition of the Myers collection helped to replace some of what was lost.

———. "The Restoration of Jewish Libraries, Archives, and Museums." *Contemporary Jewish Record* 7 (1944): 253–57. An address delivered at a conference in London, April 1943, sponsored by the Jewish Historical Society of England. The author expresses concerns over the fate of Jewish books and cultural treasures in Nazi-controlled Europe and calls for collaborative efforts to rescue what was not destroyed.

Rozier, Gilles. "The Medem Bibliothek: The Yiddish Library of Paris." *Shofar* 14 (1996): 138–43. Includes a brief description of the hiding of the library during the occupation.

Scheiber, A. "The Fate of Jewish Libraries and Jewish Books in Hungary under Nazi Occupation." *Yad La-Koré* 1/10–12 (1947): 249–51. In Hebrew.

Schidorsky, Dov. "*Confiscation of Libraries* and *Assignments to Forced Labor:* Two Documents of the Holocaust." *Libraries and Culture* 33 (1998): 347–88. Examination of two documents written by Dr. Ernst Grumach, testifying to the confiscation of libraries and the forced cooperation of Jewish scholars and professionals in the exploitation of these libraries.

———. "Das Schicksal jüdischer Bibliotheken im Dritten Reich" [The fate of Jewish libraries in the Third Reich]. *Bibliotheken während des Nationalsozialismus,* 2: 189–222. Ed. Peter Vodosek and Manfred Komorowski. Wiesbaden: Harrassowitz, 1992.

Schmidt, Schulamith. "Jüdische Bibliotheken in der Zeit des Nationalsozialismus" [Jewish libraries in the world of National Socialism]. *Bibliotheken während des Nationalsozialismus,* 2: 509–14. Ed. Peter Vodosek and Manfred Komorowski. Wiesbaden: Harrassowitz, 1992.

Schochow, Werner. "Jüdische Bibliothekare aus dem Detschen Sprachraum." In *Antisemitismus und jüdische Geschichte: Studien zu Ehren von Herbert A. Strauss.* Ed. Rainer Erb and Michael Schmidt. Berlin: Wissenschaftlicher Autorenverlag, 1987.

Schwartz, Pinchas, ed. *Herman Kruk: Bibliothekar und Chronist im Ghetto Wilna.*

Hannover: Laurentius Sonderheft, 1990. This book contains excerpts from the Kruk diary and a brief biography by Schwartz.

Seela, Torsten. *Bücher und Bibliotheken in nationalsozialistichen Konzentrationslagern: Das gedrucke Wort im antifaschistichen Widerstand der Häftlinge.* Contributions to Library Theory and Library History, 7. Munich: Saur, 1992.

——. "Enstehung und Entwicklung von Bücherein in Konzentrationslagern." *Zentralblatt für Bibliothekswesen* 102 (1988): 337–45.

——. "Der Katalog der Häftlings-Bücherei des KZ Buchenwald." *Zentralblatt für Bibliothekswesen* 102 (1988): 104–7.

——. "Lesen im KZ Sachsenhausen." In *Bücher und Bibliotheken in Ghettos und Lagern, 1933–1945,* 29–42. Hannover: Laurentius-Verlag, 1991.

——. "Lesen und Literarturbenutzung in den Konzentrationslagern: Das Gedruckte Wort im antifaschisten Widerstandkampf der Häftlinge." 2 vols. Ph.D. diss., Berlin, 1989.

Shaffer, Kenneth R. "The Destruction of Books and Libraries in World War II." *Yad La-Koré* 1/3–4 (1946): 57–62. In Hebrew. Part of this article appeared in *Library Journal* earlier in 1946.

Shavit, David. *Hunger for the Printed Word: Books and Libraries in the Jewish Ghettos of Nazi-Occupied Europe.* Jefferson, N.C.: McFarland, 1997. This book is the first monograph on the subject in English. It pieces together the history of the libraries in the Warsaw, Lodz, and Kovno ghettos and the Theresienstadt camp. Shavit also includes a chapter on "Books and Readers." The work is based on the following article but uses a variety of sources to create a living image of what it meant to be a librarian in the Nazi ghettos.

——. "Jewish Libraries in the Polish Ghettos during the Nazi Era." *Library Quarterly* 52 (1982): 103–21.

Starke-Goldschmidt, Käthe. "The Ghetto Central Library at Terezin." In *Terezin,* 172–78. Ed. Frantisek Ehrmann, Otta Heitlinger, and Rudolf Iltis. Prague: Council of Jewish Communities in Czech Lands, 1965.

Steig, Margaret F. "The Impact of National Socialism on Librarians." In *Bibliotheken Während des Nationalsozialismus,* 2: 7–11. Ed. Peter Vodosek and Manfred Komorowski. Wiesbaden: Harrassowitz, 1992.

——. *Public Libraries in Nazi Germany.* Tuscaloosa: University of Alabama Press, 1992.

Temkin, Batia. "Jüdische Bibliotheken in Warschau während des Krieges." Trans. Maria Kühn-Ludewig. In *Bücher und Bibliotheken in Ghettos und Lagern, 1933–1945.* Hannover: Laurentius-Verlag, 1991.

Tory, Avraham. *Surviving the Holocaust: The Kovno Ghetto Diary.* Cambridge: Harvard University Press, 1990. Buried in five crates, three of which survived, Tory's diary and supporting documents constitute a valuable wartime archive. The diary includes brief passages on the confiscation of books and recounts his efforts to preserve this historical record.

Toussaint, Ingo. *Die Universitätbibliothek Freiburg im Dritten Reich.* Munich: Saur, 1984.

Trunk, Issiah. "Religious, Educational, and Cultural Problems of Eastern European Ghettos under German Occupation." *YIVO Annual of Social Sciences* 14 (1969): 159–95.

United States Holocaust Memorial Museum. *Hidden History of the Kovno Ghetto.* Boston: Little, Brown, 1997. This book features many excerpts from diaries and other writings from the ghetto, including some from the Avraham Tory documents. The book features photographs of Tory's Kovno Ghetto Yearbook and other documents.

"Unseren jüduschen Kollegen, die unter dem Nationalsozialismus gelitten und das Leben verloren haben, zum Gedenken!" *Bücherei und Bildung* 4 (1952): 853–59.

Utitz, Emil. "The Central Library in the Concentration Camp Terezin." In *Terezin,* 263–66. Ed. Frantisek Ehrmann, Otta Heitlinger, and Rudolf Iltis. Prague: Council of Jewish Communities in Czech Lands, 1965.

Vodosek, Peter, and Komorowski, Manfred, eds. *Bibliotheken während des Nationalsozialismus.* 2 vols. Wiesbaden: Harrasowitz, 1989–92.

Weisberg, Moshe. "Unzere Bibliotheken un die Statistik fun die Leyener." *Literarishe Bleter* 117 (1926): 503–55; 123 (1926): 603–5.

Weltsch, F. "Library Life in the Theresienstadt Concentration Camp." *Yad LaKoré* 1 (1947): 247–49. In Hebrew.

3. PUBLISHING

Jews were greatly involved in publishing and bookselling (both Judaica and general works) before Hitler rose to power. Like other aspects of publishing history, this remains an area which scholars have only begun to explore. Israeli and German historians of print culture have recently produced a number of publishers' biographies, only a few of which are listed here.

Baron, Salo W. *The Russian Jew under Tsars and Soviets.* New York: Macmillan, 1964. This classic study discusses Hebrew and Yiddish publishing before and during the war (chap. 14). Baron finds that much of what was published had little Jewish content.

Dahm, Volker. *Das jüdische Buch im Dritten Reich.* Munich: Beck, 1993.

Freeden, Herbert. "Das Ende der jüdischen Presse in Nazideutschland." *Bulletin des Leo Baeck Institut* 65 (1983): 3–21.

Hale, Oron J. *The Captive Press in the Third Reich.* Princeton: Princeton University Press, 1964.

Herzberg, Arno. "Last Days of the German Jewish Press." *Contemporary Jewish Record* 5 (1942): 145–53. This article describes the disunity within the ranks of journalists and the German government's exploitation of this in its attempts to shut down the Jewish press.

————. "The Jewish Press under the Nazi Regime: Its Mission, Suppression, and Defiance. A Memoir." *Leo Baeck Institute Year Book*, 1991, 367–88. As editor and manager of the Jewish Telegraphic Agency in Berlin, Herzberg was in the forefront of efforts to defy the German government and keep the Jewish press alive. Herzberg here gives a fascinating account of his role in the struggle.

Kermish, Joseph. "The Jewish and Polish Underground Press as Sources of History." In *From Hatred to Extermination: Seven Lectures Delivered at the Second World Congress for Jewish Studies, the Section for the History of the Jewish People*, 77–106. Ed. Benzion Dinur et al. Jerusalem: Yad Vashem, 1959.

Kowalski, Isaac. *A Secret Press in Nazi Europe: The Story of a Jewish United Partisan Organization*. New York: Central Guide Publishers, [1969].

Lipstadt, Deborah E. "The American Press and the Persecution of German Jewry: The Early Years, 1933–1935." *Leo Baeck Institute Year Book*, 1984, 27–55. Lipstadt analyzes American press coverage of Germany's early mistreatment of Jews, as well as editorial responses.

Moore, Bob. *Victims and Survivors: The Nazi Persecution of the Jews in the Netherlands, 1940–1945*. London and New York: Arnold, 1997. A well-documented study which includes a few references to the purging of libraries and the banning of Jews from the publishing industry.

Pinkus, Benjamin. *The Soviet Government and the Jews, 1948–1967: A Documented Study*. Cambridge: Cambridge University Press, 1984. The section on cultural activities evaluates Yiddish publishing in the Soviet Union during and after the war.

Rayski, Adam. "The Jewish Underground Press in France and the Struggle to Expose the Nazi Secret of the Final Solution." In *The Holocaust and History: The Known, the Unknown, the Disputed, and the Reexamined*, 616–28. Ed. Michael Berenbaum and Abraham J. Peck. Bloomington: Indiana University Press, 1998.

Segal, Simon. "Poland Fights Back." *Contemporary Jewish Record* 5/2 (1942): 171–86. Underground newspapers helped to keep the resistance in Poland alive by providing up-to-date information and by unifying the movement. This article describes the press and its activities, and also the efforts to shut it down.

Szeintuch, Yechiel. "Einführung in die Forschung zur jiddischen und hebräischen Literatur in Polen und Litauen zur Zeit der nationalsozialistischen Herrschaft und das jüdische Verhalten im Holocaust." In *Beter und Rebellen*, 329–54. Ed. Michael Brocke. Frankfurt, 1983.

4. ALFRED ROSENBERG AND THE EINSATZSTAB REICHSLEITER ROSENBERG

Although the Nazis had several agencies that destroyed or confiscated Judaica collections, the Einsatzstab Reichsleiter Rosenberg (ERR) was directly in charge of seizing the cultural assets of Jews and others.

Akinsha, Konstantin. *Beautiful Loot: The Soviet Plunder of Europe's Art Treasures.* New York: Random House, 1995. This deals with the ERR in its beginning stages. Although it does not deal directly with books as loot, it is suggestive as to what may have happened to some of the Judaica collections which were in the Soviet-occupied area.

Bollmus, Reinhard. *Das Amt Rosenberg und seine Gegner zum Machtkampf im nationalsozialistichen Herrschafts-system.* Stuttgart: Deutsche Verlagsanstalt, 1970.

Cecil, Robert. *The Myth of the Master Race: Alfred Rosenberg and Nazi Ideology.* New York: Dodd, Mead, 1970.

Collins, Donald E, and Rothfelder, Herbert P. "The Einsatzstab Reichsleiter Rosenberg and the Looting of Jewish and Masonic Libraries during World War II." *Journal of Library History* 18 (1983): 21–36. Describes the activities of the ERR and the beginnings of American efforts to restore seized property after the war.

Hoogewoud, F. J. "The Nazi Looting of Books and Its American 'Antithesis': Selected Pictures from the Offenbach Archival Depot's Photographic History and Its Supplement." *Studia Rosenthaliana* 26 (1992): 158–92. Remarkable photographs of the activities of the ERR during the war and of the sorting of books at the Offenbach Depot. Hoogewoud's introductory essay puts the photographs into context.

Nicholas, Lynn. *The Rape of Europa: The Fate of Europe's Treasures in the Third Reich and the Second World War.* New York: Knopf, 1994. This popular book emphasizes artwork but also includes information on the ERR, the JCR, and postwar repatriation of cultural treasures.

Office of United States Chief of Counsel for Prosecution of Axis Criminality. *Nazi Conspiracy and Aggression.* 8 vols., supplements. Washington, D.C.: U.S. Government Printing Office, 1946. This series of volumes presents the documentary evidence collected by the American and British prosecutors at the Nuremberg trials. Supplement B contains an interview with Rosenberg in which he describes the confiscation of art and libraries and gives his justification for this. Vol. 3 has documentation of the establishment of the ERR.

Vries, Willem de. *Sonderstab Musik: Music Confiscations by the Einsatzstab Reichsleiter Rosenberg under the Nazi Occupation of Western Europe.* Amsterdam: Amsterdam University Press, 1996. This book contains the most information on the ERR's confiscation of cultural property, especially music but also books and libraries. It uses extensive documentation and follows the careers of ERR officials.

Weinreich, Max. *Hitler's Professors: The Part of Scholarship in Germany's Crimes against the Jewish People.* New York: YIVO, 1946. Weinreich has two chapters on Alfred Rosenberg: one is an informal biography, and the other is about his work with the ERR.

Yahil, Leni. "Einsatzstab Rosenberg." In *Encyclopedia of the Holocaust.* Ed. Israel Gutman. 4 vols. New York: Macmillan, 1990.

5. Jewish Cultural Reconstruction

Despite and sometimes because of Nazi looting of Judaica, large amounts of Judaica were recovered in storage facilities and libraries in liberated Europe. The problem was especially difficult for Allied occupiers. Jews did not want their stolen treasures to be sent back to *Judenrein* communities which were associated with mass murder. As a result, the occupation forces were encouraged to recognize an independent organization to apportion Jewish books and cultural works to libraries and museums in Palestine and in diaspora. Important Judaica experts such as Salo Baron, Hannah Arendt, Lucy Davidowicz, Shlomo Shunami, and Gerschon Scholem became involved with the Jewish Cultural Reconstruction program and its Offenbach Depot, where the material was sorted. The articles listed below are mostly contemporary reports, as a comprehensive history has not yet been completed.

Blattberg, Wolf. "Recovering Cultural Treasures." *Congress Weekly*, 30 Oct. 1950, 5–6.

Born, Lester K. "The Archives and Libraries of Postwar Germany." *American Historical Review* 51/1 (1950): 34–57. The focus of this article is the restoration of property after World War II. The author discusses problems in the administration of programs to return archives and books. The focus is on German archives, but the issues and sources are the same as those for Jewish books.

Commission on European Jewish Cultural Reconstruction. Letter to General J. H. Hildring. 5 June 1946. Hebrew Union College, Klau Library, Cincinnati, Special Collections. This document outlines the commission's plan for preserving looted books and expresses the urgency of the situation.

———. "Tentative List of Jewish Cultural Treasures in Axis-Occupied Countries." *Jewish Social Studies*, supplement to 8/1 (1946): 5–103. In order to recover looted Jewish books and restore libraries destroyed by the war, the commission compiled this list of known collections and libraries. The result is a goldmine of information about Jewish books and libraries before the war. This source is indispensable for the study of this subject.

Deutsch, Elaine. "Jewish Cultural Reconstruction, Inc." M. A. thesis, University of Southern California, 1989. This thesis only scratches the surface and fails to examine primary materials.

Dicker, Herman. *Of Learning and Libraries: The Seminary Library at One Hundred.* New York: Jewish Theological Seminary of America, 1988. Chapter 4 discusses the activities of the Commission on Jewish Cultural Reconstruction. As several tables in the appendices make clear, JTS was one of the repositories for books that could not be returned to their owners.

Goldreich, Gloria. "The Doomed Libraries. Rescued: Half-Million Jewish Books in a Dramatic Search." *Hadassah Magazine*, May 1962, 6+.

Jewish Book Council of America. *Report of the Committee on Books for Devastated and Other Libraries Abroad.* 31 Dec. 1945. Hebrew Union College, Klau Library, Cincinnati, Special Collections.

Kurtz, Michael. *Nazi Contraband: American Policy on European Cultural Treasures, 1945–1955.* New York: Garland, 1985. Chapter 7, "A Special Concern: The Jewish Inheritance," describes the formation of the JCR.

Lowenthal, Ernst Gottfried. "Jewish Cultural Reconstruction." *Encyclopaedia Judaica.* 18 vols. Jerusalem: Keter, 1972.

Poste, Leslie I. "Books Go Home from the Wars." *Library Journal* 73 (1948): 1699–1704. This article became the Offenbach chapter in Poste's dissertation, but here the material is presented in a more narrative fashion.

———. "The Development of U.S. Protection of Libraries and Archives in Europe during World War II." Ph.D. diss., University of Chicago, 1958. An account of the author's experience in the Monuments, Fine Arts, and Archives Program, which was responsible for ascertaining ownership of books and art objects looted by the Nazis. The author recounts the activities at the Offenbach Depot in detail, drawing statistics from monthly reports. Poste also analyzes the destruction of libraries in general and evaluates the restitution program.

Scholem, Gershom G. *Briefe* [Correspondence]. Ed. Itta Shedletzky. 2 vols. Munich: Beck, 1994. Several letters describe Scholem's work at the Offenbach Depot and his reaction to the JCR.

Starr, Joshua. "Jewish Cultural Property under Nazi Control." *Jewish Social Studies* 12 (1950): 27–48. This article concentrates on Alfred Rosenberg and the activities of the ERR. It also discusses the movement of confiscated books after the war. Starr was the executive secretary for Jewish Cultural Reconstruction.

6. DOCUMENTATION CENTERS AND ARCHIVAL RESOURCES

Even when it was an illegal act, Jewish scholars, journalists, and writers documented life in the ghettos and camps. This material was preserved along with Nazi documents after the war in Yad Vashem in Jerusalem and in several archives which focused on preserving oral and written evidence of the Shoah. This section lists articles on these institutions as well as some catalogs of select archival holdings.

Archives of the Holocaust: An International Collection of Selected Documents. Ed. Henry Friedlander and Sybil Milton. 18 vols. New York: Garland, 1990. This set of books is a valuable resource that makes some archival holdings more accessible. Each volume contains reproductions of photographs or documents from the archives of a particular institution, including YIVO, the Robert F. Wagner Labor Archives of New York University, and the Israel State Archives. There is no general index, but each volume has a list of its items with sources and dates.

Barkow, Ben. *Alfred Wiener and the Making of the Holocaust Library.* London: Vallentine Mitchell, 1997.

Berenstein, T. "Documents in the Archives of Poland: A Basis for Historical Research Concerning the Jewish Population during the Nazi Occupation." In *From Hatred to Extermination: Seven Lectures Delivered at the Second World Congress for Jewish Studies, the Section for the History of the Jewish People,* 67–76. Ed. Benzion Dinur et al. Jerusalem: Yad Vashem, 1959.

Binderman, Abraham. "Archival Collections: Living Memorials to the Holocaust." *A. B. Bookman's Weekly* 81 (1988): 1735–36.

Brachman-Teubner, Elisabeth. "Sources for the History of the Jews from the Eighteenth Century to the Twentieth Century of the Former DDR." *Leo Baeck Institute Year Book,* 1993, 391–408. The author describes the organization of archival material in the DDR after 1990. She surveys the holdings of individual archives and discusses the fate of archival material from Jewish communities during the Holocaust. Cataloging bureaucratic disputes, damage from mold and dampness, and intentional destruction of community files, she documents the loss of pre-Holocaust documentation for some seventy-seven communities.

Chamberlin, Brewster S. "The Archival Resources of the U.S. Holocaust Research Institute of the United States Holocaust Memorial Museum." In *The Holocaust in Hungary: Fifty Years Later,* 759–71. Ed. Randolph L. Braham and Attila Pok. Rosenthal Institute for Holocaust Studies, City University of New York; Institute of History of the Hungarian Academy of Sciences; Europa Institute, Budapest; Social Science Monographs, Boulder, Colo.; distributed by Columbia University Press, 1997. This article describes archival resources, most on microfilm, which may be useful in any study of Jewish print culture during the Holocaust. The records described include the files of many Jewish organizations.

———. "Holocaust Memorial Museum: New Approaches for an All-in-One Resource Center." *Journal of Information Management* 19 (July 1986): 36+.

Chepesiok, Ronald J. "In Memory of Millions: The Holocaust Museum Library." *American Libraries,* May 1996, 44–46.

Dobroszycki, Lucjan, and Gurock, Jeffrey, eds. *The Holocaust in the Soviet Union: Studies and Sources on the Destruction of the Jews in the Nazi-Occupied Territories of the USSR, 1941–1945.* Armonk, N.Y.: Sharpe, 1993.

Friedman, Saul S., ed. *Holocaust Literature: A Handbook of Critical, Historical, and Literary Writings.* Westport, Conn.: Greenwood Press, 1993. This collection includes articles on Holocaust historiography and the development of documentation centers. The book is a useful guide to beginning research.

Maier, Kurt. "The Library of Leo Baeck Institute." *Journal of Library History* 12 (1977): 176–86. Maier writes about the founding of the institute, the sources of its collection, and the ways in which it has been used for research.

Pelzman, Frankie. "In the Beginning: The U.S. Holocaust Memorial Library." *Wilson Library Bulletin* 67 (1993): 61–62.

Posner, Marcia W. "The Library of Yad Vashem." *Judaica Librarianship* 2 (1985): 63–64.

Ross, H. "The Holocaust Research Center." *New Jersey Libraries,* Summer 1994, 22+.

Sable, Martin. *Holocaust Studies: A Directory and Bibliography of Bibliographies.* Greenwood, Fla.: Penkevill, 1987.

Stern, Stephanie M. "The Leo Baeck Institute: Programs, Collections, and Organization of the Library." *Judaica Librarianship* 2 (1985): 57–59. Stern, then the chief librarian at Leo Baeck, gives an overview of the library and archive, their resources, and their mission of documenting German-speaking Jewry.

Thorner, J. Lincoln. "The Unimaginable Made Real: Center for Holocaust Studies." *Wilson Library Bulletin* 61 (1987): 19–21.

7. HOLOCAUST DENIAL AND LIBRARIES

Deborah Lipstadt's study of Holocaust denial writings introduced the topic to much of the Jewish community. Librarians, however, have been aware of this literature for some time, and fall into several schools—those who collect anti-Semitica, those who advocate freedom of expression, and those who believe that even discussing the issue shows a lack of respect to the victims. This conflict is captured in the ideological debate between John Swan and Noel Peattie. On these occasions librarians, who acquire and catalog all types of materials, are forced to make philosophical decisions which have implications outside of their building.

Anderson, Arthur James. "Collection Insurrection: Purchasing Holocaust Denial Titles for a College Library." *Library Journal* 120 (1995): 52+.

Berman, Sanford. "Whose Holocaust Is It, Anyway? The 'H' Word in Library Catalogs." *Reference Librarian* 61–62 (1998): 213–25.

"Book Shredding Ignites Furor." *PNLA Quarterly* 59 (1995): 18. The destruction of a Holocaust denial book in Canada.

Drobnicki, John A., et al. "Holocaust-Denial Literature in Public Libraries: An Investigation of Public Librarians' Attitudes Regarding Acquisition and Access." *Public & Access Services Quarterly* 1 (1995): 5–40. This work was prepared by several MLS students at Queens College CUNY's Library School to study attitudes toward Holocaust denial material held by East Coast public librarians.

Gleberzon, William. "Academic Freedom and Holocaust Denial Literature: Dealing with Infamy." *Interchange* 14/4–15.1 (1983/84): 62–69. The experience of Holocaust denial material through the perspective of a Canadian in the mid-1980s.

Goldberg, Beverly. "Groups Challenge Library's Holocaust-Revisionist Titles." *American Libraries,* Sept. 1988, 640.

Grunberger, Michael. "Controversial Materials in the Jewish Library." *Judaica Librarianship* 3 (1986/87): 1–2.

Hupp, Stephen L. "Collecting Extremist Political Materials: The Example of Holocaust Denial Publications." *Collection Management* 14 (1991): 163–73.

Kaplan, Paul. "Legacies: Librarians' Responsibilities Recommending Books about the Holocaust." *Public Libraries* 37 (1998): 287.

Katz, Jeffrey. "Revisionist History in the Library: To Facilitate Access or Not to Facilitate Access?" *Canadian Library Journal* 48 (1991): 319–24.

Klein, Adaire. "The Handling of Holocaust Denial Literature in a Special Library." *Judaica Librarianship* 3 (1986/87): 55–57. The author is library director at the Simon Wiesenthal Center.

Landesman, Betty. "Holocaust Denial and the Internet." *Reference Librarian* 61–62 (1998): 287–99.

Nelson, Kristina L. "Erasing the Horror: Revisionism and Library Access." *Current Studies in Librarianship* 22/1–2 (Spring/Fall 1998): 12–19.

Peattie, Noel. "Cardinal Mazarin Is Dead." In *Alternative Library Literature, 1986–1987,* 66–69. Jefferson, N.C.: McFarland, 1988. The California Library Association's reaction to a controversial anti-Holocaust exhibit.

Stauffer, Suzanne M. "Selected Issues in Holocaust Denial Literature and Reference Work." *Reference Librarian* 61–62 (1998): 189–93.

Swan, John, and Peattie, Noel. *The Freedom to Lie: A Debate about Democracy.* Jefferson, N.C.: McFarland, 1989. In this interesting work, two American librarians debate the issue of social responsibility versus the freedom to acquire "hate literature." This was written in response to the denial of a publisher's application for a booth at a California Library Association conference.

Weinfeld, Morton. "Librarians Have a Role in Holocaust Denial." *Judaica Librarianship* 3 (1986/87): 51–52.

Wolkoff, Kathleen Nietzke. "The Problem of Holocaust Denial Materials in Libraries." *Library Trends* 45 (1996): 87–96.

8. YISKER BIKHER

Rosemary Horowitz has analyzed these remarkable documents, which were compiled by survivors as memoirs of Jewish communities destroyed by the Holocaust. For years, it seemed, genealogists used these much more than historians; however, Jack Kugelmass and Jonathan Boyarin's collection brought the genre to a wider audience. As younger historians approach these volumes, it will be interesting to see how they situate them in postmodern studies of social memory.

Baker, Zachary. *Bibliography of Eastern European Memorial (Yizkor) Books: With Call Numbers for Six Judaica Libraries in New York.* New York: Jewish Genealogical Society, [1992]. This is an excellent starting point, although researchers should be cautioned to check library catalogs or contact librarians before making a trek. Bibliographic databases such as RLIN include holdings across the United States. Researchers should also understand that many libraries do not make *bikher* available by interlibrary loan.

Grunberger, Michael W. "Yizker-bikher: The Literature of Remembrance." *A. B. Bookman's Weekly* 77 (1986): 1798–1803. A bibliographic essay.

Horowitz, Rosemary. *Literacy and Cultural Transmission in the Reading, Writing, and Rewriting of Jewish Memorial Books.* Bethesda, Md.: Austin & Winfield, 1998. A groundbreaking, in-depth study of the cultural meanings and uses of *yisker bikher* by first- and second-generation Holocaust survivors.

Kugelmass, Jack, and Boyarin, Jonathan, eds. *From a Ruined Garden: The Memorial Books of Polish Jewry.* New York: Schocken, 1983; rpt. Bloomington: Indiana University Press, 1998. This is the most accessible collection of materials collected and translated from a variety of *yisker bikher*. It also contains Zachary Baker's excellent bibliography, along with a useful cross-referenced list of locales in Yiddish, Polish, and Russian.

———. "Yizker Bikher and the Problem of Historical Veracity: An Anthropological Approach." In Yisrael Gutman et al., eds. *The Jews of Poland between the Two World Wars,* 519–35. Hanover, N.H.: University Press of New England, 1989.

9. Additional Topics

Several other aspects deserve exploration, such as foreign reactions to the Nazi book burnings and firings of Jewish librarians, the reception of Holocaust literature, and exile literature and publishing. These are only raised as beginning points for research.

Cazden, Robert E. *German Exile Literature in America, 1933–1950: A History of the Free German Press and Book Trade.* Chicago: American Library Association, 1970.

Nazi Book Burnings and the American Response. Washington, D.C.: Library of Congress, [1983]. This brief exhibit guide consists of writers' and media reactions to the Nazi 1933 book burnings.

Stern, Guy. "The Burning of the Books in Nazi Germany, 1933: The American Response." *Simon Wiesenthal Center Annual* 2 (1985): 95–113.

NOTES ON CONTRIBUTORS

DINA ABRAMOWICZ began her career as a librarian in 1939 at the Jewish Children's Library in Vilna. After the German occupation of Lithuania in 1941, she worked at the Vilna Ghetto Library. Later, she escaped to a camp of Jewish resistance fighters. After the war, she studied librarianship at Columbia University. She joined the YIVO Institute for Jewish Research in New York, where she was Head Librarian until 1987, and subsequently Research Librarian. She died on 3 April 2000, at age 90. This book is dedicated to her.

ZACHARY M. BAKER is Reinhard Family Curator of Judaica and Hebraica Collections at the Stanford University Libraries. He was Head Librarian of YIVO from 1987 to 1999, and he has compiled *The Bibliography of Eastern European Memorial (Yizkor) Books* since 1980. He is editor of *Judaica Librarianship*, and from 1976 to 1999 he contributed the Yiddish books bibliography to the *Jewish Book Annual*.

ARLEN VIKTOROVICH BLIUM was born 30 March 1933 in Melitopol', Ukraine. After his father was arrested in 1936, his grandmother took him to Orenburg in the Ural Mountains, where he finished high school. (He learned only in the late 1950s that his father had been shot in 1938.) Blium went on to complete a doctoral degree at the Bibliography Department of the Leningrad Library Institute and has been teaching there since 1965. (Today it is known as the Department of Information and Library Science of the St. Petersburg Academy of Culture.) While still a graduate student, Blium became interested in censorship research, but at that time he could only publish work about pre-Soviet Russia of the eighteenth and nineteenth centuries. Nevertheless, in the 1970s, he quietly began to study Soviet censorship. The advent of *perestroika* in the late 1980s finally gave Blium access to archival materials that had been off limits. All of this work resulted in two recent books. The first is *Za kulisami "Ministerstva Pravdy": Tainaia istoriia sovetskoi tsenzury, 1917–1929* [Behind the scenes at the "Ministry of Truth": The secret history of Soviet censorship, 1917–1929] (St. Petersburg: Akademicheskii proekt, 1994). Donna M. Farina has translated one chapter from this work, "Forbidden Topics: Early Soviet Censorship Directives" ["O chem nel'zia pisat': tsenzurnye tsirkuliary"], published in *Book History* 1 (1998): 268–82. The excerpt translated here is from his latest book, *Evreiskii vopros pod sovetskoi tsenzuroi* [The Jewish question under Soviet censorship] (St. Petersburg: Peterburgskii evreiskii universitet, 1996). Letters to Arlen Blium can be sent to: Russia/Rossiia, 191104 Sankt-Peterburg, ul. Belinskogo, d. 5, kv. 75.

GEORGE DURMAN was born in 1941 in Kirov, Russia, where his family was living in evacuation during World War II. He received his master's degree in Russian literature and language from the Moscow Pedagogical Institute in 1967. From 1968 to 1979 he was a Senior Fellow at the Moscow Literary Museum, giving lectures and writing articles. He immigrated to the United States in 1981 and received master's degrees in Slavic literatures and library science from the University of Illinois at Urbana. He is Senior Librarian at the Bayonne Public Library in New Jersey, where he has worked since 1986. Durman's research interests are Russian intellectual history, Russian literature, and Russian rare books.

DONNA M. FARINA received a Licence de linguistique and Maîtrise de sciences du langage from the Université des Sciences Humaines, Strasbourg, France, and a Ph.D. in linguistics from the University of Illinois at Urbana-Champaign. She is an associate professor at New Jersey City University. She has worked on dictionary projects for Cambridge University Press and Oxford University Press and as a reader in the *Oxford English Dictionary* North American program. Her main research interest is the history of lexicography, especially Russian dictionaries. She has published articles in *Lexicographica: International Annual for Lexicography, International Journal of Lexicography,* and other journals.

DAVID E. FISHMAN is Professor of Jewish History and Chair of the Department of Jewish History at the Jewish Theological Seminary of America and Senior Research Associate at YIVO. He is the author of *Russia's First Modern Jews* and coeditor of *YIVO-bleter,* YIVO's Yiddish-language scholarly journal.

LEONIDAS E. HILL, Professor Emeritus of History at the University of British Columbia, has edited *Die Weizsäcker Papiere, 1900–1932* (1982) and *Die Weizsäcker Papiere, 1933–1950* (1974). He has published articles about Ernst von Weizsäcker and German foreign policy, the German foreign office in the Nazi era, resistance to the Nazi regime, the 9–10 November 1938 pogrom in Germany and Austria, the political memoirs of leading Nazis, Walter Gyssling and the Centralverein, and the legal trial of Holocaust denier Ernst Zundel in Canada. He also edited and wrote an introduction for Walter Gyssling, *Mein Leben in Deutschland vor und nach 1933, und Der Anti-Nazi: Handbuch im Kampf gegen die NSDAP* (Bremen: Donat Verlag, 2003).

ROSEMARY HOROWITZ is Associate Professor of English at Appalachian State University, a unit of the University of North Carolina. She is interested in the study of literacy, writing and the teaching of writing, the theory and practice of translation, and writing in the Jewish community. She is the author of *Literacy and Cultural Transmission in the Reading, Writing, and Rewriting of Jewish Memorial Books* (Austin & Winfield, 1998). Most recently she edited the collection *Elie Wiesel and the Art of Storytelling* (McFarland, 2006).

YITZCHAK KEREM teaches Sephardic history at the Hebrew University in Jerusalem and modern Greek history at the Aristotle University in Thessaloniki (Salonika). He is the founder and Director of the Institute of Hellenic-Jewish Relations (University of Denver), editor of *Sefarad* (the monthly Sephardic e-mail newsletter), co-host of the Hebrew weekly radio show *Diaspora Jewry* (Kol Israel), coauthor of *Guidebook for*

Sephardic and Oriental Genealogical Sources in Israel (Avotaynu, 1996), a board member of the Casa Shalom Institute for Anusim/Marrano Studies, and cofounder of the International Forum for Tolerance and Peace.

JOY KINGSOLVER is Director of the Chicago Jewish Archives, a component of the Asher Library at the Spertus Institute of Jewish Studies. She has written articles for *Jewish Women in America, A Reader's Guide to Judaism,* and the *Dictionary of National Biography.* She is researching a book about Fanny Goldstein, librarian at the West End Branch of the Boston Public Library.

CHARLOTTE GUTHMANN OPFERMANN was born in Wiesbaden, Germany. Most of her family—including her father, a prominent attorney and head of the Wiesbaden Jewish Congregation—were killed in concentration camps. After the war she immigrated to the United States, where she became a high school and college teacher. She frequently returned to Germany for lectures and teach-ins on the Holocaust. Her book *Stationen* was published by Fournier Verlag in 1993. After a brief illness, she died on 22 November 2004.

ANNETTE BIEMOND PECK was born in Amsterdam in 1928 and pursued a career in social work. Since 1969 she has lived in the United States.

SIGRID POHL PERRY was born in Wedel, Germany, and immigrated to the United States with her parents. She received a doctorate in English from Northwestern University, where she now works in the Charles Deering McCormick Library of Special Collections. In 1992 she curated an exhibit of Dutch clandestine publications from the Second World War, which she adapted for display at the 1996 Drew University conference on "The Holocaust and the Book." She has also pursued research on Charles G. Dawes, vice president of the United States under Calvin Coolidge.

STANISLAO G. PUGLIESE is Professor of History at Hofstra University. He is the author of *Carlo Rosselli: Socialist Heretic and Antifascist Exile* and *Desperate Inscriptions: Graffiti from the Nazi Prison in Rome.* He edited *The Most Ancient of Minorities: The Jews of Italy* and *The Legacy of Primo Levi.* He is presently editing a new collection of essays, *Answering Auschwitz: Primo Levi's Science and Humanism after the Fall,* and writing a biography of the Italian writer Ignazio Silone.

ANDRÁS RIEDLMAYER directs the Documentation Center of the Aga Khan Program for Islamic Architecture at Harvard University's Fine Arts Library. A specialist in the history and culture of the Ottoman Balkans, he has spent much of the past decade and a half documenting the destruction of libraries, archives, and other cultural heritage during the wars in Bosnia-Herzegovina (1992–1995) and Kosovo (1998–1999). He has testified about his findings as an expert witness before the International Criminal Tribunal for the former Yugoslavia in The Hague, in the war crimes trial of Slobodan Milošević, and in the genocide case brought by Bosnia-Herzegovina before the International Court of Justice. The author of more than forty articles published in scholarly and professional journals and edited volumes, in five languages, he currently serves as president of the

Turkish Studies Association. In 1994, he helped found the Bosnian Manuscript Ingathering Project, an effort to trace and recover still extant microfilms and photocopies, "shadows of lost originals," representing some of the thousands of manuscripts that were destroyed when archives and libraries in Bosnia were burned by nationalist extremists during the 1990s.

JOHN RODDEN is the author of *Repainting the Little Red Schoolhouse: A History of East German Education, 1945–95* (Oxford University Press, 2002), *Textbook Reds: Schoolbooks, Ideology, and Eastern German Identity* (Penn State University Press, 2006), and *Every Intellectual's Big Brother: George Orwell's Literary Siblings* (University of Texas Press, 2007), among other books. His most recent studies of German culture and society are *The Walls That Remain: Eastern and Western Germans since Reunification* (Paradigm Publishers, 2008) and *Dialectics, Dogmas, and Dissent: Stories of East German Victims of Human Rights Abuse* (Penn State University Press, 2008).

JONATHAN ROSE is William R. Kenan Professor of History at Drew University. He served as the founding president of the Society for the History of Authorship, Reading and Publishing, and is now coeditor of the journal *Book History*. His books include *The Intellectual Life of the British Working Classes* (2001) and *A Companion to the History of the Book* (coedited with Simon Eliot, 2007).

SEM C. SUTTER is Assistant Director for Collections at the University of Chicago Library. He has published articles on religious toleration in seventeenth-century Schleswig-Holstein and curated exhibits on German book history and Jewish bibliophilia. In the course of ongoing research on the fate of European libraries and archives during the Second World War, he has written articles on the Jewish libraries of Vilna and the Frankfurt "Institut zur Erforschung der Judenfrage," Nazi looting of Jewish book collections in France, and the fate of books confiscated in the Möbel-Aktion.

ANDREW B. WERTHEIMER is Chair of the Library and Information Science Program at the University of Hawai'i at Manoa. He has a Ph.D. in library and information studies, with a minor in print culture history, from the University of Wisconsin–Madison. His research focuses on library history and Japanese-American print culture from the Meiji period to World War II. He is a member of the editorial board of the journal *Library History*.